South Sea Journey

South Sea Journey

GEORGE WOODCOCK

Fitzhenry & Whiteside
Toronto Montreal Winnipeg Vancouver

ISBN 0-88902-047-7

Fitzhenry & Whiteside Limited
150 Lesmill Road
Don Mills, Ontario, Canada

Printed in Great Britain

Contents

Acknowledgement

Journeys of this magnitude inevitably generate complex patterns of obligation, and the number of people to whom I am indebted for their kindness in giving help, hospitality and information is more than the sum of people who are actually mentioned in this book. It would be impossible to thank them all individually, so for the most part I must make a collective acknowledgement and hope that this kind of expression of gratitude will be accepted with understanding.

However, there are some special acknowledgements that must be made: to Gordon Babineau, without whose faith in my abilities as a writer I would never have made this trip; to the Canadian Broadcasting Corporation for having offered the contract that enabled me to do it; to Air Pacific and its staff for having in so many helpful and generous ways facilitated our journeys among the islands; to the editors of *Saturday Night*, the *Canadian Forum* and *History Today*, in whose pages some of the material used in this book was first tried out; to Mrs. Tina Harrison for so capably looking after my affairs and forwarding my mail during my absence from Vancouver; to Mrs. Marian Crosson for preparing the typescript.

G.W.

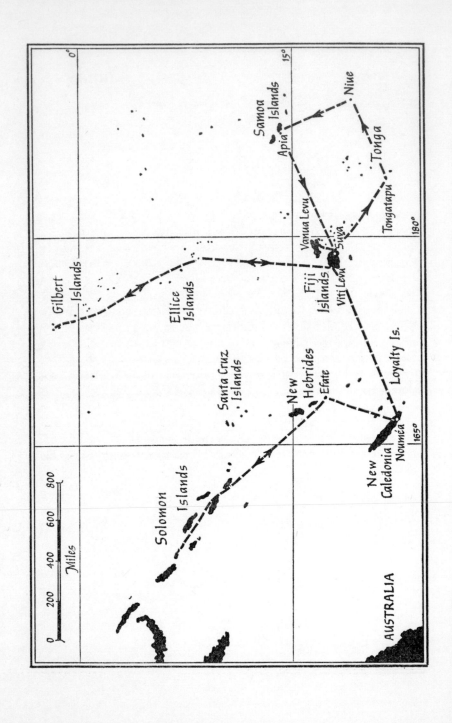

Gilbert
Islands

Ellice
Islands

Solomon
Islands

Santa Cruz
Islands

New
Hebrides

Efate

Loyalty Is.

New
Caledonia

Nouméa

AUSTRALIA

Vanua Levu

Fiji
Islands

Viti Levu

Suva

Samoa
Islands

Apia

Niue

Tonga

Tongatapu

0°

15°

180°

165°

Miles

0   200   400   600   800

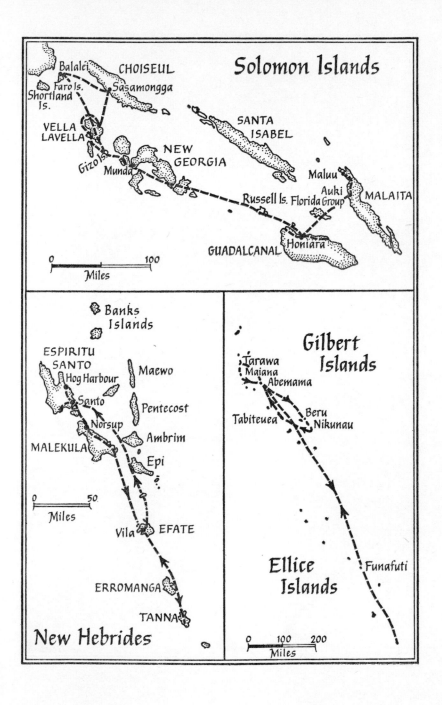

Solomon Islands

Balalei
CHOISEUL
Sasamongga
Faro Is.
Shortland
Is.
SANTA
ISABEL
VELLA
LAVELLA
Gizo Is.
NEW
GEORGIA
Munda
Maluu
Auki
Russell Is. Florida Group
MALAITA
GUADALCANAL
Honiara

0   100
Miles

New Hebrides

Banks
Islands
ESPIRITU
SANTO
Hog Harbour
Maewo
Santo
Pentecost
Norsup
MALEKULA
Ambrim
Epi
Vila
EFATE
ERROMANGA
TANNA

0   50
Miles

**Gilbert
Islands**

Tarawa
Maiana
Abemama
Tabiteuea
Beru
Nikunau

**Ellice
Islands**

Funafuti

0   100   200
Miles

Prologue

In the spring of 1971, when the Canadian television producer Gordon Babineau invited me to join him in an expedition to the South Pacific to record in films what remained of the traditional cultures and how change had been affecting them for the past two centuries, neither Inge nor I felt any hesitation. Earlier travels had taken us no nearer the region than Singapore to the north-west and the coast of Peru to the east. The South Sea islands had made their evocative appeal to me ever since as a boy I had read *Coral Island* and *Typee*, and by coincidence I had just completed the introduction to a Penguin edition of *Typee*, so that the lore of the region was fresh in my mind. We accepted Gordon's proposal on our first meeting.

Our intent involved the encompassing of a veritable continent of cultures, though a continent of water rather than of land, for the seas that contain the 10,000 Pacific islands cover a third of the world's surface, 60,000,000 square miles. Numerous though they are, these islands are so lost that one can fly between groups for two hours in a fast propeller plane and be wholly out of sight of land; among them, one ceases to wonder that Magellan sailed right through them and made his first Pacific landfall at Guam, ninety-nine days from the Straits that bear his name.

The total land area of all the scattered archipelagos of the South Pacific is in fact only about 50,000 square miles, the size of England without Wales. New Caledonia, the largest individual island of the traditional South Seas, is just over 6,000 square miles in area. If one adds New Guinea, the total land area is increased by about 350,000 square miles – but still the population of the groups that fall outside the Europeanized sector of Australia and New Zealand is little more than 5,000,000, which leaves more than ten square miles of ocean – but only a few acres of often ominously barren land – for every South Sea islander.

Yet because of local geographical conditions, because of the distances dividing groups, because of mountain barriers that split large islands into steep and barely accessible valleys, the South Seas when the Europeans discovered them formed probably the most culturally varied region of the whole earth. In eastern, Australian-governed New Guinea alone, there are 700 native languages, each with its finely differentiated culture – roughly one to every three thousand people; New Caledonia's 50,000 native Melanesians speak thirty-six languages.

Yet despite this complex variety, the South Seas in the late eighteenth century formed three major geographical regions, and each exhibited certain common cultural characteristics. In Polynesia – the realm of the Many Islands which roughly corresponds to eastern Oceania, the people were tall, light-skinned and rather softly handsome in a way that appealed to devotees of the noble savage; their languages were closely related, which seemed to bear out their legends of a common origin, and they had developed similar hierarchical systems of chiefly rule by priest-kings whose orators became mayors of the palace and virtual political rulers.

North-west of Polynesia, straddling the equator, lay the Little Islands of Micronesia, inhabited by a smaller, dourer-looking, more Malayan people than the Polynesians. Their territory formed a vast sweep of 50° of longitude and ocean from the Gilberts west to the Carolines. Except for a few high volcanic islands, these were the classic coral atolls, rising no more than a few feet above sea-level where the waves had piled debris on the reefs, and palm-trees had taken root; hard for mariners to find, they embraced within their narrow ramparts of living coral vast lagoons whose warm shallow waters teemed with marine life. From the sea or air, a coral island appears lush and green; the arid dazzle of its white sand impresses one immediately on landing with a sense of austerity, and the beauty of this austerity colours one's memories of the coral islands, their life and people; the sturdy, proud Micronesians, originating no one knows where, with the vast remembered genealogies of their landowning clans, with their extraordinary canoe-sailors' skills, with their bitter civil wars and vendettas over corners of coconut groves, and their ghost-ridden world of the imagination.

Spread so far, fragmented into so many local clans, multilingual, the Micronesians nevertheless shared a culture which the sameness of atoll existence had given a degree of cohesion, so that even today people of the British-ruled Gilberts feel an affinity with related islanders in the American-governed Marshall Islands. It was in the Black Islands of Melanesia, so named for the dark skins of their inhabitants, that cultural and racial variation was most pronounced and the sense of a common tradition most rarely existent. The Melanesians themselves are by no means a homogenous people. There are variant minglings of Australoid and Negroid strains all the way from New Guinea east to Fiji. In the western Solomons and Bougainville, the Negroid strain is so strong that the people are probably the blackest men on earth. In New Caledonia the Australoid strain predominates and many of the native people might easily be taken for Queensland Aborigines. In Fiji, Polynesian influence seeped westward from Tonga, and left not only a strong physical influence leading to tall stature and light skins among people in the Lau Islands and on the main island of Viti Levu, but also a system of hereditary high chieftainship similar to the Polynesian.

Except for the Fijians, Melanesian societies were rarely highly organized. Political structures tended to be minimal, based on the local landholding clan descended from a common mythical ancestor, and clan hamlets rather than true villages were the units of social organization. Power, where it existed, was wielded by self-made 'big men', who acquired prestige through property, which enabled them to establish networks of dependency and obligation, and who initially acquired property by unusual skill in farming or trading or by the possession of some psychic power.

What we found surprising before we went to the South Pacific, and no less so when we travelled there, was the tenacity of certain aspects of traditional life. There is no more interesting testimony to the durability of South Sea cultures than the fact that the first Fijian to be chosen in 1973 as Governor-General should be Ratu George Cakobau, great-grandson of the high chief Cakobau who in 1876 sent his warclub to Queen Victoria to symbolize the cession of his realm. Similarly, in independent Samoa the Head of State is leader of the most important of the old high chiefly clans known as the Four Royal Sons. In Tonga a kingdom founded before the battle of Hastings still persists, and its throne is occupied by King Taufa'ahau Tupou IV, descendant of George Tupou I, who gave the realm its constitution in 1862: the parliament he regularly opens with echoes of Westminster pomp is really a feudal assembly of fifteen noblemen who hold ancient chiefly titles and only seven popularly elected commoners. Such political traditionalism is only one aspect of a multiplicity of cultural survivals in the life of the South Seas, ranging as far into the Neolithic past as the use of shell money to buy brides in the Solomons and the sale of stone implements for actual use in New Guinea markets.

These survivals are all the more impressive when one considers how intensively the people of the region, living on their small and all too accessible islands, have been subjected to European intrusion. The first century after Cook's arrival in Oceania two hundred years ago was an era of sustained depredation. Whalers, sandalwood traders, black-birders, traffickers in copra, pearl and bêche-de-mer, gold-miners and itinerant traders, assaulted and demoralized the people even before the more superficially respectable figures of missionary, planter and colonial official made their appearance, followed, as the most recent in this succession of cultural assailants, by the anthropologist. The islands were stripped of everything valuable, their rare woods looted, their guano and phosphates scraped away, their nickel (in New Cale-donia) and gold (in Fiji and New Guinea) ripped from their soils; their people were captured by force or trickery for serfdom in Queens-land or Latin America; those who remained killed each other with guns introduced by the traders, or died from alien sicknesses, and even if they survived for a normal lifespan seemed to lose the reproductive urge so that their numbers declined from decade to decade; their lands were taken away from them, especially in New Zealand, New Cale-donia and the New Hebrides, by speculators whose dishonesties were upheld by colonial judges; their old religions were destroyed, their fetishes burnt, their dances forbidden, by a variety of new creeds that varied from Catholicism to Seventh-Day Adventism, from Anglican-ism to Mormonism, and from Methodism to Bahai.

Yet in spite of these multiple violations, the peoples of the South Seas have emerged from the last two centuries with their will to live renewed and with amazingly large areas of their culture intact. Except for some of the Maoris, they have kept their languages. In New Guinea and the larger islands of the Solomons, pagans continue to live by Neolithic custom. Even on islands where the people have been con-verted to Christianity, sent to school, dressed from neck to ankle, given independence and received as acceptable political societies into the United Nations and the Commonwealth, astonishing areas of tradi-tional living remain untouched: ways of building, farming and fishing, marriage and funeral customs, village organization and systems of land tenure, respect for hereditary titles and social rituals like the kava ceremonial. Old dances and songs survive or are revived; ancient ghosts still haunt, even though the old gods have departed.

Yet Oceanic cultures have survived largely because of their ability to adapt and assimilate. Except for remote bush tribes on the largest islands, they have been adapting ever since Cook in the 1770s opened the long parade of European visitors. But now the process seems to be accelerating so rapidly that adaptation may no longer be a means of cultural survival. Ironically, the balance between adaptation and conservation is being tipped partly because the island groups are regaining their ancient freedom and becoming nations in their own rights. Since 1962 Samoa, Tonga, Fiji and Nauru have all gained sovereign independence, and New Guinea and the Cook Islands have gained internal self-government, with all the developments involved in political change and in the need to achieve balanced economies. But balanced economies are precisely what most of the Oceanic archipelagos find it difficult to achieve in twentieth-century conditions. Except for New Caledonia with its nickel deposits and New Guinea with still incompletely explored mineral riches, the islands depend on resources that are either vanishing or declining in cash value. The phosphates of Nauru will be exhausted in a quarter of a century; those of the Gilberts in a decade. Sugar, copra, bananas – the main crops – are highly vulnerable commodities in world markets. Meanwhile population is growing so fast that in many groups the traditional subsistence economies cannot long be sustained without Malthusian disasters.

One after another, following the examples of Hawaii and Tahiti, the island countries are accepting the conclusion that tourism is the appropriate therapy for a dwindling trading economy. Already in Fiji tourism has replaced sugar as the leading industry. Samoa has reluctantly abandoned a policy of discouraging visitors so as to preserve fa'a Samoa (Samoan customary life) and is embarking on an experiment in controlled tourist development. Hotels and resorts are appearing on remote beaches of the New Hebrides; New Caledonia has its miniature Côte d'Azur. It seemed that we had chosen a crucial time. A decade's delay, and we might easily arrive too late. In making our plans, we decided that we could not explore the whole vast area from Hawaii to New Zealand and from New Guinea to Easter Island. We quickly eliminated Hawaii and Tahiti, because there the processes of assimilation and corruption were already too advanced, and the Marquesas and Easter Island because they were far outside what we finally decided must be the circle of our efforts, an area roughly 2,000 miles in diameter, containing both independent countries and colonies and also representative examples of the three great cultural groups. Proceeding from east to west, we would visit the Polynesian groups of Samoa and Tonga, the racially and culturally mixed nation of Fiji (with its large Indian element), the British-administered Gilbert Islands in Micronesia, and in Melanesia the British protectorate of the Solomons, the French province of New Caledonia, and that strange political anomaly, the Franco–British Condominium of the New Hebrides.

In December 1971 the Canadian Broadcasting Corporation finally adopted our scheme and we were able to complete our plans. Gordon left at once for Fiji; Inge and I planned to reach Samoa at the beginning of February.

2

It had been a bad winter in Vancouver. Often we sit snug between sea and mountains in the wind-swept misty green of our rain forests, with barely a scattering of snow and the roses stubbornly blossoming to meet the snowdrops. But occasionally the land punishes us, bitter winds sweep down from the Yukon, the roses wither over night, traffic clogs to a standstill in feet of snow, and the travel agents take down their Green Winter posters and substitute the white and dazzling ones that advertise the Skiers' Paradise. Such a winter, chill Christmas shuddering into bleak New Year, was that which drifted from 1971 to 1972. It was indeed a winter for escape.

It was night when we flew out over the Pacific. Hours later Hawaii span below us, a midnight glitter of lights. Hours later again, having slipped back a day in history as it crossed the international date line, the plane descended to Nadi on the main Fijian island of Viti Levu.

Rain was falling heavily through the thick darkness of the hour before tropical dawn. Small thin Indian girls in orange uniforms stood at the plane's door, opening tartan umbrellas and thrusting them into our hands to shelter us as we ran over the asphalt to the airport buildings. The clothes in which we had shivered in Vancouver seemed like clammy heated armour as we trotted past tall hibiscus hedges whose red blossoms nodded under the downpour; over the drowned lawns giant frogs hopped and splashed.

The plane for Samoa was due to leave three hours later, and we sat on the airport veranda, sweating gently into our tweeds and watching the dawn slowly reveal the face of the island. The rain still fell, beating crimson flowers out of the tall flame trees behind the airport buildings, and a dense veil of fleecy cloud obscured what would normally have been a middle distance view; we saw the bright green pikemen's squares of sugar-cane in the near-by fields, and little painted wooden houses where Indian farmers lived, and tree-tufted knolls crested by buildings which we later learned were hotels. As the sky brightened, the Indian mina birds that hopped among the frogs on the sodden grass set up a high bubbling chant, and crested bulbuls sang in the hibiscus bushes. A girl in an orange sari brought us sandwiches and spoke in a soft singsong. For a moment it seemed we were back in India, on the airport veranda of Trivandrum or Bangalore, waiting for the plane to Delhi. Then the low clouds stirred and quickly disintegrated, and the landscape became new and unfamiliar, the hills of Viti Levu rearing up to their rocky inland ridges, their saddles green with savanna, and woods clambering up their slopes. The rain ceased; we walked out on the splashy lawn, enjoying the coolness of a sudden breeze; there were familiar heavy tropical scents of earth and flowers and something tantalizingly acrid that we had smelt before in similar climates but never identified. Then, as suddenly as if a sluice had opened in the sky, the rain belted down again and we ran for shelter.

The lounge filled and emptied as planes arrived from Japan and Los Angeles and left for Sydney and Bombay. I wandered lethargically around the reception lounge, buying stamps with exotic bird designs at the postal wicket and looking with an unfulfilled hope of finding something interesting in the debris of duty-free electronic goods, bogus French perfumes, pandanus hats and comic heads carved from coconuts that feebly invited attention at the gift stalls. I observed – without giving it the significance it attained when we later stayed and travelled in Fiji – the racial division of functions. The airline clerks were Indian. The barmen who dispensed ink-flavoured coffee were sallow-faced Euronesians. The policemen and the porters were Fijians, dressed in the wrapover kilt (called the sulu) reaching just below the knee.

Except for one gigantic turbaned Sikh, the Indians were small and slender, with delicate hands and dark finely cut features. Compared with Indians in India, they looked prosperous, unworn by labour, yet sombre and withdrawn, as if beset by some overbearing collective anxiety. There seemed little in common – except for sharing a land – between them and the Fijians, whom they appeared to regard with an apprehensive suspicion which the Fijians countered with a gentle aloofness their physique enabled them to maintain convincingly. For they were tall, erectly walking people, and if one's first reaction to their irregular and slightly Negroid features was that in comparison with the Indians they seemed coarse and earthy, there was a vitality in their expressions that I found immediately attractive; in the end I learnt to prefer the Fijians in character and even in looks to other Oceanic people of more obvious beauty and more demonstrative charm.

PART ONE
The Royal Sons of Samoa

1

At dawn we boarded the Air Pacific plane that flies a leisurely course to Apia, via Suva, Tonga and Niue. We flew first over land, the southern side of Viti Levu, with the long white surfline of the reefs lying always out to sea on our right. Around Nadi, the land was a bright patterning of small fields, with the dark green of sugar-cane predominant, and here and there a mosaic of flashing mirrors of water where rice was being grown in paddies. The houses were mainly set on hillocks for coolness and to escape the mosquitoes, and their metal roofs semaphored from crest to crest in the morning sunlight. But we could see no house at all when we flew over the maze of hills in the centre of the island, their forests broken by great stretches of savanna covered with tall golden grass. We descended over another region of green farms, along the river Rewa, to the airport of Nausori, which serves Suva.

From Nausori we flew out over the ocean, east towards Tonga. It seemed at first a shining blue monotony, and so it was for many miles, an endless sea with neither island nor ship in sight. Only the strange curving lines, where wave patterns met, varied its even surface, which I thought of as an oceanic Shield of Achilles, concealing beneath its enamel surface an infinity of cruelties and secrets. The eventual jewels of that shield were the first coral islands I had ever seen. I realized with a shock of delight that because I was seeing them from the air they had an extraordinary abstract beauty, of pure colour and form, which the navigators had never described because they had never seen it. The first was an atoll that drifting fruit and seed-bearing birds had not yet begun to turn into an island; its reef was covered daily by the tide. But there it lay in a magic complex of concentric circles of intense colour: the deep indigo of the sea, modifying to paler blue on the edge of the white ring of surf that broke over the reef, itself moss-green, with the tone turning just within the lagoon to copper-green and shading to deep turquoise at the centre, the whole thing like the eye of some cosmic Argus. Almost immediately afterwards I saw another atoll where the chromatic pattern was enhanced by the presence of a little round island covered with light green scrub and ringed with a yellow beach, placed like a gold-set emerald in the very centre of the lagoon.

It was these small, half-formed, uninhabited atolls that were the true sea-jewels. Tongatapu, the main island of the Kingdom of Tonga, where we first put down, was a large raised atoll, a great slab of coral limestone bitten and scarred by the sea and lop-sided as well, since there was no reef on the western side. Dense regiments of coconuts rushed up to meet us as the plane descended to the grass-grown airstrip which the Tongans retain to discourage American and Australian airlines who wish to import whole battalions of tourists.

At Tonga the jurisdictions of two little Oceanic airlines meet – Air Pacific, which is centred in Fiji, and Polynesian Airlines, whose main reason for existence is to enhance the national prestige of Western Samoa, which owns it. The Air Pacific clerk at Nadi had told me to confirm at Tonga that we were indeed booked to Apia; it was known, he claimed, for passengers to be taken off the plane and stranded without a room in Tonga.

I ran into the little airport shed and faced a gigantic Tongan in khaki – the immigration officer – flanked by two equally massive policemen in blue lavalavas and slouch hats pinned at the side like Australian soldiers'. They accepted my explanation without asking to see my passport. 'I could have vanished into the island!' I said to Inge when I told her; she laughed and answered, 'How long do you think *your* protective colouring, white hair and green eyes, would last on a Polynesian island?'

The building was crowded with hefty Tongan men and women, towers of flesh garlanded for departure and wearing, over their other clothes and their prominent abdomens, pandanus mats tied with coconut fibre ropes; these ta'ovala are the national garments without which no Tongan feels decently clothed or can enter the presence of a man of standing. A youth in a large floppy coconut-leaf hat, with a spray of orchid hung over his ear, sat on the floor strumming a mandolin. There was much laughter. The flight clerk was in a state of excitement approaching hysteria, fending off a trio of Americans in expensively ragged jeans who had been trying to get off the island for a week and

had arrived to demand that promises be kept and they board our plane.
I realized it was indeed urgent to confirm our seats, and pushed my way,
waving tickets, into the argument. The clerk was glad of an excuse to
escape these justly angry men, for he immediately took my tickets and,
without checking his list, led me at a bounding trot back through the
customs shed and over the turf in a humid 80° to the plane. There he
demanded that I identify our baggage, and once I had done so he
shouted, 'Seats confirmed, sir!' and scampered back to ward off the
Americans; they were not on the plane when we departed.

We flew over the whole Tongan archipelago, its three groups
parted by trenches of open ocean: Tongatapu, the Ha'apai group of
true coral atolls, and the Vavau group, a spectacular assemblage of
high volcanic islands with sheer conical summits and, in their midst,
one of the finest harbours of the South Seas, a gleaming vastness of
dark green water held by the dark fingers of steep islands, and populated
when we flew over, by a single schooner. There is little copra in Vavau
and the Tongan government wisely procrastinates on tourism.

Crossing the dateline back from February into January, we flew over
many more miles of Reckitt's blue afternoon sea and at last came into
view of the grey whalebacks of Samoa's larger islands. White geyser-
like plumes rose high along the shoreline of Savai'i as the tide pushed
through the blow-holes in its coastal apron of lava, but we passed
south of them, descending over the little islands of Apolima and
Manono, and swinging low above the lagoon to land on the airport
that lies like a wound among the coconut groves near the western tip
of Upolu.

2

Gordon Babineau, with a face like a nervous Caesar, and the CBC
Unit Manager Mike Morgan, calm and heron-tall, were awaiting
us beyond the plywood gate where Samoan policemen stood guard
in their uniforms of grey bush-shirts and lavalavas with white bobby's
helmets. Gordon and Mike had brought their hired car, and we drove
to Apia, the capital, along the road that skirts Upolu's north-western
shore. For the first few miles we traversed a great coconut grove
originally planted by the Germans; having been confiscated by New
Zealand during World War I, it now belonged to the Samoan state.
Like all such plantations, there was a robot-like monotony about its

endlessly repeated rows of palms, their trunks rusty with lichen, rising out of a thin undergrowth of grass and small bushes where Hereford cattle grazed, tended by Samoan cowboys. Walls of grey lava blocks, like miniature Inca fortifications, fenced the grove from the highway, and trains of little donkeys carried panniers of nuts to the copra drying sheds.

Once we had passed through the plantations, the Samoan villages began and continued, with little break between them, all the way to Apia. Samoans are sea people; they may cultivate land in the interior of their islands, but they like to live on the shore, beside the lagoons which provide a great proportion of their food, and the consequence on Upolu (where more than 100,000 people live on a little over 400 square miles) is that the coast is crowded while there are large inland areas, up in the jungle-covered hills visible south of the road as we drove into Apia, which are almost uninhabited.

The villages were oriented to the road but also to the mirror-smooth expanse of the lagoon where there were always canoes passing to and fro, and men and women wading waist-deep into the shallow water and occasionally submerging themselves to gather crustaceans and molluscs from the sandy bottom. Passing from one village to the next, our eyes were always caught by the oncoming church which dwarfed every other building; there were sometimes two or three in a village, reminding one in their Gothic or Baroque magnificence, beaten shabby by the monsoons, of those vast medieval churches one sometimes finds, islanded by time, in a European village from which most of the population has long departed.

In the Samoan village the disproportion was less between church and population, for there were always plenty of brown-limbed children playing by the road, than between the strange European ostentation of the church and the Polynesian simplicity of the houses. For only a few of them were palangi houses (or wooden bungalows);[1] almost all were native fales each consisting of a thatched and peaked roof supported by an oval of upright tree-trunks, raised in turn on a platform of piled freestone. Mats were laid on the floors of the fales, and within

---

[1] Palangi, the generally used word in Samoa for a white man or any of his products, means literally sky breaker, deriving from the belief that, since the world was assumed to be limited and known (as the Greeks before had assumed their world to be) the strangers who appeared 200 years ago in their great winged ships must have broken through the atmospheric integument of the sky.

them life went on in the public eye, the people sitting cross-legged against the posts, with their wealth displayed to the world in the form of painted cupboards and chests, and great double beds piled high with brightly coloured pillows and German feather quilts never used because everybody slept on the floor on mats. There were matwork blinds to be let down not for privacy – of which Samoans have little sense – but for shade.

Village after village passed, with little space between them; each with its vast churches, and its dozens of open fales laid out beside the road, with the grass neatly cut around them and usually a bush or two of hibiscus and a few flowering plants. There would be horses grazing on the green near the church, and graves before the houses decorated with streamers of coloured plastic, and little stores of unpainted planks decorated with advertisements for Player's and Coca Cola, and boys standing by the roadside holding up strings of mullet for sale. Very occasionally, when a fale belonged to a rich and powerful man who chose to follow fa'a Samoa, it would be two-storeyed.

Even in these places on the busy highway to the airport one had an immediate (and quite accurate) sense of the extreme traditionalism of Samoan life. In contrast the first – and the lasting – impression of Apia was one of shoddy makeshift and impermanence.

Apia is not only the capital; it is also the only place in Western Samoa that can be called a town. Apia grew as a trading community in the days when Germans, British and Americans were manœuvring for the possession of Samoa. In 1899, when Britain withdrew from the contest, the Americans took the small eastern islands and the Germans the larger western ones; Apia became a colonial capital and after 1914 its overlords were the New Zealanders, who had annexed the islands in the early months of the war and became for almost fifty years the local representatives of imperialism.

We slipped almost imperceptibly from the village world into Apia. The outskirts of the city were evident only in a denser placing of fales among the coconut groves and bread-fruit orchards, until we came to the wide bay where the city stands – essentially a single long one-sided street, its buildings facing out to the shore with only the roadway separating them from the blue waters of the harbour. One realized immediately how appropriately The Beach is used as a term to describe these seashore trading communities of the South Seas which were built when communication was entirely by ship and shore-hugging canoe. From a little way out to sea Apia looks impressive because of the towers and façades of its rival churches, softened and magnified in the humid light, but driving along the front on that first day we were much more aware of the mud-spattered fronts of decaying wooden stores and warehouses, often bearing on their façades the fading names of German traders; such relics still outnumber the modern buildings that have arisen since independence. Like most places in the South Seas, Apia is slow to shake off the marks of its trading origin.

3

At the far end of the front at Apia, near the pier where the freighters and the occasional cruise ships unload, is Aggie Grey's, the only hotel that in early 1972 was not decaying like the old German stores along the front. There we spent our weeks in Samoa. Behind the original Maughamesque wooden building, still used as a dining room, featureless concrete air-conditioned rooms had been built, like rooms in any international hotel in any part of the modern traveller's world. Yet there was a warm eccentricity about the running of Aggie's that made it one of the most agreeable hotels in the South Seas. Aggie Grey, a national character whose portrait appears on Samoan postage stamps, is a strong-willed and still attractive septuagenarian, half Samoan and half New Zealand; according to the records, she was the daughter of the local apothecary; according to a legend she does not deny she was the original of one of the more spectacular characters in Michener's *Tales of the South Pacific*.

Aggie managed the hotel with her daughter and daughter-in-law, two equally attractive and autocratic women, and the rule of the trio had enough caprice and personal attentiveness to alleviate the impersonality of most hotel life. At lunch and dinner, announced by slit gongs and served at large communal tables, the roast beef and New Zealand lamb were varied by abundant and unannounced Chinese and Polynesian dishes; there were always Berliner pfannkuchen for breakfast, and the house treated one unpredictably to wine. Bunches of ripening bananas hung from the beams of the verandas to be freely plucked, and each morning dishes of sliced pineapple were put in a little refrigerator in one's room.

At least once a week, and sometimes more often, a Polynesian fiafia (literally 'happiness') would be held for Aggie's guests in the great fale by the swimming pool, beginning with a gargantuan meal of roast sucking pig and chicken, fish and crustaceans, molluscs and seaweed, taro and palusami, yams and bread-fruit, with great garnishings of coconut cream sauce. Afterwards girls from the local villages performed Europeanized Samoan dances; male dancers twirled flashing silvery swords and then rotated flaming torches in amazing arabesques of fire; a hawk-nosed transvestite of local fame performed seductive Tahitian hulas. And always, as the high point of the evening, Aggie and her daughters in turn performed the siva, that intensely personal dance of the Samoan, in which every woman seeks, by intricate gestures of the hands and arms even more than by movements of the body, to express her own proper personality; all sivas, hence, are different, and all sivas become refined with age, gaining intensity from the body's growing limitations. Aggie would mount the stage with rheumatic and almost elephantine step, and one would expect something pathetic, revealing only age, but now it was only the fingers one watched, and in their movements, still precise, eloquent, sharply beautiful, all the fire and spirit of this woman who has become a legend in her lifetime manifested themselves. It was not merely one's hostess dancing for her guests; it was the last poignant dance of that long love affair between northern man and the sunlit islands of the southern ocean.

4

But we had not come to Samoa to lounge in a genial hotel, though the variety of people on many missions we met at Aggie's contributed much to our understanding of Samoa. We had come to observe how its people lived, and began at the top, which is not difficult in a country of about 150,000 inhabitants with a small, tightly knit ruling class centred on a few noble clans. After dinner on our first evening, we drove to Samoa College, in the hills just behind Apia, to meet Al Wendt, the Principal. Samoa has no university – the nearest thing is an Agricultural College – and Samoa College is really a public school which imitates Christchurch College in New Zealand and is run by the state for the benefit of the children of chiefs.

Al Wendt's house was new, white and airy, filled with books and furnished to the taste of his wife Jenny, an open-faced New Zealand blonde. Al was short and small-limbed for a Polynesian, with a mop of curly black hair and the rather Apollonian good looks that sometimes come from the mixture of Polynesian and northern bloods; his grand-father, the original Wendt, had been a German, but the family had retained its Samoan links, and Al's father was the matai (the customary chief) of a clan in one of the villages of Upolu.

Tupuola Efi and his wife were the other guests. Tupuola was Minister of Works, tall, broad-shouldered and young; looking, in his blue shirt and blue-flowered lavalava, worn with bare feet, like a fine example of the traditional Polynesian nobility, which indeed he was, for he belonged to the same clan as the incumbent Prime Minister, and was regarded as a leader of the younger generation of Samoan politicians, likely himself to head the government when the men who came to power with independence in 1962 begin to show their age and lose their influence.

The conversation that evening wandered through the valley between two worlds, for Al was a scholar and poet highly conscious that his literary veins led elsewhere than the roots of his belonging, while Tupuola, as a rising politician, was aware of the vulnerability of small countries in the modern world, and thus saw his land's future in a double context few village Samoans would have understood.

Al had spent long periods studying abroad, mainly in New Zealand, and even now, though he accepted that his life's work lay in Samoa, he found that he had to escape now and again to satisfy the thirst for learning and literature he had developed away from home. For me, he became a prototype of the South Sea intellectual in the later twen-tieth century; I found many more who resembled him as I went on through the islands, men who were the first of their kind but already perhaps too late for the enormous task of reconciling their ancestral insularity with their acquired universality. Al saw himself as a man of two cultures, drawn back to the traditional life of his people whenever he went away, but, as soon as he had been back in his village a couple of days, already bored and nostalgic for the larger world. His were the longings of a poet and a novelist in a country with little written litera-ture; the important book in Samoa has always been and remains the translation of the King James Bible. If one uses the Samoan word for writer – Tusitala or teller of tales – the name most islanders associate with it is that of Robert Louis Stevenson, whose grave on Mount Vaea is still one of the places to which visitors are expected piously to climb; nevertheless, I found it impossible to buy a single book by Stevenson in Apia or, indeed, anywhere in the South Seas. Nor could I buy a book by Al Wendt, who is regarded by many people as the leading young Samoan writer, for the simple reason that when I knew him he had not succeeded in publishing a novel or a book of his poems; I had to search out his work in little New Zealand magazines or in that compendium of South Seas information and writing, the *Pacific Islands Monthly*.

Al's desire to feel that he was touching the edges of world literature made him question me at length and searchingly on the writers I had known. He was pleased that I had been a friend of Orwell and Dylan Thomas, and had studied and corresponded with Camus. Whenever we met again, he would turn the conversation to these writers. He saw them as men who – though for different reasons – were divided like himself; their sense of isolation in a great culture seemed to reassure him about his own frustrations in the simple and insulated culture of Samoa.

Tupuola seemed more in control than Al of his two worlds, perhaps because of the assurance of high status, wealth, and an education that had given him an almost perfect English accent. This smiling giant was, in the tradition of Polynesian noblemen, soft spoken, and often, listening to him talking and to his quiet giggling laugh, I would be reminded of the Dalai Lama and my conversations with him years ago in India.

Tupuola was a sophisticated modern politician, but his roots, like those of all Samoan leaders, were in his rural territory. The name by which everyone knew him – Tupuola – was actually his hereditary title, meaning something like 'living king', and by virtue of it he swayed the group of villages on the island of Savai'i whose matais voted him to parliament. A Samoan leader who lost touch with his villages – Tupuola insisted – would inevitably fail, for Apia, though it has attracted almost a fifth of the Samoan population, provides no power base; the loyalties of its Samoan inhabitants remain in the villages where they retain their membership of the aigas or landholding clans. But this did not mean that high chiefly politicians who depended on village votes were themselves rustic. Most of them, like Tupuola, had been educated in the English-style public schools of New Zealand or Australia, and some had attended university.

We could not hope to understand Samoa, Tupuola insisted, unless we went to the villages. We had already engaged a tall and rather taciturn young man named Sione, to act as our interpreter and guide on Upolu after Gordon and Mike went on to Tonga the next day. But

Upolu, though the most populated and most Westernized island, was not enough, Tupuola insisted. 'You must go to Apolima. It is a tiny island, just the stump of a volcano, but very beautiful. You will find people there living more traditionally than anywhere else, and you will see a historic place. Long ago there was a great rivalry between the Polynesian islands, and once the Tongans invaded Samoa and captured the whole group, all but Apolima. One day out of the harbour of Apolima the hero Malietoa, who is the forefather of our present head of state, led the canoes and warriors that drove the invaders home. When you go there you will see why Apolima held out. It is a true fortress of the sea.'

Tupuola was even more insistent that we should visit his own island of Savai'i, more than half as large again as Upolu, but sparsely inhabited owing to the volcanic eruptions that have made much of it infertile and turned its southern coastline into a desert of lava beds. We must circle the island, he said, and on our way stay at his own loyal village of Faleolupo on the north-western tip of Savai'i, from which the dead take their departure to the other world. He was going to Savai'i tomorrow, and would make the arrangements. All we need do would be to take a few presents according to Samoan custom for the chiefs who would entertain us; a tala (about 50p) or so for each matai, a little more for the tulefale or village orator, and a case of tinned fish as a present for the fono or village assembly. 'It is a strange thing, but a good Samoan will exchange the best fish of the South Seas for a little tin of English pilchards in tomato sauce!' We accepted Tupuola's invitation, not suspecting how curiously it would end.

Tupuola talked much on the choice between tradition and modernization that faced Samoan politicians and the Samoan people. Most Samoans are devoted to the manifestations of customary life – the beloved fa'a Samoa – which they retained when their conversion to Christianity brought them at least nominally into the sphere of European civilization. The churches became substitutes for the old temples, the London Missionary Society's pastors took the place of the pagan priests, a few European goods were introduced for use or more often for display, but the essential structure of Samoan native life had remained untouched, and the political leaders had sought to conserve it. For many years – ever since the waning of German rule – land sales to outsiders or even to Samoan individuals have been forbidden; land must belong to the traditional clans or be vested in the state, and only a few foreign-owned plantations survive from the colonial past. The effect of tourism on native cultures in Hawaii and Tahiti had been observed, and early Samoan governments tried to control it by allowing only short visits, by building a small airport, and by discouraging the building of hotels.

It was bleak economic reality – Tupuola remarked – that had forced a revision of this attitude. Samoa was a small country with a rapidly growing population. There were still only 150 people per square mile, but much of the land was mountainside or barren lava bed. The world market for copra, Samoa's main product, was shrinking. Bananas and cocoa, the other important crops, had proved equally uncertain. No mineral resources had been discovered. The oceans beyond the reefs were full of fish, but the Samoans were inshore fishermen and disinclined to venture into deep seas. There was timber in the interior of Savai'i, but the arrangements made with an American lumber firm were not working out well. Emigration had provided a certain relief from population pressures; probably a fourth of all Western Samoans were working abroad in New Zealand, Hawaii and California, and sending money home to their families. But that outlet could not last forever, and Samoa must recognize its situation as a static subsistence economy based on farming and fishing, with small exports, and a population whose increase family planning has so far failed to reduce.

Tourism seemed the only way out; if Samoa took its share of the boom from which Tahiti and Fiji were profiting, it would improve its economic chances. 'We are extending the airport for jet traffic,' Tupuola explained. 'We have bought a small jet for our own airline, and you will see its first flight. We have regretfully authorized leases of land for four hotels. It is necessary – and sad. The tourists who find room in Aggie's are so few that they have little effect on our lives. But once the other hotels are here, everything will change. There will be millions of strangers and many of them will be vulgar and insensitive people. They cannot fail to influence our life. All we can do is make sure they do not dominate it.'

'Why should they?' Al protested. 'We absorbed Christianity and fa'a Samoa survived. The Germans came, they left some of us their names, and they introduced us to Berliner pfannkuchen, but fa'a Samoa still survived. Why should the tourists be any different?'

'I hope you are right,' Tupuola answered. 'But we did not depend on the Church or the Germans for our living, and we shall depend on the tourists. We have escaped from political empires. I only hope it is not to become the subjects of airline imperialism!'

5

The Prime Minister of Western Samoa received us in one of the old white-painted plank buildings which the New Zealanders built when they uneasily ruled Samoa in the face of a fluctuating but never wholly dormant opposition, led openly or covertly by the chiefly families and encouraged by some European merchants. The Prime Minister, Tupua Tamasese Leafoli IV, played his part in the independence movement called Mau, which began under the German administration and continued under the New Zealand mandate; his uncle, then head of the Tamasese clan, had been killed by the police when he was trying to prevent his followers from using violence in a demonstration during the 1930s. But there was none of the fire one might expect of a resistance leader in the man we met, nor, indeed, any of the volatility of his kinsman Tupuola.

Tamasese was a thickset man with a smiling secretive face, dressed in a black worsted jacket and the black lavalava or kilt which Samoans of status and substance wear in public. He did not strike one as a charismatic leader or, indeed, in any way an exceptional intelligence or personality. In Samoa he did not have to be any of these, since his position as a local chieftain guaranteed his election to Parliament and his rank as a Royal Son ensured that he would be high in the running for office.

Having offered us Cuban cigars, Tamasese began by explaining that he was not a party leader. 'We have no political parties in Samoa. Every Member of Parliament is elected on his own merit, and then the Ministers are chosen by the consensus of Parliament.' A realistic interpretation of this statement would be that Members of Parliament win their seats by local power and titular privilege, and the Prime Minister is chosen after a complex factional intrigue in which the four high chiefly clans operate like political parties. Tamasese gained power in a three-cornered struggle with Mataafa (another Royal Son who was the first prime minister of Samoa) and Tupuola Efi, but owed his success to the fact that when the first vote was indecisive Tupuola observed clan loyalty and told his vassals to vote for Tamasese.

The conversation led naturally into the question of a political system based on the traditional patterns of land ownership. Universal suffrage exists in Samoa only in two Apia seats reserved for non-Samoan minorities. All other Members of Parliament are elected by the matais, or heads of local land-holding clans, and must themselves be matais. Tamasese argued that the system was in fact more democratic than ours. 'It's true that there are only ten thousand matais and a hundred and fifty thousand Samoans. But the matais themselves are elected in an extremely democratic way. The members of the aiga discuss who among them is best suited to be matai, which is very important to them, since the matai manages their lands and their finances. Sometimes the discussion goes on for weeks. Everyone's opinion is heard. The women have equal voices, and even the children are consulted. The clan goes on talking until everyone is agreed upon the most suitable person. It need not be the oldest son, and sometimes it is a woman if she is the best manager. So what we really have is a two-stage democracy, with literally everybody, including the children, electing their matais, and the matais electing their Parliament.'

'But aren't the matais a conservative group who resist change?'

'Not all change. And even if they do, when you see what has happened in some of the new countries of Africa, perhaps it is better to go slowly and keep our tried old traditions until we know we can do without them. It is interesting to watch our young people. They go away to complete their education. When they return they are restive. They say we must have universal suffrage like New Zealand and Britain. But before long you see them discovering the merits of the matai system and eventually becoming matais themselves.'

Like Tupuola, but with less evident reluctance, the Prime Minister placed his economic hopes in tourism. He described the difficulties of starting local industries, and claimed that while his mainly Catholic cabinet had tried to do something positive about family planning, they had been hindered by the puritanical prejudices of the Protestants. The average Samoan family, he remarked, has six children (I found the figure was even higher – 6.7), and Samoans loved children so much that it was difficult to teach them moderation. 'We still have a lot of unoccupied land, even in the hills just behind Apia. That gives us some leeway. We can subsist. But our people want to educate their children and make them more than subsistence farmers, and as we cannot keep on letting our best young people migrate to New Zealand, tourism is our only alternative.'

We talked about Samoa's sense of its place in the world. Tamasese felt that it had a role of regional leadership, since it had the largest Polynesian population outside New Zealand and might act as a counter-balance to Fiji in the South Pacific. But unlike some neighbouring countries (and here I suspect he was referring to Tonga's Lilliputian military establishment) Samoa had no ambition to gather power in the old-fashioned ways; it had decided not to spend its scanty means on an army that would be useless against a determined aggressor. When a guard of honour was needed, the police provided it; even they were only 150 strong and mostly concentrated in Apia. There was little need for policemen in the villages, where the matais kept order through their fonos or local councils.

'I am always ready to help you,' he said as we left. 'You have only to call me or any of my ministers.' One felt the burdens of office in this little realm, for all its problems were so slight that we might have sat another hour chatting quietly, with long slow pauses, and smoking those excellent cigars. Instead we went down to the street outside, from which the clamour of a procession had been floating up during the last minutes of our visit.

It was the grand parade initiating the national cricket tournament. Cricket is passionately followed by the Samoans, but it is an antique form of the game, learnt from English sailors long ago and using great three-sided bats that look more like South Sea war-clubs than any cricket bat seen in England for a century and a half. Today the teams had come in from all over Upolu, Savai'i and the smaller islands, and they followed a band playing 'The Boys of the Old Brigade'. The cricketers marched briskly in white shirts and lavalavas of brightly flowered print, with green shades over their eyes, and their bats, painted the vivid colours of their teams, carried slanting over their shoulders; they shouted the names of their villages as they marched. Three evenings later we would see them returning, the winning teams carrying their trophies high and marching to the triumphant blowing of whistles, and the losers trailing behind, shouting threats of revenge next year. An old Samoan told me that cricket arrived opportunely at the very time the first missionaries were trying to persuade the chiefs and their followers to abandon the endemic civil warfare that in pagan times had torn the islands; the aggressiveness of a warlike people was sublimated into the mock battles of cricket, with village warring ritually against village, and the worst barrier to the acceptance of Christianity was overcome.

But the martial spirit that characterized the Polynesian peoples was never entirely lost. Some of it was dissipated in theological debate, in which the Samoans delight, or consumed in the efforts of building the vast churches that mirror local rivalries. Some, in recent years, has been channelled into the factional intrigues of politics. But enough traditional bellicosity remains to find a ritual manifestation in the revival of the ancient war-dances.

This we found later the same day when we visited Dr. Fan'aafi Larkin, Director of Education and one of the most powerful women in Samoa. Women of strong mind and will have always played their part in Polynesian life. In Samoa men appear to rule at all levels from village to parliament, but we found that women's committees in the villages were strong counter-organizations to the fonos of the matais, and that in Apia the large women's centre, one of the few attractive modern buildings in the capital, was a power source nobody chose to ignore. The women of Samoa led some of the great non-violent demonstrations of the 1950s which persuaded New Zealand and the United Nations to give Samoa complete independence in 1962 rather than mere internal home rule. Al Wendt remarked that there was an even more basic reason for the influence of women. 'The men sit around and talk and think they make decisions. But the decisions are only carried out if the women agree, because it is the women who do most of the work in Samoa.' But women's influence is not always so indirect, for Polynesians have always regarded them as capable of ruling, and there have been great queens in Hawaii and Tahiti and Tonga.

The aura of the traditional Polynesian chieftainess was enhanced in the case of Fan'aafi Larkin by the prestige of being Samoa's first Ph.D. Her offices, set in a grove of rain trees outside Apia, reflected the disciplined mind she applied to what in a developing country is one of the most important areas of administration. While the Prime Minister was content with the unreconstructed office of some New Zealand official, she had created a setting of her own in new buildings with an air of North American efficiency; she had even put her typists into uniform. For herself, she had adopted the rather classical-looking dress of modern Samoa, the long wrapover skirt reaching to the ankles, and the loose tunic hanging down over the hips. It fitted the robust dignity of a high-born Polynesian woman, which Fan'aafi Larkin assumed without abandoning the mental sharpness that had made her

the obvious person to plan an educational system suited to a poor
country that could never be scholastically self-sufficient.

Dr. Larkin had to reshape a system that had never taken into account
the actualities of Samoan life. Missionary schools had unimaginatively
followed English models; when the New Zealanders began to set up
public education, they tied the curriculum in Samoa to their own
examination system.

'We have been using nothing but New Zealand textbooks. When
our children study botany, the examples in the books they study are
plants that cannot be grown in Samoa. When they study geography,
they find Samoa given a passing mention, and they grow up in such
ignorance of their country that the other day I showed a teacher,
twenty-eight years of age, a blank map of our islands and asked him
to point out the site of his own village. He had no idea where it was!'

Samoa was only the first example of a problem we were to find
everywhere in the South Seas; that of small countries with one or more
small language groups, neither numerous nor prosperous enough to
support effective book publishing in their own language or anything
better than a rudimentary periodical press. The difficulties Al Wendt
experienced as a writer in publishing his poems were encountered by
Fan'aafi Larkin in her efforts to create a curriculum appropriate to
Samoa and yet sufficiently flexible to let some Samoans take a university education in New Zealand or at the newly founded University of
the South Pacific in Fiji.

Education is neither universal nor compulsory in Samoa; to make
it so would be beyond the country's means, for even now the schooling
the islanders ardently desire for their children can be provided only by
straining resources on many levels. The state trains and pays teachers
for village primary schools, but the villages must erect and maintain
the buildings. Secondary education is offered partly in state-run schools
and partly in missionary schools. The churches run theological colleges;
the state runs Samoa College and the Agricultural College and con-
tributes to the costs of the University of the South Pacific. Finally, the
child's parents must pay for its uniform, books and stationery.

'The average family pays a twelfth of its cash income for every
child it sends to school. You can imagine what that means when there
are eight. Several thousand children get no education at all and never
will get an education unless we pay their expenses. Even so,' Fan'aafi
Larkin added with the pride that prevents Samoans from admitting

the worst about their circumstances, 'we are better off than most people in the South Pacific, as you will see.'

The pride in being Samoan ran in other directions as well. I was incautious enough to mention the Maoris approvingly. A glint came into Fan'aafi Larkin's eye. 'Our very junior cousins!' she remarked sharply, and led us out over the lawn behind her office to the teacher's training college. 'No doubt you saw how the Maoris pass off their caperings as Polynesian dancing. I will show you the authentic dances of our tradition.'

Polynesian music is simple, even simpler today than it was in the past. The traditional nose-flute survives only among a few old people in Tonga, and the forty young men and women we now watched in a bare wooden hall danced to the sound of their own voices and the rhythm of two small wooden slit gongs, beaten with sticks. Their instructor was the most astonishing maître de ballet I have ever encountered: a middle-aged chief named Iono, a veritable man-mountain in motion, more than six feet tall, with a belly and hips that made his lavalava stand out so that he seemed like an enormous bell of sweating brown flesh, supported on vast columns of legs. He must have weighed more than three hundred pounds, yet as we entered the hall I saw him flex his knees and leap into a ferocious war-posture with the litheness of a European dancer half his age and weight.

As this was a rehearsal for the coming South Pacific Festival, where these dancers would represent Samoa, the girls were in their cotton frocks and the men in flowered lavalavas, with bare tattooed torsos, but the first dances were so palpably authentic that we forgot in the exotic expressiveness of action the lack of traditional regalia. The whole troupe performed a sasa, the dance used to limber up for battle, in which all the muscles are rhythmically exercised to the staccato sound of slapping flesh as the dancers' hands move over the muscular parts of their bodies in a kind of elaborate self-massage. Then three of the girls danced their individual sivas, showing how personal this dance becomes to each woman who performs it and invents the hand movements she thinks proper to her nature. Afterwards there were three dances to lilting Samoan songs, but these had been devised to attract the international audience at the Festival, and the intensity of feeling projected by the other dances – the sense of a martial mass will in the sasa and of an intense personal pride in the siva – no longer forced their way into one's mind.

As we walked away from the dancers, Fan'aafi Larkin asked about our plans, and when I remarked that we had not yet made arrangements to go to Apolima, she offered to make them for us. 'It has the reputation of being a very uncomfortable trip. The passage through the reef is the worst in Samoa. But I went there myself to open the school two years ago, and as you see, I survived. It will probably be Monday. You must be ready to leave Apia by dawn. The seas are bad if you go too late. I will send a good man to introduce you.'

I said we had an interpreter already, but when I mentioned Sione she shook her head in a way that revealed to me more sharply than any explanation the character of Samoan society. 'I know the person,' she said. 'If you want someone merely to interpret, he will pass. But when you go to a Samoan village you are judged by your companions. This person has no title; he is not even a matai; he has no standing at all in our society. Apolima is a traditional village, and you will only be welcome if you go in the company of someone they respect. I will make sure a man of title goes with you and finds you a good boat's crew.'

6

Gordon went on to Tonga, and Inge and I occupied ourselves until Monday wandering around Upolu with Sione, whom we had chosen for his good English, which everyone admitted, and perhaps because his rather flat and sombre face, topping six feet of good Samoan muscularity, reminded us of the inscrutable figures of Easter Island, an impression enhanced by his laconic manner. Here, it seemed, was the primordial Polynesian, but speaking our own language, and we looked forward to an easy unravelling in his company of the secrets of Samoan life.

We found that Sione was not merely a man without title; he was also a man with little of the kind of knowledge we were seeking. His interests and ours were opposite rather than complementary. He had become our interpreter because his ultimate aim was to escape from Samoa and be absorbed into the fascinatingly exotic society of North America. He saw every foreigner who employed him as a possible means to escape, or at least as a source of information on the earthly paradise of his imagination. He had gone so far as to abandon his village church for a Pentecostal group directed from California.

Despite its small area, Upolu comprises a number of distinct regions. There is the stretch of closely packed villages through which we had travelled from the airport east to Apia – the most populated rural area in the whole country. From the airport around the western tip of the island the villages are more widely spaced, giving an appearance of rustic self-sufficiency. East of Apia, the coast is bitten into a series of spectacular bays, and again the villages are scattered, largely because of the irregularity of the coastline and the difficulties of fishing in the heavy swell. The road does not continue all the way around Upolu; the southern coast, a region of broad beaches and secluded coves and inlets, is reached by three roads that cross the mountainous core, where some of the jagged volcanic peaks reach 3,600 feet; this is a region of its own, its dense forest cover broken by stretches of lush savanna. The eastern corner of the island is the most isolated and the least affected by the influence of Apia; some of its villages can be reached only by boat or by foot-trails over the hills, and the coast has a starker feeling than any other part of the islands.

Always, in Samoa, we found ourselves making comparisons between the first and second look at a place. The first would almost always leave an idyllic feeling in the mind. The neat open houses, set in their lawns of carefully cut grass, the vivid flowers, the jewel-like colours of the lagoon, the great ornate churches and the children walking to school in their neat garb of white shirts and bright lavalavas; everything gave the impression of a life in perfect Christian order, straight out of one of those old London Missionary Society reports I remember poring over in childhood not because of their accounts of the great harvests of souls reaped in the mission fields, but for their pictures of exotic places.

Here, in moving life and high tropical colour, were those very places. Families were thatching their fales with sugar-cane; once we saw a house-raising bee, with the village menfolk busily fixing the posts and tying with sinnet the poles that served as rafters. Coconuts were gold-ripe on the trees, and copra dried outside the houses, as did the leaves of pandanus, which the women would later weave into fine mats, the indispensable gifts at the critical points of Samoan life, from baptism through marriage to death. The bread-fruit trees were loaded with green cannonballs, and women came wading in from the lagoon in the drenched cotton dresses they wore even in the water out of Christian modesty, with baskets of green coconut leaves filled with shellfish. Under a palm-leaf shelter the preparations for a feast were going on – men wrapping taro root in its big leaves to cook in earth ovens, and wringing the juice out of shredded coconut to make the sauce for the splendid Samoan dish known as palusami (taro leaf cooked in coconut cream). Children were cutting grass with cane knives like small machetes, but other children were dancing in the shallow water of the lagoon, and on village greens young men and girls played cricket with a kind of merry violence. The young people of both sexes wore hibiscus flowers over their ears; the publicity photos had not lied.

On a second look we would become more aware of the signs suggesting that this idyllic old balance of Polynesian life was in fact shifting towards breakdown. We realized that we were witnessing the first effects of a growth in population unaccompanied by the technological advances that might neutralize it. It was not merely that, like most South Sea islands, Samoa has little electric power, and the people have to make do with paraffin lamps in their fales and with foodsafes instead of refrigerators; that can be endured if one is used to nothing better. A more serious symptom was the fact that sanitation had not progressed beyond the tiny huts of palm-leaf or corrugated iron at the end of rickety catwalks over the lagoon which serve as latrines; their spidery rustic outlines were repeated monotonously along the shoreline. Throughout the South Seas the tide is still regarded as the great cleanser; garbage and ordure of all kinds are habitually consigned to it. Perhaps such reliance on the sea's self-purifying action was justified fifty years ago, when Samoa's population was a fifth its present size, but now the enclosed waters of the lagoons are being polluted faster than they can cleanse themselves, and very soon they may cease to be the rich reservoirs of marine food which they have been ever since men began to fish them. In Europe and North America we have been inclined to associate pollution with industry; the contamination of the beaches along the north shore of Upolu, where there is no industry, supports the view that the ultimate cause of the destruction of the environment is not industry but the unrestrained increase of the human race.

At the western end of Upolu, where people and villages became fewer and the palm-trees leant out over silver-white beaches, the sea and the sands were still little defiled, and on the morning we first went there the whole landscape was washed into sparkling brilliance by one of those lashing tropical storms which at any time between November and April are liable to blow up without warning. A couple of hours before, when we left Apia, the skies had been clear and brilliant. Now the rain was so heavy that we could look no more than a hundred yards out to sea, and over the road itself the rain beat so heavily that its spray created an iridescent mist. The Samoans accepted the storm either with indifference, walking nonchalantly with their soaked lava-lavas moulded against their legs, or as the children did, with delight, dancing and leaping naked like imps under the downpour.

Eventually the rain ended almost as abruptly as it began, but there was still a high wind on which floated dead palm-fronds and brown bread-fruit leaves like oak-leaves a foot long. Great vivid flowers – red and yellow and deep purple – had been dashed out of trees whose names neither we nor Sione knew, and in places they formed a veritable millefiori carpet over the road.

In one village a woman waved to us from a rocking chair on the veranda of a large palangi house built in an arched Spanish style unusual in Samoa. In enormous letters across the façade was painted the motto La Nuanua Ole Alofa (The Rainbow of Love). It was the pastor's house, as the woman told us when we stopped to look at the large tomb that stood before the door. This was decorated with ribbons of blue and red paper hanging from wire arches, and with silver bells, tinsel stars and fresh hibiscus flowers strung on the thin ribs of coconut fronds. It was the tomb of the pastor's wife. 'She died five years ago,' the woman told us. 'But every day the pastor makes us put fresh flowers, and every week he hangs new paper so that the colours will always be bright.' 'It is his rainbow,' said Inge. 'His love,' said the woman.

After we left, I remarked on the size of the house, which was the largest in the village. 'It is always so,' said Sione. 'A matter of village pride. The pastor is a stranger. He belongs to none of the local clans, and for the honour of the village he must be given a big house where he feels comfortable.' 'Does the village pay the pastor?' I asked. 'Pastors do not like it to be said that they are paid,' Sione answered, with a dry irony inspired by his dissent from the prevailing orthodoxy. 'They prefer to say that they receive offerings.'

A great rocky headland ended the western road just beyond the next village of Matauuta, but Matauuta was our destination; we had heard of the great church completed only five years before, to the chagrin of all neighbouring villages. It was indeed an extraordinary structure, even from the outside, with its tall Gothic tower and its perpendicular windows. The gate into the churchyard was heavily padlocked; the elders were taking no risks with jealous rivals. But Sione went to the pastor's house and found a small boy who came with the key and a company of other children. Inside, the church was even more spectacular than the exterior had led us to expect. The boy with the key said that it held a thousand people, and counting in the baroque gallery to which we ascended, I am sure this was true. Yet the total population of the village was only six hundred, and the size of the building was a matter of prestige, not utility. The ceiling was elaborately vaulted and coffered with a variety of fine woods inlaid by an obviously skilled master, and the windows were of brilliant stained glass; if their Congregational patterns were not so elaborate as those we later saw in the Catholic churches of other villages, the total effect was still that of a small cathedral rather than a mere church. It was hard to reconcile such splendour with the severe conventicles that were the Congregational chapels of my childhood, and I reflected on the ironic fate of nonconformist sects that become – like the Congregational Church in Samoa and the Wesleyan Church in Tonga – the centres of conformity. The Spartan plainness that was the badge of dissociation from the established church became inappropriate when the dissenters became the establishment.

Everywhere in Samoa outside Apia, the stranger is a source of demonstrative or discreet interest. At Matauuta the interest was demonstrative, and we emerged from the church to be surrounded by the children who had chosen to stay away from school that day – a dozen lively little creatures the colour of old ivory, with large dark eyes, dancing around us, shouting 'Goodbye!' and 'Palangi!', their bodies so spritely that it was impossible to imagine they would ever grow up into the massiveness which the adult Samoan sustains with vast meals of yam, taro and bread-fruit. Photography aroused them, as it did most Samoan children, to intense excitement, and to get shots of the church I had to pretend with one camera to take snaps of the circle of grinning faces while Inge took the real pictures with the other.

In Matauuta the adults were equally curious about our presence. A policeman in white helmet, shirt and lavalava, with a black belt and black briefcase, came sauntering over the village green. He slapped his case expressively, and explained that he was going through the villages with warrants for people fined for offences in Apia. If they paid him, the warrant was cancelled. If not, he arrested them and took them back. I asked if anyone ever resisted arrest. 'Never! You see, a man who decides not to pay the fine does so because he thinks it will be more profitable to accept a few weeks' hospitality from the government. If he has a job, he pays. If he has no job, he goes to prison. The food is good, the work is light, and his friends think him a very clever fellow.'

By now our presence had been noticed in the school across the green, and a white-gowned, brown-skinned Juno emerged to join the policeman. She was the headmistress, and invited us to see her school. Samoan schools aim to accustom children to Western ways as well as Western knowledge, and so they are all built with walls and windows like palangi houses. Yet when we entered their classroom the forty youngest children were sitting cross-legged on the floor, being taught English by a pretty girl just out of training college. In high and slightly metallic voices – and in a precise English they had learnt by ear and did not understand – they sang 'For he's a jolly good fellow', and then 'My bonnie lies over the ocean', which struck me as a strange fate for a Jacobite song about an exiled prince. A little girl, no more than eight, was monitor of the class, and after the singing she gave a demonstration of Samoan teaching methods: the rote chanting of a series of English words written on the blackboard, during which she vigorously applied the ruler which she used as a pointer to the heads of those small boys whose attention wandered.

As we left the school and thanked the headmistress, Inge remarked on the number of children for so small a village. 'We love children,' she answered. 'I have only five. Other women are more fortunate.' All peoples, I thought as we went away, have their destructive passions which take the delusive shape of love – love of wealth, of war, of ease, of display. With the Samoans it is love of children, the hardest of all loves to condemn but for that reason perhaps the most insidiously destructive.

7

Whichever of the roads one chose to take into the mountains from northern Upolu, it was a quick transition from the populousness of the coastline to the desertion of the volcanic highlands. The road that went south from Apia circled around the base of the forested cone of Mount

Vaea, and past Stevenson's house at Vailima, a big black and white wooden mansion visible between the trunks of a large palm-grove; the house is now used by the Head of State – the Ao-o-le-Malo – and so a writer's home has been transformed into a palace, which is according to the Samoan scale of things.

Along the rising road, we passed other symbols of hidden power – the splendid gardens from which the houses of the New Zealand High Commissioner and the manager of Burns Philp (largest of the South Sea traders) looked out on Apia (almost lost in verdure) and over the reef-bounded harbour. On this road the Germans long ago cleared land for cattle rearing. Cattle still grazed on the open ground, and in odd corners rose great elephant-eared leaves of taro, but the land was reverting, bracken spreading as the forerunner of forest. It would have seemed a temperate moorland, had it not been for the enormous old banian trees, supported on dense Gothic structures of trunk-roots fifteen or twenty feet across that had been left in the pastures for their great green domes of foliage to give shelter to the cattle.

At the crest of the range, the air was cool, the ditches rushed with muddy water, the road was ruined by the constant summer down-pours, and the savanna that had replaced the ferny pastures gave way to a dense jungle over which we looked southward to the sea. Tree fern and wild palm formed tangled walls of green on the cliffsides; we left the car and walked along a faint path through the bushes to the edge of an immense cylindrical chasm, the cup of an ancient volcano, into which the Tiavi Fall plunged in a single sheer ribbon cascading whitely down the fern-green precipices, tumbling almost three hundred feet into the gorge by which it drained to the sea.

Descending on the southern slopes, it was often hard to tell where the jungle ended and plantation began, for the Samoan is a poor weeder, and growth is so rapid that only if one recognizes the trees that spring out of the underbush does the difference between wild and cultivated land become evident. In the plantations, coconut palms, mangoes and bread-fruit trees form the high growth, and where the sun filters between grow the green flags of bananas, and cacao trees with strange fruit hanging like mauve lanterns in the shadows, and dark-leaved coffee bushes spotted with clusters of red fruit. We learnt eventually to recognize the real jungle at a glance by the prevalence of tree ferns and the tangles of lianas looping from tree to tree.

On the south of Upolu the road ran inland through tiny hamlets where trucks collected copra from the stores and at the same time unloaded groceries; the big Apia traders double their profits by acting at once as food wholesalers and copra gatherers. Some villages lay off the road, by the seashore, and once we turned from the highway and down the dirt track which the village maintained; the ruts were so deep that the bottom of the car scraped constantly on the high ridges left in the centre. The village was called Sa'anapu; to reach it we had to drive gingerly over a narrow bridge of palm-trunks that spanned a mangrove-fringed inlet into which the tide was running.

There are courtesies to be observed going into a Samoan village, though they are diminishing. In the days before cars and highroads one was expected to ask a chief's permission to enter a village, just as, approaching a fale, one still stands at the edge of the house-platform, with a hand resting on the mat, waiting for the invitation to climb up and take one's place on the floor. On the main roads where there is through-traffic, these courtesies are no longer observed, but in places off the highways the customs survive, and when Sione went at Sa'anapu on our behalf, and stood at a house-platform to make a petition to view the village, the courtesy was clearly appreciated.

Sa'anapu was a place in the old Samoan style that prevailed when villages were oriented merely to the sea. It stood on a circle of flat land, between the channel we had crossed and the beach; the houses were clustered concentrically rather than in linear formation. There was no real road – just the hard sand over which one bumped between the houses – and here, unlike Matauuta, interest was discreet, not demonstrative; nobody came near us, but the women over their cooking fires and the men smoking pipes and playing cards in the fales watched our progress with the closest attention.

We returned several times to this southern coast, with its fine empty beaches of silver sand where the village boys would ride their pack-horses into the surf towards sunset, and its beautiful inlets like that at Fausaga, mirror-smooth, and surrounded by sandy spits along which the mangroves formed a dark border to the shadowing palms.

But only once did we go, along rough roads where red-headed bush-hens ran in and out of the jungle at our approach, to the villages at the east end of the island where life took on a harsher, greyer tone than anywhere else in Samoa. The reef was close on this coast and the thunder of the high breakers piled up by the south-east wind was so loud that people walking on the road did not hear our car until we were almost upon them. The spray from these pounding waves hung in the air, softening and subtilizing the strong colours of the midday sea and sky, and off the point of Cape Tapaga lay small, forbidding islands with precipitous shores, like fragments of Upolu sliced off by some gigantic axe.

Here, as on the north shore, the villages were close together, but the fales were shabby, with old, decayed roofs; the people dressed in faded, ragged garments, and the clothes hanging on the lines looked worn almost beyond usefulness. The men who worked beside the road had a strangely arcadian look, for they wore chaplets of wild fern to shade their eyes from the sun, and once beside a stream we saw women squatting, beating their washing on the rocks with thick cudgels. In the village of Vailoa a group of men worked on a boat of thin planks; the stem was a curved branch they had carefully selected in the jungle, but they were fixing the planks with galvanized nails instead of sewing them with sinnet in the traditional manner.

In another village we encountered the only European working in this part of Samoa. Wayne was a marine biologist attached to the Peace Corps, a well-barbered Californian carrying on an experiment in turtle rearing. The hawksbill turtle, which at maturity weighs 130 pounds (of which 90 pounds is good edible meat), was once a major item in the island diet, but the species has been declining because the people have little idea of conservation; the previous year they had killed the remaining females on the nearest offshore island, which ceased to be a breeding ground. Fortunately the other islands are more difficult to reach, and from them the workers of the rearing station gathered eggs, often at great risk because of the high seas and lurking sharks. Wayne was still shaken by the fate of his companion, another young biologist who ten days before had been gathering seaweed for turtle fodder off one of these islands when a tiger shark – the first seen here for a generation – attacked him and bit off his head. Two of Wayne's Samoan helpers were out when we arrived, gathering eggs on one of the islands, and as he told his story he kept looking towards the entrance to the Upolu lagoon for a sign of their returning boat. The islet to which they went had so narrow an entrance in its tiny reef that one had to anchor the boat and swim ashore; the ordinary reef sharks were easily fended off, but the appearance of the great tiger sharks made the operation suddenly perilous.

Wayne's project was as simple as it was imaginative. In piles of sand, protected by wire netting, the eggs were hatched. When the young turtles emerged, they were put in concrete tanks to grow, and when they had reached a reasonable size were let loose in the ocean, which obviated the perilous march over the beaches to the sea in which they were the prey of all kinds of predatory birds. The first year 4,000 turtles would be bred; a few hundred might grow to maturity and provide food. Wayne knew that in this humble but useful task he was risking his life as much as his companion had done; tiger sharks rarely appear singly.

In a village called Selea-aumua a few miles beyond the turtle hatchery we heard they were making a boat – a fautasi – to run in the Independence Day races. When we got there, we found almost the whole male population busy around a long coconut-leaf shelter where the boat was being built. The *Magic Tree*, as it was to be called, was a massive craft for forty-four rowers, two abreast, with a coxswain and a drummer to beat the rowing rhythm on a biscuit tin. The form of the nineteenth-century whaleboat had been used, but so lengthened that a stout beam was laid from stem to stern through the bottom of the boat, reinforced by iron clamps and dogs. Because Samoan woods are brittle, every plank had to be steamed, and a strange Heath Robinson contraption had been built, of oildrums heated by wood fires from which pipes led the steam into a long wooden box covered with wet sacks, in which the planks were laid. Softened to take the needed curvature, they were fixed with copper nails. While most of the men were engaged on the boat, others were shaping the oars, first adzing them roughly out of planks and then truing them with small planes and spokeshaves. I never saw Samoans working so hard or with such excellent co-ordination to earn money as these villagers did for the honour of their community, and I realized now how the industry was generated to build the great churches.

The contrast between the vigour of the village base of Samoan life and the ineffectuality of centralized authority in the islands was demonstrated by the neglected hospital we found that afternoon. We had been seeking a place to eat lunch, and had found the beaches either too windy or too populated by seafood gatherers. At last, behind a bleak and weather-beaten building which looked like a barracks on a deserted shore, we found a sheltered beach of firm golden sand, facing a turquoise fragment of lagoon with the waves throwing the spray on the reef a hundred yards away and a fine view of the offshore islands.

Even here we were not alone, for a girl of twenty appeared and accepted our invitation to join us; Aggie's box lunches were always enough to feed any guests we might acquire on our outings.

'In Samoa we are very free,' the girl remarked, rather self-consciously. 'We do what we like.' There was something stilted about the statement, as if she had learnt it by rote, and her voice became more natural when she told us that she was a nurse, had just completed her training in Apia, and for three months was in charge of the local hospital which, it appeared, was the bleak building behind us. She was alone, except for an old couple who acted as caretakers; there were no in-patients and a doctor looked in three times a week. Once, she had been told, there was a resident doctor, and several nurses, and the wards were full of beds – but that was long ago when the palangis ruled.

She went off to swim in the lagoon, fully clothed. On our way back to the car we explored the hospital. The two wards were empty of furniture, the windows broken, dust and dead insects lying in piles on the floors; they had obviously been deserted for years. A room with shelves of bottles was evidently the dispensary where the nurse worked, and in another room with ragged curtains she must have lived. The whole decrepit establishment spoke of the constriction of social services that independence had brought; what was presumably an effective and certainly a needed hospital on this remote end of the island had been reduced to a meagre clinic.

It was a Saturday when we visited the eastern villages, and late Saturday afternoon, when we turned back to Apia, was the most active time of the Samoan week. In the hills, as we returned, the people were riding on horseback from their holdings, their produce carried in baskets hung like panniers; often they rode in tandem, a man and his wife, or a couple of children, on the same horse. We drove on into the wild savanna region, passing rainbow-misted falls and crossing the mountain spine whose steep crags were curtained by great banians tangled together with lianas. At the pass of La Mafa we drove through the narrow defile, and a vast view opened, the green slopes running down northward, chequered with groves and gardens, to the brilliant sea. We descended beside lucid mountainside streams, over an iron bridge built by the Germans, and past Falefa Falls, where we walked in an old cemetery under the rain trees; lava stones, splashed orange and green with lichen, were piled on the graves, and the water span in great whirlpools under the falls and then flowed wide and deep and serene between tall bosky cliffs into the lagoon.

The lowland road was again packed with people: no horses now, but human shoulders bearing shared poles conveying bunches of coconuts and bananas, bundles of taro and taro-leaf, fruits of the garden and jungle in leaf baskets, and sometimes live pigs. It was the great gathering of the weekend food for the Sunday feast after church. In the deep-bitten bays, men with scoop-nets were forming the arc of the fish-drive, enclosing shoals of mullet in their narrowing circles. Small boys stood in the surf, jigging with cane rods and using white fragments of chicken feathers as their lures. The fish they caught were small creatures that flashed in the sun like knives; as each was caught it was killed by biting the spine. These tiny fish are eaten raw – popped into the mouth and sucked whole until all the flesh is absorbed, when the debris of bones and scales is rather disconcertingly spat out.

While all this last ingathering of food was going on, the women and girls were working around the houses, hacking the grass, burning rubbish in little stinking fires, and brushing the yards of grey crushed coral with besoms of coconut midriffs, making the houses clean for the sabbath.

8

It is only on Sunday, when the churches are open and, passing by, one hears the pastors bellowing from their dark recesses over the great white-clothed congregations, that one realizes the full power of religion, or at least the full pressure of religious conformity, in Samoa.

Out of the goodness of heart that compensated for his other shortcomings, Sione decided on our first Sunday on Upolu to absent himself from his own Pentecostal services and take us to the Congregational church in the village of Moata'a, just east of Apia. Afterwards he invited us to lunch at his own house.

In Apia there was no possibility of failing to wake in good time for church. At half past four the bells in the Catholic cathedral just down the road from Aggie's began to toll for early mass. The whole island was up betimes, and as we went to breakfast pungent smoke drifted over the little river behind the hotel from the fires the men were lighting to heat the stones in the earth ovens where pigs for the feast after morning church would be cooked.

At Moata'a the church stood on the shore of the lagoon, a massive thick-walled building with an arched colonnade shading the door, and an ornate little detached canopy, rather like a pagoda, standing in front of the doors to shelter the bell which one of the deacons was ringing. The children were singing hymns in a white-dressed circle on the grass. Inside the church, the congregation arranged itself, men on the left, women on the right, except for the choir, at least a hundred strong, in which the men stood behind the women. The women were all in white, with little plate-like straw hats perched on their heads. The men wore white or black jackets with white lavalavas, and everyone wore ties and carried palm-leaf fans which were vigorously used as the heat built up inside the building.

The church had been built during the German era, and there was a distinctly Bavarian flavour about the interior, with its wooden baroque arches supporting the vaulted ceiling, which was decorated with painted wooden medallions; around the windows were painted floral patterns like those of Alpine churches. Most striking was the great pulpit gallery that overbearingly filled the whole end of the church; it was made of finely carved and polished wood, approached by flights of stairs on either side, and hung with red plush draperies. Thence, with his Bible resting on a great red cushion, the gaunt grey old pastor looked down on his flock, like Jehovah on the Day of Judgement, with four solemn deacons sitting below him like lesser judges. Obviously, the church had been arranged to enhance the role of the pastor as a man of God, but also perhaps, in a lingering, half-conscious memory of the past, to suggest his role as something resembling the God-man which the pagan priests had been.

The sermon, in Samoan, we could not understand, though Sione interpreted fragments from which we gathered that it concerned the nature of signs and appealed to the Samoan taste for theological abstractions. The choir's unaccompanied singing was magnificent, an organ in itself, creating spine-shivering waves of sound as the men and women sang in counterpoint. Here at least, one felt, the Samoans had received compensation for what the missionaries made them lose in the good aspects of the old pagan religion.

Not that our reflections on paganism were welcome when we reached Sione's house and met his wife, a secondary school teacher, and their seven children. Sione had wedded money, the gossiping barmaids at Aggie's had already told us; he had acquired a widow with a good job and a rare freehold lot. On that fragment of land, among palms and bread-fruit trees, mangoes and bananas, stood a new palangi house with glittering windows, and a Samoan fale decorated in our honour with green palm-fronds plaited around its poles. Sione's wife was proud of her status as a professional woman, but she insisted on entertaining according to fa'a Samoa. She served her husband and his guests, fanning us assiduously while we ate; only when we had taken our fill of the mixed Samoan-European meal of taro and palusami with sausages and onions did she and the children eat in a lesser fale down the garden. Later she joined us to chat over a cup of tea as if she were an English hostess and the earlier ceremonial had not occurred.

Fresh from seeing the Samoan villagers in their Victorian Sunday best, Inge reflected warmly on the iniquity of the missionaries who had forced their converts to substitute such hot and ugly clothes for an easy and healthy semi-nudity. But, despite the pride Samoans take in their past, this was not a point of view that pleased them, as Sione's wife quickly made clear. John Williams and the other early missionaries were still the heroes who had brought them out of pagan darkness, and now they regarded Christianity as their natural religion, and their conversion as destined.

Outside the great enclosed fale where the Samoan Parliament meets in Apia, there is a stone wall with an inscription that reads: Fa'avae i le atua Samoa (Samoa is founded on God). Most Samoans believe it fervently. They look back on their warrior past, but even here their emotions are divided, and they think of those epic days as belonging to the brave but ignorant youth of their race, the time before the missionaries gave them to eat of the tree of knowledge and made them – like Eve and Adam – go clothed.

9

On Monday, as the early sun began to stir the mists in the hills behind Apia, Fan'aafi Larkin's delegate arrived in a government car. He was the Chief School Inspector, a tall, thin, didactic man named Sao Tonga, highly conscious of his rank and responsibilities. Driving along the front, where the Apians were already opening their shops and taking produce to the market, Sao Tonga explained that he was merely taking us to the wharf at the western tip of Upolu where the boat was waiting to sail us to Apolima. The local School Inspector, who held one of the best hereditary titles in the west of the island, would accompany us. 'It's time he inspected the school in any case,' Sao Tonga remarked. 'As you've doubtless been told, it's sometimes a dangerous trip, and my inspectors are inclined to neglect it. It is a year and a half since anyone has been. You have given me a reason to insist.'

We left Apia by the road towards the airport, and as we drove through its interlinked villages Sao Tonga drew our attention to the modesty of the school buildings. 'Unfortunately,' he commented, 'our Samoan people are afflicted with a number of burning desires which they refuse to recognize as mutually contradictory. No Samoan believes his manhood has been established unless he has a large family whom he would like to educate so that they all become office workers in Apia. We are not a very poor country. There is still enough to feed us all, provided we restrain our increase and tend our gardens, including that blue garden on which the sun shines so benevolently . . .' He gestured grandly towards the lagoon. 'But perhaps we are too poor to sustain a population that spends its time beating typewriters and filling forms. That is what our people want, nevertheless. Yet they are not willing to pay the price. They prefer to spend their village funds on other things.'

He paused, gave a doubtful sideways look at the expressionless face of the driver – a Chinese half-breed – and decided he would be offending no deep sensibilities as he pointed to an especially large and ornate baroque church. 'Look at that!' He waited until a hundred yards or so farther on we passed a small, low-built school. 'And look at that! I leave the comparison to you. Do not imagine I wish to criticize the churches. Still, there is a time for rendering to Caesar as well as a time for rendering to God, and with us the rendering to God becomes confused with human pride.'

'So the pastors' influence militates against education?' I remarked.

'The pastors' influence? Not in the least, sir! I cast no blame on God's servants. It is not the pastors who build big churches or ask for big houses. It is the villagers who offer them.'

'But the pastors do accept.' Inge laughed ironically. Sao Tonga looked at her distrustfully, and fell silent as we drove through the long green shadows of the great government coconut groves.

In the next village, little girls were walking beside the road carrying extraordinary floral constructions made by threading red, pink and yellow hibiscus flowers on supple stalks of coconut leaves until they bent over with the weight and then thrusting them into a core of fern pith to make a delicate springy bouquet like a small fountain of flowers. Sao Tonga revived at the sight. 'Charming! The children gather the flowers as soon as they get up. They do it for love of their teachers. Suffer the little children . . .' He assumed such a pious air that I was prevented from adding sardonically '. . . to come unto Caesar' only by the car stopping outside a large palangi house. A dark-featured man, so solidly built that he seemed short, though he was in fact nearly six feet tall, got into the car with a briefcase in his hand. He was Afamasaga, the local chief metamorphosed into a school inspector who would take us to Apolima.

A few minutes later we reached Apolima Fou, or New Apolima, the village on the mainland where many of the people of Apolima have come to live since their island became crowded. The two places, Apolima Tai and Apolima Fou, form one community, and most of the families have representatives living on the ancestral lands of the island, so that the mana of the community, its essential being, is still located there. We were to encounter the people who lived in Apolima Fou later on, but today it was necessary to get to the island without delay because of the sea's uncertainties.

A primitive jetty of piled blocks of coral jutted out from the shore; beside it lay a battered whaleboat, its white paint worn grey by the seas. It had a rough awning of torn canvas and an outboard motor; the crew consisted of three youths, the oldest no more than eighteen. Sao Tonga handed us on board, promised to have the car back at Apolima Fou in the late afternoon, and hurried away. The boat began to chug out into the lagoon. 'It is quicker to go with a motor,' said Afamasaga, who discovered his tongue as soon as Sao Tonga departed, and added in a reluctant afterthought: 'But it is more difficult to get through the entrance at Apolima.'

At this moment it was hard to imagine any difficulty, for the lagoon seemed as smooth as a mirror, and the near-by island of Manono as well as the cone of Apolima stood out clearly from their glittering sea; beyond we could make out Savai'i as a grey distant mass. The lagoon was dotted with small outrigger canoes from which men were catching fish with spear and line; some canoes floated empty, and we imagined they were drifting until we began to see heads with dark goggles pop up beside them, and realized that their owners were diving for seafood on the floor of the lagoon. The smooth water continued as far as

Manono, a fairly large island that rose to a sharp central peak; there were many coconut palms, and clusters of fales scattered among the groves. Upolu's reef embraced Manono, but just beyond that island began the three or four miles of open sea we had to cross to Apolima. As soon as we passed through the wide passage that took us beyond the reef, we ran into a heavy swell; on its long powerful waves the boat began to rock and shudder as if its worn planks at any moment would burst apart.

Afamasaga began at this moment to speak in his shy, soft voice, perhaps to sustain our courage, perhaps to reinforce his own. He opened with a familiar Samoan gambit. 'Did you leave your family at home?' 'Our cat is our only family, and she is in good hands.' His reply to that was also characteristic. A Samoan woman, assuming the liberties of her sex, would have given a look of great commiseration – as many did – and cried out: 'How unfortunate to have no children! You must be sad!' Afamasaga handled the matter diplomatically by saying, with an air of subtly mingled pride and self-deprecation, 'I fear I have six children,' and passing quickly on to a new tack. 'Last week I had a letter from the teacher at Apolima, whom you will meet. He was unhappy because as he went through the passage there the boat capsized and he lost his shirts and some of his books.' Then, thinking he had perhaps been tactless, he hastened to add, 'But today, of course, we have a very good crew!'

By now we were approaching Apolima, and as we sailed towards the high bare cliff of lava that plunged sheer into the sea from the southern face, it seemed a totally inaccessible place. 'The entry is on the other side,' Afamasaga explained. 'The name Apolima means Held-in-the-Palm-of-Your-Hand. You will see why.'

Apolima was the top of a volcano of which one side had broken down to sea-level so that there was a great horseshoe of high cliffs formed by the rim of the crater, sheltering the island on three sides, and on the fourth side a little harbour biting into the flat ground of the crater's bed. It was protected by a most unusual reef, for around Apolima the coral did not grow to the sea's surface, and its place was taken by the remains of the broken lava wall, which formed a bar of great rock slabs. As we swung round on the eastern side the inner amphitheatre opened before us, its slopes as densely tangled with green growth as the outer cliffs had been bare of any vegetation. We spontaneously cupped our palms and raised the fingers as protective barricades around them to make the perfect image of Apolima. Soon our attention was held by the reef, which we were now approaching closely. The waves broke heavily over the barrier, and the water returned in a seething white race. At first we could distinguish no break, until Afamasaga pointed to an area where the flow, though no less powerful, seemed at least less white and broken. The boat moved into position. 'They always wait for the seventh wave,' Afamasaga explained, as the boat tossed and the crew shifted into their posts. One clambered into the bows and stood poised with a pole in his hands. The second climbed on the awning, and sat watching the water, with his hands dangling on each side so that the steersman in the stern could see them. The man in the bows made a gesture, the engine sprang into life, and suddenly we were moving full speed with the blue-green wave towards the gap, and in a few seconds were between the brown rock masses that loomed in the tumbling water. The passage ahead seemed hardly wider than the boat. The man on the awning gestured frantically, left hand and then right hand. We wavered slightly, and then we were in the passage, forging ahead and curving as we went, with the poleman fending off the rock on the port side as we swung round through the L-shaped kink and out with the last rush of the wave into the bay, the calm water and the sudden release of fear.

I looked at Afamasaga. He laughed softly. 'Only men from Apolima can do that. Now you see why it was a great fortress. No Tongan boat ever sailed into this harbour.'

A tall and sturdy man came walking down to the beach from the fales we had seen half-consciously as the boat plunged through the entrance. He wore a tartan shirt and a flowered lavalava, and as we motored in I saw his grey hair *en brosse* and his strong angular face. The boat beached; the crew leapt into the shallow water and carried us ashore, forming chairs with their clasped hands. The man who welcomed us was Tautai, the tulefale or orator of Apolima. He expressed ritual astonishment at our arrival, though we knew a message had been sent on a boat that touched at the island the previous day. He led us up the beach on to the green where the fales of Apolima were laid out. The actual area of the village was small, for the ground sloped quickly to the walls of the crater, whose lower levels were a pattern of palms, bread-fruit trees and banana groves; above, reaching to the grey rock comb of the crest, climbed the darker tangle of wild forest, and high above that a red beacon perched on its silvery scaffold.

Tautai walked before us to a large oval fale which contained no household possessions and stood apart from the actual residences, on a natural platform overlooking the bay – its wooden columns outlined against the sea like some primitive Sounion. It was the fale of the village fono, and two men were waiting there, one a preternaturally thin old man with a narrow hatchet face and long aquiline nose like a Blackfoot Indian, and the other a fat man in a gaudy Hawaiian shirt, with the heavy legs and down-weighted hips usual among Polynesians. The thin man was the head chief, the ali'i – not merely an elected matai but also the heir to an hereditary rank; the fat man was the pastor, God's vicar on Apolima.

The fale's floor was laid out with coarse pandanus mats on which we took carefully designated places. Afamasaga and I sat cross-legged, supporting our backs against the posts, opposite the ali'i and the tule-fale respectively. Inge sat beside me in the slightly less honorific position accorded to a woman. The pastor sat in his special seat on the same side as the guests; his position outside the village clan structure did not allow him to join the chiefs.

No sooner had we sat down than two girls appeared with coconuts whose tops had been cut so ingeniously that little lids remained attached by shreds of shell even when one opened them to drink. Green coconuts are symbols of welcome in most South Sea islands; by tasting the clear sweet water we accepted the welcome. A young man came with a bunch of bananas, the gift of the pastor, which were put on enamel plates before us. Such gestures of hospitality made, it was Afamasaga's turn to introduce us. Samoan protocol is complex and oblique. It would have been impolite for the chiefs to ask about us, since in Samoan society one is expected to know the identity of anyone of consequence. It would have been undignified for me to identify myself, since, as a person of consequence, I had a right to be known. Only a third party could properly resolve the problem, and this Afamasaga proceeded to do in such a way as to leave no doubt that in our own world we were people of title. Inge, whose father is the heir to an Austrian baronial line, presented no difficulty. I claimed a different nobility, for the title under which I appeared (not of course forgetting the elaborately explained doctorates and fellowships listed on the card I had printed for such occasions) was that of Tusitala, which Stevenson's extraordinary popularity in Samoa had made a prestigious calling.

The pastor made the first welcoming speech. It was obvious, he declared in terms too flowery to record, that important persons had arrived on Apolima. Not often did visitors come across the world to their small island, and they were thankful to the Lord Jesus Christ who had brought us safely through the perilous waters and the difficult passage. Afamasaga, having quietly told me to reserve my own speech until later, spoke in reply. Then Tautai remarked that, unexpected though our visit might be, Apolima knew its duty to honourable guests.

The two chiefs disappeared, and returned quickly, each carrying a woody, bleached stem about four feet long, with a gnarled sprout of root at the end; holding them in his open palms, Tautai explained that they were the roots of kava, the sacred plant of Polynesian peoples. When such roots passed from one man to another, there must be peace between them. He begged me to accept these roots as tokens of their goodwill. I took them and laid them before me. Now began the true kava ceremony, conducted with the curious mixture of ritual and earthy matter-of-factness which South Sea islanders share with the Chinese. A girl and two young men appeared, carrying a tin bucket, a shallow bowl of carved wood about four feet in diameter which stood on squat legs, and a coil of fibres that looked like raffia. The girl seated herself beside the tulefale, with the kava bowl before her. One of the young men sat beside her. The bowl, and a cup made from the polished half of a coconut shell, were rinsed. Then more water was poured into the bowl, and the girl dipped the coil of fibres, dipping and wringing, dipping and wringing. 'They are hibiscus fibres,' Afamasaga explained. 'The shredded kava root is inside them.'

After many rinsings and wringings, the water took on a cigar-brown colour, and was ready to serve. The young man beside the mixer set up a high-pitched shouting chant, which we all accompanied with a rhythmic clapping of the hands. 'He is celebrating the drinking of kava as a symbol of peace and friendship between the chiefs of Apolima and their guests.' The second young man filled the cup with kava, and, approaching with flexed knees and the cup held at arm's length, presented it in order of precedence, first to the ali'i, then to Afamasaga as the titled Samoan guest, then to me as the titled stranger, then to the tulefale, then to the pastor, and finally to Inge, an act of courtesy that surprised her, since women are usually not expected to partake of the holy drink. Each carefully spilt a few drops on the grass behind us as a libation to the ancestors of the community, and then drained the cup in a single draught as our companions clapped three times and shouted 'Malo!'

I had expected some special atrocity of flavour from a brew that looked so unappetizing, but the kava was distinguished only by a slightly disagreeable flatness. A Victorian traveller who drank it in Fiji described it as tasting like a mixture of Turkey rhubarb and magnesia, flavoured with sal volatile, which places it fairly accurately in the spectrum of unpleasant medicinal flavours. It is said to sharpen the perceptions, but after the cup had gone round three times mine remained unchanged. It is said also, drunk in large quantities, to paralyse the leg muscles while leaving the mind clear, so that a man standing up after many cups will stagger and appear drunk. The only physical effect I felt was a slight tingling numbness at the back of the mouth, but this had no effect on my speech, which was fortunate, since we had reached the point where I would have to prove myself in oratory, the most appreciated in Polynesia of all the arts.

After the triple drinking of kava, Tautai embarked on the ceremonial speech of welcome, to which the pastor's speech had been merely the informal prelude. It was long, and punctuated at the end of each flowing period by grunting exclamations from the other Samoans present. Afterwards it was my turn, and I was grateful for the metaphoric verbosity acquired in childhood from listening to revivalist preachers in the Welsh marches. I spoke of the great history of Apolima, of its place in Samoan legend, and its role in the great war against Tonga; I declared unashamedly that its fame had reached Europe and North America; I lavishly and in detail enumerated and praised the welcome we had received; I called sanctimoniously for the protection of God to extend itself over this jewel island of incomparable beauty. As Afamasaga translated, fragment by fragment, I was reassured; the chiefs grunted regularly and loudly, finding the phrases eloquent and the sentiments congenial. I had started on a course of flamboyant speechmaking that would not end until finally we left the South Seas.

No sooner had my speech ended than a long file of young men and girls appeared, weaving over the village paths. Each bore a coconut-frond mat with a banana leaf laid on it as a cloth for the food that was offered. It was a traditional island feast; roast bread-fruit, boiled taro and steamed yam; baked reef fish, octopus stewed in its ink, and fragments of muscular chicken; various seaweeds, eggs and cooked plantains; thick coconut cream was the sauce into which everything could be dipped. There was even a crumbled mass which Tautai called pisupo; it was actually Australian corned beef. (The first tinned food to arrive in the islands was pea soup and the name was later transferred to the more popular corned beef, a standard dish in many Samoan feasts.) Bowls of water were brought, with towels, and we washed our hands before and after eating with our fingers. The girls sat cross-legged before us with fans, driving away the flies and offering choice titbits. It was, like most Polynesian food, extremely bland, with no herbal seasoning and little salt. We washed it down with strong sweet tea, served without milk.

Afterwards we settled into a conversation that became a ritual contest; I was anxious to learn how the matai system worked on the local level, while the chiefs and the pastor were intent on finding what advantage might be reaped from this windfall visit of a palangi whose power, thanks to Afamasaga's flowery introduction, they imagined to be great and far-reaching.

Tautai was more than willing to answer my questions about village organization, since he was able to talk at length – puffing furiously on the cigarettes we provided – on the dignity of his own role. On Apolima island, where a mere hundred people remained, there were only the two matais – Tautai and the ali'i; the other twenty-three clan chiefs lived among the 400 people who had migrated to Apolima Fou. Together they formed the fono of the combined village. Within the fono, there were gradations of status. A few of the matai were ali'i, of noble lineages. The tulefales, of whom there were two, were the local political leaders who led debates on village policy; how they attained their rank we never fully understood. The fono acted as both municipal council and customary court. It administered village finances, raised levies for specific purposes, and supervised such communal activities as the building and maintenance of church, manse, school and roads. The fono also passed village by-laws, which often included curfews for children and even adults; it policed the locality effectively because its members knew everything that went on in the open fales; it imposed fines of money or goods on those who broke the village laws, and in extreme cases it wielded the penalty of expulsion from the village, which meant that a man lost his rights to a share of the land's produce.

The picture of Samoa that emerged from this view at the bottom of the pyramid was of a highly decentralized society built on traditional social patterns. The village maintains many of the services that in other societies are provided by the state. The lack of national welfare programmes is neutralized by the fact that the aiga automatically sustains old and incapable people and orphans from the produce of the common land or the money active members earn. It seemed a society with much stubborn strength, capable of adaptation, but largely dependent on the traditional rural occupations of farming and fishing. Any change that would take people away from the rural areas – like the growth of tourism or industry – might drastically weaken it. I remembered how anxious Tamasese and Tupuola had been to avoid rapid modernization, and as we talked in Apolima it seemed to me that this concern must have been due not only to a desire to preserve customary ways but also to a fear that any hasty shift in the rural power base would disturb the political equilibrium of the whole small country.

But Tautai had more on his mind than explaining the system in which he played a part. Not every matai, he continued, was the leader of a landholding clan. A village could adopt a stranger as a matai. Already they had elected two such matais on Apolima, a UNESCO official and a Norwegian anthropologist. 'Now we have another guest among us who is worthy of our regard. Should we not make him also a matai?' The ali'i and the pastor grunted approval. Then, with sly jocosity, Tautai asked me what I would think if it were suggested that I become a matai. It was like the devious face-saving procedure by which a man is sounded out on whether he might accept a knighthood. Afamasaga translated Tautai's remarks. 'If you say no, it will be acceptable,' he explained. 'But if you say yes or show hesitation, the tulefale will make a ceremonial speech offering you the mataiship; then it will be offensive to refuse.' He smiled quizzically, awaiting the reply my vanity might dictate. But I had been forewarned by Al Wendt: 'If you accept, you will have to provide a large feast and give lavish presents to all the matais; you will be expected to use the influence you are imagined to possess for the benefit of the village, and you will never be free from requests for aid.' I expressed my appreciation and gently indicated my probable refusal of an honour so manifestly undeserved. Tautai accepted the situation with ironic amiability. 'Nevertheless,' he remarked, 'this is your village and this is your clan. You will always be welcome among us.'

Suddenly, there was a great shouting of children from the beach, and we all rose and went to look down into the bay. A high wave had come sweeping in over the reef and lifted our boat, so that it lay broadside and tilting on the beach. It was soon righted, but the leading boatman came to tell us that we should not be too late in leaving, for the wind was blowing up in the channel between Apolima and Manono.

Afamasaga had still to inspect the school and discuss with Tautai the ticklish fact that it was only an open-sided fale, while government regulations demanded a palangi building. The pastor, who alone spoke a little English, offered to show us the village, and we set off, walking among the houses and back into the shadow of the coconut groves where the gardens and the pig-pens and the cemetery lay.

The slopes around us, dense with intricate vegetation, and the grey crags above; everywhere the brilliance of flame trees and hibiscus and the scent of frangipani; no mechanical sound to disturb the natural harmonies of insect and bird; it seemed as if we had reached the true South Sea island of literature and fantasy. We walked to the trickling runnel which the pastor called the river of Apolima. It was the only constant spring on the island. As we stood watching it flow slowly through an algae-choked pond into a surprisingly clear pool below, where several speckled fish and one little red fish were swimming, the pastor explained that legend attributed it to the good offices of a 'fairy'. 'But I believe', he intoned with great unction, 'that it is a little miracle granted by the grace of our Lord Jesus Christ.'

The houses of Apolima, even the pastor's and those of the two chiefs, were traditional fales, and here also a miraculous moral could be drawn. In the heart of the village stood the cracked and tottering concrete posts of the one palangi house that had ever been built on Apolima. 'It was destroyed by the hurricane in 1966. My fale blew down over my head, but the Lord preserved his servant. This man built a house where he thought he would be safe, but his time had come and he was the only person who died on Apolima. Since then we build our simple fales as our fathers did and trust in the Lord Jesus!'

The heat of midday was upon us. The men were sleeping in their fales or sitting on the edges of their platforms chatting softly. The women sat together in the special fale of their committee, making the fine white mats of treated pandanus fibre that provided Apolima's only industry; the mats were in demand as far away as Tonga. We walked back towards the beach.

'We are a poor island,' said the pastor. 'We feed ourselves, but many things we need. Our only link with Upolu is the boat, but the boat

you came in is very old. We need a new motor-boat to take our fish
to market in Apia. We need a radio transmitter to call the doctor.
We need a windmill to pump water out of the ground. Now, Sir
Doctor Tusitala, you are a man of power . . .' I laughed deprecatingly.
The pastor continued unperturbed. 'You can speak to the great men
who never visit us on Apolima. Our government will listen to you.
And if they do not, a man like you can send these things.'

I saw now the unfolding of the strategy begun when Tautai offered
to create me a matai. The Apolimans did not intend to miss any
chance of modernizing their sheltered microcosm which had seemed,
in that moment up among the trees beside the stream, so idyllically
perfect. I had no illusions about my influence with the Samoan government, but it would have been an act of supererogatory frankness to
say so, and I merely remarked that I would do what I could. This, I
gathered several months later, was interpreted as a promise, and my
failure to send a boat or a windmill or at least a radio transmitter was
gravely censured by Tautai in conversation with the next palangi
visitor.

By the time we got to the beach, the leading boatman had returned
to insist that we must leave; further delay would be dangerous. Nevertheless, we had to sit down, drink more green coconuts, eat more
bananas, smoke the remaining cigarettes and deliver final speeches.
I made customary presents to the chiefs and the pastor – two talas each
as Afamasaga instructed me. The notes were touched to the brow in
thanks; Tautai remarking that next time a gift of pisupo would also be
appreciated.

Then we went out to the boat. Baskets of bread-fruit and coconuts
were put on board. The pastor decided to accompany us to Apolima
Fou, and we all climbed into the boat, while Tautai and the young
men of the village waded into the bay to bid us farewell. We shot the
reef in great style, going out on the receding wave, but the boatmen
had been correct in their warnings; it was an uncomfortable and at
times an alarming voyage back. The swell rose high, and the boat was
rolled like a shell on a beach, sometimes shuddering through all its
fragile timbers on the impact of a wave, and sometimes rising before a
crest like the boat in Hokusai's famous print, and scudding down
sickeningly into the trough. Many times we shipped water, and the
boatmen bailed steadily most of the way. I felt that any moment we
would be swamped or capsized, and so did Inge, though we did not

exchange our fears until we reached dry land. Afamasaga looked grave, which perturbed me in a man who knew these waters. The pastor closed his eyes and muttered incessant prayers. The only people completely unmoved by our situation were the three young boatmen who in the end brought us skilfully through the entrance of the reef near Manono, and who regarded the feat as so unexceptional that they were astonished when I made them a small gift after we landed at Apolima Fou.

10

Compared with our trip to the island of Apolima, our visit to Savai'i was a bizarre fiasco, unexpectedly redeemed. On the day after our return from Apolima we heard that Tupuola had made all the arrangements for us to be received on Savai'i. We had merely to catch the seven-seater plane from Upolu at nine the following morning, and a government driver would be waiting with a car to take us over the long road to Faleolupo. This time, since our way had been prepared by the most important chief of Savai'i, there was no reason why we should not take Sione.

We arrived in good time at the airport, with a case of tinned pil-chards dominating our luggage, and our wallets stuffed with tala bills to present to the matais we expected to entertain us in the kava cere-mony at Faleolupo. The plane was a ramshackle craft; my seat had no belt and on flight and landing I hung on to a stanchion and hoped for the best. It was a clear day, and the young New Zealand pilot made a good flight of it, skimming low over the lagoon and the reef, passing right above Apolima, which seemed more than ever like the palm of a rocky hand, and then across the channel to Savai'i. The beaches were jungle edged, and beyond them the forest was broken by coconut groves. It was obviously far less inhabited than Upolu, for we had not seen a single village or even a habitation by the time the plane dipped to a runway among the palm-trees and taxied up to the large open fale that served as an airport building.

There was no car waiting, nor any means of establishing contact on the island, since the radio telephone in the airport shed communicated only with Upolu, and the nearest village was much too far to walk there in the late morning heat. In any case, it was unlikely that we would have found transport even if we had reached it. So we sat waiting as the heat built up, reflected from the sandy soil of the runway. An hour passed, and then two. No car arrived, and finally, when the plane returned at 11.30 and there were empty seats, we flew back to Upolu.

In Apia it was what in the South Seas they call Steamer Day. A Swedish cruise ship had arrived, and its four hundred passengers, swarming along the front, gave Apia an unaccustomed feeling of cosmopolitan activity. Most of them were ordinary wintertime American tourists, but there was a considerable contingent of homosexuals bedecked in ornate lavalavas and welcomed by their local counterparts, who are called fififines. (Homosexuality is open and frequent in the islands where the culture is wholly or even partly Polynesian; I was accosted by male prostitutes in Apia, Nuku'alofa and Suva, but never in the true Melanesian islands or in Micronesia.) Aggie's was in high turmoil, for a fiafia was being put on for Steamer Day, and it was when we were looking down from the balcony of our room at the sword dancers gyrating to the music of slit gongs and biscuit-tin drums that a servant came breathlessly to announce the Minister, and Tupuola appeared, apologetic and obviously angry that he had lost face through the neglect of a minor official who had forgotten to send out the car that morning. 'They are all waiting for you at Faleolupo.' But it was too late already to go. The planes from Savai'i were full the rest of the day and all the next day, and to go the day after would mean missing the plane we must catch to Nuku'alofa if we were to keep the audience with the King of Tonga that Gordon had gone to arrange.

To compensate for our disappointment, Tupuola invited us to his house for dinner, and that evening we went up with Al and Jenny Wendt to the vast wooden house in the foothills which he and his family inhabited. It was set in a splendid garden of flowering trees whose big lush blossoms, wet with rain, glistened brightly in the car lights. The house itself had been built in the German era; it had wide verandas, and vast lofty rooms with arches of carved wood and elaborate fanlights over all the doors.

Mrs. Tamasese, who was Tupuola's mother, greeted us. She was a lively, ivory-skinned woman in her sixties, the widow of the Prime Minister's uncle. Her father had been a member of the Swedish trading family of Nelson, whose members intermarried generation after generation with the Samoan high chiefly families, to their mutual advantage, for the Nelsons became prosperous and supported the high chiefs in their agitations for independence under New Zealand rule. Now Mrs. Tamasese was head of the clan that inhabited the house. It included two sons and two daughters, a daughter-in-law and a son-in-law, a clutch of grandchildren and a dozen or so girl servants. The house was large enough to give a little privacy to every subdivision of the great joint family, but the bar and dining room seemed to be common territory. It was typical, we gathered, of the big noble households of Apia and its environs; each chief, of course, would have an equally large but more traditionally constructed house in his own village, as Tupuola did on Savai'i.

The evening followed a pattern customary, it appeared, in Samoa. Tupuola was not immediately present, and the first hour belonged to the matriarch. We sat in a circle surrounding Mrs. Tamasese, with new guests adding themselves every few minutes, and listened to her recollections of how, having been brought up in an Apia trader's mansion and precisely educated at a very English boarding school in Australia, she married a high chief and went off to live in his village. She described in a racy finishing school slang – spattered with Edwardian expressions like 'My giddy aunt!' – how she had been exasperated with the lack of time-consciousness, with the untidiness, with the general *dolce far niente* of the village women, who applied a genial passive resistance to her efforts to teach them how best to spend their time. It was an interesting illustration of the limits of conversion in Samoa; the islanders accepted the liturgy and the theology of the missionaries, but the Protestant work ethic did not impress them. Throughout the South Seas, people work hard when it is necessary; to describe them as lazy is unjust. But they never work from a sense of moral compulsion. Work for its own sake is to them a meaningless concept.

When Tupuola finally appeared, he greeted no one and did not join the circle. Instead, he stood by the bar, offering a rival focus of interest, and one by one, nothing having been said, the male guests slipped away and joined him. Apart from Al Wendt, they included Rowen Osborn, the Australian High Commissioner to Fiji; Karanita Enari, Secretary to the Government and senior Samoan civil servant; a New Zealand agricultural adviser and two other Samoan civil servants, who remain anonymous in my memory for the simple reason that I was never told who they were; indeed, there were no introductions, and it would have been impolite to attempt an exchange of names, though Osborn and I did so in privileged defiance of Samoan manners. The ego must be resolutely masked in Samoan society, and one way of telling a man of high family in a crowd is said to be his avoidance of talking about himself – though on ceremonial occasions his orator is allowed to make up for the ritual modesty the chief displays. This does not mean that the Samoan is without pride, for the assumption that one's claims to fame are known and therefore need not be advertised betokens a special form of arrogance.

Once established, the division between men and women persisted throughout the evening. Even when the Polynesian dinner was laid buffet-style on a gigantic oak sideboard, the women ate at the dining table and the men took back to the bar their sucking pig and octopus and the oysters and wild pigeon Tupuola had brought in from Savai'i that day, and we ate and talked as we drank our wine and brandy.

All the Samoans present had been educated outside the country; they represented the young Westernized faction in the government, and their understanding of Samoa's place in the world was very different from that of the matais of Apolima. Yet they tended to defend the varying constitutional patterns in the newly liberated South Pacific countries as experiments that might show how to avoid the political disasters of those African and Asian countries that attempted too precipitately to create democracies on the models of Westminster or Washington. When we arrived in Tonga, they pointed out, we would find a feudal kingdom in which the greatest share of power was in the hands of the king and a few noble families, which renewed themselves by incorporating brilliant commoners through marriage. In Fiji we would find a parliamentary system arranged to prevent the Indian majority from gaining power; the Fijian territorial chiefs had regained much of the authority they lost when the islands were ceded by King Cakobau in 1876.

Samoa's own constitution, with which we were now familiar, had been a pioneer in these departures from accepted Anglo-Saxon governmental patterns. Strong arguments had been necessary not only to persuade New Zealand that Samoa was ripe for complete independence in 1962, but also to convince the dogmatic democrats in the United Nations that the matai system was an authentic variant of democracy. The Samoans had succeeded only because they had a persuasive advocate for their case in the Australian constitutional expert, Professor

J. W. Davidson, and only after a mechanism for removing unsatisfactory matais had been incorporated in the constitutional machinery.

Everyone admitted quite freely what we had already surmised – that there was a real structure of power in Samoa differing from that established by the constitution. An hereditary title which meant that one belonged to the ancient Samoan aristocracy conveyed more than prestige; and it was the shadowy structure of chiefly lineages, unrecognized constitutionally, but wielding enormous power, that determined who would control Samoa's political destiny. Perhaps it was a retrogression; Tupuola for one was willing to admit that it might be so. But it was better, everyone seemed agreed, for power to slip back into the cautious hands of traditional nobles than into the impetuous hands of traditionless soldiers or bureaucrats.

It was an evening when I wished I could have extended an ear into each room, for Inge joined me full of the stories Mrs. Tamasese had told at the women's table about the resistance to the New Zealanders in the 1920s, when the Nelson girls had followed their father's leadership and taken an active part in the agitations. On her marriage, Mrs. Tamasese had retreated to the village, and then had gone with her husband to live in England for twenty years; returning in the 1950s, she had set about organizing the women in the renewed struggle for independence. She was proud that the women had started the crucial demonstrations that brought Samoa freedom on its own terms, so that its people did not feel they were starting anew in the perilous world of modern politics but that they were taking up again, after generations of foreign rule, the ancient traditions. And all this, Mrs. Tamasese insisted, had been done by wholly non-violent action, a strategy she claimed the Samoan women had developed for themselves, with no thought of imitating Gandhi.

11

Because of the missionaries, the English has been the most pervasively influential of the European cultures that have helped to shape the hybrid society of modern Samoa. The quarter of a century of German influence and rule left a few material relics like the feather quilts and the Berliner pfannkuchen and the custom of giving presents on Christmas Eve rather than Christmas Day. It left also a few memories. People still talk of the German officials as hard taskmasters, and one old man said to me that if the Germans had stayed another generation they would have turned all the best lands into plantations and driven the Samoans into the hills. Yet though the public effects of German occupation were so temporary, it is an ironic fact that in human terms the German strain has been persistent. Al Wendt was only the first of many Samoans we encountered with German names and a proportion of German blood; indeed, such people were numerous in the official and business world of Apia, largely because their German forebears made sure their Samoan descendants were educated to take a part in the commercial life which they regarded as the future of the islands.

Because of the strange working of the land laws, most of the few planters left in Samoa were also Germans, whose ancestors had acquired land before or during the period of German occupation. By 1914 about an eighth of the land of Samoa, mostly on Upolu, was in the hands of German planters; it was, generally speaking, the best land. In 1914 the German plantations were alienated by the Allies, and worked by the New Zealand Trust Estates; when the war ended the estates were confiscated except where German planters had married Samoan women or were of part-Samoan ancestry. Enough of them qualified to ensure the survival of a small planter class which is partly Samoan in ancestry but mainly German in language and culture.

Hermann Retzlaff was the most important of these Germanic planters; he owned three plantations, maintained a merchant warehouse in Apia, ran a small tourist service, and had established a resort which we had seen on one of the remoter beaches of southern Upolu; it was called the Hiderway [sic] Hotel, and on the day of our visit there was not a single guest to step from its thatched luxury fales on to the silver sands, but Retzlaff, said the gossips in Apia, had foreseen the change of government policy regarding tourism and had quietly prepared himself to profit thereby. He had much earlier assured his good standing with the ruling Samoan oligarchy by marrying the other daughter of the merchant O. F. Nelson; thus Tupuola Efi was his nephew by marriage, and he maintained tenuous but real links with the rest of the powerful Tamasese clan.

On our last day in Samoa we went out to visit Retzlaff in the company of a Lufthansa pilot, Captain Rathje, and his wife; Rathje, a pioneer flyer into Mongolia in the 1930s, was a good example of the kind of people one encountered at Aggie Grey's, full of exotic tales of Shanghai and northern China at the period of the Japanese invasion.

Our directions for reaching Retzlaff's plantation were strange and confusing. Signposts are virtually non-existent on Samoa; one relies on local knowledge, and at the hotel we were told to drive out on the main road east of Apia and to ask persistently for Telefoni; and sooner or later someone would tell us which side road to take. Retzlaff's father had installed the first telephones when he was German postmaster in Samoa sixty years before, and the name had clung to the family ever since. Few people knew Retzlaff; thousands knew Telefoni.

Fortunately we did not have to rely on this method of finding our way, since Frau Thieme, who managed Aggie Grey's office, decided to accompany us with her husband, Hans Thieme, Director of Health for the Samoan government and head of the Apia Hospital. Frau Thieme had come from Germany twenty years ago, had gone home more than once in anger at Samoan fecklessness, but had always been drawn back by the islands, though at least once or twice a day one would hear her voice raised in an exasperated shout of 'Typically Samoan!' Hans Thieme, a small dark man with scars on his cheeks, had a curious history. His father had been German, his mother Samoan, and in the 1930s he was sent to Germany to receive the training that would make him the first Samoan medical doctor. He was still there in 1939 when World War II broke out, and because his father was German he was treated as a native and conscripted into the *Reichswehr*. He fought all through the war, and when it was ended returned to Apia, where he found that most of his friends had fought on the opposite side. But, the place being Samoa, there were no hard feelings either way, and in Apia it is told with relish how every year on Armistice Day Hans Thieme will put on his Iron Cross and his faded German uniform to march beside the Anzac veterans in the parade to the cenotaph. It was the duelling scars of that German interlude which turned out so differently from his anticipations that he wore on his Samoan cheeks.

Retzlaff's house was one of the biggest and newest palangi houses in Samoa, set in the middle of his coconut groves and surrounded by a garden jewelled with bright orchids and hibiscus bushes with mauve and orange flowers. Mrs. Retzlaff, the other Nelson girl, had the same dry-witted volubility, the same Edwardian slang, and the same ivory complexion as her sister; she busied herself preparing large pink gins and producing orchids for the ladies and cheroots for the men. Hermann Retzlaff, who sat drinking Coca Cola out of a great red brandy snifter, looked like a solid blond farmer from Friesland. But his German, I noted, was as accented as his English. He did not – as Thieme did – speak it like a native, and he must have sensed what passed in my mind, for he volunteered that he had spoken Samoan as a child, and had only learnt German when his father sent him to the homeland to be educated; he had not stayed long enough to be trapped in the Nazi war machine.

From Retzlaff I first heard the lamentations that issued from the lips of almost every planter we encountered anywhere in the South Seas. He had inherited his father's three plantations, which made him, next to the government, the leading copra grower in Samoa. Since nobody had been able to buy land for half a century, there were no more than a dozen other planters left; some of them owned small plantations of 150 acres, which, at the world price of copra, seemed to Retzlaff completely unviable. Copra is the most important single product not merely of Samoa but of many other South Pacific island groups. For many years it has been suffering from the competition of temperate climate sources of vegetable oil, such as mustard and sunflowers.

'I am getting only 65 talas a ton,' Retzlaff complained. 'I have to pay 11 talas a ton for the copra to be cut and dried, and 1 tala a day for the workers who tend the plantation. Wages and the world market are killing the industry between them.'

One tala is 50p, or in North America about $1.20, and even in Samoan terms it is a low daily wage. Because of a stabilization fund that imposes levies on planters in good years, the Samoan copra growers were in a good position relative to other South Sea planters in 1972. Retzlaff was left, after he had paid for the main operation of splitting the fallen nuts and sun-drying their flesh, with 54 talas (£27) a ton out of which he had to find the cost of keeping the coconut groves clear – most of which was performed by beef cattle which could be sold to the shops and hotels of Apia.

It was obvious that the great profits that had been made on copra in the boom years were no longer there, and a small grower might indeed find it difficult to keep in business from the produce of a few acres; we met people like this in other parts of the islands where equalization funds like that of Samoa did not exist. But we never met a large, well-organized planter who looked as if he were about to go out of business, and Retzlaff, as he quite genially admitted after he had delivered his tirade against the times, was not doing badly enough to abandon his new glass-and-timber mansion and his impeccably kept gardens.

That evening, when we were back at Aggie's eating our last Samoan dinner with Al and Jenny Wendt, the special justice of the Samoan situation was impressed upon me. It was not that Samoa was a place where political and economic equality prevailed; it did not, and perhaps one of the reasons was that no single person we met seemed to regard that as important. The preservation of fa'a Samoa, of Samoan custom, was important. It had not been possible to preserve everything of the Samoan past, and no church-going chief or commoner would think of this as desirable. As Tupuola Efi remarked to me when we were talking about the authenticity of the dances which the Samoans were to perform that year at the South Pacific Festival: 'If we really wanted to be faithful to the past, we would have to stage war-dances by naked men with their penises stimulated to erection! I do not think our church deacons or our women's committees would approve!' But as much of the past as the modern world allowed must be preserved – which was why Samoa had so easily slipped back into a political system based on the gradations of chiefly rule – and whatever was adopted must be effectively naturalized. It was noticeable how quickly in Samoa the churches had ceased to be missions. Except in one Catholic church, we never encountered a non-Samoan pastor. The willingness of Polynesians to intermarry, combined with the general lack of racial prejudice on the part of Europeans towards Polynesians, had meant the virtual dissolution of rigid racial barriers. One met scores of people with German, Scandinavian or British names; almost all had Polynesian features, perhaps refined a little, among the girls especially, with paler skin tone or lighter facial structure. The 'German' planters turned out to speak German with Samoan accents; the European traders turned out to be half-breeds linked with the native chiefly clans. They prospered because they had taken their place in fa'a Samoa.

So far as an alien population existed, it consisted of a few New Zealanders who acted as governmental and financial advisers, a few employees of the big Australian-based South Sea trading firms like Burns Philp and Morris Hedstrom, and the staff of the only diplomatic mission in Samoa, the New Zealand High Commission. All were temporary residents; the white man who wishes to settle in Samoa and laze out his life there is no longer encouraged, any more than he is elsewhere in the South Seas. The beachcomber is almost extinct, and I use the word *almost* only because my memory is still haunted by one Apia figure, a man who would come out at evening and sit on the low wall beside the Catholic cathedral to take the last rays of the sun falling low and warm across the water from the west. He had a classic Viking head, the beard and the long hair still merging from corn yellow into white; he dressed like a Samoan, in a cheap print lavalava and sandals – nothing more; his torso was bare and fair; he supported himself on a carved walking stick that seemed to belong to another era. I greeted him once in English; he looked at me blankly. And I wondered whether he was really, as he seemed, the last of those wandering Melvillian sailors, fetched up at last to die upon some distant strand, or whether he was a Mendelian throwback, grandson or great-grandson of the original beachcomber, his line long taken into the absorbent and infinitely tolerant fabric of fa'a Samoa.

12

Late that last night at nearly eleven, I went to the desk to ask the clerk in charge, a very attractive Samoan-German-Chinese girl with whom we had become friendly during our stay, to make sure we were awakened to catch the 5.30 a.m. bus to the airport for the Tonga plane. She noted our time, and then said: 'I come on duty at five. I shall be here to see you go.' We were taken aback at the thought of such industrial revolution hours. 'I hope you're paid overtime!' Inge remarked. She shook her head. 'Samoa is not like other countries,' she said simply and sadly. Sure enough, she was there as we left, to hang the garlands of coloured pandanus over our necks and kiss our cheeks.

The bus struggled along in the thick darkness out of Apia. In many fales lights had been lit and the mosquito nets hung over the sleeping mats in white luminous cubes like ghostly tanks. In ones and twos the airport workers boarded the bus in the villages; a boy in a wide straw hat rode his horse beside the road and resembled a Mexican charro in the bus lights. The churches looked vast in their ornateness, like strange Asian temples in the breaking dawn. A new kind of morning broke for our departure. A grey-white diaphanous cloud veiled the sky, thin enough to let the dawning sunlight through; the lagoon was no longer the dark intense azure to which we were accustomed, but a pale metallic blue with an extraordinary luminescence that seemed to come up from the heart of the water.

PART TWO
The Kingdom of Tonga

Tonga differs from all the other island states of the South Seas because it alone has remained a monarchy. Its king, Taufa'ahau Tupou IV, rules over a small realm. It has two hundred islands, every one of which was visible in the coloured map of land and ocean we flew over from Samoa to Tongatapu, but their total area is a mere 269 square miles. Yet, small as it is, Tonga is an ancient kingdom, and its durability is doubtless due to the fact that more than a thousand years ago, before the Norman conquest of England, it was ruled by a line of highly venerated priest-kings, whose rule centred on the large island of Tongatapu – or Sacred Tonga. These kings, the Tui Tonga, had undisputed authority over the local chiefs who governed in the various island groups that formed and still form the kingdom; they appear also to have had a degree of spiritual authority in other parts of the Polynesian world which may account for the Tongan invasions of Samoa in the Middle Ages and for Tongan attempts to interfere in the political affairs of Fiji as recently as the mid-Victorian age.

The rule of the Tui Tongas came to an end gradually. First of all, during the Middle Ages, they retreated into sacred isolation, leaving the actual tasks of government to other chiefs, so that a situation arose similar to that in Japan where the Emperor ruled in theory but the Shogun in reality. It was a relatively peaceful realm that Captain Cook visited in 1777, when he accorded Tonga its English name – the Friendly Islands, in ignorance of what we now know: that the Tongan chiefs plotted to kill him and seize his ships, an operation that failed only because the conspirators could not agree beforehand on proper division of the spoils. Cook's apparently idyllic Tonga passed away when the Tongans, towards the end of the eighteenth century, became engaged as mercenaries in the bitter wars between the chiefs of Fiji. Fijian society had at this time reached a peak of brutal degeneracy, and cannibalism was practised on a scale unknown before; every victory being followed by a great feast of human flesh. The Tongans who fought in Fiji were infected by the ambient ferocity, and returned to provoke in Tonga a series of internecine conflicts in which the office of the Tui Tonga lost what influence it had retained, and actually lapsed, though the Tui Tonga's descendants survived as one of Tonga's noble lines. Power increasingly fell into the hands of Taufa'ahau, a chief of the outlying Ha'apai group; he gained control over Vavau in the north, and eventually, in 1845, overcame his opponents on Tongatapu and reunited the tiny kingdom under his rule.

Taufa'ahau was a man of exceptional political acumen; and thanks to his statesmanly manipulations his great-great-great-grandson, also Taufa'ahau, now rules over a kingdom that is not merely independent but, alone among the South Sea island groups, has never been a colony; for even while it was a British protectorate Tonga enjoyed complete internal autonomy. The first Taufa'ahau realized early in his contact with Europeans that the best means by which a small realm could survive and maintain its distinctive culture was by the development of protective mimicry. It was obviously impossible to resist the intrusion of the white men who in Victoria's reign were spreading rapidly over the southern ocean. But one might mitigate that intrusion, and Taufa'-ahau combined two surprisingly effective ways of doing so. First he became converted into an enthusiastic Methodist Christian, taking for himself the name of George Tupou as a calculated compliment to the Hanoverians of Britain, and – with the assistance of a politically minded missionary named Shirley Baker – establishing his own separate Wesleyan Free Church of Tonga, the only offshoot of English nonconformity to acquire the standing of a State Church.

Taufa'ahau's political shrewdness went beyond binding the missionaries to him as allies against the more rapacious forms of white men. As George Tupou he proceeded to create an imitation Victorian monarchy. In 1862 he abolished the condition of serfdom by which his people had been bondsmen to their various chiefs – for in Tonga the basic democracy of the landholding clan which survives in Samoa had been submerged by the great power of the territorial chiefs. Yet the progressive George was not divided from the traditionalist Taufa'ahau when in 1875 he promulgated the konisitutone or constitution by which Tonga is governed to this day, to all appearances as a Victorian limited monarchy, but in fact as a Polynesian feudal kingdom. The konisitutone provides for a parliament and a cabinet. But the cabinet is appointed by the King, who often presides over its deliberations, and the cabinet, headed by the King's brother, Prince Tu'ipelahake, consists of noblemen selected from the thirty-three chiefly families of Tonga. Parliament also is constituted so as to safeguard the power of these hereditary chiefs. It has twenty-two members, of whom eight are the ministers and local governors appointed by the King, seven are noblemen elected by the thirty-three chiefs, and the remaining seven are commoners elected by universal suffrage – women enjoying an equal vote with men. Thus in every parliament fifteen of the twenty-two members are noblemen who represent the landholding interests.

In the question of land, which is vital to a country that like most South Sea island groups still depends mainly on subsistence farming, and where the density of population is already more than twice as high as in Samoa, the same ambivalence in fact exists. The constitution has some splendid provisions relating to land, and none better than that which has saved Tonga from the problems of alien landholding that have afflicted almost every other South Pacific country. 'It shall not be lawful for ever', says that document in its resounding Victorian tones 'for anyone of this country, whether he be the king or any one of his chiefs, or any one of the people of this land, to sell one part of a foot of ground of the Kingdom of Tonga.' The land, in true feudal style, belongs theoretically to the King, but in fact about 60 per cent is held in fee by the noblemen and by a few of the matapules or traditional heralds; in practice these estates are treated as the personal domains of the nobleman, even though in the distant past the land seems actually to have been held by faahinga, landholding lineages of which the nobles were originally the heads.

Another section of the constitution provides for what in appearance is a most enlightened form of land distribution among the commoners – possession without the kind of ownership that enables a man to sell his land and other men to accumulate it. According to this provision, every male Tongan on reaching the age of sixteen is entitled, on application to the Minister for Lands, to receive for use during his lifetime an api or plantation of $8\frac{1}{4}$ acres, worked out as being the equivalent of a piece of land 100 fathoms each way, together with a plot in the village for his house. It is impossible to discover whether at any time in the nineteenth century this clause of the constitution was actually fully implemented. Nowadays young men usually have to wait to inherit the landholdings of their fathers; the nobles would rather cultivate or rent out their land than allow the people of their villages to use it, and the competition for Crown land is intense. One man of forty-five told us that at last, after nearly thirty years of waiting, he finally hoped to be granted his 8¼ acres. Obviously, with a population that has increased in forty years from 30,000 to 90,000, it is impossible for the constitutionally approved area of land to be given to every man who applies, but so far nothing has been done to devise a system that would actually work. It is only because families with land help their relatives without land under the very durable local kinship system that Tonga is not already faced with the problem arising from a large and – at the present stage of industrial development – only sporadically employable agricultural proletariat.

These are the basic social and political facts which explain the peculiarly contradictory impressions one gains of Tonga on first arriving. One has to know the two Janus faces of Tongan life so as not to be astonished when things turn out to be very different from what they first appear. One of those faces is English in a forgotten way, Victorian English and rigidly Christian. The other is Polynesian and pagan. Both faces are authentic; both belong in this strange little kingdom. By imitating the Victorians, the Tongans grew to resemble them; we were told in childhood that if you pull faces long enough one of them will stick, and Tongans are caught with the face of seeming to those who visit them the last Victorian Englishmen on earth. But they are also, one quickly realizes, almost the last of the authentic Polynesians, ruled by their ancient chiefs within a cage of custom that history has not shattered.

2

We were engrossed in the strange variations of Tongan life from the moment we left the plane at Fua'amotu airfield, and found waiting for us beyond the customs barrier not Gordon, but a massive six-foot Tongan in a black shirt and a black vala (the Tongan lavalava), with a great pandanus mat tied with a rough coconut-fibre rope around his waist. He introduced himself as Pinai Sekyea, a government servant, and explained that Gordon had already hurried on to Suva so that he could check on clearing our camera equipment through the customs.

As we took our luggage out to Pinai's Morris Moke, we heard the thump of rhythmic music issuing from a little knot of Samoans gathered outside the airport lounge. 'It's the Bishop,' Pinai explained, 'the Catholic Bishop!' I sensed a kind of forbearing sectarian superiority in the way he spoke, and knew immediately that Pinai belonged to the dominant Wesleyan Church. 'The Bishop is leaving us today. He has been here for thirty years.'

We edged our way into the circle. The Bishop sat in the midst, grey and ascetic, withered by the sicknesses of a life in the tropics. Young men garlanded with hibiscus were plucking and beating on guitars; an old man thudded away on a big drum like a barrel covered with sharkskin; six brown and bouncing young women in skirts of pandanus fibres, with green leaves round their ankles and plumes in their luxuriant black hair, danced before the Bishop, legs and buttocks swinging with athletic vigour, hands conveying in delicate motions the message of fondness and farewell. They sang in strident voices. The Bishop sat there, motionless, his grey face melancholic and unmoving; he seemed tired and sad. One felt he should have left long ago or not at all, stayed for ever in the land that had consumed his life or gone home while there was still some fire left to burn in his own country. One foresaw the quick dwindling in a homeland that time had made alien, and the memories slowly losing their vividness in a lonely existence deprived of meaning and of power.

Catholicism occupies a special and almost political position in Tonga; the supercession of line of the Tui Tonga was not accepted with unanimous enthusiasm, especially on Tongatapu, and the adherents of the sacred kings became the ready converts of the Catholic missionaries, partly because this was a way of defying the Wesleyan usurper George Tupou, and partly because the Catholic fathers, as elsewhere in the South Seas, were less insistent on every fragment of the old pagan culture being destroyed and forgotten. Several of the Tongan noble families have remained Catholics largely in symbolic loyalty to the memory of Tui Tonga and they still constitute one of the basic power-groups within the Tongan political equilibrium.

The importance which the noblemen retain within the pattern of Tongan life was quickly made evident to us, for as we drove away Pinai explained that he was wearing black because the head of one of the noble lines had just died. Not only must his own villagers and his numerous kinsmen throughout Tonga go into mourning, but also the whole of the government service, yet this nobleman held no great office of state.

As we drove north-west over the completely flat land of Tongatapu, between coconut groves and bread-fruit gardens, towards the capital of Nuku'alofa, the differences between the two Polynesian countries of Tonga and Samoa immediately began to show themselves. To begin with, the Tongans were darker and more rustic in appearance; one felt that, thanks to George Tupou's policies of keeping strangers at a distance, there had been less racial intermingling here than anywhere else in the Polynesian world, a fact that seemed to be borne out by the virtual absence of European names among the Tongan people; a foreign name here indicated a foreigner, which it certainly did not in Samoa.

Even more striking than the difference between the two peoples was the difference between the look and feel of their villages. While most Samoan villages were neat and aesthetically rather pleasing, with their rows of open fales, their well-kept lawns and their splendid churches, all displaying a certain competitive pride, the villages of Tonga were, with a few exceptions, shabby, chaotic and unappealing. The Tongan house is called a fale, like its Samoan counterpart, and it is also thatched and oval. But there the resemblance ends, for the Tongan fale is closed and secretive; in its most primitive form it has walls made of woven palm-leaf, but most of the modern fales are sheathed with upright planks or, more rarely, with the sides of tea-boxes, sheets of tinplate or even flattened cardboard packing cases. Whenever a villager can afford it, he replaces his thatched roof with corrugated iron, which needs renewing less frequently and which also catches rainwater, an important consideration on an island which has no single running stream and must rely on its wells and its weather to be saved from thirst; corrugated iron, however, corrodes quickly in the moist and salty air of Tongatapu, and most roofs of this kind are rusty and pitted. As a result each village presents a ragged mixture of shabby houses built of various materials in various stages of decrepitude. The churches are hardly more impressive than the houses, being either large oval-ended thatched fales, or little wooden chapels in a vague colonial style with the paint long weathered away, or rain-beaten structures of crumbling concrete.

A few villagers grow gardens around their fales, but usually there is nothing more than coarse grass under the rain trees and coconut palms, roughly pitted with holes dug by the rooting pigs, so that one has to watch one's step always to avoid a twisted ankle. There had been a great deal of rain in the weeks before our arrival, and in some of the lower-lying villages the fales stood among pools of undrained, sewage-smelling water, where the pigs and children amused themselves with the floating garbage.

It was evident that local pride was not being projected into village competitiveness as in Samoa, for obviously no village was making much effort to do better than the rest. The difference seemed to lie in the fact that while Samoa possessed a decentralized policy, in which the village was all important, Tonga was – and had been as long as history recorded it – centred on the abode of the king, which at first meant Mu'a, the capital of the Tui Tonga, and in recent times Nuku'-alofa, where the palace of the king, to which the villages take their tributes, is the centre of the Tongan world and the source of prestige, which runs down through the local nobility to the ordinary people, and is conversely sustained by the tribute which, to this day, at certain seasons of the year, the ordinary peasants give to the noble as part of their feudal dues so that he may provide his own fitting tribute to the monarch who in recent years, through the marriage of members of the two royal lines, has united within his one person the sacred and temporal monarchies.

Nuku'alofa means Abode of Love. Love is a great deal talked of in Tonga, where the customary toast is 'My love to you', but the vague image of some erotic Polynesian paradise which the name evokes in our minds was quickly dispelled as we drove down the dusty main street towards the shore of the lagoon. That street, indeed, was wide enough for an imperial highway, but the royal capital of Tonga reminded one at first sight of a rather meagre set for a Wild West film; little single-storey shops along wooden sidewalks with awnings and hitching posts to which a couple of horses were tethered. Two barns faced each other, displaying the film posters one remembered from ten years ago. There were billiard saloons and dark curtained places where afterwards we learnt kava is served convivially, and a single café whose Italian founder is vaguely remembered. The main difference between the buildings was that some had gingerbread fretwork decorating their eaves and coats of fresh white paint, and others were weathered to the soft satiny look of driftwood.

Against the wooden walls men squatted, selling coconuts and little paper bags of peanuts. Gaudily decorated three-wheel cabs, operated with motor-bike engines, skittered among the pedestrians who walked indiscriminately on the sidewalks and in the middle of the street. Down the side roads there were wooden cottages with white palings bordering the grass verges and sometimes with lych-gates made out of the bleached porous jawbones of whales in memory of the lost past when the whaling ships came sailing in between the palm-tufted islands that framed the horizon and the lagoon. It was only near the shore itself that any of the attributes of a metropolis appeared, and then on a miniature scale that even a tiny European capital like Vaduz or San Marino would have found rustic. A new and modernistic post office was the most impressive building in Nuku'alofa (properly enough, since among Tonga's most reliable exports are the bizarre, gilded and many-shaped decals that serve it as postage stamps), drawing one's attention away from the South Sea version of a Scottish turreted castle which housed the main government offices. A swing round to the left led us past the green with its big wewa trees where the parliament building stood like a white New England chapel, and close to it the single-storeyed Government Treasury, which also served as Tonga's only bank, and the glorified cricket pavilion which was the head-quarters of the Tonga Defence Force. We had seen the Whitehall of Tonga.

Half a mile on, facing out over the lagoon, stood the Dateline Hotel, a featureless structure in the international tourist manner, owned by the government, run by a German manager and wholly out of character with the country; we continued to live there nevertheless, since its only rival was an Edwardian South Sea boarding house that was falling into decrepitude because the government had for years been blandly ignoring the pleas of its proprietor to be given an actual lease of his land. This was an example of how Tongan policy appears to be oriented towards gently discouraging the remnants of the European trading class; certainly there were no well-to-do merchants deeply involved in Tongan economic and political life like the Nelsons and the Retzlaffs in Samoa. The tightly knit Tongan feudal system left no room for it.

One could indeed never accuse the Tongans of being xenophobic; their manner to the stranger was always impeccably friendly. And yet there was a relationship between their walled-in fales and their attitudes. One had the feeling of being allowed into the country, not of being welcomed. In Samoa and Fiji the native houses were open to one; in the Gilberts one was always invited into the great maneabas or village halls where social life went on. In Tonga we were hardly ever asked to step inside a dwelling, and when this happened it was rarely that food or drink was offered. The Tongans always seemed on guard, and one could hardly resent it, since such guardedness was what had saved them and may still save them from being submerged by alien influences.

3

Though we had intended otherwise, Nuku'alofa remained the centre of our activities in Tonga, which alone illustrates the difficulties of travelling in a country that, though minute in land area, extends over a stretch of ocean about 400 miles from north to south and more than 100 miles from east to west. There were, when we reached Tonga, no internal air services, and the only regular means of transport between the three groups of islands was by means of a white boat with low graceful lines called the *Olavaha* which we saw gleaming at the end of the Queen Salote Pier when we arrived in Nuku'alofa. There was something familiar about the *Olavaha*, and sure enough, when we went to book our passage on her to the atoll of Lifuka which is the capital of the Ha'apai archipelago, we discovered that she was in fact the old *Queen of the Isles*, which used to ply between Penzance and the Scillies.

Alas, our trip to Ha'apai, like our trip to Savai'i in Samoa, became the victim of the caprice of circumstance. We had planned to leave four days after our arrival in Nuku'alofa, and Pinai had taken us to meet a man from Ha'apai who was going home on the *Olavaha* and would help us there. On the way, as we looped through the sandy streets, with their little white houses and their atmosphere of a Long Island seaside village at the beginning of the century, Pinai talked about himself. Tongans are less inhibited in this than Samoans; even so, it is a dubiously polite activity, and has to be preceded by a suitable apology. 'Excuse me for telling you this,' Pinai began; a heavy pause ensued, during which I wondered with resignation what story of calamity would ensue. But as soon as I had asked him to continue, he embarked on the story of his second career as a pillar of the Free Wesleyan Church of Samoa. Unlike Samoa, where the pastors form a professional elite and engross to themselves both the prestige and the profit of church-manship, the service of religion (which in a way is also the service of the state) tends to be universalized in Tonga. Any man who is articulate becomes a local preacher and takes his turn on the circuit, preaching where requested; even King Taufa'ahau himself is an accredited preacher, and two or three times a year he enters the pulpit of some rural church and exhorts his subjects.

Pinai's pietism, however, went somewhat beyond the customary Tongan expectations. He was so taken with his own homiletic abilities that he was building a chapel on a fragment of his api. Recently he had been one of the fortunate Tongans to be picked for a six months' period in New Zealand. He had found work there on the assembly line in the Chrysler plant, and the proceeds of those weeks in the world of *Modern Times* he had carefully saved and brought home to begin his chapel, which a few days later he showed us – looking like a ruin of cement blocks among the palm-trees. The news of his venture had reached the King and one day ('Excuse me for telling you this also') His Majesty had stopped his car, made a gracious suggestion for raising money (for Taufa'ahau is nothing if not an inventive monarch), and promised to be present on the day of Pinai's first preaching. 'I shall have,' Pinai mused, 'to preach from the lectern, so that His Majesty can sit above us all in the pulpit.'

Piety, in Tonga, is a quality to be fought for and guarded. Pinai was a twice-married man, with a double share of children. 'My wife died. I married again to resist temptation!' But if temptation came easily, so did the intimations of beatitude. On our way that day we passed a little public garden, rather spottily planted with hibiscus bushes, a few flowering trees, some little copses and bowers that seemed admirable for intrigue though in fact they were unpopulated. Pinai halted the Moke to take us on a quick stroll along the paths. As we returned he looked at us with his great Polynesian eyes, swimming with the tears that come easily to Tongans: 'I always think,' he said in a voice of dreadful sanctimony, 'I always think when the rain has fallen here and the bushes are pearled with water, that this is just how the garden of Eden must have been!'

We never discovered the status of the impeccable little house where we met Ma'ama Motilika, Pinai's friend from Ha'apai, though it certainly belonged to relatives, and I suspect had been loaned in their absence, since nobody was in evidence but Ma'ama and his wife Moana and his daughter Mele, who was eleven years old and extraordinarily pretty. She resembled her father, a grave and handsome man of fifty, with a long Orwellian face so un-Tongan in character that I surmised the whalers must have been more active on Ha'apai than they appeared to have been in Tongatapu.

Though in the end Ma'ama never did introduce us to his native island, the mere meeting with him gave a glimpse into the life and aspirations of a Tongan commoner from the outer islands. Ma'ama was not quite an ordinary commoner. To begin, he had a hereditary duty at the Palace in Nuku'alofa, which carried with it some small privileges. He was one of those who every new year came from Ha'apai with the boats loaded with pigs and coconuts, yams and bread-fruits, taro roots and green kava bushes, to present the offering of the First Fruits to the King, before which no man may partake of the new crops. He had also been for many years a leading representative of Ha'apai in the conference of the Free Wesleyan Church; one day after our meeting I saw him walking in the market of Nuku'alofa carrying a briefcase and looking solemn and important among a group of parsons.

At the same time Ma'ama was a working Tongan peasant. Like most of his fellow countrymen, he lived a mainly subsistence existence, combining fishing and farming. Sitting in the locally made wicker chairs among the giant shells and old sepia photographs which decorated the little Nuku'alofa parlour, with the breeze stirring sluggishly into the close air under the open shutters, we listened as he recounted what must be the day's routine of thousands of Tongans. He had an api; it was only four acres, but given the especially chronic land shortage on Ha'apai, he considered himself fortunate to have even that. It was sufficient, but he only made it so by cultivating it more intensively than the people of more loosely populated Tongatapu would do. Half of his land he devoted to growing coconuts; some were used by the family and from the rest he cut and dried copra. This accounted for part of his cash income, though nowadays, with the fall in world prices, he could not expect to earn more than about 60 pa'anga (£30) a year from copra. He also grew the customary Tongan root crops – yams, taro and tapioca or manioc, as well as bread-fruit, papayas and pineapples. Bananas provided him with a further source of income, and when a Produce Board boat was due at Lifuka he would load whatever of the fruit was ready into his little one-horse cart and take it to the wharf 1¾ miles away. He reared a few chickens, and, like every Tongan, kept a few pigs, partly from prestige, partly to meet the demands of his noblemen at celebrations, and partly to ensure a constant supply of sucking pigs for the feasts that in Lucullan manner mark the calendars of Tongan lives.

Ma'ama found that if he devoted his mornings to farming, the time was sufficient to keep his api in good shape. His farming operations were simple, and the most exacting task was clearing land for new cultivation, since the Tongans use no fertilizer and instead observe a three-year rotation of yams, taro and tapioca, after which the land is allowed to run fallow for several years in order to renew itself. By ten, when the sun was getting hot, Ma'ama would usually finish his garden work and return home for his large midday meal. In the afternoon he would go fishing, in the lagoon and sometimes beyond the reef, where he would catch vala, a kind of tunny. In the reef, he would take langoustes and octopus. Sometimes at night he would join his friends and go out to spear by the light of Coleman lamps, and this was usually the best fishing of all. Whatever fish the family did not eat fresh, Ma'ama would dry and pack so that it could be sent over and sold in the market at Nuku'alofa.

It was the typical Tongan rural life, and, apart from his church work (which had taken him on his only foreign journey, to Fiji for a youth congress), it was the life Ma'ama had followed ever since he left school. Yet, like many of his fellow countrymen, he had an extraordinary passion for education, which with him represented a family tradition. He, his mother and his grandfather had attended the same Methodist college. Now he was making sure that his children received as good an education as he had done – if not a better one – and to do this he was quite prepared to mortgage almost all his cash income. Four children were at school, with fees diminishing with their youth, but altogether involving 128 pa'anga a year, more than twice the income from his copra crop. He had also to pay for books and stationery, for school uniforms, and for material to make clothes so that the children could keep up appearances when they were out of school. And, since there are no schools in Ha'apai up to Ma'ama's standard, his children had to attend colleges in Nuku'alofa. He could certainly not meet the boarding charges, so that during term time his wife lived in Nuku'alofa with relatives, and looked after the children, while Ma'ama sent them farm produce and dried fish from Ha'apai. Almost everything he earned was consumed by this vast educational budget; since he lived on what he caught, and dressed simply when he was at work, his other expenses were very slight: paraffin and salt, sugar and a little tea, fishing lines and twine to repair his nets. Such luxuries as corned beef, dear to the Polynesian palate, he bought only for feast days.

Despite his rustic background, Ma'ama was a man of intelligence and even sophistication. His palace and church responsibilities had led him to mix with a wider variety of people than the ordinary Tongan villager. Though more taciturn than most Polynesians, he was, according to Pinai, a 'smart' preacher, and he certainly understood the project on which we were involved. It seemed to him an excellent idea that, after Tongans had seen the life of people in Europe and North America projected on the cinema screen, other people now should see how they lived. This was an attitude we found surprisingly widespread among people in the South Sea islands, few of whom were likely to see the films they might help us to make. In Ma'ama's case it seemed a natural outgrowth of his passion for education; the light of knowledge should be spread in any way God had allowed man in his ingenuity to devise.

But Ma'ama's willingness to help us in Ha'apai was as frustrated as our desire to get there. On the morning the *Olavaha* was due to leave, Pinai came over to tell us that the sailing had been cancelled. The engine, which had already done good service in the Scilly Isles before it began to ply the inner seas of Tonga, had broken down. It would undoubtedly be ready tomorrow. But it was not ready tomorrow, or the next day, or the day after that, until in the end we had to cancel our passage. Only on the morning when we left Tonga for Suva and the Gilberts did we finally look out to the end of Queen Salote Pier and see the white outline of the *Olavaha* no longer there; it had sailed away during the preceding night, taking Ma'ama home at last to till his yams and entice his octopus from their crannies in the reef.

4

In Tonga a touch of divinity still seems to hedge a king. Taufa'ahau is on one level a devotedly modern man, a university-educated lawyer, an omnivorous reader, an observant traveller, and a diligent dabbler in scientific and social experiments. 'He is a dreamer,' one of his old retainers remarked to me, 'but he is an active dreamer!' and that seemed an accurate description.

At the same time, he is trapped, however much he may seek to diminish this aspect of his role, in the special protocol that survives from the days when the monarch was regarded as semi-deity. When he participates in the Royal Kava ceremony, neither woman nor foreigner nor commoner can be present; only the nobles and the heralds of the land. No one must ever sit above him, or enter his presence without the ta'ovala, the rope-bound mat which as the characteristic Tongan garment has a touch of holiness attached to it. The tribute of the First Fruits is a ceremony surviving from pagan times when it was associated with the king's fertility-ensuring function. Even bodily the king is regarded by his subjects as reflecting the well-being of the land. Polynesian traditions equate prosperity with amplitude, and the prosperity of a land has among them always been associated with the amplitude of its ruler. Big men, Tongans believe, are likely to be lucky men and to bring good fortune to those with whom they associate. The King of Tonga is 6 feet 2 inches tall; he weighs more than three hundred pounds, and when he flies out of his country he occupies two seats on the plane and special straps are provided. While the king may not keep himself deliberately at this weight, it is one of the reasons for his popularity. A thin monarch would have a hard time in Tonga, and palace-watchers there are already speculating on the difficulties the Crown Prince may encounter if he has not filled out his present trim Sandhurst figure by the time he ascends the throne.

It was not difficult to see the King. In fact, we could hardly have escaped without an audience, since in his lonely eminence on that distant island, he finds the visit of any stranger other than a mere tourist a potentially interesting event. Certainly everything was done to make sure that the meeting went off agreeably. On the morning before our audience we were summoned to the little mock-castle of the government offices to confer with the Prime Minister's Establishment Officer. Victor Zakarian, of Austrian descent, with Armenian remotenesses in his ancestry, was a member of the British Colonial Service who had been seconded to Tonga, one of the small group of Europeans who hold important positions in Tonga without belonging to the actual governing élite.

Zakarian took up a great deal of the pleasant hour we spent sipping his strong tea in giving us an idea of the basic structure of Tongan government. Most of this we already knew, but there were certain nuances he added which helped to bring the King's role into perspective. For example, because of the Polynesian conception of kingship, the government is not responsible to Parliament but to the King, who appoints the cabinet. This means that, in the unlikely event of nobles and commoners uniting in Parliament against the ministers, the government would not fall. It would continue until the King chose to dismiss it. This remnant of absolutism, not uncongenial to the Tongan outlook, imposed on the ruler in modern times a peculiar burden of awareness. He must avoid the example of the Tui Tongas who had retreated into sacred isolation, and develop his sensitivity to the moods of the people. This, Zakarian felt, the King's mother, the great Queen Salote, had done admirably; she had kept amazingly close to the pulse of her people's life, and it was her understanding, as well as the marvellous expansiveness that won British hearts to her at the Coronation, which explained the extraordinary devotion which the Tongans felt for her, a devotion that continues and has spread its aegis over Taufa'ahau precisely because he is the great Salote's son. But in disposition, Zakarian felt, the King was quite unlike his mother. He was a man of good will but a shy man and a natural scholar, and his channels of awareness were less open towards the people than his mother's had been. Loyalty was sustained largely because Tongans still lived to a great extent within a tribal perspective. The individual was less important than the group. The custom of sharing goods within extended kin groups not only meant that the islanders were cushioned against the effects of unemployment or economic crisis but also that there was less likelihood of militant social discontent. But times might change, Zakarian admitted sadly. There was already discontent over the unavailability of land. The growth in population, and the increasing number of young men educated for white-collar careers that did not even exist in Tonga, would aggravate matters. 'Whoever rules Tonga in the 1980s,' Zakarian concluded, 'will have a harder task than good old Queen Salote ever dreamed of.'

'Still,' he brightened, 'I wouldn't have missed this for anything in the world. I've found the Tongans entirely intriguing. Sometimes I think this is the real Lotus Land, where a man forgets to worry. When I worked in Whitehall I was in a state of perpetual excitement over world problems. On top of the anxieties of a British civil servant, I suffered from those of a man of central European background, the heir of a world of perpetual crisis. Since I came here I have found those anxieties month by month receding. I am content to live my life among these people as it happens, from day to day. Every day I learn something new, but it is never anything fearful or threatening. The only anxiety I have is that one day I shall have to leave.'

This was an attitude I found common among the Europeans in Tonga. Another British official spent an evening pouring out the tale of his frustrations in trying to induce the Tongans to conserve their resources. 'They're a terrible people to work with,' he concluded. 'But to live among – that's another matter. It's not that they accept you. In fact they tend to leave you alone. But the atmosphere is so easy that if the King can be persuaded to let me live out my retirement here I shall accept this as the greatest of my rewards.'

If Europeans felt affected in this tranquillizing way by the atmosphere of Tongan life, it was not surprising that Tongans themselves were mentally oriented within the ocean boundaries of their islands. But of one Tongan, it seemed to us, this could by no means be said. The King was certainly more sensitive than any of his fellow countrymen we met to his tiny realm's position in the world.

His palace lies behind greens and gardens, sheltered by tall lines of Norfolk pines and spreading ironwood trees, on the opposite side of the Nuku'alofa's main street to the government offices. Its gardens run down to the lagoon, and it is protected by a low wall and a khaki-uniformed Palace Guard of thirty-six men who form one wing of Tonga's miniature military establishment. (The Tonga Defence Force of fifty men forms the other wing and there is a navy consisting of one patrol vessel armed with a machine gun; four small cannon are installed on the waterfront near the palace, facing out to sea, and until an invader appears they are used with enthusiasm to fire off blanks on ceremonial occasions.)

The palace itself, like the royal chapel beside it, is built entirely of wood, with much fretwork, a porch at the front by which the royal family and foreign visitors enter, and an enormous veranda at the back where the King or his representative sits to receive his subjects and their tribute. It reminded us of an Indian hotel of modest dimensions built in the Victorian era.

We went first to the palace office where, under the watching eyes of George Tupou I and Salote and the other Tongan rulers who had lived in the age of the camera, we were inspected by Meile Tonga, the King's private secretary, mainly to make sure that I was wearing a tie, the principal sartorial requirement for a foreign visitor, and then taken by a minor, black-garbed official to the palace porch, where the royal aide-de-camp, in his gold-frogged khaki uniform, waited to take us into the palace drawing room, which also served as an audience chamber.

As we entered we saw, outlined against the end window, a massive presence, his gigantic bulk ominously magnified by the fact that his front was in shadow and our eyes had not become adjusted to the curtained light of the room. The King advanced, his massiveness hardly reduced in proximity. He was dressed in a semi-military semi-traditional garb of his own devising, consisting of a khaki gabardine jacket with a high Chinese collar, and a khaki vala, with a coarsely woven ta'ovala tied around his waist and sandals on his feet. He wore a black armband for the nobleman whom Tonga, it appeared, universally mourned.

He welcomed us in the breathless, drowning voice of the obese, shook our hands, and motioned us to two armchairs whose legs had been trimmed so that when he sat on the sofa, which he filled as if it were an ordinary armchair, we were three inches or so below him. It was important that we should sit first so that at no moment were our heads higher than his.

At first one was almost obsessed by the King's mere physical presence, and there are some people who never get beyond that stage. A fastidious Fijian Indian politician whom I met later in Suva was virtually unable to talk of Tonga in objective terms because of the distaste which the King's obesity inspired in him. Inge has remembered vividly how, from the angle at which she was sitting, she could see his vale perpetually blowing up in the breeze of the fan (he kept pushing it down like a woman smoothing her skirt in a draught) and how the thigh that was thus revealed seemed as thick as her waist, while his arms seemed thicker than her thighs. For myself, I was possessed with the thought that this was not far different from Gulliver's first audience with the King of Brobdingnag, and I wondered whether it was possible that, by way of Tasman or Dampier or some other earlier voyager in the southern seas, an intimation of the massiveness of Polynesian sovereigns had reached Swift before he placed in the Pacific Ocean, the imaginary lands of *Gulliver's Travels*.

Like the King of Brobdingnag, Taufa'ahau of Tonga was revealed, as the conversation took its way, to be a man of immense dignity, true intelligence, and considerable humour, so that we, at least, became quickly accustomed to his sheer volume and found our voices adapting themselves to the slight deafness from which he suffers. The conversation was slow in gaining momentum, for the King is a smiling shy man, but we won his attention by the wideness of our travels, and very soon he was talking animatedly of his own.

His wandering and observant eye was immediately evident from what he said; in spite of the difficulties which security requirements impose on modern Heads of State, he had seen a great deal and had remembered the kind of details that are revelatory. He talked of human adaptability and drew out as an illustration the Indians he had seen in Calcutta living drily and cheerfully in enormous sewer pipes. He talked with sympathy of the plight of old people rejected in Western cultures, and of the need to help them to maintain their dignity by finding ways in which they could work as long as they had the necessary faculties, and he remembered seeing in Tokyo the clerks taking their shoes to be shone by old people who had established little booths for this purpose in the great office buildings.

'A sense of his dignity, and a feeling that other people respect it! That is what every man needs most of all,' he remarked. 'Riches, even independence, are secondary. Here in Tonga there are very few rich people, but nobody starves, and that is because we are not a very individualist people. We preserve our kinship loyalties, and they pre-serve us, because custom decrees that our kinsmen – and they may be very distant kinsmen – must always see that we do not want. In that way we perhaps lose a little independence, but we retain our dignity, because what we are given does not come from charity or from the welfare state. It comes to us because our traditions tell us that the property of anyone should be at the disposal of his kinsmen who are in need, and nobody resents it, because everyone knows that one day it may be his turn to ask for help and receive it freely.'

It was obvious that the King relished as much as his predecessors had done the adroitness with which Tonga had kept its autonomy by walk-ing the razor's edge between Westernization and tradition, and when I quoted Thailand as perhaps the only other similar example in the whole Pacific region, he gleefully pointed out that even Thailand had not escaped the twin evils of American infiltration and military dic-tatorship, while Tonga had avoided both. And, while he insisted on the stabilizing effects of the conservative elements in the Tongan constitu-tion, he could not resist drawing a sharp comparison with neighbouring Samoa by pointing out that even if the common people of Tonga elected only seven Members of Parliament, at least for those seats the suffrage was universal. Men and women voted alike while in Samoa only the matais voted. That very day voting was taking place in the broad sunlight of Nuku'alofa.

We had to admit that this was true, for that morning we had seen the people lining up at open desks in the main street, and even though we had felt a little doubtful about the secrecy of such a ballot, we had to grant the King's point that there was no chance in such circumstances of any returning officer stuffing the ballot boxes. Admittedly, there were no political parties in Tonga. But, the King remarked, partisan politics was the product of societies which grew so large that people no longer knew each other and personal politics became impossible.

'But Tonga is a small country and the people who are in office live the lives of goldfishes because everyone knows everything they do, and when they do it, and they cannot keep any of their lives or actions secret. In that way, you see,' the King continued, gleefully mixing metaphors, 'there is a real watchdog on everything that happens, twenty-four hours of the day. So that when individuals run for office, or are appointed by me to office, everyone knows their record, the good parts of it and the bad. The word goes round, and the women talk, and the women are a great power here in Tonga, for in the old days we were a matriarchy. All this means that no really bad men can get into public office here, and that is a kind of democracy, even if it does not follow Westminster to the dotting of every i.'

The King rang a bell, and a boy appeared with a tray of glasses of highly gaseous lemonade, a product of Tonga, as His Majesty assured us when he toasted us in non-alcoholic solemnity. It gave him an excuse to proceed on one of his favourite topics – the fact that Tonga is at present the only territory in the South Seas with a favourable trade balance, and the programme he himself is carrying on to maintain that happy position. Tourism – of course, but within limits. In his view, Fiji and Samoa were going overboard. He was content to expand gradually; a small resort was being set up in Vavau, but he intended to watch and see how it developed and how it affected local life.

After all, an ingenious government had many alternatives. Rock melons for example! He had been growing them successfully on one of his estates. And hats! He had just designed a fine sun-hat based on those used by Chinese and Japanese peasants; the materials were available and cheap in Tonga, and there was a ready export market. And honey! All those hibiscus flowers should be put to some use. And fish! Why should the Samoans spend all their money on English tinned pilchards when the Tongans could supply them with tinned mackerel?

But there were bigger things for Tonga in the offing, the King assured us, and he rang the bell again. The boy came running in with a large photograph which the King proceeded to hold before us. It represented a small and very ordinary looking freighter, but the King displayed it with obvious pride. 'We have already established a navy to protect our fishing rights, and now we are starting a merchant navy. We have leased this ship from Japan for two years to transport our products from Fiji to New Zealand so that we shall no longer be dependent on the caprices of the shipping lines. If the experiment proves successful we shall buy her.' And then, as an obviously calculated afterthought: 'You know, we are drilling for oil. If we strike it, and there is every reason to believe we shall, we shall be able to buy and pay for everything that Tonga needs.' A dreamer indeed! But, alas for the dreamer, it was not long after we left Tonga that the oilmen finally decided the islands were as dry as a barren cow.

However, the King of Tonga has never been a man with a single scheme in his quiver, and I am sure the failure of oil drilling has merely inspired him to ever more varied schemes for the welfare of his minute kingdom. Certainly his interests, at least in practical and scientific matters, seemed inexhaustible, and he not merely discussed the general idea of the film we would be making in Tonga, but proceeded to talk of aspects of the craft of film-making which caught me lamely at a loss for answers, since I had gladly left such matters to the competence of Gordon and the cameraman.

'Are you by chance interested in sports?' the King asked, with a gleam in the eye which suggested a more than ordinary enthusiasm. I confessed to a mild enthusiasm for cricket, provided I were not required to play. 'I am endeavouring to interest my people in soccer,' he continued. 'Owing to the proximity of New Zealand, we already play a great deal of rugby, but since our connection with Britain is more than sentimental, I think it would be a good thing for our young men and our young women to become proficient in a British sport. Perhaps one day we shall be able to send a Tongan team to Britain. Tomorrow I shall be attending a soccer match of which I am patron.'

And on that note we withdrew, for King Taufa'ahau, the descendant of the priest-kings of Tonga, is known to be so devoted to the rituals of sport that unsuspecting visitors are liable to be conscripted into attending the games he attends. As we were leaving I thought of the incongruity of this immense and breathless monarch perspiring in a suitably elevated seat as he vicariously followed the achievements of his loyal athletes. But a few days later, in the dusty, jumbled little shed that serves as a museum for Tupou College – Tonga's Eton – I saw a fading photograph of a slim figure riding high and horizontal through the air. It was the prince who would become King Taufa'ahau, setting what has remained the unchallenged pole jump record for the Kingdom of Tonga.

5

Tonga is famous in the South Seas for its Sundays and its funerals, Sunday observance, indeed, is enshrined in the constitution. 'The Sabbath day,' says that document, 'shall be sacred in Tonga for ever and it shall not be lawful to do work or play games or trade on the Sabbath. And any agreement made or documents witnessed on that day shall be counted void and not recognized by the government.'

To this day this clause of the constitution is severely enforced. No taxis or buses run on a Sunday and only the King's car drives out, and that merely to church. It is a crime on the Sabbath to go fishing or to work in one's api. Shops are tightly closed, the market does not operate, and the only island of activity is the bar of the Dateline Hotel, which is kept open for the benefit of unholy foreigners. It is not even possible to get in or out of Tonga on a Sunday, for boats may not enter or leave the harbour, and aeroplanes may not fly in or over the Kingdom. The only occasion in history when the airport on Tongatapu was opened on a Sunday took place during our visit. Because heavy rains had made the turf runway unusable, a number of dignitaries, including the Australian High Commissioner, and a high official of Qantas, had unexpectedly been trapped for several days and must return urgently to Fiji. Sunday was the first day on which the runway would be dry enough for a plane to land and take off, but the Tongan cabinet had to meet on Saturday night and pass a special decree before this could be allowed. There were pious members of the Free Wesleyan Church who whispered prophecies of dire consequences to Tonga for this desecration of the Sabbath that had been preserved so punctiliously since the good days of old King George Tupou.

Nuku'alofa indeed was transformed on Sunday. The cars were replaced by droves of pedestrians and cyclists (for bicycles, being manpowered, are at least tolerated) all dressed in their best clothes, all carrying Bibles and prayer books, and all hurrying in the direction of

one of Nuku'alofa's many churches. Apart from our interest in the
religious activities which played so large a part in Tongan life, there
was nothing to do on Sunday in Nuku'alofa except to attend church,
and since Pinai was off on a preaching trip to a remote corner of the
island, for which he must leave by bicycle early in the morning,
Ma'ama undertook to take us to the Centennial Church, Tonga's
equivalent of Canterbury Cathedral, so that we could see the Royal
Family at worship. He was there early standing outside the Hotel,
but refusing to enter, with a look on his face as if he regarded it as one
of the halls of Babylon. He was dressed in an impeccable white jacket,
and wore a tie and a ta'ovala of remarkably delicate white pandanus
fibre, which looked like an example of fine lacework; he explained that
it was an heirloom that had descended through several generations in
his family. Such ancient waistmats are highly valued in Tonga and
never sold.

In the Centennial Church, as in most modern Tongan churches,
there was none of the warmth of colour or inventiveness of decoration
that made the Samoan churches so extraordinary. The old church had
been one of the oval buildings with vaulted roofs made of poles lashed
with sinnet, raised on thick wooden pillars and deeply thatched with
sugar-cane leaf which were built in the Victorian era and of which
only a few now survive. (There is a particularly splendid example – a
tribute to the vanishing native architecture of Tonga – still in use as the
chapel at Tupou College.) The present building was a bleak rectangular
concrete hall without harmonious proportions or inspiring decoration.
But since the singing, like all Polynesian singing, was pleasing, it was
at least a merit – though doubtless an accidental one – that the church
had good acoustics.

Singing had already begun when we entered. The two hundred girls
of Queen Salote School, with white dresses and blue ribbons setting off
their richly brown skins and oiled black hair, were seated in a solid
block in the centre of the church and they continued to sing hymns in
unison until the service began. Gradually the church filled until its
thousand seats were taken. The choir filed in to take their places in the
front of the church. The choirmaster climbed into his rostrum above
the choir, and the preacher into a pulpit above the choirmaster, and
finally a door opened at the end of the church and the Royal Family
entered their pew which was above everything; the King, who had a
throne-like seat a little higher than the rest, and the Queen, a handsome,

light-skinned woman (descendant of the Tui Tongas) rather badly dressed in black, and the Princess, and finally the Prince Prime Minister (who is the King's somewhat less massive younger brother) and his wife.

As was doubtless intended by whoever designed the church, one's attention inevitably wandered back towards that pew elevated above all common mortals, but with a sympathetic discomfort, for the day was hot, and much of the service was taken standing as the choir sang prodigiously its rather staid eighteenth-century Methodist hymns to the tune of cornets and French horns and the King stood there, bundled in his Chinese jacket and his thick waistmat, with the sweat streaming from his face even under the electric fan that blew directly upon him. Immense and motionless like some hieratic statue, his great head leaning forward, his arms hanging rigidly by his side, he seemed to personify the very immobility of absolutism, and it was hard to imagine the quick light of intelligence that had flickered over his countenance so often and so unpredictably when we had met him face to face.

After the service we left Ma'ama and walked down to the green outside the palace, where we sat on a bench under one of the great Norfolk pines, looking out over the harbour. Everything was peaceful in its Sabbath stillness, the very waters mirror-like; the only person in sight was a man who sat under a tree at the water's edge, looking like a brown Verlaine, with immense beard, long hair and satyr face; he read from one of a pile of folio volumes that lay on the grass beside him. As we lingered there a police motor-cycle came into sight, driving along the waterfront road towards the palace, and behind it the bullet-proof and air-conditioned royal limousine, flying the Tongan ensign. The King recognized us, smiled and spoke to the Queen, who waved at us as if she were the lady of some Victorian manor and we the deserving poor.

In the evening Pinai was back from his preaching, and we went with him to the service in the royal chapel beside the palace. It was, apart from the old native church at Tupou College, the only attractive ecclesiastical building we saw in Tonga, and that, I suspect, only because the rulers of Tonga were inspired by the example of the one monarchy they thought worth imitating – the British monarchy. The chapel was a charming late Gothic Revival structure in wood, the outside white-painted, and the inside all of brown wood with white trim, elaborately fretted. To the left of the eagle lectern, where the minister would stand, the three crowned thrones used in ordinary services by the King, Queen and Crown Prince were elevated on a low platform. At the back of the chapel, elevated even higher, stood the coronation thrones, richly carved and gilded. It was Westminster in miniature, the scale modulating into Biedermeier, the manner *gemütlich*.

The Sunday evening services were for Europeans, and specifically this meant the Australian and New Zealand Wesleyans, who are strongly present in the Tongan educational system and represent the largest contingent of resident foreigners. There was lusty singing and embarrassingly bad sermonizing. After church we took Pinai back to the Dateline for dinner, or rather for the simple Tongan meal served on a Sunday, of yams and taro and a very tasty dish called lu pulu, consisting of meat and onions marinated in coconut milk, wrapped in taro leaves and cooked in an earth oven. We sat beside the bathing pool until the mosquitoes drove us away, trying without success to penetrate Pinai's Tongan aloofness. We never succeeded in getting beyond that polite and rather eloquent person who doubled as the accomplished preacher and the civil servant loyal to his monarch. The nearest thing to a confession came when, in a state of moist-eyed exaltation, he said once again, 'Excuse me for telling you this!' and then proceeded to recount the greatest day of his life, when he had sung baritone to the Queen's soprano in a performance of *The Messiah*.

6

George Frederick Handel was a name almost as familiar in Tonga as George Tupou the great constitution-maker, and one of the scenes that lingers most vividly in my mind's eye and ear is a funeral in which he figured as prominently as in any British royal obsequies.

We had been in the country and were returning to the town beside the royal mausolea whose white marble pinnacles and weeping angels cluster on the western edge of Nuku'alofa near the Queen Salote School. The pagan kings are buried elsewhere; here lie the Christian monarchs and princes from George Tupou onwards. Beyond the royal mausolea is a cemetery for commoners, characterized by that combination of the bleak and the bizarre which marks such places in Tonga. The graves were covered with high mounds of grey-brown coral sand, and their edges were marked by lines of large smooth pebbles or upturned beer bottles; most of them had headstones, but the more remarkable decorations were the sheets embroidered gaudily with tinsel and hung on poles beside the newer graves to represent the kia-kias or fringed dancing skirts that were used in the past.

In this cemetery we had seen, two days before, a grave being dug and lined with bricks. 'They must be expecting a death,' said the Australian teacher with whom we were returning from a visit to the theological college in western Tongatapu. 'You know,' he added, 'it is a strange thing that I have seen often in Tonga. An old man will have a foreknowledge that he is about to die. He may appear healthy, but he will not let that influence him. He will announce his coming departure, tie up all his worldly arrangements, and often give detailed instructions for his funeral and order the grave to be dug. Then, feeling he has left nothing undone that may induce him to return and haunt the places of his life, he will be at peace and slip quietly away.'

It was the man whose grave had been dug that we met coming to occupy it on our second journey past the cemetery; an extraordinary combination of the two aspects of Tongan life passed before us in procession as we halted the car beside the road and got out to stand respectfully bowing as Tongan custom prescribes. The dead man, though not a noble, had been a man of consequence, and at the head of the procession marched the Tonga police band, the best in the country. The sounds of the Dead March from *Saul*, played impeccably, surged among the tamarind trees and sent the frigate birds soaring and screaming from the windy palms. Behind came a truck serving as a bier, with the man's wife and daughters, their hair hanging in veils over their eyes, sitting beside his open coffin, and keening in the high-pitched tones that custom demands. Behind, solemn and black, prayerbooks in their right hands and rolled umbrellas in their left, a dozen parsons marched in ranks. And then, like an upsurging from the pagan past, the women kinsfolk tramped like sorrowing maenads, barefoot and clad in rusty and ragged black, with ancient tattered mats around their waists, their hair hanging uncombed and tangled over their shoulders, and great bunches of showy flowers clasped in their arms. It was these women who afterwards, like living caryatids, held up the great sheet of tapa to encircle the grave and to make the actual burial as private an act as the rest of the funeral had been public.

'The Tongans are very professional about their mourning,' Tupuola Efi said to me, taking a dry look at the rival Polynesian culture when he visited Tonga during our presence there. The mourning for the nobleman who had already died before we reached Tonga and been buried on the morning of our arrival was still going on. There were so many kinsmen and vassals and dependents that all the time in the streets one encountered companies of bedraggled mourning women, padding barefoot to and from his house where, when we passed, we would see them sitting silently in circles under the trees, continuing the wake. Even high officials were involved, and one afternoon, when we went to see the Honourable Ve'ehala, the Governor of Ha'apai and one of the most powerful of Tongan noblemen, we found that he was mourning at the nobleman's house. Pinai went to fetch him while we waited on the enclosed veranda of his own house, the walls of which were hung with old photographs, and oleographs of the saints, and red satin sacred hearts. Ve'ehala, a short man for a Tongan, with a pudgy, humorous face, came uttering apologies for not having welcomed us. He explained that for ten days after a funeral the dead man's friends would sit within the house, in a perpetual circle that continued day and night, as the participants came and went. 'We drink kava, and we tell over and over again the same anecdotes about the dead person, and we recount all the stories of ghosts we have ever heard, and we chew over the topics that come into our heads, endlessly. It becomes very boring. I am grateful that you have provided me with a respectable reason to withdraw for a little while.'

We arranged ourselves according to the formal patterns of Tongan custom with Ve'ehala as a noble taking the largest and highest chair, Inge and me sitting just an inch lower, and Pinai as a commoner sitting cross-legged on the floor at a respectable distance and keeping out of the conversation.

Apart from his functions as the mainly absentee Governor of Ha'apai and as a member of the cabinet, Ve'ehala was also the keeper of the royal records and reputed to possess more knowledge about the ancient customs, the old songs and dances, than any other man in Tonga.

We sat drinking whisky – for Ve'ehala had no patience with the Methodist extremities of some of his countrymen – and talking about the dances which he would be re-enacting when he led a troupe of a hundred Tongans to take part in the South Pacific festival.

'Many of the dances are so old that even I can no longer understand the chants that accompany them. They are like the words of No plays in modern Japan, meaningless to modern people. My own belief is that both the dances and the chants came originally from Asia. When you hear them you will recognize that the music is very Oriental in flavour, a little like the music of Bali, except that we use only the drum and the human voice. And another thing that of course is very similar to Balinese dancing is the importance we give to hand movements which almost take the place of speech, since they are used to portray both action and emotional states.'

Ve'ehala remarked that in the early days of conversion to Christianity there was a real danger of the traditional songs and dances being suppressed by George Tupou and his Methodist adviser Shirley Baker, who regarded them as relics of heathenism which must be swept out of the way to turn Tonga into a Christian state.

'Fortunately the last of the Tui Tonga was still alive at that time, and he resented bitterly the way George Tupou had usurped the rights in Tongatapu which he regarded as his own. So when Father Chevron came along and started to teach Catholic doctrines, the Tui Tonga was amenable to the idea of supporting a rival church. Besides, the ritualism of the Catholics appealed to him, and when Father Chevron said that there was nothing wrong with the old customs provided they did not interfere with Catholic dogma, the Tui Tonga was converted and so were several other noble families, including my own.'

Ve'ehala explained that in these families the dances and songs had been preserved, but the interest had diminished, and fewer and fewer people felt they had any meaning in the Tonga of the constitution and the Methodist Church.

'Fortunately, our great Queen Salote was not like her predecessors. She believed our traditions should be preserved. She had learnt many of them in her childhood, and when I was a young man at her court she picked me out and passed them on to me. Until a few months ago I was the only person left who remembered some of the chants. But the festival has given me an opportunity. I am teaching what I know, to as many people as possible, and I hope that one or two of them will carry it on. We still have many old customs left, but it is our songs and our dances that are the heart of the tradition, and if that heart is not kept alive the rest will soon vanish and we shall be independent for no purpose because we shall have no culture of our own.'

He invited us to attend the rehearsals he was holding in the public gardens, and one day we went, and saw in a great open fale the men performing, to the sound of a wooden drum, the sacred me'eut'upaki, the dance celebrating the migrations that had brought the Tongans to their islands in the days before history. It was danced exactly as Cook and his men had seen it 195 years before, with the dancers 'each holding in their hands a little light thin wooden instrument, about two feet long, and in shape not unlike a small oblong paddle. . . . Their motions were at first slow, but quickened as the drums beat faster, and they recited sentences in a musical tone the whole time which were answered by the chorus; but at the end of a short space they all joined and finished with a shout.'

Ve'ehala told us, when the dance was finished, that this was the day when the mourning for the dead nobleman came to an end, and in a little while they would be going to the palace to celebrate the occasion by dancing a lakalaka, the great Tongan dance of tribute. So we walked along the front in the direction of the town.

The morning was perfect, a flawless sky, a silvery gleam on the blueness of the lagoon, the islets of the reef standing out in sharp relief on the horizon. A soft, cool breeze was blowing as we sat waiting under the Norfolk pines, watching the red dragonflies and some satiny black butterflies whose wings were spattered with blue spots like sapphires, and listening to the doves calling in the palace grounds. 'I could stay here the rest of my life,' said Inge. And it was true, I felt instantly; in that moment – and there were few others like them on our journey – we felt completely at one with our setting, and understood the lost English-men who could think of no better privilege than to end their days in this remote realm. We saw many more splendid spots in scenic terms than this, in the Solomons and the New Hebrides, and even in Fiji, but nowhere else did we find such an intensity of colour and light and peace, combined in such a pellucid harmony.

Soon the voices of the dancers aroused us from our meditation, and we hurried over to the palace office where the private secretary hastily checked to see that I was wearing my tie, and then an attendant took us in past the guards and round to a vantage-point where from the side we could see what went on.

Along the wide back veranda, seated cross-legged with their backs to the wall, four men in black were ranged at regular intervals. These were the matapules, the royal heralds. Inside an open door in the middle of the veranda, but invisible to us, the Queen was seated. She would remain royally immobile while the matapules spoke on her behalf.

Meanwhile, the dancers had gathered in a wide double line across the lawn, the men ranged on the right and the women on the left. When all was ready, they suddenly burst into a loud and strident song, and the antiphonal choruses continued, male surge answering female surge, as the dance swept forward and backward over the lawn, the men prancing and gesticulating like furious warriors and the women swaying and interpreting the meaning of the song with the motions of their hands and arms. As the dances went on, the matapules from the veranda uttered hoarse shouts of approval. The whole scene had an extraordinary primitive power and it brought to my mind more vividly than any narrative had done what the first explorers must have felt when they came and saw the Polynesian culture at its uncorrupted height. At the end the chief matapule delivered a speech in a high-pitched oratorical voice, accepting the dried kava stick that Ve'ehala came to lay on the veranda before him, talking of the time of mourning and its ending, praising the dancers. Then Ve'ehala came forward again to receive the kava root back, and the dancers danced their way out of the palace grounds.

7

Tongatapu really falls into two areas which culturally are quite different. Just east of Nuku'alofa, a double-lobed arm of the lagoon which on the charts looks like a pair of lungs bites deeply inland, and to the east and south of this lies the region which in pre-European times and in modern independent Tonga alike has been the most advanced – the centre of the rule of the Tui Tongas and now – with its colleges and airport, hospital and military encampment – the most important single region in the country outside the capital. Here the villages project their relative modernity either in a very self-conscious neatness of trimmed lawns and flower-beds and well-kept fales, or in the opposite extreme, the untidiness of places built out of the detritus of the technological age. West of Nuku'alofa and the great lagoon, the villages are more traditional, more naturally rustic, and, to all appearances, more closely dominated by the landlords.

It was to the eastern side that we made our first expedition, and instead of Pinai's open Moke we hired for the dusty country roads one of the few local taxis. For the occasion Pinai insisted on garlanding us, Inge with white frangipani blossoms and me with red ginger flowers;

we quietly removed them after the first mile, but as long as we stayed in the car their fading fragrance surrounded us.

The day happened to be Steamer Day, for a cruise ship had put in, and the event rippled like a great activating wave over the whole island. In Nuku'alofa the green in front of the parliament building was already crammed with stalls selling mats and tapa cloth and wood carvings and baskets as big as the jars of the Forty Thieves, while dancers were rehearsing before the assembled small boys of the capital the comic combats with which they would entertain the visitors. Out in the country the roads were full of little blue and red two-wheeled carts, which are the regular form of rural transport in Tonga, carrying goods to the places where the buses would stop with their loads of tourists.

The first of these was Cook's Tree. Despite the Tongan plots on his life, Cookie, as the Tongans call him (he is Toote in other parts of Poly-nesia) has become a great figure of myth; until 1966 a tortoise reputed to have been left by him still wandered in the grounds of the palace and was treated with great reverence under the honorific name of Tui Malinga. And today the ovava tree near Mu'a where he is reputed to have rested on landing is marked by a stone and is one of the pilgrimage places for visitors. Already, when we got there, the village women had spread their goods under the trees, and were sitting silently beside them. It was a splendid view over the water where Cook's ships moored, with the shores before us coming together to make the inlet into a funnel lined with dense vegetation, and the vista opening through its mouth towards the distant islands, flat and tufted, that guarded the lagoon's farther extremities. The red roofs of the royal summer palace showed among the trees; the shores were lined with tall mangroves, whose dark green accentuated the brilliant blue of the water, over which a solitary white bird flew.

Mu'a, the ancient capital of the sacred kings, had fallen away to a village of shabby plank huts, but the grandeur of the old culture was at least suggested by the massive terraces of blackish stone, furred over with grass and lantana, which lay just outside the village. These were the Langi, reputed to be the tombs of the prehistoric Tui Tongas. There is no doubt that they were used for burial purposes, but they resemble so closely the ceremonial platforms which existed in other Polynesian societies – and notably in the Marquesas – that it seems fair to assume that they were actually multi-purpose sacred sites, used for the rituals connected with the sacred monarchy and rendered all the more holy by the mana emanating from the bodies buried under their great slabs.

On the broad beaches beyond Mu'a the fishermen's huts were built, with nets drying on the pandanus trees that grew around them in the sand, and pigs rooting in the shallows. Brilliant wild flowers, red and magenta, grew around the huts, and the men, with their valas twisted between their legs like loin-cloths, waded into the water, casting their circular throw-nets. It seemed, on this poor corner of the island, as if nothing had changed since the Tui Tongas reigned.

But change was there, as we learnt with dramatic abruptness, for just beyond the fishing village we swung a little inland along a narrow coral road bordered by a kind of mimosa with large white bubbles of blossom. As we were turning a corner, at a quiet 15 miles an hour but dead in the middle of the road, another car came round at what must have been a good 40 miles an hour, the highest speed possible on these twisting island roads. The collision was inevitable, but both drivers mitigated it by frantic swerving. The sound of crumbling and rending tinplate was dramatic, but though we were all thrown violently about, the only casualties were Inge's grazed elbows and my bruised shins.

We climbed out and stood in the road, facing the plump young man who extricated himself from the other car. There was a curious quiet after the din of the crash – nothing of the shouting that would attend such an event in Italy or in India. Inge, indeed, provided the only excitement, soundly berating the other driver for driving so recklessly. Pinai waved his hand nervously and then came forward. 'Let me introduce you! This is the Prime Minister's son. He is His Majesty's nephew!' 'I'm glad to meet you,' Inge retorted, 'but you should still be ashamed of yourself!' 'Strange meeting!' said the King's nephew and smiled.

A peasant passing on a motor-bike had informed the police who were directing traffic at Cook's Tree, and a Land-Rover came racing up with the Chief Inspector for the Mu'a district. He was a tall, smooth-featured man, with an almost impeccable English accent. 'Sorry about all this!' he said, shaking our hands. 'Never do have accidents in my territory! Almost never! Only seven last year! And now it happens to guests in our country!' I noticed that he spoke obliquely, never directly reproaching the King's nephew, who nevertheless looked uneasy at the implied reproach. 'I was trained in the U.K. – Scotland Yard,' the Chief

Inspector remarked, and proceeded to show his expertise by examining the tyre marks and drawing elaborately in his notebook. But when the time came to measure distances, nobody had a tape. The King's nephew tried to remedy this by plucking a piece of dried liana from one of the mimosa bushes which he and the constable who drove the Land-Rover began to drag over the ground and knot in various places. The Inspector considered such a procedure most improper, and unbuckled his belt so that everything could be given a look of regularity by being measured in Sam Browne lengths. When all this was over a peasant appeared with a long pole and we tried to prise up the buckled mudguards and bonnets in the hope of getting the cars moving again. But the damage was much too drastic for makeshift remedies, and the Inspector took us in his Land-Rover on the next stage of the journey, to the great megalithic trilithon of Ha'amonga. On the way he talked with pride about the peacefulness of Tonga. Most of the crime was petty – theft and drunkenness and minor brawling. Despite their repute as warriors in the past, the Tongans had ceased to be notably violent, and the kingdom averaged about two murders a year. 'We are like Britain in that as in other matters,' he remarked, and it was interesting that he stressed resemblance rather than influence. 'In Pago Pago, where the Americans are, there are many murders.'

At Ha'amonga the Inspector arranged for one of the tourist buses to take us back to Nuku'alofa, and then, before they left with him to make their depositions, the King's nephew and the taxi-driver both came up to us to apologize for the accident. The Inspector had already taken our evidence and asked how long we would be in the kingdom and available to present our testimony.

Not doubting that justice would be done in the spirit of the famous constitution, we turned our attention to the most imposing monument of Tonga and indeed of our whole journey in the South Seas. The Ha'amonga, whose very form suggests that the ancestors of the Polynesians were affected by the great megalithic culture which swept from Britain and Brittany down through Malta and the Levant to the southern tip of India, looks at first sight like one of the trilithons of Stonehenge, but in fact there is a marked difference, since the horizontal member, which is 19 feet long and weighs about 40 tons, is not just laid on top of the 16 foot uprights, but is actually slotted into them. Away from the trilithon, down a long alley in the surrounding coconut plantation, stands an isolated monolith.

Until recently it was believed that the Ha'amonga was either the gateway to a royal compound or itself a kind of shrine. But the King, with his scientific interests, had other ideas, and pointed to a pattern of crossed lines on the centrepiece. Relating this to the isolated monolith, he concluded that the Ha'amonga was in fact a gigantic cosmic calendar related to fertility festivals, and in 1967 he proved his theory by tests at the summer and winter solstices which showed that the line between the monolith and the markings on the trilithon was perfectly oriented to the rising of the sun.

Science, it seems, flourishes more readily in Tonga than ideal justice. Our accident created a great deal of attention, and that evening we received a telephone call on behalf of the Prime Minister inquiring about our well-being. We fully expected to be called as witnesses; our evidence would have shown that while the taxi-driver was at fault for not keeping to his side of the road, the prince was even more so for driving far beyond the speed limit on the twisting country roads. We were not called, and the reason seemed evident when, three months later, we returned briefly to Tonga to make the final arrangements for film, and found that the taxi-driver had alone been found guilty. He told me the story quietly and without complaint; his only comment was conveyed in the obliquity of his smile.

8

To the west of the island we went many times, for it was the villages in this direction that, with Nuku'alofa, we eventually decided to make the locale of our film. Partly it was because here one could see most clearly delineated the pattern of feudal relations, and the way of life was less modernized. Partly it was for visual reasons, since these places were also more traditional in form, and the vegetation was more luxuriant, with large old mangoes and rain trees shadowing the little houses. Old fales with plaited cane walls were still common, and some of the original oval churches survived. There were few cars on the roads, but many of the little Tongan carts, and often at evening we would meet processions of men returning on horseback from their apis, looking like ancient warriors as they carried on their shoulders the long spades which are now used for digging out the deep roots of yams but were originally introduced by the whalers for flensing blubber.

One of our journeys took us to the village of Houma on the south-western shore of Tongatapu, where there is no lagoon and the ocean breakers sweep directly upon the cliffs of the island's raised edge. We went on this trip with an old taxi-driver called Sam who came from this district. Sam led us off the coral roads that served as highways on to the narrow lanes that ran between the plantations, which at this season were so luxuriant that often we seemed to drive through solid walls of green, though we had only to stop and find an opening with cart ruts going through it to enter a complex of cultivated patches and haphazardly planted trees, each of which made its contribution to the traditional Tongan economy.

Sam was the ideal companion for this kind of journey, since he knew the whole process of Tongan agriculture with the enthusiasm of a man who hoped very soon to become himself the possessor of a holding. He would take us into an api, whether the farmers were there or not, and demonstrate how things were done, and nobody seemed to be in the least concerned by our invasion of their privacy. Indeed, the people appeared to be intrigued and amused that anyone should be interested in their agricultural methods, which in fact were simple in the extreme. A small piece of taro root with a purple eye, heeled in, was enough to start a plant; a stick of tapioca with a small fragment of root could just be stuck in the ground and left to grow; a yam could be chopped into small pieces each of which, planted, might well produce a great starchy root weighing 30 pounds; the fresh shoot from a pineapple that had fruited need merely be put in the ground, and the rich brown powdery soil would do the rest. So far as I could tell, apart from following the usual South Seas pattern of rotation, the only aid which the farmers gave to growth beyond their own labour was the practice of planting according to ancient lunar timetables. A few of the nobles on their estates had apparently taken to intensive cultivation with the use of fertilizers, but no ordinary man cultivating his api could afford such modern refinements.

Apart from food, which had to be supplemented by fish caught in the lagoon, the api grew everything needed for a traditional Polynesian existence; and one could envisage the Tongans, if the ships and the planes ceased to call, returning to living off the land in a way it has become impossible to think of Europeans doing. The coconut tree provided materials to construct a house and its nuts fibre for rope and cups for drinking; the pandanus gave material for baskets and mats and elementary garments; the fruit of the candlenut made excellent torches; and there was the paper mulberry, a rather unassuming little bush with palmate leaves which before the traders came provided the Tongans with cloth. In one of the apis Sam tore off a shoot of the mulberry and stripped the outer bark to reveal the silky underbark. A little later, in one of the villages on the way to Houma, we came across the women gathered in a big open shed and turning the mulberry bark into tapa. They were beating it with short clubs until it was as thin as India paper, and several times its original width. The strips they made in this way were joined with a kind of vegetable glue into squares and rectangles of various sizes, and on the grass outside the shed a row of women were sitting at the end of a great sheet which they were decorating with black and brown designs – geometrical figures and conventionalized birds and fish – painted with vegetable tinctures on the soft ivory-coloured fabric. I paced out the size of the sheet; it was approximately 10 feet wide and 35 feet long, and this, one of the women told me, was not large. For occasions of state, cloths 500 feet long had been made; like the fine mats of Samoa, such tapas were regarded as both material and symbolic wealth, to be stored away for its mana and its monetary worth alike. Tongan tapas are regarded as the best in the South Seas, and this art that most authentically transmits the ancient culture, for it has been far more effectively preserved than the songs or the dances, is entirely in the hands of the women. In Tonga the women are the most conservative and traditional element in the population, and a powerful element in view of the vestiges of matriarchal custom that still survive, notably among the nobility, whose titles descend through the female line.

Outside Nuku'alofa, Houma was the largest settlement we visited in Tonga, a sprawling place with houses in every style from traditional coconut-leaf fales to ugly structures of precast concrete blocks, each standing in the centre of its town lot, so that the place seemed as if it had been loosely shaken out over the open grassland.

The attraction of Houma, which brought the buses there on Steamer Days when the roads were not impassably muddy, was the blow-holes. We went down a winding boggy lane out of the village, through a grove of toas with feathery foliage like tamarisks and hard gnarled trunks which are used for making dugout canoes. Then came a belt of pandanus trees through which we emerged on to the clifftop that faced out to the blow-holes. As we came out into the open we could see the white leaping of geysers of water and feel the salt spray falling like a gentle and persistent drizzle.

The clifftop was actually a raised coral terrace, covered with a peculiar vegetation of dwarf leather-leaved shrubs that clung close to the rock, and spiky rushes, and creepers with thick glaucous leaves. Below stretched another terrace, which was really the reef that at this point joined the coast of the island. Here the great ocean waves broke, forcing the water up through holes in the coral so that it rose hissing and vaporizing in columns 30 feet high. Between the two capes that bounded our view there must have been two miles of these terraces, and along the whole distance the geysers rose and fell above the white turbulence of the tumbling breakers.

'Today is nothing,' said Sam. 'On a stormy day the blow-holes shoot so high that the pandanus trees are constantly drenched. When the storm is over people come from the village and scrape off the salt that clings to the leaves.'

9

It was the north-western corner of the island, a few miles north of Houma that we finally picked as the site for the village sequences in our films. Here, on a peninsula that projected like a horn from the main body of the island, lay a cluster of settlements – Foui and Ahau, Ha'avakotolo and Kolovai – which were not only more isolated than the rest of the island from the influences of Nuku'alofa, but were also of considerable historical interest. Grassed-over mounds on the outskirts of the villages delineated pre-European fortifications; the Queen's family were nobles in Ha'avakotola, which formed a rival nucleus of loyalty to Nuku'alofa because of their links with the line of the Tui Tongas; the various villages vied for the honour of having been the first to welcome the pioneer missionary John Thomas, who landed on this coast. And in Kolovai the tall trees in the centre of the village were bare of leaves, but garlanded during the day with the dark hanging shapes of thousands of fruit-bats, at times breaking their sleep with shrill squeakings and at sunset rising in clouds and flying off to feed in the plantations. These were sacred beasts; only the King or members of his family could kill them.

In these villages, though we rarely penetrated the tight curtain of privacy that guards a Tongan house, we watched the people at work and play and in fact observed all but the most intimate details of their lives, since their work was done out of doors, the men splitting the coconuts and drying copra outside their houses, the women working on tapa in the communal sheds or sitting in circles on the grass deftly plaiting coconut leaves for walls and roofs and making their mats and baskets of the pandanus which lay bleaching in the sun beside them. Out of doors, also, the cooking took place, in little unwalled kitchens beside the houses, and here the meals were eaten in perpetual alfresco style.

Here too we met the types of people who wielded authority in the villages, and observed how deeply the Tongan life was affected by the characteristic mingling of feudalism and democracy. We found a curious balance of forces, consisting of the Church and its ministers, the elected officials who theoretically represented the King, and the noblemen, with their matapules forming petty courts around them. To an extent the orders interlocked, since almost everyone of any importance was a preacher in a church, while the town officers who represented the central government were tenants of the nobles and owed them tributary services.

We encountered rural religion when we stepped into the little church of Ha'avakotolo, where the Queen's family of Ahom'e kept their country seat in a circle of small fales within a compound, much, I imagine, like the chiefs' compounds in the past, except that now the fales were of freshly painted wood. The church was also of wood, with a red corrugated iron roof, but it was in the traditional shape, with the original frame of poles, tied with sinnet, that had been built for the first missionary. Inside, the pews were blacked with time and worn by generations of pious buttocks. On a blackboard, the words of a hymn were written in Tongan, and over a massive octagonal black pulpit hung a coloured banner on the wall with the word, AMELIA embroidered upon it in great capitals. As we were looking at it a man we had passed on the road came hurrying in. He wore a dark vala, and the shirt and tie of the man who no longer belongs to the land; his ragged ta'ovala and his bare feet suggested a mingling of poverty with respectability, yet he had the well-fed look of a man familiar with feasts.

He spoke in a squeaky falsetto. 'I believe God told me to walk faster, so that I could be of help to you people,' he fluted, with the usual Tongan assumption that the deity is personally involved in the smallest of the island's affairs. 'My name is Faletoa Vailea. I am schoolmaster at Kolovai, but since the pastor has three villages to look after, he has given me special care of this church at Ha'avakatolo. It is a great

honour for me, since here we believe it was the chief of Ha'avakotolo
who first served the Lord by welcoming his great emissary, John
Thomas.' The theme was a favourite one with Faletoa; another day,
when we saw him outside his school beating the ship's bell with a
great bite broken out of its side which the villagers had saved from a
wrecked schooner generations ago, he came quickly back to that aspect
of local history. 'When a member of the Ahom'e family became Queen
of Tonga, we believed that God had elevated her because of her ancestor's generosity to our first missionary.'

In Faletoa's company we first met Sitani Pani, the town officer of
Ha'avakotolo. It was one of the blue and golden days when the light
assumes a peculiar softness and Tonga appears at its most charming.
(And *charm* rather than anything so dramatic as *beauty* is the characteristic Tongan mood.) We heard the clatter of hooves, and a handsome
young man dressed in khaki overalls came cantering down the main
road of the village, shouting at the top of his voice while the people
stood outside their fales to listen. 'He is calling the people to a fono,'
Faletoa explained, as Sitani reined up his horse beside us. In Tonga, it
appeared, the fono was not a meeting of clan chiefs, as in Samoa, but a
village meeting, which every person over sixteen was expected to attend.

The next time we met Sitani he was acting in his private role, bringing home a cartload of coconuts to add to those already drying outside
his weather-stained plank house in the middle of the village. When we
reached the house, his family came out to meet us – a monumentally
massive wife and three strapping daughters. But, as always in Tonga,
there was no suggestion that we should enter the house, and we stood
outside talking about his farm, which was three miles away in the bush,
so that his horse and cart were a virtual necessity. He was one of the
lucky men, for the api had belonged to his father, and it only came to
him because on the father's death his elder brother decided to live in
Nuku'alofa and withdrew in Sitani's favour.

By now, in Samoa or Fiji or the Gilberts, the coconut of welcome
would have been offered, but this was not the custom in Tonga, and
we had to accept our thirst, and wander off with Sitani on his weekly
walk around the village to make sure that the grass had been cut and
the refuse cleared away around the houses. He fined the untidy house-
holders, but he was unable to discipline the pigs who roamed freely
about the village, tearing up the grass and digging pits for the unwary
walker.

The noble, Ahom'e, was away in Australia, and Sitani took us instead to visit his matapule, whose name was Kavafusi. Kavafusi lived in an unpainted frame house, larger than most of the dwellings in the village. He was sitting by his cookhouse, clad only in trousers, when we came up, and hurried into the house to put on a clean white shirt before he came to talk to us. Like most Tongan nobles and heralds, he was a tall and strongly built man, with heavy features that normally looked like a mask of melancholia, but would light up almost unrecognizably when he laughed. As I stood there talking to him, I was intrigued by the alien feeling of the scene before me: the cooking house, a mere open shed with a thatched roof supported on poles, with half an oil drum forming a semi-cylindrical brazier on which blackened iron pots were cooking with the flames darting between them; outside the shed, on boxes and barrels, sat Sitani, and Kavafusi's wife, a dark and rather Mexican-looking, woman and a couple of children, and a horse was tethered to one of the posts. It was a scene that called up in my mind descriptions of the Argentinian pampas in the novels of W. H. Hudson and R. B. Cunningham Graham; it resembled in no way one's pre-conceptions of the South Seas.

It was evident from Kavafusi's description of his function that a matapule was much more than a mere herald or orator; perhaps the frequently used expression, 'talking chief', best describes his role. He was a necessary link in the aristocratic system in Tonga and even in the system of authority as it exists in fact rather than in law. Tribute to the King, like the First Fruits, being a matter of custom rather than law, is the nobleman's responsibility, but it is the matapule who makes sure that the goods are gathered from the tenants and who actually goes to Nuku'alofa to perform the ceremonial presentation. When the noble-man attends a function, it is the matapule who speaks on his behalf. When the noble is away, it is the matapule who acts in his place. And it is the matapule who, as the payment for his services, receives the gifts, such as pigs or produce or fine mats or tapa, that are publicly offered to his noble.

Like most ceremonial roles in Tonga, that of matapule runs in lineages, but is not necessarily passed on from father to son. Kavafusi's father was not a matapule; he inherited the role from his grandfather, who saw, when Kavafusi was a boy, that he had the proper qualities for a matapule – dignity of bearing, a sonorous voice, an ability to learn the special and rhetorical forms of traditional oratory and the various forms of address, and a memory capable of retaining and reciting at will the genealogies of all the noble families and all the matapule lineages in the kingdom. As in many highly traditional and aristocratic societies, like that of old Tibet, there are in fact several usages of Tongan, governing one's contacts with different classes, and every matapule must know the royal language to be used in ceremonial relations with the King and his family, and the honorific language to be used in addressing nobles, and the ordinary form of address – plain and laconic in comparison – to be used when speaking to commoners. In ancient Tongan society the matapule was not only the noble's spokesman but also his confidential adviser and his most intimate bodyguard, and matapules were expected to sacrifice their lives – if necessary – to save their chiefs. It was obvious, from the way Sitani addressed Kavafusi, that the matapule was even now a man of more real authority in the village than the town officer, even though the latter was elected by the people and officially represented the government in Nuku'alofa; at one village fono we later witnessed, the noble sat on the mat of honour and the matapule virtually conducted the meeting and dictated its decisions.

At Foui, the village down the road from Ha'avakotolo, the noble was in residence. His title was Va'hai; the name is linked to the estate and can be assumed only when a noble's right to inherit the land and title is confirmed by the King in a royal kava ceremony. We gained easy access to Va'hai because by a lucky chance it was his two brothers we addressed when we stopped in Foui to ask the way to his house. The older, a tall man with a sorrowful equine countenance who dressed in a green Hawaiian shirt, khaki trousers and well-made brogues, introduced himself as Solo, the town officer. Sione, the younger brother, looked like the Sancho to Solo's Don Quixote, a machete-flourishing ragamuffin in trousers that had been savaged off at the knees, a filthy shirt, shoes too big and worn far down at the heels. Sione pointed out the great, bleak frame house that served as Va'hai's mansion, and ran over to it. He came back a quarter of an hour later, time to sweep and put down mats and clear the women into the back rooms, and we were ushered into the only house we entered in any Tongan village.

It was a strange uncomfortable dwelling, a vast room in which the studs had only been partially sheathed with painted wood taken from another house and nailed on so haphazardly that the various colours – white and green and pale blue – formed a bizarre pattern to which one's eyes kept returning with a disconcerted fascination. The floor was covered by two immense mats, but there was hardly any furniture to fill the emptiness of the room; a glass-fronted dresser, a large bed without sheets over the green mattress but with a traditional Tongan wooden pillow at the head, and the chairs in which we and Va-hai sat, while his brothers assumed their lowly positions on the floor.

Va'hai was a man of formidable presence, with a great bald head and a face of massive sculptural quality that reminded me of early Japanese wooden sculptures. He had a positively hieratic look as he sat solidly in his chair, dressed in black shirt and vala, with his great knees apart, and his stiff waist-mat jutting out to complement the monumental folds of his garments. He seemed, as one looked at him, like the very personification of all that was conservative in Tongan society.

And, indeed, we could have come to no one more inclined than this rustic landowner to give us the viewpoint of the noble class, a viewpoint which we quickly realized was appreciably different from that of the Westernized intellectual who finds himself cast in the role of King of Tonga. According to Va'hai, vigorously supported by his brothers, it was the nobles who had made the common people a gift of parliamentary representation, though history in fact seems to confirm that this concession to democracy was a measure initiated by King George Tupou, to which the nobles only assented with the greatest unwillingness. Another myth Va'hai zealously sustained was that the assignment of land provided for in the constitution was also a gift of the noblemen, and that apis were still being given to young men on reaching maturity, though even the official statistics of the government of Tonga admitted that this was not the case. But perhaps the most interesting feature of his remarks was the primitive ideology the nobles evidently felt the need to work out in justifying their role and their privileges. It was an ideology peculiarly fitted to a coral island, essentially based on the idea of society as a kind of vast zoophyte in which the members perform their various roles willingly and for their mutual benefit. What joined all layers of society was a sense of unity that went deeper than reason; the phrase 'from the heart' kept cropping up as Va'hai and his brothers stressed the inner sense of loyalty that united nobles and common people in reciprocal love and also united the nobles themselves, so that if anyone were visited with calamity, help would come from all parts of Tonga. Va'hai was intent on disputing any suggestion that compulsion – either physical or moral – might enter into the relationship between

the commoners and the nobles. When the people contributed towards
the tribute of First Fruits, or even towards a gift which the noble sent
to the palace on some more special occasion, it was – he insisted – 'just
a feeling inside' that prompted the people.

'If the people contribute so much and so freely,' I asked, 'what is the
noble's contribution?'

There was a momentary look of astonishment on Va'hai's massive
face. I am sure he had never before thought a noble had any other duty
but to be noble. But he quickly recovered his imperturbable calm.
'His duty,' he said, 'is to give an example, such as going regularly to
church!'

10

Like other visitors to Tonga, we sensed rather than perceived under-
currents of discontent. Tongans are masters at the art of keeping their
own counsel, and while most of them would talk frankly about problems admitted by the government, such as the unavailability of land,
one never heard from them any overt criticism of the monarch or the
system.

Even if political discontent existed, there were no means by which
it could readily be made public. No independent press existed, for the
only newspaper – a weekly appearing in English and Tongan – was
operated by the government. There were no political parties, and if
candidates for election represented anything, it was regional rather than
political rivalries.

One day we thought we were on the track of an opposition, when
we saw over the doorway of a little wooden shack on the main street
of Nuku'alofa a sign saying that it was the office of the lawyer to the
Tongan National Political Society. We went in. A white-haired man
in black shirt and vala called us into a musty inner room. To my first
question he answered vaguely that the Tongan National Political
Society was intended 'to help the Tongan people'. 'In what way is it
political?' I asked. 'It is a society of people of various professions who
are willing to advise Tongans.' 'Advise in what way?' 'We tell people
how to get to New Zealand so as to find work.' He would say nothing
more, but our impression of pretentious futility was deepened when
he called us back as we were walking away to tell us, that he was the
proprietor of the Way Inn, Tonga's only motel. 'If you have already

made your arrangements, kindly tell your friends! I am charging only 4 pa'anga a day, room and board!'

'We go away,' I noted in my diary, 'feeling that something has been concealed, but we are not sure even of that. That is the feeling one often has in Tonga. Are there undetected depths waiting to be plumbed, or is what one sees in fact all there is to see? One has at times the impression that this is a mentally two-dimensional society, as flat as the coral plain on which it exists; that Methodism has swept all but the political superstructure clean and flat.'

The only occasion on which I was able to talk to a Tongan with any frankness on this subject strengthened my impression that whatever discontent existed in Tonga, it was not politically oriented or expressed. At a faculty party at the University of the South Pacific in Suva I was intrigued by the behaviour of the only Tongan present. He spoke with an enthusiastic radicalism when he was discussing the affairs of other South Sea territories, but immediately fell silent when the conversation turned to Tonga and the Fijians began to criticize its feudal structure. Later on I asked him directly why he had nothing to say about Tonga. Was it because he feared his criticisms might be repeated at home?

'Nothing as simple as that,' he answered. 'It is really that I prefer not to say things I would not want to say at home.'

'Do you mean dare not say?' I asked.

'No. I mean that I can live and act like a radical out of Tonga but not inside. I was in an American university at the height of the student disturbances of the 1960s, and I supported them. Here in Suva I am considered a radical on the faculty. But when I go home to Tonga I seem to sink into a soft bed of contentment and indifference, and I think that happens to all Tongans. I can still make mentally the criticisms of our society which I make outside. But I no longer feel any urge to act.'

11

Life on Tongatapu, because the island was flat and therefore almost entirely arable, is not as oriented to the lagoon as it is in Samoa. It was rarely one found a village built close on the seashore. Yet, living as we did on the harbour at Nuku'alofa, the lagoon provided one of the most familiar backgrounds to our life in Tonga, and when I think of the country in physical terms, it is that great water, with all the variety of its light and life, that first flashes into my memory.

The strand itself was a panorama of Tongan life. Sitting on the balcony of our room, we would look down and watch the people strolling along the seawalk, and especially the majestic stride of the Tongan women, who were altogether a freer breed than the men; they smiled at one frankly in the street and they liked to transmit their friendliness by touching one on the arm or shoulder, though never on the head, which throughout the South Seas is taboo as the source of mana. Sometimes a young Tongan noblewoman would stroll there, and her walk would be aloof and stately, as her maid sheltered her pale face from the sun with a lace-trimmed parasol; she would ignore anyone below her own status.

In the water there were always girls bathing in wet dresses moulded tightly against their bodies, so that prudery was usually frustrated, and men fishing with cast-nets. The men would walk gently along the edge of the water, looking out for the glint of silver or the movement of thin shadows over the floor of the lagoon. Then they would cast the carefully folded net with a flick of the wrist so that it fell on the water in a perfectly spread circle, allowing it to sink before they waded in to raise it gently and take the trapped fish, often half a dozen in a throw. These were small fish, 4 inches long at most, and shaped like oval leaves; some were silver-grey, and other brass-yellow, and yet others a coppery-red.

At evening the fishing boats would come in to the wharf below the hotel; the fishermen would stand on shore and blow their whistles, and the women would come hurrying down, to bargain for strings of silver mackerel or red mullet, or for the dark bloody chunks of tuna caught beyond the reef. A little later boys would come cantering down to ride their horses into the water and scrub them down. And then the sun, levelling out before its quick fall below the horizon, would pick out in dazzling white the coasting steamers lying along the wharf, and its rays would spread to illuminate the whole lagoon in a great sheet of electrum on which the little boats floated incandescently, as if they were about to burst into flame. One evening great double rainbows hung over the harbour, and at the end, when all else had faded, a fragment lingered for a long time over one of the little islands of the reef like a prismatic plume rising from a flat and shaggy green cap.

It was to that or another island that we went on our last afternoon in Tonga; I remember the occasion particularly vividly because it served so appropriately as a prelude to our departure the next day for the lagoon and atoll world of the Gilberts. We went out with two Australians, an English girl and Pinai. At Nuku'alofa there is a live, submerged inner reef, and an outer reef of dead coral reaching above low-tide level. My diary tells the rest:

'We sail out over the inner to the outer reef. It is hard to describe such a haunting visual experience, but perhaps the most astonishing aspect of it is that, though one has read a great deal about living coral, one still has fixed in the mind until one actually sees it an image of the pink substance Italians make into necklaces, or of the white bleached fragments of stag-horn found on beaches; but the coral *does in fact live*, in a dramatic way, moves and sways in the movement of the water, and is coloured vividly and livelily, so that one seems to be looking down into a strange surrealist garden in which the fishes are the birds. There are clumps of purple coral that might be giant heather; the tips of the stag-horn are startling brilliant blue and the fish that swim among them are of the same electric colour; there are great yellowish-green flat corals which look like tree fungi, magnified gigantically; there are vast yellow structures that resemble brains 3 feet across; there are green fronded growths like Brobdingnagian mosses. Among them the fish swim in endless variety, as though the Monaco aquarium has liberated all its inhabitants at the same time, so many strange creatures in metallic colours and emblematic forms move below one. Starfish lie where the coral temporarily gives way to sand, occasionally one sees the wavy lips of a giant clam 3–4 feet wide, and to remind one that ugliness enters into the most paradisial garden of the real world, turd-like sea-cucumbers lie inert and hideous upon the ocean floor. The anchor is thrown down among the coral, and the others swim while we remain in the boat, watching as it drifts over new and ever-changing stretches of coral, moving at the end of its long tether. We also watch the fishermen who have moored their sailing dinghies and dugout canoes on the dead brown exposed crests of the reef, where the noddies perch, black birds with white heads, and sweep low over the water.

'Later we sail to one of the islands of the reef. It is called Fafa, a few acres covered with palms; its broad golden sands are edged by an intermediate zone of seashore plants and broad-leafed bushes. It is uninhabited, perhaps because it is the property of the Prime Minister (the next island belongs to the King) and reserved as a noble domain. There is one little fale on the beach where workers shelter when they gather the prime ministerial coconuts, and sometimes the fishermen camp on its shores; it is they who brought the flies that plague one walking along the otherwise perfect beach. We poach some of the coconuts, and the boatman thrusts a sharpened stick into the sand and bashes them on it until the husks break away. The juice is fresh and cool, and flesh is jelly-like and delicious. On such an island one could survive, living on coconuts, on the shellfish abundant in the eel-grass that grows close inshore, on sea-slugs and other food to be got by wading out to one's waist. Tongans in fact do survive like this. Only recently, on one of the uninhabited islands of Ha'apai, some boys were found whose boat had gone astray and who had been given up for lost; they had survived almost a year in good health and excellent spirits. Doubtless one has in such modern adventures the models, if only one takes them in retrospect, for the human settlements of all these thousands of South Sea islands in the past before history.'

PART THREE

Remotenesses of Sea and Sand

1

I was considered more than a little eccentric in the Gilbert Islands when I kept on talking about the Canadian Arctic. After all, the Gilberts stride the equator. They are, probably more than any other group, the archetypal coral islands: the places one conjured up in the mind's eye of boyhood – or at least of my boyhood – from reading Ballantyne and Robert Louis Stevenson. The symbiotic work of trillions of minute organisms, that grow only in the warm waters of tropical oceans, built them up by patient architecture from the ocean floor. Their shallow profiles are made tall by vast groves of coconut palms through which even the sunlight filters with such poetic softness that the Gilbertese named one of their own islands Abemama – Island of Moonlight. The temperature in the Gilberts never falls below 80°, and rarely rises much above. When I attempted to describe snow, sitting among the elders in a Gilbertese maneaba, the great meeting hall built of palm logs lashed together with sinnet and roofed with pandanus thatch, they would look curious, and then they would laugh uneasily, because they could not tell me they thought I was lying, which among them would be a mortal insult, to be wiped away with the stroke of a knife.

Yet, inappropriate as it seemed, I kept thinking of the Arctic. It was not because of the historical associations, of the fact that the whalers began the destruction of the traditional Gilbertese culture just as they began the destruction of the traditional Eskimo culture. It was rather because I felt the austere marginality of a people who had chosen to live on infertile coral soil and had developed a culture as specialized and as delicate of that of other marginal peoples, the Bedouin, and the Eskimo whose life I knew. Even more, I felt the kinship of the Arctic through a sense of absolute remoteness as intense as I had felt on the treeless tundra beside Baker Lake in the North-West Territories, or flying over the tarn-spattered solitudes north of the Thélon River.

Like the Arctic, the Gilberts are one of the ends of the earth, and since the waves of traders and beachcombers, whalers and black-birders, finally ebbed early in this century, not many travellers have visited them except on official business. In 1972, according to the statistics of the British officials who still administer the group as part of the Gilbert and Ellice Islands Colony, only thirty tourists visited Tarawa, the main island of the Gilberts, and of those I doubt if more than a dozen found their way to any of the outer islands. Tourism is not even encouraged, for the simple reason that fresh water is too hard to find on the atolls for large hotel developments to be feasible. There are no comfortable cruises like those in Fiji, no Hawaiianized resorts, and the one tiny hotel in a million square miles of ocean, the Otintai on Tarawa, makes a habit of wiring to prospective visitors: 'Absolutely no room. Repeat, absolutely!' That, we later discovered, was a test by which Peter Barker, the young Australian who runs the hotel on behalf of the Wholesale Society (a government-sponsored agency aimed at fostering a co-operative economy among the Gilbertese), sorted out the enterprising goats who, he felt, would accept the difficulties of travel among the islands, from the sheep who would prefer to be guided. 'If you want to go,' said the Australian girl who booked our plane tickets in Suva, 'you go.' And so, although we received the routine telegram, we went.

The sense of remoteness builds up relentlessly on the long day it takes to travel north-west by north to Tarawa from Suva, which is the nearest point where urban civilization of any kind approaches the Gilberts. That nearest point is 1,365 miles away. We left the baroque splendours of the Grand Pacific Hotel in Suva at half-past four in the morning on the long drive through the Indian villages beside the river Rewa to Nausori Airport. The front seats of the little Air Pacific plane had been taken out and the space stuffed with mailbags. A flock of white-robed nuns, French and Australian, settled in the seats behind them. A brace of civil servants from Whitehall, in Bermuda shorts, with brief-cases and authentically rolled umbrellas, sat on the other side of the gangway from a pair of Gilbertese youths whose catlike Micro-nesian faces were crowned with chaplets of hibiscus, jasmine and coco-nut leaves. The smell of the flowers and the twittering of a thousand day-old chicks in the back cabin wafted through the plane. Fat Poly-nesian women from the Ellice Islands lurched on board with baskets. It was like being on an airborne country bus. At dawn we flew north over the volcanic hills of Viti Levu, unpeopled and as sharp-edged as crumpled paper, and above the other islands of Fiji, dark and shaggy within their green lagoons.

Then, hour after hour, it was the open sea, dazzling blue as it almost always is in these latitudes, without a ship or an island, a fluid Sahara. The Gilberts and the Ellices, their fellow archipelago to the south, are lost in an ocean so immense that after the Spaniards found them in the sixteenth century, no European sighted them again until 1765, when a Royal Navy captain nicknamed 'Foulweather' Jack Byron (grand-father of Byron the poet), discovered the Gilbertese island of Nikunau by chance as he was sailing on a short-cut course from South America to Canton. Fortune, which played many tricks on 'Foulweather' Jack, has also robbed him of the credit for his discovery; Nikunau, for a time called Byron Island, has long reverted to its native name, while the group as a whole is named after Captain Thomas Gilbert, who came in 1788, more than twenty years after. The Ellice Islands were not even named after a navigator; they took their name from Edward Ellice, a London merchant and financier of wide imperialist interests who was also a leading figure in the Hudson's Bay Company, and who thus in a way anticipated my own inclination to link the coral islands of the South Seas with the snowy wilderness of the far north; not exactly 'From Greenland's icy mountains/To India's coral strand', but the same kind of nineteenth-century sweep of interest and power.

The Gilberts and Ellices, with a few outlying islands that are ad-ministered with them, form one of the last fragments of the British Empire. The colony stretches over two million square miles of salt water, but the actual land area consists of some 370 square miles, divided among thirty-nine small islands and atolls scattered in the fluid immen-sities. They are inhabited by 60,000 people, divided between less than 10,000 Polynesians in the Ellices, about 50,000 Micronesians in the Gilberts, and, as in all the South Sea island groups, a few hundred half-breeds descended usually from European traders, and a few hundred far from pure-blooded Chinese, whose ancestors appear to have inter-bred quite freely with the Micronesians.

By ten o'clock the first islands came into sight: they were the Ellices, the southernmost group. Some of them were drop-shaped solid islands, or raised atolls, set in the turquoise jewels of their lagoons. Others were harp-shaped true atolls, which are like fences of coral enclosing great stretches of salt water, their eastern reefs built up into series of narrow islands green-pelted with coconut palms, and their western reefs mere shoals where the ocean broke in white rims, beyond which the depths dropped down to indigo.

We landed at the atoll of Funafuti, on the ragged grass strip which the Americans created during World War II by ruining the islanders' gardens. Funafuti is a place of some note in scientific history, for it was here that Edgeworth David came in 1897 to drill the hole, 1,100 feet down into the island's mass, which proved the validity of Darwin's theory of the origin of coral islands. Now it is an outpost of Empire so classic that it approaches caricature.

We had, in fact, landed at a native village which served as a marginal capital, for in these remote islands even the basic urbanization that exists in Apia and Nuku'alofa has not taken place; they were never wealthy enough for traders to gather and form anything resembling a town. At Funafuti a coral track lined with white spider lilies led down towards the lagoon through a grove of palms and of pandanus trees growing on high stilted roots. There are no roads in the Ellices, and there is only one jeep, which the District Commissioner keeps for prestige.

From the modest bungalow called the Residency, the District Commissioner had emerged with the Fisheries Officer, who was the only other British representative, to join the crowd of giggling, flower-crowned Ellice Islanders who came to meet the plane. He was barefooted, wore worn-out khaki shorts, and seemed to have relaxed into the last and easiest of a long line of colonial postings. A look of anxiety passed over his lean imperial face when I mentioned the talk that some day the colony might become independent, and that the Ellicemen had even asked to become independent separately from the Gilbertese.

'It's economic nonsense,' he answered. 'The Ellice Islands have nothing but coconuts. In twenty-five years even Nauru, which is the richest place in these regions because of its phosphate deposits in the South Seas, will run out of its resources and start living on its investments. The Ellices have nothing to invest. They can't even be a banana republic because the climate is too unreliable. They're condemned to copra, and no country can be economically independent on copra alone. Now that's the voice of good sense. But good sense doesn't have much influence in a world where nationalism is the favourite sickness of small peoples. If you ask me to prophesy, I would say, Yes, in spite of all economic sense the colony will get its independence, and under the impulse of economic insanity the Ellices will demand their freedom from the Gilbertese and end up as the most precarious of all the world's new nations. And then, I suppose, I shall have to resign myself to the Falklands. By that time there won't be much left but Hong Kong and the Falklands, and Hong Kong is the kind of plum that isn't likely to come my way.'

We wandered down to the lawns that had been made beside the lagoon. A government launch was moored there, and some outriggered dugout canoes were drawn up on shore. (The Ellicemen carve out their canoes while the Gilbertese sew theirs together.) We went into the shack that served as a substitute for a hotel and drank gin slings until an old man on the airstrip beat an iron triangle and we all trooped back through the palm-groves to rejoin the plane.

After the lushness and flowery brilliance of Fiji and Samoa, I was struck by the land's meagreness on Funafuti; the palms sent down their roots into the limy aerated soil under the grey rubble of dead coral, and prospered, but the green undergrowth was scanty, and the only spectacular flowers seemed to be those of the hibiscus. But at least the Ellices were, in terms of this region, relatively rainy islands. Drought increases as one draws nearer the equator; and Tarawa, after we had flown over the more southerly atolls of the Gilberts, was just north of the line. Here, as we landed on the airstrip at Bonriki, it was evident that we had advanced considerably farther into barrenness. On Tarawa there was usually no green at all beneath the trees. It looked lush from the sea, because of the verdure of the palms, but in their shade the ground was always arid and grey, a desert with trees.

2

On any ordinary map of the South Pacific, Tarawa, if it appears at all, is shown as a single dot, and one imagines, if not a town there, at least a closely knit settlement. In fact, Tarawa is an angle whose two sides are in all forty miles long, consisting of the fifteen narrow islets, divided by tidal channels, which form the southern and eastern reefs of the Tarawa lagoon, a saltwater lake so vast that to the north, looking out from the Otintai Hotel, its waters dipped down over the horizon without any land being visible. The part of Tarawa that functioned as capital of the Gilberts was scattered for almost twenty miles among the villages of the southern islets. The airport was a stretch of grey packed coral sand at Bonriki, the easternmost of these islets. Travelling westward, the hotel, the hospital and the training college were on the island of Bikenibu; the bishop's palace and the headquarters of the Sacred Heart Mission were on Taborio, the British administrative headquarters and Government House were on Bairiki, and the harbour facilities and commercial centre were on Betio. All these islets except the last were linked by causeways; the wide gap between Bairiki and Betio was crossed by a ferry.

Nowhere, except among the warehouses and offices near the wharf at Betio, which is more thickly populated than anywhere else in the Gilberts, does one ever have the feeling among these islands that life has begun to congeal into an urban state. As we drove in one of Tarawa's two taxis from Bonriki to the Otintai Hotel there were few places where we were out of sight of the little stilted houses of the Gilbertese, built under the palm-trees that provided all the materials out of which they were constructed, and equally few places where we did not see the life of the people going on openly, for during the daytime the mats that formed the walls were rolled up as in Samoa and all was open to the public gaze. Yet the houses were scattered discreetly among the palm-trees, without any of the open spaces that were features of the Samoan or Tongan villages, and without any real sense of coalescing into communities.

All this, as we afterwards realized, was linked with the essentially decentralized character of Micronesian as distinguished from Polynesian life. Though on one or two islands, like Abemama and Butaritari, certain lineages had contrived with the help of European weapons and beachcomber ministers to set themselves up as ruling dynasties, the usual pattern of Gilbertese life is closer to that suggested by the name of one of the largest atolls: Tabiteuea – the land forbidden to have a king. The villagers meet daily in the great steep-roofed maneabas which are the focuses of social life, but even within the maneabas the very ground on which the men sit, and the roof-supporting pillars of roughly hewn coral rock against which the elders lean, are divided as scrupulously as the coconut groves between the various landholding lineages or utus. Clan traditions are carefully preserved by oral transmission, genealogies are punctiliously remembered, and in the pre-European age questions of honour and land became so important that the islands were in a state of perpetual internecine warfare, with shifting clan alliances constantly warring against each other. On most islands the elders, who remembered the ancestries and interpreted the traditions and customary law, were the real centres of power. No high chiefly system like the Polynesian was able to develop, and the scattered nature of the archipelago, and even of the settlements that fringed each lagoon, discouraged the concentration of power. The introduction of European weapons intensified the negative and fissiparous aspects of this society of proud and martial men, and the Gilbertese seemed well on the way towards mutual extermination in a disastrous series of land wars when the British established a protectorate in 1892.

The fact that land more than any other cause provoked the wars of the Gilberts illustrates the preciousness of even the most remotely fertile fragment of land in these islands of meagre soil and scanty territory. After the British had stabilized the situation which wars made fluid, and had forbidden foreigners to acquire Gilbertese land, inheritance became the principal way in which land was transferred, and inheritance has usually meant subdivisions in each generation between all the available heirs, so that now, as the population pushes on the edge of viability, one often hears of men whose heritage is a piece of land big enough to grow six or five or even three coconut palms.

I bring these facts so early into my narrative, because almost from the beginning we were aware of them, and they conditioned our view of the Gilberts. Except perhaps for the commercial nucleus of Betio, where people from all over the islands have gathered in a unique pattern of semi-urban alienation, there is nowhere in the Gilberts where one feels removed from village life. At the Otintai Hotel we were always conscious of the local people living their rustic lives publicly around us. We did indeed find a room there, and learnt that no one who defied one of Peter Barker's famous telegrams had ever been turned away. The Otintai was in fact a very modest little hostelry whose verandas faced out on to the often literally dazzling vistas of the lagoon. There were eleven rooms, but one was regarded by the staff as haunted, and only the officials who came from Whitehall on unpopular and unproductive missions of investigation were lodged in it. In the rest stayed the air-crews, people on official missions from other South Sea islands, the rare travelling salesmen, even rarer tourists, and the self-styled King of Abemama when he decided to take a holiday from his little realm. Peter Barker ran the place with genial Australian hospitality; he was deeply committed to the islands and his wife Rose, the loveliest girl we met in all the South Seas, was herself a Gilbertese, with those dashes of Chinese and European blood that produce such attractive combinations. Peter and Rose, who have since become our very good friends, were from the beginning perfect hosts, spending hours with us explaining local customs and beliefs, retailing anecdotes about the old guard of imperialism who dominate the local colonial administration, telling the tales about the anti – the ghosts and goblins surviving from pagan days – that still circulate among the Gilbertese, and helping us to find means by which we could explore the outer islands.

The hotel was built between the lagoon and the coral road, along which the traffic went to the other islets of Tarawa and on which it was held to be unwise to accost a stranger walking northward in case he were a spirit making his way to the abode of the Lord of Death on the distant island of Makin where all Gilbertese go on their way to the afterworld. The little houses of the village clustered close around the hotel, and the girls from these houses worked there, cooked the lagoon fish and reef lobsters for us, cleaned our rooms, and chattered to us in high light voices that turned English into a language of birds.

The rooms, already inhabited by honey-coloured gecko lizards that chirped to us in the night, and by brown cantharides beetles, out of the coconut trees, whose mere touch on the skin could raise a painful blister, were built right along the edge of the beach, and we learnt much in the first days, merely watching and listening. At dawn I would get up and go out to see the white reef herons flapping down to fish in the shallows, and the silhouettes of the islanders going out on trembling catwalks of sticks against the lilac sunrise to their palm-leaf outhouses. During the morning there would be the usual South Seas waterfront parade of men fishing with castnets and women wading in to gather shellfish, and little boys jiggling with lines on sticks and swimming naked and plastering themselves with the fine white silt until they looked like dancing ghosts as they clowned and gesticulated before us. In the middle distance the outriggered Gilbertese canoes, their lateen sails spread like great white butterfly wings, skimmed with incredible lightness over the lagoon; these canoes are built extremely narrowly, for speed, of thin planks sewn with coconut fibres; operated by a man sitting on a platform poised between the canoe and the outrigger, they are among the fastest non-mechanical craft in the world, and it is said that an expert sailor can travel in them as fast as twenty-three knots. At evening, in a long necklace of moving lights, the boats would slip out into the darkness for the night fishing on the reef.

Every dawn, and every night at dusk, we would hear, filtering down from the great leaf-tuft of one of the palms before our room, a high-pitched song that had a strangely Arabic lilt; another voice echoed down the beach, and another farther off, like cocks answering each other in the last hour of darkness. They were the boys cutting the spathes of coconut flowers for toddy; they would come scampering down as if the trees were ladders, each with his sharp knife and his coconut shells of nectar. Palm toddy is the Gilbertese native drink, and like every product of the coconut it can fulfil a number of needs. Sweet toddy, which is not yet fermented, is a bland and pleasant drink that forms one of the main sources of vitamins in the local diet. Sour toddy is a potent and treacherous intoxicant, for alien heads at least. Toddy, boiled down into a thick syrup, served as a sweetening substance before sugar was introduced, and is still sometimes offered at feasts.

Fishermen, toddy cutters, children, women cooking and drying fish outside their houses, cyclists carrying burdens on their shoulders or heads, men repairing their boats and nets on the shore; there were always people in view, and one was always observed, yet the houses were so scattered among the palms, and the villages lapsed so loosely into each other, that one was rarely oppressively conscious of human presence. But occasionally we would find ourselves unexpectedly in a crowd, as we did one night when we went with other guests from the hotel to the island's only place of collective amusement, the outdoor cinema. We drove in the hotel Moke, dangling over the side the cane chairs we had been warned to take with us. We entered a great stockade of coconut logs like an old trading fort and planted our chairs at the back; the Gilbertese sat in rows cross-legged on the ground. The moon rose behind the shivering palms above the screen. The films were incredibly antique. The main feature was an epic about ancient Rome called *The Revolt of the Slaves* but actually dealing with early Christians, not with the followers of Spartacus, and the audience followed the action at least with a good deal of interest, for they laughed derisively in the amatory scenes and shouted with delight when, at the end, the cruel and vindictive villain was savaged to death by his own bloodhounds; the newsreel was actually ten years old, bringing to Tarawa man's earliest ventures into space! My attention wandered, and I found myself trying to count the heads of the people sitting below, and failing, and realizing for the first time in human terms what I already knew from books, that population in the Gilberts is an even greater problem than it is anywhere else in the over-peopled South Seas. Much of the small land area of the colony is actually on the largely barren Christmas Island, far from the Gilberts, which have only a 100 square miles of solid but not very fertile land; 500 people must draw a living from every one of these square miles.

Yet, strangely enough, there were times on this crowded island when I would experience the same sense of remoteness and isolation as I had felt flying up on the long day from Suva. I would stand by the lagoon. Phalaropes ran on the beach and called like peewits. Frigate birds swooped and glided. The far islands were a mere furry line of palms on the horizon, and the great stretch of water seemed as much a fluid microcosm, a world caught in its own distances, as the great lakes of the Canadian north. Yet the fragment of land on which I stood was so narrow that I could turn round, walk yards through the coconut grove and stand on the ocean shore, with the Pacific breakers beating up the beach of white sand on to the outcrops of coral rocks and creating a fine veil of spray under the overhanging palms. The nearest other island, even of the Gilberts, was far out of sight. At such times I would feel out of the world and out of time, as if my past and my future had no real connection with this space-besieged present. I was drifting free.

3

On a coral atoll it is difficult to think of land apart from water. The waves are rarely out of earshot, the water rarely out of sight, and in the subsistence economy to which most Gilbertese still owe their living the sea is as important as the land. Because there is little fresh water, and the ground is too porous to hold what there is, not many plants grow in the Gilberts, and few of those that do are of any use in sustaining human life. Even bananas and bread-fruit trees grow only in the southern islands. At times there are long droughts – one that lasted eighteen months had ended just before we arrived – when the fresh water gained by digging deep into the coral is replaced by water seeping from the sea, water with a taste of salt, water that hardly quenches human thirst. Then such exotic plants flag and die, and when we went to the island of Tabiteuea, celebrated for its bread-fruit, most of the trees had already dried into barkless skeletons like great stark candelabra. There were places on Tarawa where in that great drought even the hardy coconuts were reduced to bare frondless poles.

In most of the Gilberts, apart from the coconut, only two plants are at the best of times of much use to human beings. One is the tall, stilt-rooted pandanus tree, which here assumes an almost geometrical angularity of form; in most parts of the South Seas, the pandanus is despised, but in the Gilberts – in default of better food – its coarse orange-coloured fruit, like gigantic pine-cones the size of melons, are part of the diet. The other edible plant is babai. In every village, as well as the narrow wells, there are deep wide pits dug 10–12 feet into the coral to the water table. Here grows the babai, a coarse and giant relative of the taro and like it a distant congener of English lords-and-ladies. It is the only known root crop that thrives in brackish water. Looking down into the pit from above all one sees is a dense cluster of immense, dark green leaves, but on scrambling into the slimy depths, one finds that each of the plants with its great tuft of foliage is carefully nurtured, the root being surrounded by a circular dam of plaited pandanus leaves, like the basket around a flask of chianti, which is filled with laboriously gathered humus. The result is an enormous root, grey in colour and dense in texture which, however it is cooked, is among the world's most indigestible foods. Yet the leaves are beautifully veined, and once among them I found a yellow cylindrical flower in a pale green sheath, cool and lily-like.

When the narrow islets with their scanty vegetation are so ungiving, it is inevitable that the Gilbertese should continue to live largely by food-gathering, and that the lagoon, the reef and the ocean assume special importance, since there are no land birds or mammals to be hunted. Nothing that comes out of the water and is not poisonous is ever wasted. The boys jig for small fish and when they reach adolescence catch octopus from the reefs by enticing them out of clefts in the coral, using their own bodies as bait. The men often gather for the great fish drive, when they surround a large shallow area with nets, and advance shouting and splashing to the centre of the circle where the fish congregate in a threshing mass and are easily speared or – in the case of the smaller kinds – are killed by a sharp bite. At other times they sail their canoes beyond the reef and fish with lines, and sometimes dive into the water, armed only with knives, to play a kind of deadly *corrida* with the ferocious tiger-sharks; the great feat is to entice a shark to charge, and to swerve aside so that the fish is killed as his own momentum slits open his belly on the swimmer's outstretched knife. The men also catch marine eels in traps of basketwork and capture the rock lobsters that lurk among the brilliant growth of living coral. As the tide falls, the women and any child that can walk wade into the lagoon to gather sea-urchins and sea-slugs. They sift the damp sand for tiny shellfish. They go out with sharpened digging sticks to probe in the tidal beaches for the long white sand-worms that are island delicacies. There is nothing minute enough or strange enough to be despised as food, and as long as there are not too many mouths, as long as the waters remain unpolluted, the lagoon provides.

For the Gilbertese the lagoon is not merely a kind of great marine farm; it is also a highway, since in travelling between the various parts of the atoll one naturally avoids the dangerous ocean sides of the islands, and one can hardly have a real conception of life on Tarawa without sailing the lagoon.

On our second day Peter took us in his speed boat to the islet at the north-eastern corner of the lagoon which was originally the headquarters of the Catholic mission and, like the island where the Bishop now lives, is called Taborio. Now it is the site of one of the few Gilbertese secondary schools, the Immaculate Conception College for Girls. We managed the journey to and fro in the time between early lunch and sunset.

For unpigmented skins, the midday light of the lagoon is cruel in its intensity, and before setting out we tied sunhats on our heads, put on long-sleeved shirts, laid towels over our bare legs, and plastered other exposed surfaces thickly with Nivea cream. Even so, there were gaps in our protection, and in sundry unlikely parts of our body we suffered painful burns for a long time afterwards.

We sped across the lagoon, with the propeller at the rear cleaving a deep green trough behind us, parallel with the southern shore until we were north of Bonriki; then we turned to parallel the eastern islands. The sun was so bright, and the sea such a brilliant and opaque surface of turquoise, that it was hard to see much in its depths except when we slowed to cross the submerged reefs, whose approach we could always tell by the darkening green of the water; then we saw shoals of large fish, and turtles flopping up and down like brown sacks on the waves. The tern swept high above us, and occasionally would plummet sud-

denly into the sea; so intense was the reflection from the sea that over-
head they seemed a pale, ethereal green.

We passed sailing canoes, with their owners sitting cross-legged on
the platforms and fishing by handline. We overtook a mail launch,
lumbering awkwardly and slowly inshore over the submerged reefs.
Later we met a big, heavily loaded ketch making an almost equally
slow course, sails spread, between the islands. 'It's the *Nautasha*,' Peter
explained. 'A co-op boat. It belongs to the Island Council for the eastern
part of Tarawa.' Both the ketch and the dinghy it towed were piled
high above the gunwales with sacks of copra and bundles of dark babai
roots, and on top of them perched men and women in bright lavalavas
and frocks who seemed to accept with the greatest good humour their
slow progress over the dazzling waters. Like most people who live in
subsistence economies, the Gilbertese had little sense of diurnal time
and even less of time as a commodity; many of them, we found later,
had worked for wages in the phosphate mines of Nauru or Ocean
Island, which is about the only way in which most Gilbertese enter the
labour market, but such periods seemed detached interludes in their
lives which had no influence at all on their customary pattern of existence, governed by no temporal pattern more exacting than that of the
seasons, of plant growth and fish migrations.

There were small villages on the islets, in each of them the great
roof of the maneaba forming the landmark, with the houses scattered
along the edge of the shore on each side of it under the palm trees.
Some of them were raised on high stilts, so that there was room below
for storage and for sitting in the shade. There were other houses of a
more private kind than the open shacks, with closed walls which we
afterwards found were made of the midriffs of coconut fronds, which
can be joined together into an elastic and sturdy kind of flooring or
walling, known in the Gilberts as tareka.

Peter drew gently through the shielding growths of coral into one
of the passages between the islets. It was a place called Tabiteuea (not
to be confused with the large atoll of Tabiteuea to the south which we
later visited). The shallow water was clear and lucid; the flying fish
were leaping before our prow as we nosed in, their scales flashing like
blue steel; the dry sands above the tide-mark were pocked with land
crabs' burrows; on the shore a solitary brick chimney and the remnants
of a wharf marked the spot where a store had stood in the days of the
white traders. We saw the flash of orange lavalavas as men walked

among the ubiquitous palm-trees. Nothing of the modernization that was creeping over southern Tarawa had even begun to reach here. 'Idyllic, don't you agree?' Peter asked. One could do nothing but agree. 'We're thinking of buying the land. You see, Rose is Gilbertese, and she can do it. And if we can only solve the water problem, we'll start a little resort . . .' Inge and I stayed silent; much as we liked Peter and Rose, we hoped the water problems would remain insoluble.

The missionaries of the Sacred Heart of Jesus consisted originally of French fathers and sisters who reached the islands in 1888, more than thirty years after Hiram Bingham of the American Board of Missions began Protestant proselytization on Abaiang. There were decades and generations of bitter rivalry, and at one point, just before the British declared their protectorate, Christian sectarianism became an element in the internecine wars that were ravaging the islands and decimating the population. Now a rough balance has been reached; the northern islands are mainly Catholic, the southern mainly Protestant (with fanaticism strong enough for a notice to stand on the beach of one southern atoll forbidding the Catholic Bishop in the name of the Island Council to land), with Tarawa and the other central islands fairly evenly divided. Only a few very old men still claim to be pagan, and proselytization is left to the newer sects, like the Seventh-Day Adventists and the Church of God of South Carolina, skirmishing on the outskirts of the established churches, which now that the government has taken over the hospitals, concentrate on retaining their hold on the educational system. The sheer lack of money in the colonial treasury favours them; without the funds which the churches send in from outside, it would be impossible out of the revenue of so poor a territory to provide schools and teachers for all the Gilbertese children, whose parents are just as convinced as those of the Polynesian islands about the magic virtues of education.

The Immaculate Conception College is one of the two secondary schools run by the Catholic mission. Recently the personnel of the mission has changed in character, and while the priests are still French and mainly Breton, as are the older sisters, the younger sisters are almost entirely Australian, with a few Gilbertese among them.

We drew slowly into the beach at Taborio. The outboard motor could no longer be used because of the reefs, and had to be tilted up out of the water, and Peter leapt out and began to pull us in towards the shore. Before long we joined him, retaining our sandals because of the risk of poisoning by coral or stonefish. By the time this slow approach had been completed, the news of our arrival had spread. Two white-clad figures stood on the shore waiting to welcome us. Sisters Marian and Peter were delighted to see visitors – any visitors – and soon they were joined by Sister Esther, an attractive blue-eyed younger woman who was obviously a capable teacher, and whose presence I welcomed as a sign of the vitality of the church in an age that has declared the death of God. As an unbeliever, I have always wished vigour to my opponents, since it is the vitality of disagreement that keeps one spiritually searching. Yet at Taborio, and often elsewhere in the South Seas, I wondered how far I really was the opponent of the Catholic fathers and sisters, whose knowledge of the islanders was so great in comparison with that of most government officials, and who seemed to have shed the sectarian prides and prejudices that have lingered in almost all the Protestant missions. Certainly the three sisters, and the girls who had come from New Zealand to teach as lay volunteers, were not only hospitable, but frank in revealing the difficulties of trying to find a form of education that would not detach their 115 pupils from their traditions and from the economic realities of island life, yet would fit them to live in the modern world during the decades ahead when independence might make the position of the Gilbertese more precarious than it had ever been before. This affected even their patterns of instruction. There were girls from both the Gilberts and the Ellices, who spoke different languages; but the language of instruction had to be English, not only because of the division in native languages, but because so small a territory as the Gilberts would always have to rely on its foreign connections, and the ability of a good proportion of its young people to speak English was obviously one of the conditions of survival.

Because the Catholic fathers and sisters intended to stay on and work with their people whether independence came or not, they often seemed to understand the basic issues of survival in a more direct and down-to-earth way than the colonial officials. I had long conversations with both the Governor of the colony and the Catholic Bishop, and of the two I found the Bishop far more realistic and also far more closely informed about the actualities of Gilbertese life than the Governor showed evidence of being. But of the Bishop I shall have more to say later. It was the Governor I met first.

4

We encountered the late imperialists who ruled the Gilbert and Ellice Islands Colony when we set out with Gordon, who had now rejoined us, to find out how we could get to the outer islands and make arrangements for our filming there. It was hard enough to travel even on Tarawa, and on the first day when we attempted to get from Bikenibu to the government centre at Bairiki it took us from eight to eleven in the morning merely to cover the ten miles between the two places. The two taxis were at the airport, waiting for a delayed plane. The bus drivers seemed possessed of a xenophobia which we did not later find characteristic of the Gilbertese, since they persistently refused to stop when we tried to flag them down outside the hotel. But in fact we need not have been so anxious about our tardiness in arriving at the compound of prefabricated huts which formed the government head-quarters. For when we did arrive it was obvious that the higher administrators had little intention of co-operating with us and, indeed, appeared to regard our presence with the utmost suspicion.

We were received by the appropriate official, correct and starched from the collar of his white shirt down to the ankles of his white knee-socks, with a studied coldness. Our very apologies for lateness brought a frigid cut. 'If you will come to a place like the Gilberts, that is what you will have to expect.' And when we requested government transport, at our own expense, he replied flatly that this was impossible. 'Let me assure you from the start,' he continued, 'that you can expect no practical help whatever from the government of the colony. We can give you information that is generally available to the public. That is all.'

We left him with the feeling that, while the administration could not keep us out as Commonwealth subjects, they would have been very glad if we had never arrived. That impression was hardly changed when we met the Governor, Sir John Field, a stocky pipe-smoking man who looked as if he had a touch of the Navy in his background, and who spoke rapidly and non-committally about government policy. It was a time of uneasy policy-making at which we arrived, since the agitation in the Ellice Islands for separate treatment from the Gilbertese had reached its height, and quite evidently instead of facing many of the issues squarely, Sir John preferred to carry out a tactical evasion behind a smoke-screen of verbosity. After we had left him,

Gordon and I both felt so overwhelmed by the flood of words that only when we sat down to analyse what had actually been said in concrete terms, did we realize that we had, as the Governor evidently saw it, been put in the places proper for inquiring writers and television men. In other words, at great length and with the utmost cordiality, we had been told nothing of importance.

Nevertheless, certain facts did emerge with a kind of insistent vagueness. It was evident, to begin, that Whitehall was anxious to reduce its responsibilities in the Gilberts, as in its other remaining possessions, as quickly and as far as was consonant with British dignity and Britain's moral responsibilities to the islanders. The reason why the British found it hard to leave was also the reason why the Gilbertese were not at that time eager for independence. Independence might very easily be politically feasible, since from the beginning there had been local self-government through island councils and also local administration of justice through native magistrates; thus the Gilbertese are not unskilled in the kind of decentralized small-scale government that would be appropriate to their conditions. Economically, however, independence would be precarious. The Gilbertese love children as much as the Samoans, and so far have passively resisted all the family planning campaigns that have been attempted. This means that the traditional subsistence pattern of living by the produce of the land and the lagoons cannot long continue. At present a favourable trade balance, which allows a disproportionately high level of government expenditure, is maintained only because Ocean Island, which is not actually within the Gilberts group, happens by historical accident to be part of the colony. But the phosphate deposits of Ocean Island, which at present account for about five-sixths of the colony's income, will be exhausted within a decade. Then the only product which the Gilbertese can sell on the world markets will be copra, one of the most unstable of all crops in terms of price and demand.

Nevertheless, though they regard independence with a mixture of fear and guarded interest, it is evident that the Gilbertese are being hurried willy-nilly in the direction of complete internal self-government, and already a kind of shadow cabinet system, with Gilbertese members of the Executive Council acquiring considerable responsibility within government departments, has come into being.

The strange feature of the situation, to an outsider, is that the British efforts to bring an end to imperial rule have resulted in an extraordinary distension of the apparatus of administration. In the classic days of Sir Arthur Grimble, a mere handful of English officers maintained a very simple apparatus of government. Today the colonial government in the Gilbert and Ellice Islands Colony has an establishment that runs into the hundreds and is actually larger than that with which Lugard ruled Nigeria so splendidly in the classic days of the Empire. Government expenditure has increased more than forty times since the 1930s; in 1936 it was about £60,000 and by 1970 it had reached more than £2,500,000 and was rising steadily. This is largely due to the fact that since World War II the Gilberts have been turned into a semi-socialist society with co-operative overtones. The white traders with their island stores and their schooners, once such an important part of Gilbertese life, have departed; even the great companies like Burns Philp and Morris Hedstrom which operate in other parts of the South Seas have given up the struggle here. The sale of copra and most of the retail trading is in the hands of island co-operatives run by the Gilbertese themselves. Commerce on a larger scale, and the whole inter-island trade and transport, is in the hands of the Development Authority, staffed mainly by Britons and Australians. The only non-governmental enterprises of any importance left in the Gilberts are the missions.

All this has meant that the traditional colonial servants, drawn in from all the corners of the shrinking Empire, must now work alongside a great variety of people – educationalists, technicians, commercial experts, agronomists, doctors and sea-captains – who were usually engaged on two-year contracts and who often had little sympathy with the traditions of the service of the Empire.

The higher officials – often inflexible personalities, unable to adapt to a new career when the Empire crumbled and unwilling to work for the new ex-colonial countries even on a temporary basis – seemed to believe that they had to maintain imperial pomp to the end. The Governor on Tarawa still on occasion appeared before a crowd of giggling Gilbertese in his full-plumed regalia, announced with the call of trumpets and accompanied by wigged and red-robed judges; outside Government House, though the colony has no military force, an armed policeman tramped up and down outside his sentry box; garden parties still took place on the expanse of coral sand which serves as the Government House lawn.

Probably nine-tenths of the Europeans now employed by the government in the Gilberts regard such anachronistic behaviour as totally unrelated to the realities of contemporary South Sea life. Many of the temporary officials are experts of some kind or another with little interest in anything outside their special field. They include a fair proportion of amiable incompetents. But we also met men and women who were really anxious to serve the Gilbertese, and who felt that the present inflated and expert-ridden administration, with its parade of constantly changing 'solutions' to the stark economic problems of the Gilberts, merely had the effect of preventing the Gilbertese from looking realistically at their own future.

With those who were more closely linked to daily Gilbertese life our encounters were more congenial than with the headquarters staff. We had been given an introduction by a New Zealand anthropologist to R. E. N. Smith, the District Commissioner who does the actual field-work in the Gilberts. To visit him we had to cross the channel from Bairiki on the Betio ferry, a primitive and rather uncomfortable vessel which I suspect was actually a converted landing-barge. The cabin at one end was raised a couple of feet above the deck, and the Gilbertese raced for it as soon as we were allowed on board, so that no room was left for us. We soon realized why; the ferry was so low in the water that as it progressed the spray spurted through the gap between the raised landing-ramp and the deck, and we stood in a stream of water at least an inch deep that flowed constantly from the bows to run away in the scuppers amidships, soaking any piece of deck cargo that had thoughtlessly been placed within its range. The knowledgeable people piled their belongings in such a way that non-perishable items were at the bottom, and perched on one such pile sat two old Gilbertese ladies with elegant chaplets of flowers and silver tinsel around their brows. One of them pulled from her bosom a little box, which contained a piece of stick tobacco (the kind of black stuff looking like liquorice which we used to call twist in my English childhood), a little roll of dried pandanus leaf and a penknife; she cut off a bit of tobacco, crumbled it and rubbed it down between her palms, cut a length of pandanus leaf as big as a cigarette paper and rolled herself a very serviceable whiff that looked like an Indian bidi.

After forty minutes of stiff sea-breeze and wet feet, we pulled into Betio harbour, bucketing past a trio of white ships that lay at anchor – the *Ninikoria*, a large passenger-cum-cargo boat that plies between the islands and sometimes down to Suva, the *Teraka*, used for training Gilbertese boys to be sailors on German merchant ships, and a smaller inter-island boat, the *Nivanga*; all belonged to the Development Authority's Marine Department. Our ferry dropped its ramp at some rough steps made of broken concrete bags; as we scrambled up to the wharf, a driver appeared who took us to the District Commissioner's car. It was immediately evident that our treatment on Betio was going to be better than at Bairiki, and so indeed, it turned out to be. Smith, who was a small dark man with the dense tan of life in the tropics, welcomed us with gin, and his wife with succulent ham sandwiches and both of them with tales of a progression that charted the narrowing of Empire, for it had begun in India, continued in Tanganyika and Nyasaland, proceeded to the New Hebrides and now mingled with many other imperial odysseys in one of the final eddies of colonialism.

It was Smith who helped us to chart out clearly where we should and could go. Tabiteuea, he declared without hesitation, was the island where life was nearest to the past, the island where we had the best chance of seeing the classic Gilbertese dance, the bino, still being most faithfully performed. But if we could, we must also go on one of the copra boats that sailed through the group, so that we could get some sense of the way the islands were related within their ocean vastnesses, and some feeling of what it was to voyage among them.

After lunch Smith took us to Captain Andy Taylor, a blue-eyed, hatchet-nosed seaman who was head of the Marine Department. Again there was the same instant co-operation, the same unspoken recognition that anyone who had come so far to see for himself deserved a receptive ear and a helping hand. Andy Taylor explained the abilities and limitations of his services. We must not expect to travel on the old inter-island schooners of romantic South Sea legend; the last survivors of that great past were down in Fiji, being used for the entertainment of rich American tourists. Even the sooty old coal-burning tramp steamers were a matter of memory. Now there were just motor vessels, of various sizes. The smallest of them, round-bottomed little vessels of 30 tons, he did not recommend. The largest, the *Ninikoria*, was about to start its big trip down through Funafuti to Suva; a pity, because its master, Captain Ward, who had been in the Gilberts for thirty years, was the greatest island mariner of them all. That left the *Nivanga*, a trim little ship with a fine master, but headed according to schedule for the Ellices. Still, if there happened to be enough copra down in the southern Gilberts, perhaps the *Nivanga* could be diverted. That was precisely what Captain Andy Taylor did. Within a day we had worked out our plans

with him. The *Nivanga*, delivering cargo and gathering copra, would
be proceeding around the southern islands and would eventually land
us at Tabiteuea, where Gordon would have gone already by air. From
Tabiteuea we would then fly to Abemama, Stevenson's island, and
then return to Tarawa.

5

The Journal of the Nivanga

Day 1. We are up before dawn. It is soft and dove-grey, with a pale
pink flush on the eastern horizon that never deepens into flamingo. The
lagoon gleams a dull silver. A tern cries and a cock crows in answer.
The taxi arrives at 7.15; Cinemascope is driving. (He is tall and lanky,
and the Gilbertese have conferred the nickname because he resembles
a man in the elongated distortion that takes place when a Cinemascope
film is shown on the narrow screens of the palm-grove cinemas.)

We drive over the islands and causeways to the ferry for Betio,
climb on board, stow our cases dryly, and while Inge finds a seat on the
upper deck, I remain below, perched on a hatch-cover that saves my
feet from the water. Just before the ferry casts off, four men come
hurrying on board, carrying a stretcher; under a clean white sheet one
can make out the shape of a corpse, and then, as the wind flips up a
corner of the sheet, his feet are visible, the grey, stiff coral-calloused
feet of an old man. The stretcher is laid on two boxes, and a woman
in a bright skirt sits impassively on her suitcase at the head, while the
two younger men stand silently beside those protruding feet. There is no
demonstration of grief, as there would be among Polynesians; the
Micronesians are a stoical race, and everyone is dry eyed; one of the
older men I see telling an obscene tale to some friends he has met on
the ferry, and vividly miming the act of masturbation.

If we were superstitious, we would turn away from this voyage,
for the appearance of the corpse is followed by another ominous
incident. Down on the sandbag steps at Betio we wait for the *Nivanga's*
orange cockleshell of a dinghy to move into position, and as we do so a
launch draws up from the sailors' training ship, and a youth in his
sailor's uniform slips as he attempts to get ashore, and falls into the
water.

This is so unexpected a mishap for a Gilbertese, bred from infancy
to the water, that we are tempted to see it as an omen, particularly

when the *Nivanga*'s dinghy runs us out over the choppy water and
draws in at the high steel side of the unloaded ship. There is no gangway
– not even a rope ladder – and the waves are so high that at one moment
we are three feet and the next ten feet below the deck. The thin
half-Chinese mate and the fat Ellice supercargo stand on the deck
gesticulating, and finally, when the boat is lifted to its highest point,
I stretch out my arms, which they catch by the wrists, and leap. Inge
follows; we both graze our bare knees on the iron deck.

The *Nivanga* is a trim little white cargo steamer, built for the island
trade, low-waisted and high in stem and stern, 125 feet long and 353
tons displacement. The cabins – there are only two – are spartan but
adequate; each has two bunks and a bench with a thin leather-covered
pallet; I soon discover that in such a small ship the upper bunk is far
too precarious for peaceful sleeping, and resign myself to the bench
and its hardness. The other cabin is occupied by Father Kerouantan;
he is a fellow Celt, from near Dinard, but I have never felt much common ground between the Breton character and my own Welshness,
and I find it hard to think of him as other than a rather rustic provincial
Frenchman. He has been here in the Gilberts for twenty-two years.
He made his most recent trip back to Europe four years ago, and the
experience only confirmed his preference for life in the Gilberts,
though he grants that without the challenge he faces, of defending the
Catholic faith on the two predominantly Protestant islands of Beru
and Nikunau, he might find too demoralizing the easy life that so many
Europeans live in the South Seas.

About ten in the morning the *Nivanga* finally sails from Betio, west
out of the lagoon to the north of that island, and then southward, so
that we see the ocean side of Betio, the ruins of the Japanese fortifications still scarring the beaches thirty years after the great battle of
Tarawa, and the shape of the great gun dominating from its artificial
eminence the whole flat prospect, a monstrous irrelevant memento of
human vanity. Now, at last, as we swing south from Tarawa towards
Maiana, we are seeing the islands more or less as mariners did when
they first approached them, for all the buildings in fact appear as minor
excrescences under those long, swaying walls of palms, 60–70 feet high,
which *are* the islands from the off-shore view.

Out at sea the breeze sharpens; for the first time in many voyages,
I feel the edge of sickness, from which I had previously thought myself
immune. Perhaps it is the peculiar roll of a small ship in the great

Pacific swell: perhaps it is the advance of age, as Father Kerouantan suggests, remarking that in his first years in the islands he was untroubled by the worst of seas, but now no longer feels comfortable at any time on board ship. Inge feels as I do, and is suffering as well from some intestinal trouble for which the doctor at Bikenibu had provided merely painkillers and pious wishes. But, since this means meeting the ships' officers for the first time, we resolutely sit down to lunch. Captain Redfern, who is part Gilbertese, has navigated the islands all his sailing life; he is reputed to be a martinet about leaving on time, so that we have been warned never to risk being left on shore by staying too late for the last launch. The engineer ,who adds a touch of Japanese to his racial mixture, has sailed for a long time out of Fiji, as well as serving on the run between New Zealand and New Caledonia. We eat our rissoles served with instant potatoes and tinned peas, toy with the tinned pears, and then retreat to the cabin to sleep our nausea off.

When I awaken, the *Nivanga* has anchored off Maiana, the nearest island south of Tarawa. We lie outside the reef, along which the sea is breaking in a line of high spray, with the palm-trees, which form the island's silhouette, swaying beyond it and a few native huts huddling in their shadow above the broad yellow beach. So the first voyagers must have seen it, for the government station, which alone might represent the changes that have taken place in the generations of European contact, is far over the lagoon and barely visible. The *Nivanga's* boats have gone out into the lagoon, loaded with cargo, and as we wait for them to return the crew is fishing amidships with handlines, using chunks of fish as bait. They have been hauling in reef fish, all of them rather deep-bodied and oval in shape. Some are ugly creatures, a foot or so long, with large greenish scales, orange dorsal fins and pink muzzles with pursed toothy mouths. Others have a bizarre beauty; they are pale blue, speckled with deeper blue spots, have deep blue tails, yellow front and dorsal fins, a yellow streak across the face. The fish are killed with short wooden clubs as they are hauled on deck. The ships' boats are mere dots as they begin their return journey over the turquoise lagoon and through the narrow entrance into the indigo waters where the ship lies at anchor. The two dinghies are towing the larger boats – a traditional wooden whaleboat, well crafted by some good old-style boatbuilder, and a clumsy square-ended lighter which looks as though it has been fabricated from plywood. The boats are lifted on board by crane, and stowed away.

As I write it is moonlight, catching the ocean waves in its glitter, faint veils of cloud moving over the stars, a satellite hurrying eastward down to the horizon. The outline of the atoll's islands is low and black, and the line of the reef is picked out by the lights of the night fishers. It is a still, peaceful, lucid night, on which one knows why this ocean, so inclined to turbulence in my own northern region, came by its name. At ten, after dinner, the tide is ready for sailing, and we leave in the direction of Abemama. Before I turn in, the engineer has come up on to the afterdeck and let out the long lines with great hooks and gaudy plastic lures which he hopes will catch us tuna.

Day 2. Just before breakfast we sail into the lagoon at Abemama, where the passage is safe and wide. A dinghy goes out with the scow to collect a generator for the Seventh-Day Adventist Mission that is going to Betio for repair. As we shall be flying back to Abemama after the *Nivanga* has landed us at Tabiteuea, we do not go ashore. From the ship, which even in the lagoon lies miles offshore, there is not much to distinguish Abemama from the other atolls: the same solid line of palm-trees giving height to the low coastline and over to the left a large village of traditional houses lining the shore. The fishermen seem to have gone outside the reef, for the only sign of activity in the lagoon is a single sailing canoe, and the only European building in sight is the store. Strangely, the lack of evident variety among these atolls does not lessen their appeal, which is partly the physical one of elemental sea and shore, but partly the ever recurrent sense of remoteness which, despite all the atrocities of two centuries of European contact since Cook and Bougainville opened the Pacific, still seems to defend these islands. The engineer shows us two 40-pound tuna which the lines caught during the night – solid, steel-blue fish as streamlined as torpedoes.

Once we leave Abemama in the middle of the morning and begin our bucking course over the open Pacific, towards the southerly island of Beru, with no land sighted before nightfall or likely to be sighted before noon tomorrow, the real vastness of the region, the true remoteness of the Gilberts not only from the rest of the world but also from each other, begins finally to assume reality in our minds, as we sit on the little afterdeck behind the cabins, and watch the parallels of the trolling lines stretching behind the ship and seeming to emphasize the infinity to which parallels point. Towards noon a barracuda is brought in on one of the lines – a small one, 3 feet long, but still impressive, silvery and lean, with a great fierce eye and an underhung jaw like a giant pike with lines of big vicious teeth.

After the barracuda has been hauled on board and clubbed with a long pole, since nobody wants to get near that ferocious mouth, the engineer sits with us talking about other ways of catching the denizens of the sea. Everywhere in the South Seas one hears of the callings. Up on Makin in the northern Gilberts there are – we have heard from Rose Barker – families that can call the dolphins; she even claims to have seen killer whales that had been called ashore and beached themselves. We have heard of dolphin-calling in the Solomons as well. The engineer talks of the callings in Fiji. On one island, at a certain season, a chief calls in the turtles; there is a famous cavern inhabited by red prawn which respond to certain calls. The engineer claims to have seen the turtle-calling, and twice to have seen the calling of mullet up a river by one of the chiefs of Viti Levu. Is there actually a rapport between these people and the creatures of the sea, as most people in the South Pacific appear to believe? Or is it merely a sensitivity to the signs of oncoming migrations?

At dinner Father Kerouantan talks of the difficulties of life on the smaller islands, like Beru. At Beru the only anchorage is far from the settlements; he himself will be eight miles away when he lands from the village that is the centre of his parish, and there is no public transport; in fact, since there are no cars at all among the island's 2,500 people, the only means of transport is a tractor belonging to the island co-operative, which drags a trailer over a rough road. Sometimes it drags the island's only truck, which broke down a year ago and has not been repaired. Those who can afford it on Beru travel by motor bike, but since there are few ways of earning the cash to buy one, most people still travel by canoe or on foot.

Third Day. Last night the ship drove through the bounding waves of a heavy sea, bucking the wind. At about ten this morning I see an atoll coming into view, a rather grey and furry outline on the horizon; shortly after eleven the *Nivanga* lies at anchor off the reef. It is low tide, great rusty expanses of dead coral heaving above the water, imprisoning the blue lake of the lagoon. Beru is a U-shaped atoll, reputed to have fine beaches on the ocean side; on this side they are coarse and broken by coral outcrops. There is a kind of wharf, a corrugated iron shed that serves as a copra store, three or four huts; the nearest village is three miles away.

Father Kerouantan is anxious to land, but a mere trickle of water lies in the passage through the reef, and Captain Redfern decrees that the boats will not attempt it until the tide begins to rise, after lunch. In consolation we are given a special meal of excellent kingfish caught early this morning, with fried potatoes, green beans, oranges and Australian Roquefort, all of which the captain had managed to get from an English ship lying off Betio. Father Kerouantan, who at breakfast was lamenting how far the quality of life and food has declined in France, now points out that the Roquefort is merely an imitation, and that even if it were real one would need a little wine to appreciate it. But then he adds sadly that in this climate there is no pleasure in drinking wine, except perhaps a little at the end of the day. He is fated to live on Protestant islands where the Councils have declared prohibition, and while the Bishop sees that he is supplied with wine, there is nobody who will dare to share it with him.

Waiting for the tide to change, we watch the canoes of Beru, sailing in flotilla, their white lateen sails making them resemble gigantic butterflies, as they seem to skim on rather than over the water, one or two men to a boat, their heads protected by conical sunhats of palm-leaves; the man in the stern operates the steering paddle with one hand and the halyards of the sail with the other. They evidently spend much of their time coursing over the water from sheer pleasure, and to see six or eight of these insubstantial little craft following each other over the bay is extraordinarily exciting and beautiful. I am reminded of the lateen-sailed craft we used to see in the channel at Penang, and the resemblance may indeed come from some distant link between Malaya and Micronesia, though the sailing platforms seem to be peculiar to the islands.

By one the tide has changed sufficiently. Where there was ugly brown reef the surf is now breaking in a lacy line of spray. The dinghy is lowered into the water on its rope slings, the lighter afterwards. Father Kerouantan says good-bye, steps gingerly into the dinghy with the look of a man who in all these years in the islands has never got quite accustomed to the maritime discomforts his vocation has thrust upon him, and as the outboard motor of the dinghy sputters into action gives a last wave and disappears across the water to his lonely parsonage. A man of great modesty, shy from isolation, and, one senses, of great goodness. He will have to wait to visit his other parish on Nikunau until another boat puts in to Beru, perhaps in two weeks, and then will have to remain, yet another two weeks, for a boat touching at Nikunau; the inter-island air services only link the four largest islands, Tabiteuea, Abemama, Tarawa, Butaritari. What one would give for a Gilbertese *Diary of a Country Priest* to make a modern complement to Grimble's great narratives! But so far none of these good fathers has written one.

The fat supercargo goes with Father Kerouantan and the freight for Beru. The captain discourages us from going ashore, since there is no village and we can see what is going on best from the ship; he advises us to wait for Nikunau, where we shall anchor opposite the village of Nukumanu. The freight for Beru suggests how modest is the dependence of these islands on the outside world: three drums of petrol, four tins of Mobiloil, a bag of mail and a couple of boxes of stores for Father Kerouantan! The only export is copra. As we waited the village tractor arrived dragging a trailer full of islanders, and now, when the lighter and the whaleboat have reached the wharf, they attack the wall of the sacks beside the copra shed, and carry them on their heads to throw them into the boats, where they are piled within rope slings for the crane to lift them when they reach the ship and lower them into the hold.

The later afternoon, as the sun is falling low, is the best time of all in the islands, especially when, as now, the tide is high, the lagoon full, the colours of the sea intense, and the level light not only illuminates the walls of palms in burning green (and, alas, in sere yellow as well on drought-devastated Beru) but also reveals, far over the lagoon, the shoreline village whose brown buildings had hitherto concealed themselves in the shadow of the palms from whose detritus they are made.

After two days on the *Nivanga*, I am impressed not only by the excellent trim in which it is kept by an entirely Gilbertese crew, but also by the vigour with which the Gilbertese will toil, *when there is work that needs to be done*. Today, after working hard for four hours to bring in copra, they have continued for another three hours without interruption stowing it in a shipshape manner to be ready for the next load at Nikunau, and everybody has pitched in, the captain, the mate, the supercargo, the wireless operator, so that I, watching from above, felt the lazy man. Yet the same men, when there is nothing necessary to do on the boat, will spend hours watching a fishing line cast over the side. The Gilbertese, of all South Sea peoples, can never have been lazy in any real sense, for the mere task of wringing a living from atoll and lagoon, and of making the tools to do so must always have required application and time as well as ingenuity.

At dinner the captain and the engineer talk of the perils of navigation in the Ellices. It is four days' sailing from Tarawa to Funafuti, which has the only good lagoon in the Ellices. Some of the other islands have no shelter at all, and their anchorages can be used only in reasonably good weather; even then it can be perilous for passengers to go ashore through the surf; boats are often overturned, and on their last trip a senior magistrate was tipped into the water, though he survived.

We go on to talk of kava. The captain shudders at the thought, but he is a Gilbertese, and there is no kava in these islands. The engineer, who has lived long in Fiji, gives us a different version from those who claim it is merely a pleasant, harmless drink. That may be so, he admits, in Samoa, where it is weak, or in Tonga where its use is ringed round with ancient protocol, but in Fiji it is made indiscriminately and of a far stronger brew than in Polynesia, while the green kava, which is more potent than the dry, is often used. He insists that it is addictive and cites his own experience, for he himself was an addict until he came to the Gilberts and found kava unobtainable. 'In the mornings I would wake up, and I would make up my mind never to touch it again. By four o'clock the craving would be back, and I would join in a kava circle, telling myself I would just take a cup or two, but always stayed to the end, which might be eight hours away. A session would begin like whisky drinking. Everybody talked and nobody listened. In the end everybody was silent.' He confirms that kava affects the motor centres to the extent of temporarily depriving a man of the use of his legs. He says that some people suffer a lasting failure of balance and in extreme cases there is permanent paralysis. He adds – and claims to know of this from personal experience – that prolonged use of kava has characteristic physical consequences; crowsfeet and lines around the mouth become more pronounced, the skin on the arms is dry and itches almost unbearably, and the skin on the legs is wrinkled in a crisscross manner so that it looks as if they are covered with scales.[1]

[1] Later, in Fiji, I met an Indian who had married a Fijian woman and largely adopted the native way of life. He too claimed to be a former kava addict, and the effects he described to me from personal experience coincided with those listed by the engineer, though he had never heard of permanent paralysis, and I suspect that this at least may have been a tall tale, since the engineer did not relate it to his personal experience.

We sail after dark, intending to make Nikunau before dawn, and to start loading in the darkness to take advantage of the tide. We sail east beside the long southern shore of Beru, shore fires flickering at intervals within the lagoon. The moon is full, scattering its path of reflections across the black ocean, and turning into silver knives the flying fish that leap out from the sideswell of the boat.

Fourth Day. During the night the *Nivanga* anchored off the village of Rungata on Nikunau, and by the time I get up at 6.30 they are bringing in the last of the small harvest of copra. The hold has been filled and closed and now the breastworks of sacks are rising on the deck. Rungata is an attractive village, with a pleasant rococo Catholic church, white and red-roofed, topped by a silvery cross that shines over the palm-trees. There are no European-style houses; everything is of palm and pandanus, and among the houses rise green mopheads of papaw and an occasional modest bread-fruit. The one ugly feature is the great concrete barn of a Protestant church which the local men are said to have built with money they earned working away from home in the phosphate mines. The blue smoke of morning fires, fed by coconut husks, begins to rise among the houses as I watch, but apart from a few men who have been helping to load copra, there is nobody about until a man in long trousers who looks like a European begins to stride along the beach with his two dogs.

At breakfast, when there is fresh papaw from Rungata and more kingfish, the engineer dilates with admiration on the intelligence of dolphins, which he says are common around Tabiteuea and love to play in the bow-waves of the ship. He asserts that though they chase flying fish and follow them with apparent impetuosity, they have never been known to take a flying fish trolled as live bait; in some mysterious way they know there is something wrong with it.

After breakfast we sail along the coast a few miles to Nukumanu. Nikunau is a raised atoll, a solid island which in places is a mile and a half across, and it has no real lagoon, but merely the reef project- ing outward from the coast, and a steep beach that at low tide gives the island an appearance of height and solidity unusual in the Gilberts.

At Nukumanu, which from the shore looks much like Rungata, the supercargo goes ashore in the whaleboat rowed with an oar over the stern; the dinghies with their outboard motors cannot go in at low tide because of the coral. For loading we have to wait for higher water in the afternoon, and now there is a feeling of almost completely suspended animation on the ship. Most of the men, who worked the night through, are sleeping. The engineer is jigging a handline over the side. The wireless operator is cutting the captain's hair on the afterdeck. The mate is fabricating fish lures with a pair of scissors and bits of coloured plastic. The steward is polishing brass and a boy is irritatingly chipping paint on the bridge just above our cabin. The boats drift out on lines behind the ship, and small boys who have swum out from the island lie sunning upon them.

We have been looking over the odd little library, accumulation of remnants from seamen's libraries all over the world, that fills a couple of shelves in the cabin, musty battered volumes dating back to the nineties, mostly forgotten books by forgotten people, but among them *The Possessed*, *Crome Yellow*, *The Flame Trees of Thika*, a volume of Sherlock Holmes. There is – perhaps one should not wonder at it – nothing on the South Seas. I am reading, of all remote things, W. H. Hudson's *A Shepherd's Life*, yet perhaps not so remote after all, for Hudson too, talking about the stark life of the Wiltshire Downs, is describing something as elemental and marginal and difficult as life in these atolls once was and may be again.

The fishermen sit in their canoes in the bay, their sails folded and masts unshipped; there are eight in sight on our side of the ship. Doubtless they have lines out, but mainly they are waiting for the tide to be high enough for them to go through the passage to the beach without smashing their flimsy boats, whose planking is a mere quarter of an inch thick, on the coral. Once a man has gone out, especially at neap tide, he often has to stay at sea for twelve hours before he can return. In one canoe there are two fine turtles wedged in on their sides.

At 2.30 the mate comes to tell me that a dinghy is going out, and as Inge is feeling sick I go ashore on my own. It is an open beach with the ocean breakers pounding in at high tide and a heavy surf and backtow on the beach. The village youths are riding the surf on pieces of coconut trunks. The dinghy goes up the beach as far as it can, but I still have to leap into the water as the wave runs before it. The sand is soft and my feet sink deeply in as I walk up the beach.

Walls of copra sacks have been built on top of the beach, and others are being brought from the shed. The supercargo is there with his list and the walkie-talkie by which he communicates with the ship. But such sophistications make little difference to the actual labour of loading copra on an exposed beach. The lighter bucks violently in the surf, held with difficulty by men up to their waists and sometimes their necks in water. On the shore two men lift a sack on to the head of another man, and he runs down over the soft beach and up to his waist in the surf to pitch it to the men on the lighter.

I wander into the village, followed by the children, excitedly chattering and shouting 'Imatang! Imatang!'[1] Apart from one board house at the far end, Nukumanu consists entirely of palm-leaf dwellings, most of them raised 4–5 feet above the ground on stilts to allow room for storing a canoe. Girls are swinging from one of the leaning palm-trees as I pass; swinging is a favourite pastime among young Gilbertese, and Rose tells me that it plays a part in courtship, for when a girl is swinging a boy will jump up to try and share the swing with her, and if she allows him to stay it means his attentions will be welcome. (I am reminded of the importance of the swing as a religio-erotic symbol in the Hindu cult of Krishna, and wonder whether this may not be another among the many suggestions of Asian origins one encounters among the Micronesians.) The women are filling with coconut husks a smouldering pit the length and shape of a grave.

I walk on to photograph some splendid pandanus trees by the beach with tall stilted roots and fine large fruit as knobbly as maces, but before I can get to them a youth is running by my side, and saying: 'Some people would like to speak to you.' He leads me to the maneaba, and I stoop beside him to enter under the deeply hanging eaves. It takes me a few seconds to get used to the shade after the bright sunlight outside, but then I realize that the place is full. It is the first time I have been inside a maneaba, for no one can go uninvited, and I am impressed by the sheer volume of space under that great vault of a roof, 40 feet high at least to the peak, and complicatedly constructed of coconut trunks lashed together with coconut fibre rope and thickly pelted with its palm-leaf thatch.

Before the posts of coral rock the old men sit, the elders of the community in the positions to which their genealogies entitle them. They

---

[1] Imatang is the Gilbertese word for white man, and it has no connotations of disrespect or hostility, for the Gilbertese believe that we are the pure race from their own mythical ancestral land of Matang (Imatang meaning 'man of Matang'), and therefore we are the only race who in their great pride they do not regard as inferior.

are all dressed in lavalavas with thick leather belts that have old-fashioned snake clasps, and their torsos are bare. The fat old man who has invited me – he is dressed no differently from the rest – is the pastor, though he is imposing enough in his presence to be at least a high chief and so bulky that he cannot sit cross-legged but stretches out one of his great legs and supports it under the knee with a round wooden pillow, a practice I observe several others of the old men doing.

I sit cross-legged on the mat before the pastor, but almost immediately a girl appears with a chair, and though I would prefer to be on a level with the rest, I cannot reject the courtesy. I make slow conversation with the old man. His English is scanty, my Gilbertese non-existent, but he grasps that I am a Canadian and a writer, and this he announces to the elders and the other occupants of the maneaba, whom meantime I have the leisure to observe. They are a mixed collection of people. At the short ends of the maneaba are groups of women and girls, among whom the younger children are playing. The posts where the old men sit are left unencumbered with ordinary people, but in the middle of the floor sits a circle of eight men playing cards. They play quietly – for the Gilbertese are rarely a noisy people – and I notice that their garb makes no provision either for pockets or for those capacious folds in which Central Asians stuff their portable possessions. Consequently each man has beside him some kind of money container; one has a lockable cash box, another a woman's handbag, and others have cylindrical lidded boxes which are carved locally from coconut wood and are also used as tobacco boxes.

After a while a coconut is brought me – the green nut of traditional welcome, and as I sip it a tall young man who speaks English appears and asks what message I have for the people of the village. I make a little speech like that of Apolima, and it is received by the elders with approving murmurs. Knowing the requirements of local behaviour, I ask permission to photograph and also to walk around the village. It is granted. I am fortunate, the young man tells me, since this is not a formal gathering of the maneaba to which I am invited as a guest; then it would be impossible to leave so quickly. I am merely the fortuitous stranger who has stumbled on the beginnings of a wedding feast and must be shown courtesy.

Marea, my guide, is a minority man on Nikunau, a Catholic in a Protestant stronghold. He is a radio operator on leave, educated in the Catholic boys' school at Abaiang. He is patient, courteous and resourceful in pointing out the things that may interest me, though I suspect he finds my mission a little absurd – for why should an outsider be interested in islands from which such educated men as he are only anxious to escape? At Nukumanu, he tells me, white men are rarely seen, which was why I was fetched into the maneaba; Father Kerouan-tan may appear three or four times and the District Commissioner once or twice a year. Otherwise the place is left to the Island Council and the native magistrates.

Here again there is an immense, ugly, half-completed concrete church built by the Protestants to celebrate the centenary of the arrival of the first missionaries. The Gilbertese resemble the Samoans in their competitive mania for large churches, but they do not have the same taste for the decorative and the baroque, so that their new buildings look shoddy and vulgar in comparison with the natural beauty of the maneabas, which fit so well into this setting of palm-tree and sand.

There are a few bread-fruits in the village, and some papaws, but only the coconuts and pandanus seem to be fruiting abundantly, and I gather that babai is hard to grow here because of the extreme saltiness of the surface water. Thus fish, coconuts and pandanus form the basic diet, supplemented, when they can be afforded, by a little rice and wheat bread. And indeed, we come upon a group of merry wives making bread for the wedding in an oildrum converted into an oven; one of them wears, over the red cloth skirt which is fashionable in Nukamanu, a native skirt or ridi, made from treated palm-leaf – the so-called 'grass skirt' of the South Sea island legend. We pass curious square structures of palm-logs that look like toy forts; they are inhabited by pigs, which are a much fatter breed than the runts that run in the palm-groves of Tarawa. We pass small pits half filled with refuse; these, Marea tells me, are the former wells, which are no longer used, since the water was always brackish and now there is an artesian well. We have worked round to the beach, and I see that in the grave-like pit lumps of coral have been placed to get red-hot on top of the glowing bed of coconut husks. 'Here they will cook the pig for the wedding,' Marea explains.

I return, wading into the surf to board the dinghy, and my legs get such a battering from the debris the sea dashes to and fro that when I get back on board the ship I am bleeding from one ankle and one big toe.

Inge and I now stand watching from the deck. On shore a great cloud of smoke suddenly puffs up near the maneaba, and we know the pig has been put on his bed of glowing stones. At the same time a crowd gathers on the beach, with much red of women's skirts and blouses. It is a farewell party, for as the whaleboat prepares to leave for the last time, they all surge down to the water's edge, and when it reaches the ship it carries, perched on the final load of copra, the first deck passengers of the voyage. They are a family of six, evidently migrating to some other island, for they carry what would certainly be the worldly goods of an average Gilbertese family: a tin suitcase, two wooden chests, a sewing machine, a kettle, some mats tied in a bundle, a basket evidently filled with fruit and two ripe, orange pandanus fruit. The father is a little stocky man in blue shorts, his arms covered with the sailors' tattoos which the Gilbertese favour now they have lost their traditional designs. The mother wears a flowered print dress, and a wreath of flowers around her brow; she has gold ear-rings and her hair hangs in a thick black braid down her back; there are two little girls, and two even smaller boys, who wear the necklaces of bright plastic beads which I had noticed were popular among boys on Nikunau. They retreat to the high foredeck to spread out their mats and settle down to sleep under the canvas awning in the open air. Meanwhile the deck amidships is piled high with copra; we have a full load for the *Nivanga* – 120 tons.

Fifth Day. When we wake this morning the *Nivanga* is already cruising off Tabiteuea, and at 8 a.m. it stops opposite the government station at Utiroa, though the land is still little more than a thick fuzzy line on the southern horizon. We are four miles out, for these are shoaly and dangerous waters where even small ships cannot find anchorage close in shore. As it is only half-tide, the lighter will not be going ashore for another two or three hours, but the captain is willing to send us in on one of the dinghies, if we are willing to wade the last half mile through the shallows. We agree, and after breakfast the captain comes to hand us down to the boat; he gives us four oranges, a present of no mean value in the Gilberts, where such fruit do not grow and are rarely seen. It seems a long ride in, choppy until we get some shelter from the coral. Half a mile from the beach, as Captain Redfern had told us, it becomes too shallow for the dinghy to proceed safely, and we get out into the warm knee-high water with a ship's boy who carries our suitcase on his head as we trail laboriously ashore. It is not an easy walk for the sand is pitted with crabs' burrows, and as we get close to the land we realize that we have to watch out not merely for coral that might graze and poison our feet, but also for the jagged edges of tin cans. On shore there is a large native-style house with solid walls of tarake, and a boathouse with several canoes, but there is no one in sight, though Gordon is supposed to meet us. At last, as we step on to the dry sand, a white man comes out of the house and stands waiting for us.

6

The white man was not Gordon, but he knew who we were. His name was Davies, and he was in charge of a project for reviving local hand-crafts and organizing them as a commercially viable undertaking. Gordon, he told us, had been misinformed about the place of our landing and had gone to a wharf three miles away. We accompanied Davies into the house. He lived there and used it as his office; it had been made by native carpenters of local materials – coconut and pandanus wood, leaf and leaf-ribs, and there was not a nail or a piece of iron, he proudly remarked, in the whole construction.

Davies made us coffee, and seemed glad to have visitors coming up out of the sea, as he put it. He confessed that he found life at once interesting and disturbing. Tabiteuea, as we had already learnt, has retained more than any other part of the Gilberts the violence and lawlessness of the old pre-British days. The name – the land where kings are forbidden – commemorates the disinclination of Tabiteueans even in the past to accept very much in the way of chiefly rule, and they did not seem to have changed, for just before we left Tarawa we heard that they had burnt down the government meeting hall at Utiroa. Everything we had heard of the Tabiteueans – especially of the men of Utiroa and the neighbouring villages – seemed to confirm the opinion Davies now expressed: that they lived very much like the Sicilians, sustaining strong and antique codes of honour with passionate violence. There were certain insults a Tabiteuean felt worthy of death; Rose Barker's father had been killed because he called a man from Utiroa a thief, and deaths among Tabiteueans were avenged according to a code of vendetta as strict as any in Italy. 'Never say or do anything without considering the consequences – that seems to be the rule for survival here,' Davies concluded.

By this time Gordon had arrived on the back of a policeman's motor bike. He was staying in the government rest-house, which stood in isolation three-quarters of a mile away, over a waste of coral and sand cluttered with brown debris from the stunted palms. Noon was still two hours off, but the sun was reflected from the sand with such intensity that we were exhausted by the time we reached the rest-house. It was another native-style building made of tareka; the thick roof and the abundant ventilation of this style of building made it relatively cool, which was a good thing, since the heat that quivered up from the coral outcrop between the rest-house and the beach was so great that I was able to venture out only for ten minutes and then retreated.

We would be going later in the day to a village called Taneang where Rose's Gilbertese uncle, Peter Kanere, had arranged for us to stay because that night there would be a feast and dancing in the mane-aba. But we had to wait, as always in the Gilberts, for transport, since the only vehicle larger than a motor bike at this end of the island was the Moke operated by two British doctors, the Underwoods, wife and husband, who were just finishing a term as family planning consultants. While we waited for them to return to the rest-house, where they also were staying, we talked to their two small and articulate boys, who told splendid tales of what they had seen, in the cool of the morning, when they went down to the rock pools on the shore below the rest-house, and especially of the great battles there between the red fish and the blue fish, and many other such wonders in which fairy tales and knightly romances became marvellously intermingled with the equally strange things seen in the underwater world of the South Seas.

About two o'clock the Underwoods arrived: she small, nervously slim and sharply intelligent in conversation; he sombrely thin and withdrawn, and somewhat self-consciously didactic, so that his real nature emerged only unwillingly, like one of those little hermit crabs of the South Seas which retreat into their shells but come looking out if one holds them before one's mouth and whistles softly. Mrs. Underwood immediately loaded us with our luggage into the Moke, and we set off for Taneang.

On the way she talked of her experiences as a family planning doctor. She claimed that the efforts of the team had been most successful on Tabiteuea, though as we drove along the narrow roads there seemed as many children playing and shouting outside the houses as anywhere else in the South Seas. There had, she admitted, been opposition, from the Catholics especially, who had their own methods of birth control which, as an orthodox physician, she naturally rejected. Finally she stated very dogmatically that we must not be deceived by the plumpness and the beautiful brown skins of the Gilbertese; they were – most of them – the victims of malnutrition. Fat and protein were deficient in their diet. They kept chickens but had a prejudice about eating eggs, which had once been taboo. They ate little fruit. And, surprisingly, in view of their life in the sun, experts had found them deficient in vitamin D. Perhaps all this was true; I certainly had no facts to disprove it. Yet when I looked out and saw the abundantly healthy looks of the women working around the houses, who here on Tabiteuea went bare-breasted and wore nothing but the palm-fibre ridi slung very low and provocatively on the hips, I could not help feeling that in the direction of malnutrition the troubles of the Gilberts lay obviously in the future rather than the present. One is not often deceived by a look of full-bodied, healthy vigour, and I felt there must be some factor in the diet or metabolism of the Gilbertese that made inapplicable criteria devised by Europeans for Europeans.

Towards Taneang the landscape – if one can give such a name to flat ground and coconut groves as open as a cathedral – became greener than we had seen since we left Fiji; under the trees it was verdant with grass, and the long drought which had made stark skeletons of the bread-fruit trees we passed had obviously ended.

At Taneang, near the big Catholic compound with its church and its school and its nuns' residence, Rose's uncle was awaiting us. Peter Kanere was a small vital man with curly black hair and a grey stubbled face like a monkey with great soulful eyes, an appearance that seemed to fit well with his restless, springy manner, always on the edge of laughter. We knew Peter's reputation already; he had been involved at the end of the war in an abortive movement, started up as the result of loose talking among American G.I.s, to get the Gilberts detached from Britain and incorporated in the Pacific possessions of the United States. It was rather like the cargo cults in the Melanesian islands, for – as Peter ruefully explained to me the day after our meeting – everyone expected that American rule would mean plenty of material gifts and lots of freedom without responsibility. Other men went to prison, but Peter's part in the affair was never proved, though he was forbidden to go near Tarawa, and instead deployed his talents on the tiny stage of Tabiteuea, where his own land lay.

And Peter's talents were considerable. He spoke excellent English. He had read as omnivorously as a man on an outer island in a remote archipelago can possibly do. He had been a wireless operator and held a mate's certificate. He had been a member of the Island Council. He became a good mechanic and an adept carpenter, without abandoning the native skills of a Micronesian man, for he provided for his family by fishing and tending the fragment of coconut plantation and babai pit that had descended to him. He had been thrice married and twice divorced, and he was the unashamed father of fourteen children. He had even been excommunicated for having advocated ecumenism long before the Vatican accepted it, and now he had found a vehicle for his universalism by having become a Bahai. He was certainly an extra-ordinary man to find cheerfully struggling for a living on an island like Tabiteuea. He had come straight from his fishing, and his hand had been lacerated by the bite of an eel he had caught on the reef, but there was no clinic where he could get it treated, and he would have passed it off with a joke if Inge had not insisted on bringing out our first-aid bag and dressing it.

Peter had persuaded the Catholic sisters – in the absence of the priest – to allow us to use a tareka-walled house in the mission compound which had been built for the Bishop's visits. As he took us in, and we felt appreciatively the springiness of the pandanus mats that had been piled several thick on the floor, he declared: 'It is the best we can do in Taneang! But if you come in a year's time, we will treat you like the Governor himself! The village council has decided to build a hotel!' It would have been ungracious to inquire how Peter and a collection of poor fishermen and copra farmers could perform such a feat and attract the tourists of whom they innocently dreamed. We were content with our hut which was good enough for a Bishop, particularly as it had not only its own catwalk and closet overhanging the sea but also a shower consisting of an oil drum perched on a scaffold with a tap which one turned to release a ragged spray.

Immediately after we had arrived, the village schoolmaster appeared with his wife to offer coconuts of welcome on behalf of Taneang, and then we all went off to visit the sisters. The experience turned out to be very different from our meeting with their colleagues at Taborio in the girls' school atmosphere of the Immaculate Conception College. Here at Taneang the sisters were running a village primary school, in direct contact with parents as well as children, but the real difference was

created by the personalities involved. Sister Damiani was a jolly, plump
Gilbertese girl prone to laughter; she came from the island of Nonuti,
which the Gilbertese pronounce – such are eccentricities of translitera-
tion – as Noonoose! Sister Columbus was ample and easy-going;
Australian Irish, I guessed. Sister Raphael was also Australian, but it was
more than thirty years since she left her native land, and she had become
– in Gilbertese terms – a historical personage. The Bishop – even the
Governor – had told us that if we visited Tabiteuea we must not fail
to meet Sister Raphael and hear her tale of how she escaped from
Abaiang when the Americans were invading the Gilberts and the
Japanese had decided to execute all the sisters, and how the islanders
had helped them at the right moments, and kept silent at the right
moments, so that in the end they had arrived safely at the part of the
atoll which the Americans held.

And indeed, the story was told and was interesting, but even more
interesting were the observations which Sister Raphael had to make on
the violence in Tabiteuean life and its links with a kind of moral austerity which in some ways makes the Gilbertese resemble the Jews of the
Old Testament; both groups emerged after all from a rigorous environment where any departure from the accepted code might have
immediate and disastrous consequences.

According to Sister Raphael, theft – not murder – is the crime most
publicly condemned on Tabiteuea, and this condemnation springs from
ancient memories of scarcity. To illustrate how harshly theft is judged,
she told the story of a woman whose husband had died and who was
desperately short of food. One night she went cautiously to a neighbour's babai pit and dug a large root which she cooked to feed her
children. But she had been seen, and she was summoned before the
elders in the maneaba and publicly ostracized. The shame of the act
clung to her and her family so long that her daughters could find no
husbands on Tabiteuea. And when Sister Raphael went and protested
to the elders at the excessiveness of the punishment, they replied that
this was their law, and if the woman was in need it was her own fault
because neither she nor her husband before her had cultivated their
land properly, which itself was something very near a crime in Tabiteuean eyes.

This hatred of theft, Sister Raphael insisted, had been the reason why
Rose's father died. When he called a Tabiteuean a thief, the offended
man gave him the opportunity to retract an accusation made in heat,

and when he refused, felt honour must be satisfied, went home to get his knife, and quite cold-bloodedly performed the killing, which many Tabiteueans openly applauded. Apart from the injury that comes from the loss of face due to an accusation like that of theft, the other accepted reason for a Tabiteuean to take the law into his hands was that of sexual outrage. 'To attack a married woman is death!' declared Sister Raphael, and she said it with a zest which suggested that she half admired these people with their code of passionate honour.

7

After dark the conches blew in Taneang, hoarsely calling the people to the maneaba, and, with Gordon and the Underwoods, we were guided into the great hall; lit by Coleman lamps hung from the rafters, it look like some vast and lofty old tithe barn. The floor was well covered with mats, and we sat in the place of guests at the head, with the men ranged along each side of the hall, the children at the far end, and the women moving in the background as they prepared the meal.

The people slowly arrived, taking their places. Questions were asked concerning our presence, and then one by one the elders rose to make speeches of welcome, and in turn we replied. The feast, when it came, was no gastronomic adventure. On tin plates were piled grey masses of babai, which turned out to be even more solid and flavourless than taro, boiled bread-fruit, some salt fish of heavy texture; poured over everything was a brown semi-liquid paste made of pandanus fruit, which looked and tasted like a kind of date jam, and which would have been pleasant on its own but did not go well with the other foods. There were green coconuts, and later coffee with sweet condensed milk. The very fact that this was feast food, and enjoyed by everyone present, was as eloquent a testimony as one could desire to the habitual austerity of Gilbertese life. Normal meals were obviously not merely less abundant but also less appetizing.

Haste had no place in the Tabiteuean pattern of entertainment, and instead of the dances beginning, there was another round of speeches, more flowery than the last, and then a long pause while the men talked idly among themselves, and we began to wonder if there would be any dances at all. But eventually one of the elders stood up and remarked slyly that if the young ones did not come forward perhaps the old ones should show them how to dance. This was evidently a kind of cue, for the men nonchalantly produced little bundles, and wrapped mats around their waists, which they bound with dark girdles made of plaited women's hair. Then the women donned ridis over their ordinary skirts and flowery chaplets on their heads and bound hibiscus blossoms on their arms with fragments of pandanus leaf. Because the maneaba was on ground belonging to the Catholic Church, the dancing would not be bare-breasted as it still is in some Tabiteuean villages.

That made no difference to the vigour and zest with which the dancing proceeded. The older men began with what they called their 'piece by piece' dances. Some of these were vigorously stamping figures which had almost certainly originated as limbering-up dances before battle; others were chronicle dances, representing myths and also historical events like the arrival of the first whalers more than a century before. Behind the men the other dancers gathered in a semicircle – women and younger men and children, keeping the rhythm of the dance with the sway of their arms and singing the appropriate chants, of which the meaning, as in Tonga, was largely forgotten. It was the old women, we noticed, whose shrill voices carried the burden of the song, and it was the oldest men who were the most possessed by the spirit of the dance. The star was a gaunt, thin, double-jointed man wearing a crown of green leaves, who played the role of clown, dancing with a boneless suppleness that reminded one of Lautrec's Valentin le Desossé, and performing, to the rhythm of the dance, the most extraordinary abdominal convulsions.

After a series of these taxing dances, everyone sat down for a while and drank strong sweet tea, and then the high point of the evening came with the classic Gilbertese bino. This is the sitting dance whose chants and gestures echo back to a mythical past. Two flower-decked girls sat in front, their legs covered with mats. The other dancers, also seated, ranged themselves in three long rows behind. And while the chorus swayed the rhythm and sang the melody proper to each item, the girls danced with their arms and hands and heads alone, every gesture of the fingers representing a phrase of the song. Some were love songs, as the gestures of hands, placed on hearts and then held out towards the male guests, transparently indicated. Others Peter Kanere was unable to explain, because they enacted legends from the pagan days whose meanings had been lost in the long decades of conversion. Yet the dances to some extent represented an ongoing present; once we realized with surprise and amusement that the song being sung was a highly harmonized version of 'Tipperary', with the words distorted (all the Ts turned into Ss and the Rs into Ls), so that Tipperary became 'Sippalally'!

These solemn dances ended, the men took over again in a series of antic clownings as they capered and tumbled to and fro across the matted floor. The two girls who had danced the bino came waltzing up to bow to Gordon and me as the most honoured guests. In true politeness we should have danced with them, but grey hairs confer privileges in the Gilberts, and since neither of us felt fit to leap – at a humid 85° – in the twist, the most modern dance to have reached those distant oceans, we made the minimum gesture of pulling from our pockets square tins of Johnson's Baby Powder and liberally sprinkling the girls' necks and shoulders as a ritual compliment to their performance.

When the dancers were thoroughly exhausted, it was time to sit down, stuff pipes with rubbed-down stick tobacco, drink more strong tea, and after a suitable interval, resume the speech-making. No less than a dozen elders had their say, so that the voice of every lineage was heard, and Gordon and Dr. Underwood and I spoke again, praising the dancers, vowing eternal memory.

After midnight we made our way back to the Bishop's house, where we slept on mats, laid on rope beds like Indian charpoys, with the mosquito nets enclosing us in filmy but breathless cubes and the smoke of mosquito coils caressing the air with a faint pungency. (They were Fish Coils, manufactured by the Blood Protection Company of Hong Kong, and guaranteed to deal swift death to all mosquitoes, sandflies and such flying pests.) We slept fitfully, disturbed by wakeful dogs and by feet crunching past now and again on the coral. I finally woke in the first dawn and lay listening to the call of the noddies over the lagoon, the crow of cocks, the singing of the toddy cutters echoing out of the distance and finally sounding high and loud in the trees above the house. At 6.30 the church bell began its cracked clanging and I walked outside; the people were treading along the boardwalks to the outhouses above the tide, girls were going to and from the brackish wells with buckets balanced on the end of poles, and smoke stood in the air.

Soon afterwards Peter Kanere appeared with an invitation from the elders to breakfast in the maneaba. They would like to talk to us as friends about our way of life and theirs. There were ten of them already seated when we arrived and took our former places at the head of the maneaba. Each had brought something for breakfast. Peter provided the coffee, another man offered ships' biscuits, a third had bread that was dark and sweet because toddy had been used instead of yeast, a fourth offered a little plate of cold dried fish, and we all ate together, using our fingers, and talking as we ate, while Peter indefatigably translated in both directions for, apart from the schoolmaster, none of them knew much English.

In spite of such handicaps, it was good, ranging conversation, for the Gilbertese are a verbally adept people with a considerable oral literature embodied in songs, epics and tales of the supernatural, and oratory is probably more elaborately developed among them than among any other South Sea people. Much of our time was taken up with answering their questions about life in our 'village'; none of them had more than the vaguest idea of the life or look of a city, and all we said was of interest, some of it of wonder and some – it was evident despite their elaborate politeness – was matter for incredulity.

About their own future they were stoical. I asked what they would do when the phosphates ran out on Ocean Island and there was no longer anywhere for them to earn money. There were grunts of approval when one of the older men replied: 'We shall go back to our own way of life.'

Inge asked then whether this was not perhaps already too late. Had not the Western education they had received already parted the young people from traditional patterns? That was true, one of the younger men replied. But the trend could be reversed. Gilbertese parents were beginning to realize that what the schools taught was not everything in life, though one could not do without it in the modern world. (This with a nod to the teacher, for it was dangerous on Tabiteuea to make a man feel he had lost face.) Fathers were now making sure that their sons would learn to live from the land and the sea. And fathers, the elders made clear, were still obeyed in the Gilberts. They had heard of the troubles we had with the young in our villages, and they felt that here they might have something to teach us. For in the Gilberts not only wisdom but also power have always been regarded as belonging to the old, and so far this gerontocracy has continued virtually unchallenged. As Peter Kanere put it: 'Among us white heads are not insulted.'

The problem that most troubled these Gilbertese elders was not the drying up of modest cash incomes, or the rebellion of the young, or pollution, for – though the fouling of the lagoon was visible enough even to us as strangers – they still believed that the sea would continue to provide all it had ever done. Even the departure of the whites they could accept with equanimity, though they hastened to assure us that they liked the Imatangs, who had stopped them from destroying themselves in the civil wars, and they still revered the memory of the great Kurimbo, as Sir Arthur Grimble is affectionately named among them. The real problem – as it had been in the old battling days before the white men came – was land. Man could not live by fish alone. He needed coconuts and good solid babai. (He needed also, though this was never said explicitly, the sense of identity that throughout the South Seas is associated with a man's relationship to his land.) The Gilbertese do not recognize primogeniture; the land a man leaves is equally divided among his children. The only relaxation of these difficulties is provided by the fact that a man can cultivate the lands of other members of his clan who are not using them.

'Look at me,' Peter explained. 'I cultivate several acres of palm-trees and babai pits because my brothers are away working in Tarawa and Nauru. But if they return, I must give back their land. I shall have about two acres left. And if my sons want to divide that between them, there will be very little for each.'

'And yet you had fourteen children,' Inge sharply remarked. Peter lifted his hands in a silent gesture that seemed to portray all the hopelessness an intelligent Gilbertese could see in the future of his people or, for that matter, in his own future.

The other men seemed to catch, without being told, the sad tenor of what was being said, for one of them remarked suddenly that speaking is all very well, but it is song that gives speech its polish. And immediately he and Peter broke into a jaunty miming ditty about a branch that is torn by the wind off its tree, and taken over the oceans and returns transformed into a splendid flower. It was, they explained, a song for visitors whom they hope will return. And now, they asked, would we sing them a song? We were rather nonplussed, since there were few songs all of us knew, until Gordon suggested that we should sing our own version of 'Tipperary', and this we did. They gazed at us in astonishment. 'But you're singing *our* song!' one of them shouted. And it turned out that none of them even knew when they had acquired 'Tipperary', though it must have come from British sailors fifty years or more ago. It had become so much a part of their dance tradition that they made no distinction between the incomprehensibility of its words and the equal incomprehensibility of some of the bino chants that belonged to an ancient and largely forgotten Gilbertese dialect.

At ten o'clock Dr. Underwood came to drive us to the coral strip that serves as Tabiteuea's airport, and we departed on our bucking journey through the rough and narrow roads, wearing the crowns of little shells which the senior elder had gravely placed upon our heads so that we might remember the land without a king and one day return like the song's magnificent flower. It was hard in that moment of friendship to remember the Tabiteuean reputation for passionate pride and violence.

8

Abemama, the island of moonlight, is also the island where Stevenson lived during the reign of the ferocious King Tem Binoka, whose special pastime was to shoot his subjects down out of the crowns of coconut-trees. Apart from Tarawa, which Grimble described so eloquently in *A Pattern of Islands*, it is the only island of the Gilberts that has any place in Western literature, and though we had no particular mission there, Inge and I decided to leave the plane while Gordon flew on to Tarawa, and to stay for a day so that we could at least savour its look and flavour.

From the air it was the most handsome of the Gilberts, an almost circular atoll, with a great emerald arc of long islets enclosing the lagoon with wide, white beaches. The airport was far from any settlement, on a hot barren stretch of coral sand at one end of the longest island. It was here that for the first time we were trapped by the difficulties of transport on these almost vehicleless islands. It took a little time to get our luggage, and then a problem arose which we had to discuss with Gordon for five minutes before the plane departed. When we had finished, we realized that the little bus which had brought the passengers had already left. The government centre was nine miles away, and we knew that it would be impossible in the midday heat, even without our luggage, to walk that far. An old man who acted as caretaker for the airport had a motor bike, and he offered to go off and send a car to fetch us. He cut two coconuts for us, and left. We waited, with the heat building up. No car came, and as an hour passed, and then two, we began to think that we would be here, marooned at the

stark airport shed, until the next day's plane arrived. It promised to be
an uncomfortable night as we lived it in imagination. We had no food
and no cigarettes, our last having been smoked by the elders of Taneang.
The coconuts were soon finished, and there was no visible supply of
water. If we did stay here overnight, there would only be the concrete
floor to sleep on.

Three hours passed, and I was going out to the line of palms along
the beach to see whether I could forage some fallen nuts when I saw
a Volkswagen bus approaching. It was the only public transport on
the island, the bus which the Island Council runs twice a day from the
government centre to the airport. Immediately the celebrated kindness
of the Abemamans (regarded as a soft people in comparison with the
Tabiteueans) displayed itself, as an old man who was a passenger got
down from the bus and insisted on loading our luggage.

The bus scuttled by devious lanes through coconut groves until it
reached the road that runs beside the lagoon. Our hearts lifted as we
sensed the special atmosphere of the island. It was softer, more lyrical
than that of the other islands; Tabiteuea and Tarawa both seemed hard
in light and dry in soil by comparison. The palms were denser, there
was an undergrowth of grass and low shrubs so that the rough coral
was less visible, and the light had a kind of greenish pearliness. Whenever the bus stopped or slowed, we could hear the cooing of pigeons,
for Abemama is the one island in the Gilberts which has a population
of naturalized land-birds.

Always with the lagoon in sight, we drove through village after
village, though there were intervals between them and it was obvious
that the island was less thickly populated than Tarawa. We passed a
big concrete slab by the shore which the old man told us was the tomb
of the famous Tem Binoka, and we reached the cluster of prefabricated
buildings that is the government station of Tabontibeke; here the
driver of the bus ran round to the store, which was already closed,
and got the manager to open up so that we could buy supplies for our
evening's dinner, since in the rest-houses the guests cook for themselves.
To our relief, the rest-house was not one of the bleak, prefabricated
buildings, but a large native-style house, with a big open veranda,
standing on a wide blue channel between the lagoon and the ocean.
A long and rickety bridge of poles and branches crossed the channel
like a gigantic millipede, and two young men were walking motor
bikes over it to the palm-groves of the opposite shore. The light was

richening, as it always does in the later afternoon of the Gilberts, and among the intense and varying blue of the lagoon a dazzling white Korean ship lay moored.

As we entered the rest-house we were suddenly and surprisingly engulfed in a welcome that made up for all the discomforts of midday. The place was already occupied by a New Zealand education officer who was on tour with his wife and their two children. As they introduced themselves – Bill McMinn and Jocelyn – there was immediately the feeling of open geniality we had experienced so often in New Zealand. The McMinns were cooking their dinner and asked us to share it. An Australian geographer who was studying lagoon ecology, and an English agriculturist with his Gilbertese girl came over from the prefabricated houses to join in the welcome and brought sheets and pillows so that our night would not be too uncomfortable. McMinn made an immense salad with tomatoes and cucumbers which he had coaxed with careful composting from the reluctant Gilbertese soil, and with tinned lamb curry and tinned fruit salad and the wine we had bought at the store we ate something better than a typical white man's island meal. Afterwards we sat on the veranda, watching the fires being lit on the opposite shore of the passage until they ran like a fiery necklace along the edge of the groves, burning the debris that had fallen from the palm-trees. The moon came up, and illuminated the white house among the trees where the so-called king of Abemama lives. And the king provided an ample subject for anecdote and conversation to while away the evening as we drank beer under the white light of the Coleman lamps.

He is, in fact, a king without crown or legitimacy. There was never in the pre-European Gilberts the same tradition of rule by sacred kings as existed among the Polynesians. The clans or utus with their elders formed the essential structure of society, but there was a hierarchy among the clans, and some were regarded as having more spiritual potency than others. It was when trade began and modern weapons were introduced that clan leaders were able to assert, in some islands like Abemama and Butaritari, what amounted to tyranny rather than kingship. Tem Binoka, with his beachcomber aides, became the tyrant of Abemama, and, as Stevenson narrated eloquently in *In the South Seas*, he set up a bloody and oppressive rule, on the strength of alien arms rather than of local custom. Significantly, it was in Tem Binoka's realm, on Abemama, that the British in 1892 proclaimed their protectorate over the Gilberts and rendered merely ceremonial the functions of the self-styled kings of Abemama and Butaritari.

Paul Toketake, the present pretender to the shadowy throne of Abemama, enjoys no legal title. He owns much land, and he has a following among older Abemama families, who still see social relationships in terms of clan hierarchies, which has enabled him to get elected to the Legislative Council of the colony; when the Governor visits Abemama it is to Paul Toketake's village that he goes first, and there he is presented the green coconut of welcome in the maneaba.

But even on Abemama times have changed, and democratic urges have spread, largely, ironically, because the shadow king has been selling his lands to keep up a style of living proper to pretenders to royalty. Since Abemama is relatively thinly populated, and fertile enough for bananas to grow, there has in recent years been a considerable immigration from the other islands of people who feel no special loyalty to the descendant of Tem Binoka, and Paul Toketake's standing appears to have declined perceptibly, though he contrives in small and curious ways to emphasize his difference from other men. This was evident next morning when we caught our only glimpse of him, a tall man wearing long trousers (which alone distinguish him from the other men of Abemama) and driving an expensive-looking motor bike with precarious daring over the rickety bridge across the channel where all other Abemamans are obliged under penalty of fine to walk their bikes.

We had spent another restless night, for this time our mats were spread on iron springs, which are a great deal more uncomfortable than the string beds of Taneang. The great maneaba-like roof-space of the rest-house, open above the mere cubicles that served as rooms, was illuminated with diffused moonlight; insects like crickets creaked most of the night through in the thatch; and a wind sprang up and rustled the palm-trees so that I kept awakening with the thought that the rains had come.

We had half a day to spare in Abemama before the plane left, but we could not get a launch or a canoe to take us along the lagoon, and spent the morning idling along the channel near the rest-house, picking up shells and watching the fishermen. One of them gave us some gold-striped and white-bellied fish about the size of a mackerel, and Jocelyn McMinn, who cooked them up for our lunch, sent out one of the children with a stick of tobacco, according to the custom by which the internal economy of Abemama appears to be carried on. It is not exactly ordinary barter, but the presentation of one's surplus – bread-fruit or babai or fish – on the unspoken assumption that the recipient will give something he has in surplus, which in the case of a European usually means tobacco or chewing gum. The custom extends so far that the kippered fish which we saw drying on some of the house-roofs along the shore are sent via family connections to Betio, whence sophisticated trade goods are sent in barter by relatives who have found employment.

This kind of casual exchange was part of the traditional Gilbertese way of life, and linked to another custom, called bubuti (and pronounced booboosee), that had developed in pre-European days as one of the necessary insurances against disaster in a marginal economy. According to the custom of bubuti (there is a similar custom called kerekere in Fiji) one can ask a relative for anything he has acquired, and he is unable to refuse to give it. This applied not merely within the nuclear family of parents and children, but within the lineage, which may include fairly distant cousins. Bubuti was a means of saving many lives at times of need or ill fortune, and on some islands, like Tabiteuea, it is still carefully restricted, so that anyone who asks for it except in genuine need is subject to social ostracism. On some of the other islands the custom is looser, so that a man merely coveting his relatives' possessions can acquire them, and on Tarawa it has become a powerful barrier to social mobility, since a man who gets a salaried post is likely to find his relatives invoking bubuti and moving into his house with great good humour to share his fortune. Bill McMinn quoted to me the cases of teachers who had come to him asking to be transferred to schools on other islands, since the demands of their relatives had made them poorer than they would have been without their jobs. Most of the white inhabitants of Tarawa lamented the situation, but it seemed to me that there might be advantages in the particular circumstances of the Gilberts to a custom that prevented even those who had jobs from getting the taste for a higher standard of living which the realities of the Gilbertese future may not allow them to sustain. Bubuti may well be a self-protective way of ensuring that the necessary austerity of Gilbertese life is not forgotten.

The danger of losing through bubuti whatever profits they might make, led the Gilbertese to support co-operative stores after the departure of the white traders rather than to take on the role of individual shopkeepers. One of the last durable relics of the old independent traders stood on the shore at Abemama, a few steps away from the rest-house. It was the copra shed of coral rock that had been built by Thomas Murdoch, the Scottish cabin boy who jumped ship at Abemama, entered King Tem Binoka's service, established himself as a trader, and in his later years joined the British government service, laying out the roads on the main islands and inducing the people to come together in villages. When we got back to Tarawa from Abemama, we met the youngest of his sons, Alex Murdoch, a large and sombre man who was now a foreman for construction work.

Alex Murdoch was unusually shy and withdrawn for a Gilbertese, but the reverse was true of Anton Meyer, the son of a German trader who had come down into the Gilberts from the Marshalls in the 1880s before the British took over the islands. Anton lived on a minute islet within the lagoon which was isolated at high tide, but he was extraordinarily fond of company, and when he heard of our presence at the Otintai he cycled down to the hotel one day to talk to us.

Anton was seventy-five. He has inherited his Gilbertese mother's brown skin, but his eyes were dazzlingly blue and he had the sharp features and the brown walrus moustache of a shrewd and genial German peasant. He spoke a pure Hamburg German, though he had never been nearer Europe than Sydney, but he also spoke Gilbertese, Marshallese and fluent English.

Anton was seventy-five. He had inherited his Gilbertese mother's encountered in the South Seas the two worlds of the islander and the white man. Once he had lived the life of a prosperous trader, having inherited his father's store, which he kept going until the Japanese came to the Gilberts in 1942. Since he was a German subject, they did not molest him personally, but his store was plundered and his business ruined, and he did not relish their rule, so that when the Americans arrived in the islands he made his way to them and offered his services as a guide. He had been a poor man ever since, for he had received no kind of compensation for the loss of his business. He lived in a native house on the scrap of land where the store had once stood, cut his copra, and every day went fishing for his own food. Yet it was hard to imagine a happier-looking man than Anton as he sat there, drinking beer, eating a great plate of fried eggs which he had chosen as his favourite food, recollecting incident after incident from his seventy-five years of life, and joyful for the unusual opportunity to speak German which Inge's presence afforded him.

Anton was obviously much closer to the Gilbertese than any of the white men who had come from outside, with the possible exception of the legendary Grimble, whom he had known well. 'Grimble . . .' he said, with a sigh. 'Ah, Grimble! He was a tall man, so thin that he looked as if he would break into two. The people loved him. He paid them the compliment of learning their language so well that if you heard him through the door of a room without seeing him, you would think it was a native speaking.'

Anton used the word 'native' constantly, and in spite of his Gilbertese blood and his way of living, regarded himself as a European, preserving carefully the rituals and attitudes that prevented him from going completely native. He rose early, as his father had taught him; he took coffee and bread for breakfast; he continued to read his father's German books, and German newspapers whenever they came his way; red-letter days came when the Catholic fathers gave him tins of sauerkraut and frankfurters. He had brought up his children and his grandchildren in a rigid north German manner, and now they were grown up he was running a little school in a hut on his islet where he was patiently teaching a few backward boys who had not benefited from the official system.

Yet if European culture existed for him in the remoteness of the Gilberts as a living thing, the traditions of the Gilbertese were equally present in his mind.

'I have lived so long because Eito, where I was born, is what the people call a strong place. When I was a child all the old women of the village took me in their arms in turn, and they performed some kind of ceremony with a coconut filled with water. It protected me from the evil forces, and now all the others have gone, and I alone am left.'

The Gilbertese, he said, believed not only in ghosts, but also in the spirits of places, though they concealed these survivals of animism from the priests. 'I have never seen a ghost,' he remarked, 'so I reserve my judgement. But I know that magic goes on and I know that it works because I have seen its effects. There are people in all the villages who still practise as sorcerers. Yes, men as well as women. They make potions of coconut-oil and other substances and activate them with spells. I used to go to them when I was a young man. I would fall in love with a girl and try and win her with trinkets I would take from my

father's store. That never worked. But if I could get one of her hairs
and take it to a magician, I would win her. Always. Many lovely girls,
and all of them dead and gone!'

He sighed, looking long-sightedly over the lagoon. 'But there are
bad sorcerers also. They give people sicknesses which no doctor can
diagnose or cure, and sometimes their victims die. It has happened even
to white people, who have offended their servants, and the servants
have taken away little things belonging to their mistresses with which
the magicians have worked.'

I asked Anton what he thought of the future of the Gilberts. He
looked at me directly and sharply. 'I have had a long life, and although
I am ending it a poor man, it has been a happy life. But I am glad
I lived when I did, and I am glad I shall not be living much longer.
The British will not stay for ever, and when they go there will be want
and strife and starvation.'

'What is the attitude of the Gilbertese?'

'Blind equanimity! They know the problems exist, but they think
the Imatangs are all wise, and they expect the government to save
them by some magic which they do not understand!'

9

Anton Meyer was a child of three when Sister Clementine left her
village near Dinant in Brittany, and came to the Gilberts, where the
rest of her life has been spent. She was ninety-four when we reached
Tarawa, and living in the sisters' residence within the big Catholic
compound at Taborio where the Bishop's palace is situated. With an
enormous amount of patient effort the sisters had made one of the few
real gardens in the Gilberts, with pebble paths edged by white crinum
lilies, and shrubberies of hibiscus, and seats under the palm-trees. Here
Sister Clementine came out, on the arm of one of the Australian sisters,
to meet us, a tiny frail woman, bent like a wind-blown tree of the
Breton coast, with the sharp, shrivelled-apple countenance of a north
French paysanne. We were a little anxious, since she was reputed to be
unpredictable with visitors, and inclined to be silent with those she felt
regarded her as a mere historical curiosity, but she looked at us
shrewdly, obviously took to Inge, and began immediately to talk to us
in a mixture of a heavily accentuated English and a dense, antique and
rustic French, punctuated by occasional Gilbertese words.

Sister Clementine was one of the few people surviving whose memories went back over almost the whole British era in the Gilberts. It was clear at times that the mists of age were closing over her mind, and sometimes her memories were obviously confused. But suddenly the light would break in and reflect itself in her expression, and everything would return so that she would be once again the young woman coming fresh from Brittany to a strange and savage world, and she would narrate in a rush of words the story of those long past days, more than a canonical life ago, when she sailed to the Gilberts.

She left France in 1899 and early in 1900 reached the little Catholic outpost on Nonuti. She was chosen immediately as one of the party to establish the mission on Nikunau which Father Kerouantan now operates. It was a foray into enemy territory, for the people were half pagan, half Protestant, and entirely hostile to the intrusion of the Catholics. The party consisted of a priest, a lay brother and two sisters, and the Bishop accompanied them to give the new mission his blessing. The people were hostile and armed, lining up on the beach with their guns and their swords and spears edged with sharks' teeth, and forbade the party to land. The 'fat Samoans', as Sister Clementine described them, were there on the beach, inciting the people; these were the Polynesians whom the London Missionary Society had sent out to convert the Gilberts. The situation was solved only when the captain of the trading schooner on which they sailed threatened not to take copra from the island and not to return unless the Catholic party was allowed to land. So eventually they came on shore, where the Bishop blessed and left them, a forlorn little party stranded on the beach with their possessions, and surrounded by the jeering, angry Nikunauans. Only one of them, a sister, knew a little Gilbertese, and even she could not persuade the islanders to give them shelter. Eventually, in half-willing compassion, the white trader offered them an unfurnished corner of his house, and so, without any material comforts, among a people whose unfriendliness was sustained by the constant preachings of the Protestant missionaries, they started work. In those days there was not much charity among Christians in the South Seas. But Sister Clementine patiently learnt Gilbertese and eventually set up a school, and remembered those hardships ever afterwards with a strange kind of joy which made them more vivid in her mind and in the telling than most of the long decades of patient work that stretched between.

Though Bishop Guichet was Sister Clementine's nephew, and had been inspired by the example of her courage to become himself a missionary priest, there seemed an extraordinary difference between the simple French countrywoman she had remained in spite of all her experiences, and the sophisticated man who greeted us in the great white bungalow which served him as a palace, dressed informally in a blue Hawaiian shirt and cotton slacks, with only his massive gold and amethyst ring suggesting his status.

The Bishop was as pessimistic as Anton Meyer in his assessment of the future that confronted the people of the Gilberts, and if Anton seemed to speak from shrewd intuition, the Bishop spoke from a wide cultural background and a close knowledge of the complexities of Gilbertese conditions. I felt that there was a slight flavour of national acrimony in his statements, and afterwards, when I visited the New Hebrides and New Caledonia, I wondered how he would have spoken of the even greater faults of French administrations. Nevertheless, considered in its own terms, what he had to say about the Gilberts presented the most convincing critical summary of the situation that we heard.

The Bishop was quite ready to admit that many things had improved. Communications were better owing to the establishment of airlines; the introduction of refrigeration had made life, at least for the whites, a great deal easier to endure. Even the Gilbertese were probably better dressed, better fed and better educated than they had been at any time in the past. But he believed that all this merely masked the realities of the situation. These he felt had to be seen within the general context of the breakup of the British Empire. Ever since the liberation of India, Britain had been steadily shedding her colonies, and not a year passed in which at least one did not receive the equivocal gift of independence. One day the turn of the Gilberts might come.

Already, he felt, the British were preparing for internal self-government with a haste that had little relation to the low degree of political sophistication among the Gilbertese. And one could not discount the possibility that some day, to gain a political advantage among the African nations of the Commonwealth, the British might suddenly decide to leave the islands to their fates, perhaps salving the national conscience with a small subsidy. One of the reasons for concern was that the British were already treating the colony as a poor territory from which there was little to be gained, and giving it only a fraction of the cash and care lavished on a prosperous colony like Hong Kong.

As an example, he pointed out that for 14,000 children of school age
there was a government expenditure on education of $500,000 (about
£250,000).

And even that money, he argued, was being spent on the wrong kind
of education. ' What we have to give the Gilbertese now, if we follow
the official curriculum, is an entirely European education. It is an education that is useless except to those who will leave the islands. Primary
education is directed towards the secondary schools, but that means it is
a waste for the 86 per cent who never go to secondary schools. And we
must recognize that most of the people on the islands will never achieve
a European way of living. They will always be dependent on their
environment, and what we have done over the past century is to allow
a culture that was splendidly fitted for that environment to be submerged.'

He paused to fill our glasses. 'But things may be improving in that
field at least. We've been experimenting in our schools, and there are
some good young people at the teachers' training college who are
working on a system oriented towards educating children for living in
their villages, for becoming better fishermen and farmers and learning
to get even more out of their environment. We're even managing to
incorporate the old men into the pattern, to teach by example their
skills of boat-building and house-building which otherwise will die out.

'From that side I'm not so pessimistic as I was some time ago. But
there are other alarming developments. Population, of course – you
know all about that. And the fact that we're relying on dying industries
like copra and phosphates. But one thing people don't say much about
is the unhealthy population shift within the islands. There's a steady
flow of people from the outer islands to Tarawa, and the flow consists
mostly of young men who come to earn money. It means that the
active people are leaving the outer islands. On some of them already
there are two women to every man, while on Betio the overcrowding
is so great that the other day one of our priests found forty-seven
people sleeping in one small house. The worst thing is that all these
young people are losing the taste for the very island life to which they'll
be condemned when the economy declines.'

He could see no easy solution. 'I'd like to believe that a people who
were resilient and resourceful enough to create such a marvellously
adapted culture in the past can face their circumstances and do it
again. But I know that those circumstances are far more heavily

weighted against them than they ever were in the past. We're all trying
in our own ways to reduce the 3 per cent annual growth in population
but it can't be stopped altogether, and the islands are already too full.
You can't bring back the phosphates, and copra will never be a reliable
crop. Emigration! They've tried it already, with small groups in the
Solomons and in Fiji, but it hadn't been very successful because the
Gilbertese are too arrogant to live easily with other South Sea people.
What they want is a place where they can be themselves and live something like the life they're used to. But there you get political selfishness
coming in. There are empty islands off the Australian coast that would
be ideal, but when I suggested they should be given to the Gilbertese,
the Australians would have nothing of it. That's because the Gilbertese
are a poor people. Their only asset is their willingness to learn. But if
large numbers don't emigrate, I fear for the future of all of them.'

10

What I learnt from the Gilberts – and the pessimistic realism of men
like the Bishop and Anton merely confirmed all I had observed and
sensed during our weeks in the islands – was that the coral island has
never been a paradise except in legend. One does not live there by
waiting for food to drop from trees, but by hard, ingenious work that
defeats the meagreness of the environment. But the fragile balance of
the traditional life of the Gilberts has already been destroyed, and now
their remoteness is no longer a protection, but the threat of an isolation
that can only be destructive. While we were there I enjoyed their
moody beauty, their pristine flavour, their proud and uncorrupted
people; they were too primitive, too distant, too poor, too lacking even
in the basic necessity of fresh water, to have been spoilt in the way
Fiji and Samoa are being destroyed by commercialized tourism. But
since I have left those islands I think of them, more than of any other
part of the South Seas, with a nostalgia that is darkened by despair.

PART FOUR
The Giant Pebble

1

We had intended, on our return from the Gilberts to Suva, to spend two weeks in Fiji, establishing a first acquaintance with the main island of Viti Levu, but it was impossible to do this now because of Inge's illness. Fortunately in Suva we fell in with good doctors, and though the Suva hospital reminded one in its primitiveness of the Paris hospital Orwell described in 'How the Poor Die', the operation she underwent was excellently done by a surgeon, Dr. Ramrakha, who is one of the leading members of Fiji's Indian community. Inge convalesced in the Grand Pacific Hotel, which with its vast rooms and rococo decor is one of the great imperial moments of the South Seas, and there we learnt by experience the good nature of the Fijian people. In a hotel a sick person is usually regarded as a nuisance, but at the Grand Pacific everyone from the manager and the housekeeper to the chambermaid and the waitresses went out of his or her way to make Inge as comfortable as possible. In a society where tips are neither customary nor expected, such good will was obviously disinterested. For my part, in days spent largely tramping over the city, I picked up a knowledge of Suva, with its mixed population of Indians and Fijians, of Europeans and Chinese, that otherwise I would not have acquired. But our experience of Fiji as something more than its cosmopolitan capital was postponed.

Meanwhile, Inge's recovery was more rapid than we had expected, and we were only two days late setting off to our next destination, New Caledonia. From the moment we hurried off the little Air Pacific plane that had taken us from Nausori to Nandi, and on to the great UTA jet that stood waiting, it was evident that we were embarking on something different from our previous expeditions. The British may be hurriedly and guiltily conspiring to shed the last of their imperial possessions. The French – despite Indo-China and despite Algeria – still cling proudly to what remains, even if they have to do so by means of the transparently fraudulent pretence that the colonies they keep are (however many thousands of miles away) territories of France. And so while the last British possessions are accessible only with difficulty by small airlines operated by Australians and owned by local governments, France runs a grand route, through its former possessions of Lebanon and Syria, to link up with its present possessions in New Caledonia and Tahiti, and so proclaim the continuing imperial glory of France.

For a little over an hour we winged again over the blank blue ocean, enjoying excellent French food and the unaccustomed comfort of a large plane, until New Caledonia came into sight, a long narrow island, its length vanishing into the north-westerly distance, and its breadth visible from the cruising height of a jet, with the surf breaking around it far offshore on the reefs. At first sight – and this was a true foretaste of our later experience – it was quite unlike anything we had so far seen in the South Seas, stark and austere in shape, its gaunt central chain of mountains darkened by scrubby bush. It was easy to guess why Captain Cook had named it New Caledonia, for swinging in from the sea on a partly cloudy morning, the mountains did indeed resemble those of Scotland; their dark pelt, which one did not then realize consisted of stunted pines and small bushes, looked surprisingly like whin outside the flowering season. But the dark was broken by the red scars of exploitation which had not been there when Cook arrived. One offshore island was half stripped of its vegetation, so that it looked like a partly flayed body; the streams were running red with the waste from the nickel mines that were invisible to us on the other side of the mountains, and a river flowed sluggishly out to the lagoon through a vast vermilion fan of a delta where its branches pushed reluctant paths through the silt with which even the indomitable mangroves had been quite unable to keep pace.

At the airport the customs and passport officers and the police were all French; even among the passengers in the lounge only a few were local Melanesians, whom we immediately recognized by the Australoid features, with remarkably heavy brow lines, that made them quite distinct in appearance from any other people we had seen so far in the islands. Mike Poole, the CBC associate producer who had gone on ahead to Nouméa two days before, was conspicuous on the edge of the crowd, with his red Viking hair and beard. He had brought a hired car, and we drove the thirty miles from the airport at Tontouta into

Nouméa through a landscape that was as different from what we had become accustomed to in the other islands as the original view of New Caledonia had been. It was green but not lush, and except for the tall column pines, the trees were small, and there were few coconut-palms, though the green shafted areca-palm, from which the betel nut is derived, was quite common. There was little recent cultivation, but the old terraces on which the Melanesians had once grown their taro gardens still patterned the hillsides as the Inca terraces do the slopes of Machu Picchu, and like the terraces of Machu Picchu they were deserted and overgrown. We drove through two small towns, each of them with a big French church and a mairie and a few of the kind of Third Republic bungalows one finds in Parisian suburbs like Meudon, and then, before Nouméa even came into sight, we saw the pillars of red fumes rising out of the great chimneys of the smelter of Dumbéa, and drove past its vast rust-coloured conglomeration of gantries and furnaces and sheds, like some Petra of the industrial revolution, into the city.

It was almost too fitting a symbol of the character of life in Nouméa that, on a road project on the outskirts of the city, we saw a white man, in shorts and a trilby hat, operating a steam-roller. Everywhere else in the South Seas employment had been sharply divided, and white men did no manual work, whether the country was colonial or independent. But Nouméa, we found, as we drove into the centre of the town, and lingered at a small café to drink a carafe of wine, and then went on down to the splendid bays where the hotels are situated, was not merely a town dominated by the French. It was an actual French town, two-thirds of whose people were French by race as well as by citizenship. The bank clerks were French, the people who served us in shops and cafés were French, the policemen were French, and so were the girls and boys who decorated the beaches and the fanatic admirers of le vélo who defied the heat as they sped along the corniche roads.

Even the beachside hotel we stayed in was French in its combination of an imposing exterior and inner slovenliness. The sheets were grey and damp; the mattresses sagged and the springs creaked; the wardrobe stank of mould; it was as if one were back in a damp room in the Quartier Latin. There was an air-conditioning unit in the room, but it was unusable until I had paid an extra four francs and the clerk had come up to insert the fuses. He was metropolitan French, and I got

my first taste of the attitudes of his kind when I remarked that the
bays reminded me of the Côte d'Azur, which was true. His look
verged on indignation. 'Ah, non, monsieur, not really like the Côte
d'Azur. Like San Francisco perhaps.' And that was true too, for Nouméa is not only a town of bays, but also a town of hills and of white
houses clambering over them, like the vanished San Francisco I knew
a quarter of a century ago. But, just though his remark may have been,
I sensed in the young Frenchman a suggestion, that though a good
effort had been made in Nouméa, France in its true form was not
transportable.

And indeed, later in the day, when we went into the city, it was
evident that, though at first sight it looked like a good imitation of a
southern French provincial town – the centre resembling Nîmes and
the bays resembling Cannes – the climate and history had conspired
to create important differences. The marble statues in the public gardens, the old brick warehouses in the back streets, the little Hôtel de
Ville dating from the turn of the century, the older villas in their shady
gardens with Monet lily-ponds, were as French as one could desire.
But the squares were shaded with coconuts and flame trees; there were,
for reasons I never discovered, no boulevards; and while there were
many plausibly French restaurants, there was only one real café, and
that had been founded recently by a metropolitan Frenchman, for the
custom of the colon families was to drink and entertain in their homes
which (as one metropolitan complained to me) meant entertaining
strangers not at all. Finally, there was always the minority of native
people, many of whom lived in the slums down by the smelter; they
were usually self-effacing in manner, but intensely visible, for the
women wore Mother Hubbards of gaudy print and the men affected
nylon shirts of acid brilliance and often bound their heads with the red
scarves of rebellion. They seemed exotic foreigners in this city that was
the capital of their country.

2

It was obvious from that first evening's glimpse of Nouméa that we
had reached a place where human and political relationships varied
widely from those we had encountered anywhere else in the South
Seas, and at this point a potted history may not be out of place. Next to
New Guinea, New Caledonia is the largest island of the South Seas,

and its very size, as well as its geological conformation, affected its destiny. Nickel, which now dominates both its economics and its politics, was actually a later complication in its history. After Cook discovered it in 1774, it was visited and its coast fairly thoroughly explored by D'Entrecasteau and De Kermadac in 1792, which gave the French the feeling that they had a kind of claim over it, though it was long before they occupied the island. During the first half of the nineteenth century it was a place of refuge for deserting seamen and runaway convicts from Australia; a few traders arrived and established connections with the Melanesian tribes. About 1840 the missionaries arrived – French Catholics and also – less predictably – Huguenots.

It was the imperial acquisitiveness of the Second Empire – newly founded and seeking easy laurels – that led the French to annex the island in 1853. The excuse was an attack three years before on a French survey ship, whose entire crew was killed and ritually eaten, but the real motive was undoubtedly to anticipate the British, who had sent a survey ship there with a view to making a formal annexation of their own. Captain Denham's ship, the *Herald*, was actually moored off the Isle of Pines, in the coastal waters of New Caledonia, when Vice-Admiral Febvrier-Despointes landed at Balade on the main island to proclaim the annexation, and the legend goes that Denham committed suicide in chagrin, though the tale appears to be apocryphal.

At first, like the British in Australia, the French were content to turn their new possession into a penal settlement, and until almost the end of the century convicts were sent there, some of whom did not complete their sentences until well into the twentieth century. These men and women included not only habitual criminals, but also many of the socialists and anarchists who had fought in the Paris Commune of 1870–1. The traditions of the left portray these exiles as languishing in an oppressive and disease-ridden land. In fact New Caledonia lies south of the malaria belt in the South Seas, which begins in the New Hebrides, and the climate is one of the most temperate of the region, with light rainfall and a cool season when the winds are constant and refreshing; until they were amnestied in the 1880s, the Commune exiles, who included many writers and artists and such celebrities as Louise Michel and Henri de Rochefort, provided a decade of high culture, with theatrical performances and literary publications, the like of which New Caledonia has not since enjoyed.

But the penal settlements were not all. The French soon began to encourage European settlers. Even before that, French and Australian farmers had arrived and now others followed and began to acquire land from the local Melanesians. It was rarely they did so by fair means, since the native New Caledonian is deeply attached to his ancestral lands and reluctant to part with them. The land seizures by force and fraud provoked a bloody native uprising in 1878, and others followed, the most recent being in 1917, when the local Melanesians imagined that the French would be too occupied with their war in Europe to bother about a remote South Sea island.

They miscalculated, and this, like previous risings, failed. The Melanesians were punished by losing even more of their lands and being confined in reservations whose area – even now after some of the lost land has been given back – is only half the area owned by Europeans. It was the good land that the French occupied for coffee plantations and also, in the western part of the island, for cattle ranching, so that the cowboy – 'le stockman' – is a common but unexpected sight on this South Sea island. Thus, unlike the other possessions which the various powers acquired in the South Seas, New Caledonia became a settlement colony. The French did not set up immense plantations to be worked by native labour. They established farms on which they themselves worked, with the result that in New Caledonia the French are in equal numbers to the native people – about 50,000 of each. The remaining 20,000 are people of many origins; Chinese and Vietnamese, Melanesians from the New Hebrides and Polynesians from Tahiti and from Wallis Island, most of them imported to work in the mines which the natives have always shunned, partly because they do not like regular work, but partly also because they believe that tearing the earth open to take its riches is an offence to the land and its spirits.

Nickel is the basis of a mineral industry that further differentiates New Caledonia from other islands of the South Seas, though recent extensive discoveries of copper on Bougainville in New Guinea may challenge its uniqueness in this respect. The French call New Caledonia Le Caillou – the stone – and the name is appropriate enough if we take it as referring to the rock out of which fortunes are made on the island though not by the islanders. It is quite possible that the French might have been as willing to abandon New Caledonia as the British are to abandon their South Sea colonies if it had been only a matter of agriculture, for coffee is no longer profitable except to native farmers who grow it on a family basis and ranching is precarious. It is nickel that since its discovery in the 1870s has formed the basis of the New Caledonian economy; the greatest power on the island, after the local French government, is La Société de Nickel, which in a good year can export nickel and nickel ore to the value of up to $200,000,000. The nickel industry of New Caledonia is an almost classic example of the parasitic nature of primary industries dominated by alien interests. The capital is French, and almost all the profits leave New Caledonia, while the mines are run by European technicians and labourers from other island groups who send most of their pay home or save it until they return. The only place in New Caledonia that benefits from the nickel mines is Nouméa, and Nouméa, of course, is an alien outpost.

Technically, New Caledonia is not a French colony. It has been since the 1950s an integral territory of the French Republic, and all its inhabitants are French citizens. The political life of the island is melo-dramatic but ineffectual, since though there are autonomist move-ments they are to all appearances irrevocably divided. The French to begin are divided between the metropolitan French, who oppose autonomy, and the colons, who would like it but only if they can keep power in their own hands. This in turn leads to divisions among the native Melanesians. Some of them believe that more autonomy can only play into the hands of the colons, and so they favour a continuation of the present subordination to Paris. But there is also an extreme native faction, known as the Foulards Rouges or Red Scarves, who would like to expel the whites entirely from the islands. The result is that there are five political parties, representing various shades of opinion, and in the last election an anti-autonomist coalition gained control of the assembly.

All this has played into the hands of the unrepentant French imperial-ists who actually administer the island, and whose attitude exemplifies the essential difference between the French and the British as colonial rulers. The British gathered their possessions for simple reasons of trade or strategy, without having a real ideology of imperialism; except in the most euphoric days, round about the Diamond Jubilee of 1897, there was no real thought that colonial peoples were being or could be turned into Britons. This pragmatic attitude served very well while the British Empire hung together, but once India was liberated the whole structure fell away, and imperial attitudes died with it.

The French, on the other hand, have been possessed – ever since the Revolution – with an ideological view of empire, a sense that since they have created the world's best culture, any man should regard it as a privilege to belong to it. This was the philosophy behind Napoleon's European empire, and we found it very much alive in both New Caledonia and the New Hebrides.

This was the explanation for many of the strange anomalies which we were to encounter in New Caledonia. For example, we found that nothing but French was taught in the schools; there is no attempt to use any of the thirty-six native dialects as a medium of instruction, and the result is that many children who have not learnt French in the family leave the school as illiterate as when they enter. And even though equal franchise has now been given to native New Caledonians, so that they vote in the elections beside colons and metropolitan French, the political control of the territory is kept firmly in French – which means metropolitan – hands. The nearest approach to a cabinet in New Caledonia is an advisory council, but ultimate power is vested in a governor appointed from Paris and always sent from France. All the key officials are French. So are almost all the police and the gendarmerie, and Bastille Day is a display in miniature of French military power, with stiffly marching troops and rumbling armoured vehicles. Since New Caledonia is politically a part of France, it is felt that general French policies and interests should have precedence–and this is of course an aspect of the attitude towards the un-French world which has justified the French atomic tests in the South Pacific. The pursuit of French glory at the expense of local interests proved disastrous in Algeria and Indo-China, but the Algerians and the Vietnamese were, after all, far more numerous than the native peoples of the French possessions in the Pacific, and so the situation, if it is similar in character to those in the colonies France so dramatically lost, is almost certainly different in its potentialities. It is unlikely that the French will leave New Caledonia until they are willing to go, and the likelihood of any such willingness emerging while the nickel lodes hold out is remote indeed.

3

The official face of France in New Caledonia was blander and more smiling than the official face of Britain in the Gilberts had been, but in practice no less impenetrable. Mike had made contact by correspondence with the Chef de Cabinet, who is the equivalent of the Colonial

Secretary in a British colony. His office was in the Old Commissariat, the former residence of the High Commissioner, an elegant single-storeyed wooden building in a shady garden where the noise of the city was completely muted. It was not, however, the Chef de Cabinet who received us, but his assistant, Captain Dufour. And with the most exemplary apologies Captain Dufour informed us that an urgent and totally unexpected meeting had robbed both him and the Chef de Cabinet of the pleasure and – he was sure – the great interest that they would have gained from talking to us. As he walked us along the corridor to the office of the Press Secretary, I could not resist reflecting that if French imperial aims are worse than those of the British, their political manners are a great deal better, for there is an art in making a snub sound like a compliment.

The Press Secretary was already involved with two other separate visitors, and he added us with a juggler's ease, talking to us in the intervals of his other business, and carrying it off with much charm and with a great deal of helpfulness in small matters. He was free with information and also misinformation, for we discovered that though all he said about the French side of New Caledonian life was correct, his statements about native life were highly inaccurate, since – we subsequently learned – he had rarely taken the trouble to leave Nouméa and visit a native village.

But, as in the Gilberts, the authorities made no attempt to impede us, even if they courteously evaded helping us, and fortunately through a New Zealand anthropologist working in Vancouver we had an introduction that opened the necessary channels of help. It was to Luc Chevalier, the Director of the Museum in Nouméa. He insisted on meeting us at eight in the morning, and as we drove along the Baie d'Orphélinat to our appointment the bugles were blowing and the signal flags were dipping and rising on the little flotilla of grey ships from the French Navy anchored beyond the thickly packed lines of yachts and launches that symbolized, as well as anything else we saw, the wealth of Nouméa.

Chevalier was waiting in the main hall of the museum, a tall blond man whose family links were with New Caledonia – or La Grande Terre as the colons often call it to distinguish it from the dependent islands. All around him were the characteristic artefacts of New Caledonia, remnants of a sculptural tradition already dead and even in its life surprisingly restricted in ways of expression, since it was used almost exclusively for the decoration of the men's houses which were also the sanctuaries of ancestors. Three kinds of carving were repeated, with conventions varying from tribe to tribe and village to village. There were the upright boards that stood on each side of the house entrance, carved in low relief with a rectangular portrait of the clan ancestor. There were the thresholds carved with human faces. And there were the tall wooden finials that surmounted the house, each presenting in highly stylized form the ancestor's profile.

We were confronting, in our first contact with a Melanesian people, an attitude radically different from anything we had met among the Polynesians or the Micronesians. Here was no recollection of an ancestral voyage from distant continents, no memory of some distant Matang populated by pale-skinned forebears. Only the land and the ancestor existed, growing together like plant and the soil. Chevalier took us out to the courtyard of the museum, where he had built a replica of the men's house, which the French call La Grande Case and the Melanesians the House of Memories. Basically the form was that of all traditional New Caledonian houses; a squat cylinder of wood and reeds daubed with mud and surmounted by a cone thatched – since New Caledonia has few coconut-palms – with thick layers of reeds. But in the Grande Case the ancestral carvings surrounded the doorway, the finial projected from the top of the conical roof, decorated with giant conch shells, and – representing the sexual polarities – taro grew on one side of the doorway and yam on the other. The god, the ancestor and the land were one. There was no mythical hint of a primordial voyage; men had been here as long as memory and myth recorded, and so the human link with the land was immediate in its sacredness.

When we came back from Luc Chevalier's replica of La Grande Case, a thin nervous young Frenchman was awaiting us: Jean-Pierre Doumenge, graduate student of the University of Bordeaux and son of the Oceanic geographer, François Doumenge, whose *L'Homme dans le Pacifique Sud* I found one of the essential texts for understanding human life in the South Seas. Jean-Pierre had made his speciality the social organization of the native peoples of New Caledonia. So far as our interests were concerned, he was the ideal adviser, since he combined an intense Gallic patriotism (he vehemently disputed our alien criticisms of French atomic tests in the South Pacific) with an uneasy feeling that French relationships with the lesser peoples of the empire were not all that the glory of his nation might require. Jean-Pierre agreed to help us, and Luc Chevalier immediately faded into the tasks of museum administration as we made our plans for a reconnaissance of the island.

The plan finally evolved was that we and Mike would go to the mines at Thio on the north side of the island. Then we would return over the mountains to a town named La Foa in the ranching country on the eastern side of the island. Jean-Pierre would meet us there, and with him we would travel on another mountain road into the district of Canala where the native villages were more thickly scattered than in other parts of New Caledonia.

4

It was a humid, misty morning when we drove from Nouméa. The roads were full of cars taking people to their work in the city (where the southern French custom of an early start to the day and a long siesta is observed) and the pavements were filled with children in smocks idling to school. We drove out westward past the great cemetery where gravestones of imported marble marched like white regiments across the hillsides. We passed the last suburban shops advertising fish and turtles, and suddenly we were in that strange frontier land which is rural New Caledonia.

It was almost startling, after the crowded coastlines of Samoa, and the evenly populated apis of Tonga, and the almost continuous villages of the Gilberts, to find ourselves in a land where, outside Nouméa (where half the people are congregated), the population is no more than eight per square mile. Settlement thinned out as soon as we left suburban Nouméa. The places that seemed large on the map turned out usually to be less than villages. There would be a church and a gendarmerie, a school and a petrol station, a modest hotel, a couple of poor cafés, and perhaps three shops. Houses were scattered at far intervals, on the edges of banana and pineapple plantations. There were thickets of castor-oil plants and mimosa along the roadsides, and occasional rusty and untended cast-iron crucifixes. The smells in the air were musky and green, and immense spiders hung spread-eagled on webs they had strung on the telegraph wires. The tall spires of century plants on the hillsides stirred memories of Mexico.

Soon we entered a savanna country of grassland dotted with a grey, olive-like tree called niaouli, a stunted and twisted kind of eucalyptus which springs up readily on burnt ground and in recent years has given a curiously African look to the dryer parts of New Caledonia. Beyond the densely islanded Bay of St. Vincent there were low hills, with small farms where Hereford cattle grazed. The ranges began to build up, fading away through veils of rain towards the central mountains. The roadside scrub changed to guava thickets where the fruit hung like golden Christmas baubles. The great ranches began, with hawks and buzzards hanging in the sky above them, and at Boulouparis, where we drank superb coffee and Alsatian beer in a hotel that doubled as a frontier store, we turned inland on a dirt road towards Thio.

It was a steadily ascending land of small ranches with rough corrals, of cattle and horses grazing around neat little Provençal houses with pergolas hung with grapes. The great leaves of taro grew wild beside the streams; soon the mountain jungle began, and quail-like birds called and ran among the lianas and wild ginger. Melanesians in thread-bare Western suits were slashing the roadside grass into Gallic neatness, and road-gangs of Frenchmen – les petits blancs – worked with spade and barrow as the highway narrowed into the mountains and we came to one-way stretches where traffic was regulated by the horaires – notice boards behind which one waited for the appropriate hour on which to proceed. It was the height of the range, where the clouds hung low, and the rain was intermittent, so that we drove often through fords where water cascaded down the mountainsides and across the road.

On these heights the mountain meadows were as brightly emerald as the June meadows above Zermatt, and the flowers had the brilliance of all high-altitude blossoms – gold coreopsis, deep red pea-vine, orange lantana, mauve sensitive plants, bright blue labiates, and great purple cups of convolvulus; the wild orange trees were heavy with jade-green fruit.

Descending towards Thio, the valley became broad and green, for this was the rainier side of the island, and above it the mountains were harlequin coloured where the green of natural slopes alternated with the orange-red of those that mining had stripped bare. Here there were floods, and once we edged cautiously along a submerged concrete bridge over a brimming river while below us a horseman forded the high current, the water near his knees and his three black hounds swimming behind him.

Thio was a company town of a kind familiar to anyone who knows the forest or mining areas of western North America. Nothing we saw could have been interpreted to suggest that La Société de Nickel were bad employers, though it was clear that they were rarely the employers of New Caledonians, for most of the people we saw in the neat little clusters of workers' prefabricated dwellings on the way to the town were Europeans, Vietnamese or Polynesians.

Down beside the beach was a nucleus of managers' houses and company stores, and a little restaurant where an excellent pâté de maison was followed at lunch by grilled fish caught that morning on the reef and an escalope de veau that did credit to the local ranches. The proprietor sat talking to us while his wife served the meal. He came from Ezes-sur-Mer, with which Inge and I had an old acquaintance through having lived in Menton, and he worked in the offices of the mine.

As he talked I felt uneasily, as I have often felt in recent years, the conflicts of loyalties to which the circumstances of the modern age impel us. For men from the islands, whose living at home was no better than what we had seen in Samoa or the Gilberts, here enjoyed under a capitalist corporation a material standard higher than that of most European workers. A man operating a machine up in the mines, the restaurateur assured us, would earn $600 a month. Yet he would also have a free house, generous state allowances for his children, free medical care and entertainment, and a store where goods were sold 20 per cent below city prices. There were workers who lived on their family allowances and saved their salaries untouched – for there is no income tax in New Caledonia.

The workers were contented. There were no strikes. The shareholders were happy with what they received. But the uneasy fact grated on the mind that the real people of New Caledonia had little share of this welfare, for there were very few of them among the 7,000 people whom La Société de Nickel employed, and the land that those native people once possessed was being ravaged in the process.

How the land was being ravaged we saw after we had been to the mine office down by the shore and the manager had delegated one of his foremen to take us in a Land-Rover halfway along the valley and then up the lacing roads of the mountainside through the forest of the lower slopes and the stunted snakewood scrub that grows on the red soil which holds the nickel. The mining at Thio, which has been going on for more than forty years, is strip mining, starting from the top of the rubbly mountains and slicing them down into great terraces that give the appearance of gigantic Mexican pyramids.

It was, unusually, a gloomy day, and the rain was falling on the mountaintop, turning the subsoil into a mire of tenacious red gumbo, while the cloud kept drifting over and creating a foggy twilight in which great machines moved and ground as if in some monstrous mechanical Walpurgis-night. We watched the blasters probing into the mountainside with long drills to loosen the rock, and the big grabs taking in five-ton bites the bright green-blue boulders of ore, which the miners give the same name – les cailloux – as they give the island. Great fifty-ton trucks took the excavated material to the crusher and sorter which rumbled and clanked away under its long shed, breaking down the ore, rejecting the useless material, and dropping the richer matter into other trucks which took it to the aerial railway on the mountain edge where the wires swung clear and took the buckets high over the valley and down to the long jetty which we could see far below us in the bay, where the ore was being dumped on to a moving belt that carried it to the dust-red ship that lay clear of the reef.

It was the kind of mining that had none of the underground terrors evoked by Zola and the other novelists of the industrial revolution. The men worked in incessant noise, and usually – the day of our visit was an exception – in stifling clouds of dust, but they ran little risk of the kind of disaster that imperils underground mining and – as they obviously knew well – their wages made them the labour aristocrats of the South Seas; even miners in New Zealand earned no more. It was the land that suffered most in paying for the good wages of the workers and the good dividends of the shareholders. It will obviously continue to pay until all the minerals are exhausted. The mountains are being shaved lower. A tenth of the natural vegetation of the island has been destroyed, including not only the snakewood brush but thousands of acres of primeval forest. Whole hillsides wash into the streams, and the rivers and lagoons are polluted. The eventual climatic result of these operations has not even been calculated, and there is no programme for conserving resources, no adequate plan for saving the environment. If present policies persist, La Société de Nickel and its possible rivals (for there is talk of Canadian nickel interests being allowed to operate) will continue to mine until the nickel is exhausted and then will abandon vast ruined areas of La Grande Terre to the slow recovery of geological time.

To reach La Foa we had to return over the mountain road to Boulou-paris, and – since it was late on a Friday afternoon – the road was filled with impetuous drivers hastening towards Nouméa for the weekend; twice we were forced off the road to avoid accidents. We stopped for coffee in Boulouparis, where bright-kerchiefed old Melanesian women greeted us as they came in from their gardens with hoes and scythes on their shoulders, and then we drove westward through winding lanes with high hedgerows and fields of wind-swept golden grass that gave the feeling of some lush temperate land rather than a tropical island.

The hotel where we stayed the night was outside the village of La Foa, a pretentious native-style hostelry that in a very French way combined extreme discomfort with an excellent kitchen. The proprietor was a colon of Flemish descent, a dour and brutal man before whom his dogs and cats cowered with terror, and he and his daughters contemp-tuously served us a splendid and abundant meal – Norman peasant soup, local fish baked with onions and herbs, and tripe à la mode de Caen, with a good Burgundy. The restaurant was a great airy place under a vast thatched roof like a Gilbertese maneaba, but we had to tramp over a marshy lawn to sleep in replicas of Melanesian huts. These were circular structures of adobe with thatched conical roofs and tiny windows. There were no fans, and no air-conditioning, for the good reason that the hotel was powered by its own generator which went off sharply and without warning at ten o'clock, leaving us with no lights. There were many mosquitoes, so that we had to sleep under the nets, but the windows were too small to create a flow of air, and the heat built up, while cicada-like insects whirred in the garden around us and we became oppressively conscious of the great cone of darkness in the roof of the hut, accentuated by the faint line of moonlight that seeped between wall and eaves. I dreamt that the cone turned into solid black rock and was descending upon us, and awoke shuddering as the cocks began to crow.

5

Early the next morning Jean-Pierre arrived with his shy young wife, a schoolteacher who looked like a member of the House of Windsor in miniature. We paid our hotel bill to one of the patron's snickering daughters and set off to La Foa. Again it looked large on the map but turned out to be no more than a crossroads, with a hotel, a bank, a café and three shops. The shops were also petrol stations, but at two of them the pumps were dry and there were neither the cigarettes nor the stick tobacco we needed for our visits to the tribal villages. In the third, where we found everything we needed, the proprietor was a man from Sète in the Languedoc, and, since Jean-Pierre came originally from Montpellier, a good half-hour was consumed with the gossip that breaks out when people from the same region of France meet abroad.

La Foa lay at the foot of the mountains, and we drove almost immediately into the narrow wooded valleys where the Melanesian reserves began. By the edge of a milky river women in faded missionary gowns were washing clothes on the rocks, and after we had crossed the shallow ford, the road ran through a large native village called Grand Couli. The old circular houses were no longer being made as dwellings, and the people were living in rectangular adobe huts whose roofs were thatched with sugar cane or covered with layers of flexible niaouli bark; a few of the most prosperous had substituted corrugated iron. Yet there was a traditional heart to the village, with a memorial house in its grove, one of the few left in modern New Caledonia.

'It is the village of a Grand Chef,' Jean-Pierre explained. 'There is his house,' he said, pointing out the only building of cement blocks in the village. 'It would be unwise to pay a visit. The old chief has just died, and there is a dispute over the title between his brother and his son.'

He explained that unlike most other Melanesians, the natives of New Caledonia had a complicated system of chieftainship. Each village had two chiefs; the political chief, who represented the village in its relations with the outside world; and another, less visible to strangers, whose role as land chief was the more revered because he was the closest descendant of the first settler of the region, the great ancestor, the primordial local Adam who was also the local deity. The relationship seemed very similar to that which had sprung up between secular and sacred kings in Tonga or between the ali'i and the tulefale in Samoa. But in addition to the village chiefs, each group of villages which shared a common dialect had a Grand Chef, elected by the village chiefs on the basis of his lineage but also of his ability. The lineages ran in the paternal line, which is curious in view of the beliefs which the New Caledonians had about the relationship between sex and childbirth. Impregnation was regarded as a kind of mystical function performed by the totem spirit of the woman's clan; it had nothing to do with the sexual act which – apart from his own pleasure – the man performed as a rite showing respect for his wife's totem.

We stopped at the memorial grove. 'We cannot approach the Grande Case without an invitation,' Jean-Pierre remarked. And though several men watched us as we got out and stood at the edge of the grove, none came forward to greet us. 'They are holding back, because there is no chief in whose name they can speak. But we need not enter. It is very simply explained.' And as he pointed out the features of the site, the symbolism of the fertility religion it served took visual form. A broad rectangular green where the grass was thick and well trimmed led up to the memorial house, identical in form and decorations with that which we had seen at the museum. On either side soared a line of tall column pines. These symbolized power, and even in villages where memorial houses no longer existed, the pines would still be planted near the house of a Grand Chef to establish his authority. On the outer side of each row of pines stretched a line of coconut-palms; these symbolized wisdom, which tempers power. Within the Grande Case, invisible to us in the darkness that lurked in its open door-way, were stored the totem figures of the village clans; outside the door, on the right side, a yam was planted, its vine trailing up a pole, and the left a taro; the yam represented the male principle and the taro the female principle. On the green before these growing symbols the dances of the tribe took place and gifts were presented to the Grand Chef, suzerain of the tribes south of the mountains.

We drove on up the roads of brown earth from Grand Couli into the mountains, threading the sides of deep valleys where many water-falls plunged from the high ridges. It seemed an empty country, yet once it must have been densely populated, for everywhere the lines of overgrown terraces climbed like great steps up the hillsides. We saw only two or three villages; one of them lay in a valley at the bottom of a deep precipice, so that we could look down on it almost from above, and observe in the patterning of thatched roofs how its very ground plan delineated its way of life. Around each small square of garden, belonging to a family, was spaced the formation of three buildings that constitutes a Melanesian household in New Caledonia: a cookhouse, a house for sleeping and a house for entertaining. These clusters of buildings in their turn were grouped according to clans, so that each of the three or four lineages lived separate from the rest, clustered around a bare earth space used for drying coffee. Here too, at the end of the village where the chief lived, towered the column pines and the tufted palms.

After threading many sharp curves in the hilly road we arrived eventually at an upland village called Le Crouen, where there were hot springs and a little wooden hotel built in a splendid verdurous bowl among the mountains. It was kept by an old Norman couple who had once owned a restaurant in Paris, and had decided to end their days in a quiet place among natural beauty. They had brought enough of France with them to create in that distant place a nostalgic island of Gallic culture. There were pieces of fine old Norman peasant furniture, and much pewter and old china, among which I was intrigued to discover a set of plates decorated with political caricatures dating from shortly after 1848, for they satirized the socialists and anarchists of that era: Louis Blanc with his national workshops, Proudhon with his people's bank, and Etienne Cabet with the misfortunes of Icaria.

Jean-Pierre proposed to take us from Le Crouen on a visit to the chief of the hill-village of Ema, and afterwards into the broad valley that opens towards the sea at Canala so that we could visit the Grand Chef of the tribes to the north of the mountains.

The way up to Ema, rising out of the valley on to wooded mountainsides, was a steep single track whose red earth had been mashed by recent rains into a slimy mud. It was difficult to ascend, even for Mike, who was a remarkably resourceful driver, but it was a route of extraordinary interest, since the damp mountainsides generated a lush vegetation, and the verges were brilliant with blue plumbago and with dense clumps of wild impatiens in a remarkable variety of colours, carmine and coral red, pink and white. At first it seemed as though these flowers were growing in the shade of a dense jungle, but soon we realized that this was the native form of plantation. There were orange and lemon trees heavy with green and golden fruit, grapefruits and bananas, bread-fruit and jack-fruit, pepper vines climbing up dead trees, coffee bushes under a dense shadow of rain trees and flamboyants, taro growing wherever there were damp depressions, tapioca with its palmate leaves, yam vines clambering like beans up bamboo poles, and bamboo itself, growing in dense and gracefully drooping clumps, the first we had seen anywhere in the South Seas. Unlike the valley villages, those in the New Caledonian hills are scattered through their upland woods and plantations, and every now and again along the steep road the trees would open out to give room for a house before which the coffee berries lay drying and blackening on the ground.

After the Gilberts such Amazonian lushness seemed extraordinary, and it was evident that, even though they had lost much of their lands, these people did not live on the same level of precarious subsistence as the inhabitants of the coral islands. In this village, Jean-Pierre told us, they had a surplus of everything, and could sell as many oranges as they wished through a co-operative that had been established to deal with native crops. The previous year, from this village alone, 200 tons of oranges were sold, and that was only a fraction of the whole crop; in the end the people grew tired of picking and allowed the rest of the fruit to fall and rot.

Eventually the road became too steep and slippery even for Mike to continue. We parked the car and walked; a hundred yards on we came to a panel wagon, its wheels wreathed in chains, which are regularly used on the slimy surfaces into which all roads break down in the New Caledonian highlands. There a tribesman of villainously ugly appearance, with a great flat nose, a low corrugated brow bound with a red bandana, and a ragged windbreaker covered with European cycling club badges, attached himself to us. He spoke an extraordinary pidgin French, and seemed mildly imbecilic. Jean-Pierre and his wife hurried on ahead, and the tribesman, babbling incessantly and without any apparent care whether we understood, took me and Inge by the hand, and led us up the mountain on a series of steep short-cuts that were as slippery as runs of ice. 'My land,' he kept shouting. And then, 'My cousin's land!' Finally he took us scrambling up a last slope to a clearing where native carpenters were putting up the wooden frames for two houses, one already roofed with corrugated iron; clearly they belonged to some prosperous member of the tribe. 'My houses!' shouted our guide, strutting out into the open space between the frames, but two women who were there began to laugh scornfully, and our doubts of his pretensions strengthened into certainty. Later we found he was one of the poorest men of the village, principally noted as the tribal alcoholic.

By now it was already obvious that he was no use as a guide, and while he was preoccupied with his squabble with the women, which developed into an angry shouting contest, one of the carpenters pointed out a path that led along an abandoned taro terrace; we followed it to find the chief's house built on a high open bank from which one could see clearly the valley and the valley roads.

The chief himself was standing with Jean-Pierre under the bell that hung from a kind of gallows outside the village church. His broad sly face was covered with a grey stubble; he wore long trousers and a bright blue Hawaiian shirt, typical garb among the Melanesians in New Caledonia, who have completely abandoned native dress. But native customs survived and as soon as we appeared Jean-Pierre, who had been chatting idly with the chief, drew himself up, made the customary ceremonial speech – he was presenting according to the traditions of the chief and his people a gift that should be regarded as a token of our respect – and handed him the customary present of two packets of Gauloises and two sticks of tobacco done up in a screw of newspaper. The chief sent into his house one of the children who were watching us, and proceeded to his own speech of welcome, which he contrived so adeptly that it drew to an end just as the boy appeared with a cardboard Heineken's beer case filled with green bananas that were his present to us.

He took us into the little church, of which he was proud, having built it himself. There was a crudely carved wooden Christ, rather like one of the distorted crucifixions of Mexico, above a simple table of an altar, but no other furniture at all; the floor was covered with a layer of reeds on which the people evidently kneeled and sat, and prayer books were scattered untidily over them. He was the political chief; the land chief who was his uncle dealt with the difficult internal problems of adjudicating land distribution; no individual ever owned the land, which was the property of the clan, but a man was allotted a patch of land and to all intents and purposes possessed it until he became incapable of working it, when it returned to the clan and was reallocated. He was not only political chief within the tribe; he also served as one of the maires adjoints for the district of Canala, whose mayor is also a Melanesian; the French have set up a system of local government, with prefects and mayors, which is identical with the system operating in metropolitan France, and, in order that this may not appear too open a challenge to the native system of tribal government, they try to incorporate local chiefs into it wherever the population contains a high proportion of Melanesians.

Later in the afternoon we drove down from Le Crouen to the valley of Canala to see the Grand Chef who rules, so far as custom rule still exists, over twenty villages of the area. From the hills we could see the broad shining inlet to which the valley led, and then we descended into green parklands dotted with immense trees that had great buttress roots. The rivers were in flood, turning the roads for long distances into shallow lakes, and once we saw a man poling a raft of bamboo through a submerged taro patch where the great leaves were standing above the water.

The Grand Chef's house was marked by the customary column pines, but it was not in itself impressive. It consisted of an adobe house in the western style, with a corrugated iron roof, which served for sleeping and entertainment, and behind it a long thatched building that served as kitchen. There was a rough lawn, and some African marigolds bloomed in front of the living house. Sacks of produce were piled beside the door, and a little metal plate announced a public telephone; every chief is given a telephone by the state and by now its presence has become one of the symbols of office.

A young man went in to announce our arrival, and shortly afterwards the Grand Chef came out to receive us, a tall man with cropped grey hair and an intellectual cast to his pale handsome face. He led us into his room. The walls were of unwhitened adobe; on one of them hung a large clock advertising St. Raphael aperitif, on another figures of Christ and the Virgin. The furniture was cheap and worn; some bentwood chairs and two old round tables, on one of which there were several piles of books. Later the chief told me that he spent much of his time reading, and when I asked him the kind of books he liked, he mentioned Victor Hugo and De Gaulle.

Jean-Pierre made his presentation of cigarettes and tobacco, a double share for a Grand Chef, and then we began to talk, the chief speaking hesitantly in a pure and deliberate French. As we talked the evening darkened, but no lamp was lit; a child crept in and sat under one of the tables watching us, his face growing dimmer and finally invisible. The darkness seemed to give the chief more confidence. He began cautiously, as if he were suspicious of us as strangers. He talked of the land question. He believed that for the present the native people had enough land; the problem now was marketing what they grew on the land they had. He was really more concerned with the way in which Nouméa had acted as a magnet for many of the younger people, who went there expecting to earn much money, but found the pattern of work was not to their taste, and lapsed into idleness in the slums. But he believed the fascination of the city was growing dim. He detected among young people a desire to repossess their inheritance; it was important now to provide employment in the country areas so that they could earn what money they needed near at hand. After all, a man with a few acres of coffee and a patch for yams and taro and some orange trees did not need much cash to get along. As long as he had the chance to be employed two or three months a year, that was enough. The chief reiterated that his people were attached to their land, and they would sooner live – if they could – where their ancestors had done than earn big money in the mines or the city.

It was only when the room was completely dark that he began to talk of what was perhaps nearest his heart. If his people were to survive as a people, he said, they must keep their traditional tribal organization, which enabled them to regulate properly the use of their land according to the rights of clans and lineages. This meant that the authority of the chiefs should not be undermined. But now that the French had introduced their municipal system, he had to share his power with the maire of Canala, who was a man of his own tribe, a man not even of a chiefly clan, a Protestant convert of the Mission de Paris while he – the Grand Chef – was a devout Catholic, and an autonomist while the Grand Chef has remained loyal to the memory of that grandest of all Grand Chefs, De Gaulle. One began to suspect that the French were adroitly neutralizing the awakening political consciousness of the native Melanesians by using the traditional imperial method of dividing and ruling. There was a tired note of complaint in the Grand Chef's voice by the time we left; it was evident that he was suffering from the disillusioning realization that neither the column pine nor the public telephone was any longer a convincing symbol of power as both once had been.

6

The mountain night at Le Crouen was cool after the sea-level nights of the smaller islands. We slept well and awoke to a dewy morning, with electric-blue butterflies dancing under the palm-trees outside the hotel. We drove back through the mountains and the soft-shouldered green foothills to La Foa. It was Sunday, and the ranchers were crowding in to the little single-storeyed hotel which, with its veranda and its swing-doors, deliberately evoked the legendary cowboy west of another land. The restaurant was packed – for the Sunday lunch at La Foa is celebrated among New Caledonians – and we were already too late to do more than contemplate wistfully a menu that began with oysters and continued through crabs, mussels and coq au vin to steak and dessert and the inevitable platter of French cheeses at the proper ripeness which one astonishingly encounters in every New Caledonian meal. We had to be content with sitting in the bar and eating sandwiches of Brie and succulent jambon de Paris (flown in on the same Paris–Tahiti planes that bring in the cheeses and the snails) while a crowd of stockmen in grey shirts and wide-brimmed Stetsons came in to drink – black-faced cowboys primed to a state of rare bonhomie who insisted on shaking our hands and exchanging rounds of beer.

Jean-Pierre was by now feeling unwell – we had dined overlavishly at Le Crouen after our return from the Grand Chef of Canala the previous evening – and he and his wife wanted to return immediately to Nouméa. We and Mike decided to go farther up island so that we could see something of the ranching country and drove west along the main road until we reached Moindou. This was an even more rudimentary centre of population than any other of the settlements though it looked as large on the map. On the main road a single store, a rough-looking hotel with saddled horses tied to the posts of the veranda, a row of decaying cottages inhabited by depressed-looking petits blancs, as near as life has ever come to my mind's eye picture of the poor-white crossroad centres of Tennessee; up a dirt road on the hill a gaunt church with the paint peeling off its walls, and a new mairie, and a large gendarmerie sheltered in a grove of high trees. Moindou made another fragment of the historical mosaic of New Caledonia; it was founded in the 1870s by French-speaking Alsatians who fled from their province rather than accept German rule after the Franco-Prussian War.

The real population of Moindou was not in this pathetic roadside hamlet, but in the ranch-houses set on the tops of hillocks which we saw when we took a dirt road out of the village that we thought would lead down to the sea. Instead it took us wandering westward, first through a savanna country where bamboos like green fountains and the gaunt white skeletons of tall dead trees stood high among the lush grass. Afterwards the land changed to a mixture of rough grass and thorny scrub. On a low hilltop we sat by the roadside eating the bananas the chief of Ema had given us and looking over the pastures at the ranches. Surrounded on all sides by deep verandas, the houses had the classic proportions of old Australian station houses, doubtless because the Australians were the pioneers in New Caledonian cattle raising. Great butterflies with black-bordered red wings fluttered over as we sat, and buzzards hovered high.

A little farther on the country became dryer, with outcrops of sand which hinted at the desert we were told existed farther west, and here we met a rancher herding his cattle beside the road. He was a sharp-faced, white-haired old man, with stiff leather leggings reaching above his knees, a blanket roll on the front of his saddle, a knife in a leather scabbard on his belt, a long black whip in his hand with which he expertly drove his stock, and a black dog at his heel. He posed good-humouredly for a photograph and then stopped for a chat and a cigarette while his dog kept cannily circling the cattle to prevent them from breaking away into the niaouli scrub on the hillside above us.

He was a colon, the old man told us. Nobody around Moindou was descended from les forçats – the convicts – he remarked, with a touch of pride. His grandfather had come here just a hundred years ago, after the Germans had burnt his farm near Strasbourg. Yes, they had been proud to be French then, and he still was. But that didn't mean he agreed with everything they did in Paris. It was time les colons had more say in running La Grande Terre. After all, they and their fathers had made it, and their sons would still be there when La Société de Nickel had made the fortune of its shareholders and departed. It did not seem to dawn on him – as it probably never dawned until too late on the colons of Algeria – that the native people might believe they had a claim to the land that was theirs even before the convicts and the ranchers came.

Ranching? Yes, he made a living from it, but on the other side of the island cattle did better. Here the land was too dry, and the bush was full of ticks. 'A gift from America!' he added with a laugh. 'The G.I.s brought them in on their mules! Ticks and Coca Cola!' He whistled his dog, flicked that long snake of a whip, and rode off driving his knot of cattle.

7

Like most other places on the edge of civilization that live in the precarious noontide of primary industry which cannot last for ever, Nouméa was a town of extraordinary contrasts. Dumbéa, both the smelter and the crowded and decrepit slum streets around it, would have reminded one of the Black Country at its worst if everything on that side of Nouméa had not been covered with a layer of brown dust that floated down from the polluting chimneys. On the eastern side of the city, however, where the winds blew no pollution and the hotels stood – and the South Pacific Commission, and the High Commissioner's residence, and the villas of nickel men and speculators, all in their splendid and umbrageous gardens – there was a flavour of the most prosperous French coastal resorts, with the difference that this face of Nouméa looked even more brilliant because its buildings were new. Within the city, indeed, the Third Republic still dominated architecturally, with its ornate villas and romantic statuary, but many modern buildings were already rising, and from the hill above the cathedral it was these that attracted one's eye questing over the city.

Since the early 1950s the French authorities have deliberately attracted metropolitan French to New Caledonia so as to create parity between the European and native populations. Largely by immigration, the European population has doubled since 1958, while the native population has increased by less than 50 per cent during the same period. One of the main attractions offered to immigrants from France is exemption from income tax. At the same time French firms have been encouraged to invest freely, and the result has been to create a free-spending boom atmosphere. Prices are inflated, but the untaxed French seem to gain in balance, though as travellers we found the city very expensive, and contented ourselves with merely looking at the shops which – unlike those in any other South Sea town – were positively Parisian in the range of expensive goods they offered.

We were glad in fact of the little cheap restaurants which the Vietnamese and the Corsicans ran in the area of bars and eating houses near the museum known as the Quartier Latin. After dinner we would go on to the only café, the St. Hubert, which in its very self-conscious imitation of a Parisian café of La Grande Epoque proclaimed its foreignness to New Caledonian traditions of privacy and exclusiveness. There we would meet the few people, all metropolitan French, with whom we had formed more than a fleeting acquaintance. School teachers, a newspaper reporter, graduate students, a young man who worked in a financial house, they looked at New Caledonian life from the outside, as transients who were in Nouméa to make money or to gain knowledge or experience, yet between them they probably had a wider sense of the realities of New Caledonian life than most of the colons. The financier would describe the artificial 'gold rush' standard of

values that had arisen because of the inflow of loose capital. The price
of land in the centre of the city had reached that of the Champs
Elysées; it was an entirely artificial valuation, because city regulations
forbade buildings more than four storeys high, so that the land costs
could never be recouped by rent. At this level speculators made great
fortunes. At the other level one of the graduate students described the
Melanesian workers who drifted in and out of Nouméa, working as
we had seen them on the docks in gangs that did three-week stints at
about £25 a week. Such men rarely settled in the city; they would
work for a period to earn the cash they needed for a year back in the
village, and because there was no kind of living quarters for transients
they would live with relatives or fellow villagers, so that often ten of
them slept in a single room.

The impression one gained from these conversations was curiously
at odds with the sunlit secure face which the city so often assumed;
it was the impression of a camp rather than a city, in which everyone,
from the officials who came from France down to the workers who
wandered in from the villages, was there to gain his share of a wealth
that would run out as certainly as the wealth ran out of the goldfields,
and leave Nouméa a ghost town commemorating the last era of French
imperialism.

PART FIVE
Three Fellow Government

1

To go from New Caledonia to the New Hebrides is to step from the bogus high drama of a society based on a boom economy to the high musical comedy of one of the strangest political situations in the modern world. For the New Hebrides is the joint responsibility of Britain and France, and its administration is so curiously complexioned that it consists not of one government but an uneasy symbiosis of three. The French and the British maintain equal and distinct presences, but direct certain matters of common interest through a third authority, the notorious Condominium. How rights and responsibilities are divided between these three governing entities is often a mystery even to people who live in the New Hebrides, and for the visitor they are frequently a matter of perplexity and sometimes of embarrassment.

The flavour of comedy appeared even before we had set foot on the soil of Efate, the island from which the benefits of tripartite government radiate to the wildernesses of Santo and Malekula and Tanna. 'In ten minutes,' declared the French hostess, 'we shall be landing at 28,000 feet.' And indeed it seemed that we had arrived at something approaching cloud-cuckoo-land when we had circled over the bay of Vila, with its inhabited islands clustering like stars within a crescent, and descended over the familiar regimented palm-groves to the airstrip. For on entering the airport building we were faced not with one but with two immigration desks. One was for French subjects and was administered by a trio of kepi-crowned gendarmes; the other, at which we were processed, was for Commonwealth subjects, and a New Hebridean sergeant in khaki with a bastard glengarry bonnet on his head stamped our passports under the supervision of a dyspeptically melancholy British officer. People of other nationalities were free to gamble on either desk. But if immigration was divided, customs was united, being administered by a genial and incurious Frenchman on behalf of the third government, the Condominium.

We drove along gravel roads through the palm-groves into Vila, the capital, an ugly town in which raw newness mingled with monsoon-beaten decrepitude along the main street that paralleled the sea-front. The name it bore, Rue Higginson, commemorated no great explorer or even a politician, but a British subject turned French who became the most notorious land-shark of the South Seas, and that fact added another appropriate fragment to the crazy mosaic of New Hebridean life. Shabby, crowded Chinese shops clustered around the rival Australian and French department stores, and in the midst stood a ludicrous assemblage of cubes, pillars and purposeless roofs that appeared to have been designed by some malaria-crazed disciple of Le Corbusier; it was the headquarters of the Condominium.

We looked at and rejected the dirty, noisy rooms of the hotel in the centre of Vila, and then drove out three miles along a dirt road that twisted through a ragged suburbia of villas and crossroad stores. At the end of the three miles was a resort hotel run by Australians and called Le Lagon; it lay on an attractive bay, and had been built, like so many similar places in the South Seas, to look like a stage set of a native village, all thatched huts which turned out to have concrete cubes enclosed within their palm-leaf integuments that were neither cool nor comfortable nor quaint. But they were quiet and clean, and we worked out a liveable pattern while we remained in Vila, using Le Lagon for sleeping and writing, and spending most of the day in the town and a great deal of it at Rossi's, the restaurant and café kept by a Corsican clan of tall sons dominated by a formidable matriarch, which is the centre of social life in Vila.

At some time of the day, either at the long bar in Rossi's or on the breezy terrace that projects like an apron into the harbour, or in the restaurant itself, one would see almost everyone of interest who was about in Vila. The food was without exception the best we found in the South Seas – better even than anything we had in New Caledonia. The fish and the crustaceans were so good and so varied that we rarely needed meat, though the veal raised in the palm-groves was excellent; the snails were tender, the salads perfectly seasoned, the crèpes served at just the right intermediate stage between crispness and succulence, the wine cheap and good, and the Calvados and Armagnac superb.

Having arranged this pattern of living to our satisfaction, we proceeded to Burns Philp, the leading merchants in Vila, whose connections in the islands make them an excellent substitute for a travel agency. The man in charge of such matters reflected the curious anomalies one constantly encounters in the New Hebrides; his name was André Lanson, but he looked surprisingly blank when I began to speak to him in French, and it turned out that he was in fact an Australian with no knowledge of the French language who had been sent to Vila merely because it was thought his name would fit into the condominial setting. But he was efficient and knowledgeable, arranged flights on the local airlines to take us on a circular trip of the principal islands – Espiritu Santo, Malekula, Tanna and back to Efate – and advised us on the accommodation we would find. On Espiritu Santo there was a hotel called the Corsica – we would see what it was like when we got there, he added ominously. On Malekula we would have to stay in the rest-house attached to the British agency. And on Tanna there was a famous trader, Bob Paul, who had built some cabins for visitors to the island's volcano. Lanson promised to radio them all, on our behalf, which he did with excellent eventual results.

2

Having dealt with these immediate questions of how to enjoy what Vila offered and how to visit the outer islands, we were free to explore the oddities of New Hebridean government, which in Vila assume a curious geographical manifestation. The French Resident Commissioner lives on a hill above Vila, and each morning he drives down in his tricoloured car to the French Residency. The British Commissioner lives on an island in the harbour, and each morning he boards a launch flying his ensign which takes him over to the British Residency. Already, shortly after dawn, the bugles have sounded outside each residency as the Union Jack and Tricolour have risen simultaneously on their respective flagstaffs. Both the French and British headquarters stand above the city, roughly at the same level; symbolically, the offices of the Condominium are placed below them, in the heart of downtown Vila. The same emphasis on the symbolism of power affects every aspect of overt political life in the New Hebrides. In the smaller centres, like Santo, where joint rule prevails, there is a flagstaff with double halyards and pulleys, so that both flags may fly, and when there is a ceremony at which both Commissioners appear, they ascend the steps together with measured steps and, as in some stately ballet, turn so that they face the audience simultaneously.

This strange and – I believe – unique political situation arose from the peculiar history of European imperial penetration into the South Pacific. The New Hebrides, like New Caledonia, are inhabited by Melanesians. A few, in the high bush of islands like Santo and Malekula, live in a traditional way that has been little affected by the impact of the modern world. They enjoy this relative immunity only so long as they remain in the almost inaccessible hill country. The fate of the coastal tribes has been quite different. In the mid Victorian age the New Hebrides more than any other group of islands in the South Seas became a no-man's-land where whalers, sandalwood traders and blackbirders plundered at will. The sandalwood traders stole the property of the islanders, who felt with an emotional intensity any diminution by unnecessary tree-felling of the land they used and revered. The blackbirders kidnapped the islanders themselves and took them to work as virtual serfs in the sugar plantations of Queensland. The New Hebrideans reacted violently. They killed some of the blackbirders, and they also killed some of the Presbyterian missionaries who arrived under the leadership of the celebrated John G. Paton; they ate them as well until the local epicures decided – as old men in these regions still tell one – that white men's flesh is at once too insipid and too salty. Despite the violence going on in the New Hebrides, between white man and natives and – after trade muskets appeared in large quantities – between natives and natives, the tensions in the South Pacific were such that neither France nor Britain at first wanted to take action in the New Hebrides, though the land speculators were already at work. It was only when Germany appeared in the South Seas, and made its intentions evident by annexing New Guinea in 1882 and sending its traders into the Micronesian archipelagos, that the other two powers decided to intervene. In 1886 they set up the Joint Naval Commission to keep order in the New Hebrides. In 1906 they created the Condominium.

In pidgin the Condominium is called Two Pella Gubment. In reality, as I have suggested, it is Three Fellow Government. The British and French administrations are equal and separate. They maintain their own police forces and courts. British residents can only be arrested by their own police and tried in their own courts, and the same applies to the French, but foreigners – which usually means Americans – and native New Hebrideans are fair game for either. A limited number of matters of common concern, such as the customs and postal services and transport, are handled by the Condominium, and the Condominium is also responsible for the Joint Court which assesses land-claims by both foreigners and natives; in typical New Hebridean style, the impartiality of the Joint Court was guaranteed originally by the appointment to the Presidency of a deaf Spaniard who spoke neither French nor English, but for a number of years the French and British judges have managed without a president. Vast areas of administration went undefined, and thus such departments as education, health and welfare were left for the French and British administrations to carry on as they saw fit. Until very recently the power of discretion allowed in these areas was interpreted to justify neglect, and until well after World War II such matters were left to the missionaries if they saw fit to pursue them. The two governments were much more concerned with protecting the interests of their various subjects who were trading and planting in the archipelago.

In recent years however, conscious of the extent to which the United Nations has evolved into a noisy forum of world public opinion, the two governments have begun to compete for the best welfare show window. French and British hospitals and clinics, British and French schools, have sprung up on all the islands, and there again with rather sadly comic results, for if the French build a clinic, the British are likely to establish a better one in the next village rather than in a more isolated village where it is really needed, and vice versa. The competition over education is even more serious in its consequences, since it acts as a divisive factor among the native people. Some children learn French in their schools; others learn English. And since New Hebrideans have no common tongue, and several different languages on each island, this means that even educated men and women often have no means of communication better than pidgin, which is an efficient lingua franca for trading – for which it was originally used by Chinese merchants – but limited as soon as one attempts to use it for transmission of even the most elementary abstract concept.

So far as we were concerned, the situation had its notable advantages. The very fact that two classic empires were in competition – even though they were competing under the shadow of the imperial *Götterdämmerung* – had made them send to the New Hebrides some of their best remaining colonial officers, so that the whole tone of the British service there was incomparably higher than in the Gilberts. Moreover, both sides were anxious to appear at their best in the eyes of inquiring visitors, and thus we encountered no obstruction of any kind, and from the British service a great deal of assistance even when we set out to establish contact with the native dissidents of the Jon Frum and the Nagriamel movements and – on a more sophisticated level – the members of the New Hebridean National Party.

We established our first and probably our most important relationship when we went to the white wooden building of the British Residency which overlooks the harbour. Keith Woodward, the senior officer who took us under his aegis from that moment until we left the islands, had been in the New Hebrides for nineteen years, longer than anyone else in either of the administrations. He appeared to one as a rather Miltonic figure. He was a man of lambent mind and wide intellectual interests, who had spent his early years in the group wandering from island to island, who had read everything that had been published in English, French, German or Spanish on the South Seas, and he could talk of the region with a greater store of information and a greater power of synthesizing it than I encountered in any other local resident. But he was now afflicted not only with a progressive and incurable deficiency of eyesight, so that he could not recognize one at two yards and had to write with his face nine inches from the paper, and was also retreating towards the silence of deafness, so that I had to pitch my rather low voice sharply for him to hear everything I said. Yet he was reputed to continue his work with undiminished application, coming to the office each morning before dawn so that he could get through as much work as before in spite of his purblindness, and spending his spare time on the task of trying to establish a New Hebridean museum when it was almost too late, since most of the good local artefacts had already found their way into the collections of Europe and North America. Certainly, he took our aims very seriously, and not only arranged our meetings with the British Resident Commissioner and with the French Commissioner's principal assistant, but also called together a group of local people with whom we could meet that first evening to acquire some educated non-official views of the New Hebridean situation.

Monsieur Fabre, the French Commissioner's assistant, was a Gallic counterpart of Keith Woodward, knowledgeable about the South Seas, rather inclined in the Malraux manner to stress the art historical view of primitive cultures, and acutely sensitive, as we found every administrator of either nationality to be, regarding the land question.

He began, it is true, by explaining the rather rudimentary attempts that have been made to introduce self-government into the New Hebrides. An Advisory Council, part elected and part appointed, exists, but it has no legislative or executive powers. Local councils are now being set up on some of the islands, but Monsieur Fabre was doubtful of their effectiveness; later we found that the French had in fact impeded the establishment of such councils, which was a British idea, because they would have preferred a municipal system like that in New Caledonia, with mayors responsible to the government rather than to the people. But any mention of local government led to native movements, and any mention of native movements led inevitably to the land question. For though M. Fabre dismissed Jon Frum as a declining cargo cult, and described Nagriamel as a reactionary return to tradition and custom, and showed a qualified approval of the New Hebridean National Party as a movement for constitutional change within the existing political situation, he had to admit that all these movements had in common was their expression in various forms of the discontent among New Hebrideans with the way in which their land had been taken away from them.

The British Resident Commissioner, C. H. Allan, a grey-haired intellectual with a New Statesmanly look who had formerly been an anthropologist, was uninclined even to talk of the political movements – he seemed to feel it in some sense incompatible with his office to do so though he did not object to frankness among his subordinates – but he too identified the land question as central to the existing discontents among the New Hebrideans: 'The Melanesian feels the land in his guts,' he said. 'Every tree and every plant has its special significance for him, so that he never thinks of the bush as useless land, even if it is uncultivated or ungrazed, since it still has many things to give him, and above all his sense of identity.'

The problem with which both Allan and Fabre were so concerned went back to the days before the joint Anglo-French intervention in 1886. Settlers began to arrive in the 1860s, and they secured title to as much land for as little money as they could. John Higginson, the Englishman turned French subject after whom the main street of Vila is named, was responsible for the worst land grabs. He would moor off an island, estimate by eye the area between certain landmarks, and assemble a group of illiterate New Hebrideans to put their marks on a deed in exchange for a few trade goods. Some of the deeds make strange and appalling reading. One that I read recorded the selling of

10,000 acres of land on Malekula for a pile of goods consisting of 25 Schneider muskets, 2 rifles, 200 cartridges, 6 pounds of gunpowder, 60 pounds of stick tobacco, a gross of matches, a dozen clay pipes and three boxes of assorted trinkets! The total value of this assemblage of trade goods in 1880 when the deed was made was 690 francs, which at the going rate of exchange was worth about £35, or a little over three farthings an acre! Such sales were registered in Nouméa or Suva, and were then recognized under French or British jurisdiction, though in fact they were contrary to Melanesian custom, which regards land as belonging inalienably to a lineage going back to the original land-holding ancestor, usually regarded as a semi-supernatural being; land can be loaned, according to local custom, but it can never be alienated from the people with whom it is almost mystically connected. The original European speculators did not understand this situation, and probably would not have cared if they had. The scandalous aspect of the situation, which now embarrasses both governments, is that the Joint Court, established to end injustices in landholding, has mainly concerned itself with legalities of form and registration, and has never attempted to interpret a case according to immemorial local custom or on grounds of equity, so that as recently as ten years ago the manifest injustice of the land sale on Malekula which I have described was condoned by the Joint Court when it confirmed Higginson's successors, La Société Française des Nouvelles Hébrides (a subsidiary of the Bank of Indo-China) in their possession of it.

By means such as this, 34 per cent of the total land-area of the New Hebrides was acquired and has been retained by Europeans, mostly Frenchmen. But even these figures give no idea of the true situation. Much of the New Hebrides is barren volcanic mountainside, useless to anyone. It is the coastal lowlands, on which coconuts grow and cattle will graze, that are profitable, and it is such land that the French planters own. Of the coastline of Malekula, 80 per cent is owned by foreigners, and 90 per cent of that by the French.

Both Allan and Fabre agreed that the situation had been aggravated by the tendency of the land claims of the planters to act like time-bombs. In some cases claims to coastal land first registered in the 1880s lay dormant, with a whole generation of New Hebrideans remaining untouched on their ancestral land, until in the 1920s, when the world demand for copra was great, copra plantations were staked out. Thus native villagers who had no memory of the original deeds suddenly found that according to the laws of the Condominium they were squatters on their own ancestral lands.

Even the coconut plantations, though they caused an immense disruption of native farming patterns, were not the worst. To make a large coconut plantation needs a great deal of capital, labour and patience, and usually the planters took over only a fraction of the great areas that had been acquired for a few miserable trade goods by men like Higginson in the 1880s and earlier. But they never relinquished their rights to the whole areas covered by their deeds, and in the 1960s a new element was introduced by the arrival of Hereford cattle in the New Hebrides. At first these were introduced as an efficient and economical means of keeping the plantations well weeded. Then, when it was obvious that profits as well as savings could be made through beef cattle, the planters looked at their maps and their deeds, and decided to fence off the bush to which the natives had retreated after being expelled from the areas now under coconuts. The natives had the alternative of moving farther back into the bush or of resisting. Some of them chose the path of resistance, and out of this choice had arisen several native movements, the most important of them Jon Frum on Tanna and Nagriamel on Santo. In addition, on other islands like Malekula and Pentecost and Ambrim, there were local examples of resistance, and even the New Hebridean National Party had been forced by the acuteness of the problem to make land reform one of its leading planks.

One sensed – it was never stated explicitly – that the land question had even become a major point of difference between the British and the French. It was true that the two governments acted together with great decisiveness when American speculators set out to complicate issues by starting an ambitious land development at Hog Harbour on the north of Espiritu Santo. But while the French seemed resolved to dig themselves in, boasting of a few token restitutions of land into which they have pressured their planters but doing nothing fundamental to disperse the large landholdings controlled by the Bank of Indo-China and similar powerful corporations, the British were inclined to seek merit in the eyes of the natives and in those of the Asian and African members of the Commonwealth by showing a willingness to make concessions on the land question. This, as we found later, promoted divisions within the British community, since British and Australian planters felt that they were not getting the same kind of

support from their representatives in the Joint Court as the French
planters were getting. Ironically, some of the most ardent supporters
of the French stubbornness in remaining in the New Hebrides are men
who speak no French.

So far as our own plans were concerned, it was evident that we could
expect a great deal of co-operation from British local representatives
who would not be in the least unhappy with anything we said about
the land situation and that the French, for fear of appearing worse than
the British, could be relied on not to hinder us. This impression was
confirmed when we went later that evening to our rendezvous with
Keith Woodward in the little museum which he was fostering in the
Vila Cultural Centre.

As we wandered from case to case and from carving to carving along
the walls, I watched the sensitive play of Keith's fingers, and realized
that these things which he had known and come to love visually were
now perceived largely by a combination of touch and memory. Yet
the patterns of the mind went on integrating recollection and narrowing perception, and from case to case he would describe the stuffed
birds that stood fading on their perches, and the artifacts that charted
already imperilled cultures. Occasionally a touch of bitterness would
enter into his voice, as he talked of the anthropologists who combined
their roles with those of collectors for museums and thus made sure
that no one again would see native life as it had been revealed to them.
But mostly it was a sense of the fascination of this flamboyant culture
that his words aroused, a culture whose complexity was exemplified
in the great grotesque carvings of treefern, some of them 10 feet high,
whose function he so carefully explained.

On many of the islands there are graded secret societies, primitive
freemasonries, through which men rise by the acquisition of spiritual
understanding and of material wealth, which in the Melanesian view
are not entirely unconnected, and these carvings represent the stages of
an initiate's ascent. On the island of Ambrim, famous for its sorcerers,
the graded societies reach their most complex development; there are
thirteen grades. As a man ascends from grade to grade, acquiring a new
name at each step, he has to celebrate his elevation by killing a number
of pigs that increases with each advance in the hierarchy. To enter the
thirteenth grade a man must kill no less than 112 pigs, and a tusked pig
is valued at about £50. This means that a man who has reached the
top of the ceremonial ladder must have collected and killed in his life-

time between 600 and 700 pigs, the equivalent, at present prices, to a small fortune of about £30,000. For a long time, under the impact of missionary teachings, the graded societies were in decay, and there is no man living who has reached the thirteenth degree of the Ambrim society, though in recent years the cult has been reviving, and Keith Woodward told us of an Ambrim man, now forty-five, who has struggled up to the eleventh grade and expects to collect before he dies the 200 tuskers that will guarantee his final elevation. A man who can carry out such a feat has shown that he possesses the virtues associated in the Melanesian islands with what is called 'a big man'; he must have been good at trading, an adept husbandman, and loyal and generous with his friends and relatives so that he will be able to command their assistance in terms of loans when the time for each great pig killing arrives and his resources are strained to their limits.

It seemed curious – and it was a sensation often repeated in these Melanesian islands – when we walked with Keith Woodward from the barbaric world of the museum along the street to Rossi's and sat down with the little group of friends he had gathered to meet us. Some of them were Europeans. One was an English lawyer just returning home after three years' working in Vila; another was a Canadian woman organizing a training centre for district nurses under the aegis of the World Health Organization. Three were educated New Hebrideans. George Kalkoa, of whom we had already heard as a kind of intellectual spokesman for the modern New Hebrideans, was an elected member of the Advisory Council; Peter Taurokotu was Assistant Education Officer for the British administration; both of them were members of the New Hebridean Party. They had all been subjected, in New Zealand or Australia, to Western ways and influences, and it was very hard to assess just how much they still had in common with the men on Ambrim who were assiduously collecting pigs to elevate their rankings in a pagan society.

Obviously these men with whom we sat so cordially drinking were temporarily attached to the British if for no other reason than a view that the British were seriously interested in making the islands independent. Peter Taurokotu laid a great emphasis on the way the British were using their schools for this purpose, carefully training native teachers, where the French still staffed their schools almost entirely with metropolitan French. He and the other New Hebrideans present talked scornfully of movements like Nagriamel and Jon Frum, and argued quite passionately with the English lawyer, who pointed out that it was the emergence of Jon Frum on Tanna, with its bizarre beliefs in abundance arriving in aeroplanes from America, that marked the beginning of native resistance in the New Hebrides and prepared the authorities to welcome their own New Hebridean National Party as a lesser evil. Yet I was amused to see the New Hebrideans at one moment off their sophisticated guard. The Canadian nurse was telling how her well-trained New Hebridean assistant had been convinced, when bad weather spoilt the ceremonial opening of their training centre, that this had been the work of a disgruntled chief with rain-making powers. Not one of the New Hebrideans thought such an explanation extraordinary. Nor, for that matter, did Inge or I.

Certainly, by the time that evening's conversation was ended, it had become evident to us that we could get a true understanding of the New Hebrides and their people only if we went to the villages where discontent was born, and so our aims became sharpened. On Tanna we would visit the Jon Frum village, even though we had been told their cult was disintegrating. On Santo we must talk in the bush with Jimmy Stevens, the leader of Nagriamel. On Malekula we must find the people whose ancestors were the victims of Higginson and his kind. And we must try to discover how far traditional elements as well as acquired Western ideas of justice and equality were shaping the character of resistance, and how far that resistance had moved from threat into action.

3

Because of the number of European plantations, the islands of the New Hebrides are probably better linked by air than any other of the South Sea groups with the possible exception of Fiji. Air Mélanesie was originally started as a bush pilot operation by planters and traders, and even now they have a share in the undertaking which mirrors the extent to which the New Hebrides remain a survival from the days when white interests were dominant in the South Seas.

Air Mélanesie runs a service of nine-seater Islanders, piloted by a curious combination of young apprentice flyers from Australia, getting in their hours of flight before they can qualify for the Qantas jets, and elderly Frenchmen, who are always eccentric and sometimes drunk. When we took our first trip in the airline, down to Tanna, it was an apprentice in the cockpit, and we flew uneventfully and at a low altitude over the sea and the forested edge of Eromanga until the smoking crest of volcanic Mount Yasua came into view and we descended between the lines of coconut palms on to an airstrip located in a fold of the ground so that the plane landed on the top of a slope, taxied down it and then up the opposing slope to come to a halt at a sign which announced Burton Field. There was little more than the sign, for all that was left of the airport building was a rubble of broken planks among which two white toilet pans glistened in the sunlight; it had been demolished in a recent hurricane. Some wild-looking women who had been watching the plane land from the edge of the bush retreated shyly as soon as we began to disembark. A cow lowed frenziedly among the trees. A tall young man with long yellow hair, piercing blue eyes and a daredevil air got down from a Land-Rover and came towards us. 'I'm Russell Paul,' he said. 'Bob Paul's my father.' He loaded our luggage into the jeep, together with that of a young German doctor working in an American institute, who had come to see the famous volcano.

Tanna has no roads – merely tracks that wind over the hills and through the groves and the jungle and turn at the slightest touch of rain into that red and slippery mud which one encounters so often on high South Sea islands. Tough vehicles with four-wheel drives are the only possible kind of transport, and Russell drove his Land-Rover with skill and an obviously intimate familiarity with the terrain. Inge complimented him on his driving. 'I should know how, ma'am, if anyone should,' he answered. 'I've been here since I was one year old. I went away for a few years to school in Australia, but that doesn't make any difference. Tanna's the only home I have, and I don't want to make my life anywhere else.' And indeed, as we got to know him, Russell Paul seemed as true a son of the islands as any white man could possibly be.

He drove us first to the big white house behind the trading store where his family lived. It was one of the wooden houses with large airy rooms and great shutters kept open with white poles, so that the breeze came in and the sunlight kept out, that are characteristic of New Hebridean traders. Shortly afterwards, Bob Paul himself came in, one of those large, loose, slightly shambling men in whom an essential toughness is combined with a great gentleness of manner. Bob Paul has been in the New Hebrides for almost thirty years, since 1946. He was one of the founders and pilots of the rough-and-ready interisland plane services that had preceded Air Mélanesie, and still served as its agent on Tanna. He was the largest trader and planter on the island. He was a member of the Advisory Council and known as a man to whom anyone, European or native, could apply for help if he felt himself the victim of injustice. He was sometimes called the King of Tanna, but it was a title he did not invite or relish, since he had learnt the inconvenience of authoritarian stances in a world as volatile as the South Seas in the 1970s, and he seemed to live at guarded peace with all men, including the militants of Jon Frum. His name throughout the Condominium was such that whenever the Advisory Council wished to put a point strongly to the two governments, its divergent groups of British, French and Melanesian representatives always united to nominate him their spokesman. He was the one man who could be relied on to reduce the passions of a situation to a fair and persuasive statement.

We were given coffee grown on the plantation, and fresh rolls baked in the Paul store; it was obvious that Bob Paul and his family had recognized that a measure of self-sufficiency was essential to the very civilized way of life they maintained on Tanna. Then we drove to the cabins, native-style huts of bamboo and palm-leaf with the necessary amenities of Coleman lamps and kerosene refrigerators, standing on the shores of a rocky cove with a few native houses on its farther shore. Beside each door a padlock hung on a hook with its key. 'There's no need to use it,' Bob Paul remarked. 'Taboo still counts on Tanna, and a padlock beside a door is now a taboo sign. You can leave everything you have without worrying. Nobody will step past that padlock.' We would have been ashamed to disregard such an assurance, and during our days on Tanna we left the cabin open with cameras and money and other usually tempting items inside it, but though the Tannese wandered freely along the shore below the cabins and through the coconut grove above, nothing was ever touched. The first night we were disturbed by noises on the veranda which sounded as if someone were about to break in, but we found it was only some of the goats which Bob Paul had introduced, before he took to cattle rearing, to keep down the weeds in his plantations.

Tanna is one of the lushest islands of the New Hebrides, so fertile that its people – unlike most South Sea islanders – live almost entirely off the land and are reputed to be poor fishermen. Nevertheless, it is by no means entirely forested, and it contains a considerable area of upland savanna. After we had decided to leave our trip to the Jon Frum village until the next day, Russell Paul suggested that we might take a trip as far as these natural pasturelands to see the herds of wild horses that now inhabited them.

The distance was comparatively slight, but travel was slow, since in this direction the tracks were particularly steep and broken down; even vehicles with four-wheel drives could travel only very slowly through the coconut-groves where the cattle and goats were grazing. There was still a good deal of devastation to be seen from the last hurricane – trees uprooted and broken off, and one palm whose trunk had been severed by a flying piece of roofing with such force that the cut reproduced the corrugations of the iron. The inhabitants were clearly fearful that the experience might be repeated; when we drove past the nondescript little European bungalows of the government station we saw that their roofs were loaded down with sandbags and blocks of cement and coral in case of another blow.

Our way took us through two native villages, and the contrast between them illustrated vividly what had happened on the island since the advent of Jon Frum. One was a Presbyterian village; we had seen nothing in the islands more dejected in its atmosphere than this shabby, rundown settlement of corrugated-roofed houses which in their pristine newness must have symbolized for some past missionary the triumph of Scottish progress and Presbyterian light. The next village was a pagan one. Its huts of cane and thatch, and its cane-walled school, all of them renewed or repaired since the hurricane, looked neat and bright, and the well-cultivated gardens around it gave the whole place an appearance of happiness and self-sufficient prosperity.

The contrast between the villages reflected the extraordinary developments by which Tanna, almost alone among the missionized islands of the South Seas, slipped back from its conversion. I remembered, from my boyhood reading of missionary narratives, how after some alarming violence and the eating of a few pious Caledonians, Tanna was brought into the Kirk by the efforts of John G. Paton and his missionary associates. It continued as a model Presbyterian island until the arrival of the American forces during World War II set going strange thoughts of material blessings, and Jon Frum arose as one of the many cargo cults of Melanesia. Jon Frum – as we realized when we began to piece the story together – seemed to base its power largely on lingering pagan emotions which the Presbyterians had only papered over with their apparent conversions, and when the Jon Frum leaders sent kava sticks through the villages with the exhortation to abandon missionary religion, many people who never thought of joining them were willing – from fear or perhaps from a long suppressed desire to be free of a Calvinist outlook – to obey the call. The Presbyterian Church, which had commanded the loyalties of the vast majority of the islanders, suddenly found itself reduced to a small sect, and it was the least self-reliant of the Tannese who chose to remain under Christian tutelage.

Beyond the villages we turned inland into steeper country, through a forest tangled with lianas, where little canary-like birds called silver-eyes skittered among the undergrowth and we saw several of the brilliant blue and white kingfishers which migrate seasonally from Siberia to the New Hebrides and back. At last we came to a plateau where the forest sharply gave way to a low maquis which eventually became grassland. Here, at a primitive gate of barbed wire and stakes, Bob Paul's land ended and native land began, and here too Jon Frum showed its first sign. Within a little red wooden fence like the surround of a grave and about the same size, stood a tall cross, also painted red. 'It's just to show us,' Russell remarked. 'Defiance, not taboo. They wouldn't try that! After all, they still like to trade with us.'

We drove on over the trackless downs, where a few cattle and some hobbled horses belonging to the local villagers were grazing, and passed a deep gorge where a great tongue of jungle taller and thicker than the forest we had passed through came in contact with the grassland, the dense woodland sweeping down one side and the almost treeless savanna down the other, and the two meeting on the sharp line of demarcation formed by the river below. Beyond this gorge the downs, dotted with scanty groups of trees, flowed down to the sea, and it was here that we found the wild horses, whose ancestors had been left to graze freely when the Tannese had no use for them. They ran in troops varying in numbers from six to a dozen, each with its dominant stallion. Kurt, the German doctor, was anxious to take film of them, so we hid in one of the clumps of trees, and Russell careered with the Land-Rover across the savanna, driving the horses so that they raced, uncut manes and tails sweeping in the wind, towards us. As each troop swept by, the guardian stallion, mane and tail held high, ran between the mares and foals and the Land-Rover. Round they would race, and then stop on some knoll to observe us, and then, surprisingly, come sweeping down to tempt Russell to a further pursuit. At first we were inclined to pity such splendid creatures who had returned to primordial wildness and then were pursued, but soon it became evident that for them this unlethal pursuit was actually an exhilarating game. As I watched them, I seemed to be looking over an unbelievable chasm of time, for it was of the palaeolithic horses of Lascaux that I was irresistibly reminded.

We lunched back in the cabin on Paris ham and excellent Vila charcuterie we had picked up at the store, and drank Gewurztraminer wondering what John G. Paton would have said to the enjoyment of such Gallic luxuries on his savage nineteenth-century island. Russell joined us, and I said to him that I had heard there was a priest on southern Tanna who knew the history of Jon Frum better than any other white man. 'Yes, that's Father Sacco,' said Russell. 'He's a marvellous man. The sharpest man at cards I've ever seen. He knows so many of the languages of Tanna that he can make himself understood anywhere on the island. The one language he won't learn is pidgin. He says it would be a barrier between him and the natives rather than a means of communication. Come on! We'll call on him!'

So we drove through the palm groves along the coast, and eventually found Father Sacco in his parsonage that looked out over a sloping lawn towards the sea. There was something immediately puzzling about him. He looked Italian but his accent was not, and into its indefinable Europeanness there would break every now and then a mystifying twang of the English north country – somewhere pretty far north of York I decided. 'A good guess,' he laughed when I told him my impression. 'I'm a Maltese, but I spent many years in Middlesbrough before the Marist mission decided to send me here. And it's not so far from Durham miners to Tannese villagers as you'd think. They both live pretty close to the elemental. They both live close to death.'

We were standing on his veranda, and he pointed across the lawn. 'Why do you think I have such a good view of the sea? Because ten years ago the church which stood just above the beach was swept away by a tidal wave. And in the last hurricane the walls of the school building collapsed and the roof fell flat on to the ground. I was all right in my parsonage because I worked on it myself as leading carpenter, and a properly braced wooden house has the right combination of give and strength to stand any hurricane. But the night of that hurricane was terrible for the Tannese. The women and children squatted down in the centre of the houses, and the men and youths stood in a circle around them, clinging desperately to the roof timbers to prevent everything flying away. Three-quarters of the houses collapsed, and some of the roofs were blown two and a half miles before they came to the ground.'

Since the hurricane, Father Sacco had built a new school, guaranteed to stand up to any wind, and he insisted on taking us on a tour of his compound before we settled down to talk. Like Catholic missionaries who live for years on their own – I have met his kind in the Canadian Arctic and the Indian jungles – he had become something of a Robinson Crusoe, learning the skills necessary for survival and a modicum of comfort. And after he had shown us his special marvels – the fragment of church wall with its niched Virgin that had survived the tidal wave, and the iron roof of the fallen school where the sand had been blown against the windward side with such force that it had stripped away the paint and brightly burnished the metal – he took us into his workshop filled with a vast variety of hand and power tools, and then showed us his never-failing pump, drawing water from deep in the coral, water which he was giving to the village people whose wells were still brackish as a result of the hurricane. Then, pausing to show us a great black and white butterfly laying its eggs on one of his small orange trees, he took us into his school, where the children rose and greeted us in a chorus of guttural French; half of them had blond heads of curly hair that contrasted disconcertingly with their charcoal black skins, but we were not astonished, for Bob Paul had already shown us the shelf of hydrogen peroxide which was a fast seller in his store.

Back in the parsonage, Father Sacco talked of Jon Frum. 'It started up when a man began to go around saying that one night he had seen a personage on the beach who was the devil, and that by magic he had been able to catch him, and use his powers. Whether the original Jon Frum was the devil or the man who caught him is not certain now even in the minds of the Tannese, but it does seem certain that Jon Frum – whoever he was – began to meet people in the dark and pretend to inject them, which in itself is a curious thing, since he appeared before the great campaign of penicillin which virtually eliminated yaws. There is a woman in the next village who claims that by Jon Frum's injections she was cured of paralysis. All this happened before the Americans came. The name of Jon Frum survived, and what we call the bush beliefs – the fragments of paganism that lingered in the interior villages – were incorporated. Though the interesting thing is that the bush people have a different name for Jon Frum; they call him Kalip Apen, and I suspect that is the name of a pagan god whose cult survived surreptitiously all through the period of Presbyterian conversion. After the Americans came, the idea of cargo cropped up. Whether it came from New Guinea or was generated here spontaneously I cannot say, but now Jon Frum became the being who would bring cargo, and his prophets multiplied. One man wandered around with a crazy woman whose vapourings he claimed to interpret like the priest of an oracle. Another used to put his ear to the ground, and claimed he was receiving messages from America.

'It was a situation ripe for a leader. A former teacher named Nambas appeared; he organized Jon Frum into a movement with himself as its leader, invented the bloody cross as its symbol, and turned it into an openly anti-Christian movement. He created a village at Sulphur Bay which became the Jon Frum mecca, and drilled his storm-troopers who marched up and down on special days with wooden imitation rifles and the letters USA painted on their chests in white clay. They still do it! It was he who sent the kava stick over the island to call for the abandonment of Christianity, and when the people in the villages received it, they drank kava openly – which the missionaries had forbidden – to signify that they renounced their conversion. Nambas died. Then came another leader called Milas. He went off to Vila, and came back with the story that he had been transported to America in what he called a "thing", and there he met two soldiers who told him that they were waiting for the Eagle to take off at any moment, after which the cargo would arrive in Tanna. Milas made his people clear airstrips in the jungle and build dummy planes to act as decoys for the real planes that would bring the cargo. Now Milas has gone, and his dummy planes have vanished, and all you will see in the jungle are the bloody crosses of Nambas. But the mecca is still at Sulphur Bay, and the leaders come and go. Frankly, I cannot tell you whom you will find in power when you go there.'

The next morning Mike and I, with Russell, the German Kurt, and a girl from Vila who was staying with the Pauls, set off for the Jon Frum village of Sulphur Bay, a journey that would take us close to the volcano of Mount Yasua. Inge was feeling unequal to the hard jeep journey and decided to stay at the cabin. We travelled by old horse-tracks – formerly the foot-tracks of trade – that took us up over the interior spine of the island. Beside the track, every two or three miles, we passed a big tramped open space in the forest, with a single great banian tree under which rough benches had been made out of tree trunks; this was the nakamel: the meeting centre for a village whose houses were scattered in the bush; the Tannese have nothing resembling the maneabas of the Micronesians, and it is in the open, under the banian, that they gather to make their kava and discuss the affairs of men. They gather, that is, when they are at home, but in most of these upland settlements the hurricane had destroyed the crops, and the men had gone to New Caledonia to earn a little money while the women kept alive by eating coconuts. In one village Russell stopped to talk to a man with one hand; the other had been blown off fishing with dynamite. He told us that apart from himself there were only two old men and two youths in the village, though there were thirty women.

The road climbed higher, through dense woods inhabited by large black-and-bronze-winged pigeons. We went into cloud and rain, at times slithering perilously down hills that the rains had turned into slopes of red mud, and then we rose through the cloud, drove along the edges of sheer precipices which fell perpendicularly into the shifting vapours below us. Twice we met jeeps which were actually taxis, and the cars would edge round each other on the narrow road like cautious animals. As we approached the volcano the roads turned into dark grey ash, very porous and firm, and then the volcano came into sight, a great grey heap of ashes towering over the neighbouring wooded hills, with just a wisp of smoke blowing from its crest. The land around its base – the Ash Plain – was bare and black, but we turned away into the woods and went by steep roads through the dense coastal rain forest of the eastern shore of the island down to White Sands beach, where we ate our lunch in the shade of great overhanging trees, watching the boys fishing with rods in the surf and a man working with an adze on a log of yellow wood, hacking into shape a dugout canoe.

We drove back into the hills and over the Ash Plain beside the volcano towards Sulphur Bay; the Plain was as firm as the finest ocean beach, so that Russell could drive over it at top speed. It was a grim impressive scene: the black ash field with a few gaunt pandanus its only vegetation; the rusty-red field of lava that cropped out of it; the grey lake inhabited – Russell told us – with black fish imported from Africa; and the black cone of the mountain in which thunder growled and reverberated until a great columnar puff of smoke rose suddenly into the sky.

Skirting the mountain on the coastal side, we came eventually to a barrier of stakes driven into the road to prevent vehicles going any further. It was Sulphur Bay. Beyond the barrier lay a great square green of well-grazed grass, and the houses of the village were situated on two sides of the green. A young man in shorts was standing casually but observantly near the barrier. If he was a kind of sentry, he gave no obvious sign of it, and when Russell talked to him in pidgin, he waved us on over the green. As we walked there we could see that Sulphur Bay was a planned community, much larger than the other villages we had seen. The houses were arranged in orderly rows leading back from two sides of the square. Some were built in a traditional manner that has died out elsewhere on Tanna, with no walls and curved roofs like Nissen huts that came right down to the ground and were densely thatched; the wooden frames of these houses were well carpentered, so that they were sturdy and gave little purchase to the wind. All the other houses had cane walls, woven neatly into herringbone or chequered patterns, with roofs of palm or pandanus thatch. There was not an iron roof in the village, which was in accordance with the resolute traditionalism of the Jon Frum leaders that seemed to contradict their hopes of salvation through cargo from the prosperous west. Four red Jon Frum crosses within their little fences were spaced over the green, and another stood in the hollow of an old banian. A second and larger banian, with benches under it, served as a meeting place and a few women were sitting there and gossiping. The young man followed us and pointed out another rectangular fence on the edge of the green. It was the grave of Nambas, the first leader of the village; some faded plastic wreaths lay on a pile of lava rubble, but there was no mark.

Most of the men, we gathered, were up on the hillsides, working in their gardens. A second young man, in a blue lavalava, was walking about with a baby in his arms, and he led us down through the rows of huts towards the beach, where a line of outrigger canoes was beached and a score of village boys were riding and tossing on the vast bounding surf that broke in the reefless bay. Seated on a log watching them was an old man with a broad greying beard who looked rather like a black Darwin. 'He's one of Nambas's successors,' said Russell, and we went up to the old man. He shook hands and smiled very benignly, but as soon as Russell began to talk in pidgin he turned and slipped away as

silently as a ghost among the huts. The young man in shorts laughed
and went into a long gabble of pidgin. It turned out that the old man
had been recognized as a prophet and leader until a few months ago,
but then there had been disputes among the faithful, and he was forced
to share his power with two of his rivals. These triumvirs were away
in their gardens, and the old man did not wish to say anything to
strangers out of their presence.

We strolled back over the green, and the clatter of bamboo drums
sounded on the edge of the village, and then up in the hills. 'Calling
pigs home,' said the young man in shorts. The clouds began to drift
over the sun, and it seemed wise to begin making our way back if we
did not want to be caught in a mountain storm. We walked to the row
of stakes that marked the gate to the Jon Frum village. A toothless old
woman in a dirty and shapeless cotton dress came up and spoke
affectionately to Russell. 'This is Marguerite,' he said. 'She was my
nanny!' Marguerite spoke better English than the rather difficult pidgin
of Sulphur Bay, and when Russell told her we were waiting for the
leaders, she laughed. 'You hear them drums?' 'Calling the pigs,' said
Russell. She laughed again. 'No calling pigs. Telling big men stay
away!' And though we waited for another half hour, anxiously eyeing
the sky, the old man remained in hiding and the other leaders failed to
appear, though some lesser men straggled down with bags of produce
on their backs.

At last we gave up and left, Mount Yasua celebrating our passing
by clanking its bowels and puffing up an even taller column of smoke
that hung in the air and shaped itself into a miniature mushroom cloud.
About half way back the rain began to fall heavily, though on the
nakamels the villagers were still sitting around tiny fires over which
they had rigged little awnings of banana leaves. We all felt the end of
the journey had come when we reached the last of the slippery hills and
the Land-Rover went out of control and slid down sideways. Luckily
it did not topple over, but then there was the opposing hill, equally
slippery to ascend; only after six runs at it did Russell reach the top.
Ours, we learnt next day, was the last car to make the journey over the
island; the others were benighted on the road and their passengers had
to sleep in native huts.

When we got back Inge told us that Bob Paul and his wife had been
to call and had invited us to 'tea' that evening. In fact tea was the one
thing missing from the splendid meal, served with aperitifs and wine

and notable Armagnac and excellent talk, that we were offered. Bob and his tall and charming wife were fine hosts, and the evening was a glimpse into the graces of planter life at its best – the life of those who refuse to let go into pseudo-native squalor and do so by holding more deliberately to the urbane aspects of life than most people nowadays in Europe or North America.

Bob Paul was not surprised by our reception – or lack of it – at Sulphur Bay. 'The movement's in flux,' he told us. 'There isn't a dynamic leader any more and the militant phase is over. The real Jon Frum people are scattered in the bush villages off the roads, and with them it's become a withdrawal. They don't want to speak pidgin or send their kids to school or have anything to do with us, and except for a few basic things they get in the barter markets up in the hills, they do very well without us. But those fellows at Sulphur Bay – they're just discontented acculturated people. Most of them hoped that when the cargo came they could turn into sham Americans, and now it hasn't come they stay on partly because it's the best run village on the island, and partly because they still hate us though they don't know what to do about it. That's why they wouldn't come to see you. You could go back a dozen times and until there's a real leader again they'll just fade away into the bush. But Jimmy Stevens up on Santo – that's another matter altogether! You'll have no trouble seeing Jimmy and his men!'

4

Tanna is the southernmost of the larger islands of the New Hebrides and Santo the northernmost, and to go from one to the other we had to fly the whole north-westerly length of the island chain. The pilot that morning, one of the genial, elderly Frenchmen, flew out over the volcano, avoiding the up-draught of the crater, but showing us the great shoulders of lava and the woods of tree ferns that grew high on the warm slopes of the weather side.

We had to change planes on Efate, and there was time enough to drive into Vila for a lunch of langouste at Rossi's. The flight north, in the late afternoon, was exciting and beautiful, for in these small island planes, flying low, one really has a kind of condor's eye-view, distant and far-embracing yet curiously intimate. The islands lay below us, new forms rising on the horizon every few minutes, like the pieces of a vast jigsaw puzzle whose bay-bitten polygonal outlines seemed to demand reconstruction. Each large island was surrounded by its satellite group of islets. The pattern one saw from above was always individual yet similar in its generalities – a reef a few hundred yards from shore, with a vitriol-blue edge where the water began to plunge to the indigo depths; then the green and brown floor of the lagoon, a dark and sombre edge of mangroves stepping out of the water, and the coconuts above the tideline, extending to the feet of the lower slopes, but never too far from the sea that would transport the copra. Inland was always the jungle mantling all but the sharpest crags, and looking, as Inge pointed out, like a densely packed bed of broccoli. To the east loomed the conical bulk of Ambrim, the extinct volcano which is celebrated and feared in the New Hebrides as the sorcerer's island, to the west the long bulk of Malekula, with the villages dotted along the shore; one never saw the bush villages, which were few and hidden in the jungle.

Australia del Espiritu Santo (the Southern Land of the Holy Ghost) – to give its full name – was the first island of the New Hebrides to be discovered. The Spaniard Quiros arrived there in 1606, and established a settlement he called the New Jerusalem, which quickly disintegrated under the combined impact of sickness and native hostility. The modern capital is a rough settlement on the Segond Channel to the south of the island; it was originally an American base, and even now it seems so indeterminate a place that no one is quite sure of its real name, though the French are inclined to call it Luganville and the British to call it Santo, like the island.

Burns Philp had made sure that a hired car was waiting for us at the airport, and this was a good thing, since we had to drive several times up and down the dusty main street of the town, with its shabby wooden shops and its decaying huts dating from the American occupation and its few new raw concrete buildings, before we finally identified the Corsica Hotel. It turned out to be one of the shabbiest relics, a large and rusty Quonset hut with a bar built out to the front, a general air of ravishment by hurricane and earthquake, and no sign. In the lounge, shabby and broken chairs were scattered around glass-ringed tables on a bare concrete floor cracked by the quakes, and on the wall hung as fine a collection of Ambrim and Banks Islands artefacts as I have ever seen in private hands. A thin gangling man detached himself from a group of talkers around a table, and approached us with a look of suspicion. He was the manager, and without a smile he showed us into a corridor with doors on each side and into a room at the end with broken linoleum on the floor, the lock torn off the door, a smell of advanced tropical mouldiness in the clothes cupboard, a smell of stale urine in the shower, and coming through the netting that served as a window a stench so formidable that I suddenly remembered Bob Paul's exhortation – 'Make sure you don't get put on the sewer side at the Corsica!' We were on the sewer side, but Inge got in her protest before me. The manager suddenly looked aggrieved and vulnerable. 'But I didn't know you were coming, my dear, till the last minute!'

The next day we graduated to the non-sewer side, and, strange though it would have seemed to me at that depressing moment when we looked at our first room, I am now sad to remember that the Corsica, having survived so many hurricanes and earthquakes, burnt to the ground with all its fine artefacts a few months after we stayed there. For the French cook was excellent in the Burgundian manner, the cellar was good, and when the manager presided at the bar, which he usually did, the drinks were always strong. He was a curious, interesting man, full of information and always willing to help us by searching up an inhabitant of Santo we wanted to meet, and considering that he had been roaming the islands for decades, he had a strangely innocent view of human nature. One night when we were staying with him there was a boxing tournament in Santo, with two minor French prize-fighters brought up from Nouméa. Brown had organized the affair, and when he came home he left the gate money – some $1,300 – plus $1,000 of his own, in the glove compartment of his unlocked car. The next morning he awoke in a panic, and rushed out, to find the money untouched. 'You are lucky,' I said when he told the story over our first noontide gin. 'Lucky be damned,' he said in a sudden fury. 'That's just how it is in Santo. Nobody steals. That's why one lives here!' Only that morning Marie-Thérèse, the little Melanesian woman who sometimes worked in the bar, had told me how her own people were in fact losing their honesty because young men went to earn good money in New Caledonia and when they returned to Santo, where work was scarce and wages small, took to thieving. But Alan Brown preferred to believe that men were good rather than that he was lucky.

We had come to Santo to talk to Jimmy Stevens, the most visible symbol of native resistance in the New Hebrides. Strange things had obviously been happening in imperial relationships, we realized, when John Wilson, the local British agent, whom we met for breakfast on the morning after our arrival on Santo, energetically set about making sure that we were taken without delay or impediment to the head-quarters of the Nagriamel movement at Vanofo, in the central bush of Santo, where Jimmy Stevens has established a kind of community that, despite vicissitudes, has turned out already to be a more durable New Jerusalem than that which the unfortunate Quiros tried to establish three centuries ago on the island of the Holy Ghost.

A civil servant, George Bule, a stocky dark man from Pentecost Island, agreed to accompany us as our guide to the mercurial being known to his followers as Jimmy Moses, to white men as Jimmy Stevens (apparently his baptismal name) and to himself and all he can impress with his dignity as Chief James Tupou Putuntan Steven Moses. We were uncertain about accepting an official intermediary, but we decided that any suspicion aroused by our arriving in such company would be counterbalanced by the fact that we had carried a letter of introduction written by K. C. Ramrakha, brother of the surgeon who had so ably attended Inge; Ramrakha, a radical Indian political leader in Suva, had acted as legal representative for Nagriamel when it petitioned the United Nations with a view to gaining independence for the New Hebrides.

We drove back from the British agency into the slums of Luganville, a series of old American Nissen huts, steadily rusting away in the sea air, where families live in small partitioned spaces. In one of them George Bule found a minister of the Church of Christ called James Karai, a tall, pleasant and rather stately man, dressed in a blue shirt, dirty white shorts and panama hat. Karai was the head man of Nagriamel in Lugan-ville, and as soon as he read Ramrakha's letter, he agreed to accompany us. George Bule went off to try and hire a Land-Rover, and we went to the hotel to get a day's food prepared. Having failed to find a vehicle for hire, Bule arrived with a government jeep, driven by a bearded VSO volunteer. We picked up James Karai, who had meanwhile donned his insignia, an armband embroidered with the Nagriamel symbol, a bunch of green and yellow taboo leaves above and a blue star below.

We drove northward along the east coast, and tried to pump Karai for information as we went, but he quite obviously regarded the dis-pensing of knowledge as the privilege of the leader we were visiting, and we got very little out of him except an admission that Nagriamel had received a proposal of co-operation from Jon Frum and had so far postponed its response. He added a few caustic remarks on the folly of expecting cargo to descend when the land was lying there waiting to be made productive if only it could be returned to the native people, and the tone of his reply suggested what the response would be.

Not many miles up the coast road we turned inland, through jungle land where bush-hens scurried and the people walked in the sun using giant taro leaves as parasols. The road was surprisingly good. It had been built by the Americans to serve their ammunition stores – earth-covered bunkers which, half concealed by grass and trees, were still visible. As we went, James Karai told one of those pathetic stories of the contacts between Melanesians and Europeans which contribute to the resentments that fuel movements like Nagriamel. Originally there were Melanesian villages in this area. But when the Americans set up their ammunition stores, they soon came to realize that the simple village people had no idea of the realities of modern war, and could not be persuaded to observe elementary blackout precautions in an area where a Japanese air attack would be disastrous. Accordingly, they displaced the villagers and sent them to live in the hills, with the promise that their lands would be returned to them when the war ended; in fact, French planters seized the land as soon as the Americans left, and none of it was ever returned to its real Melanesian owners.

Soon the highway ended, and we had to travel over a track gouged out of the parkland, dotted with great banians and with volcanic out-crops, that replaced the jungle. With its lush growth of grass, it looked ideal land for the grazing of cattle, and the French were certainly emphatic in asserting their rights over it, for in many places we saw notices reading:

Propriétée Privée
Défense d'Entrer
TABOU

We drove for miles through these well-herded pastures, protected by endless notices, barbed-wire fences and cattle grids, and we forded a good number of streams sunk in muddy declivities out of which the driver extricated us with difficulty. Eventually, we came to the lands of the Nagriamel community, and there, awaiting us at the border, was a squad of young men, some bare-torsoed, others clad in garish shirts, and one of them holding a tall longbow in his hand. I immediately realized that in some way they knew of our coming. Old South Sea hands are convinced that – especially on the Melanesian islands – a 'coconut telegraph' exists, involving normally the use of drums. We had seen it in operation at the Jon Frum settlement of Sulphur Bay, and now, when I saw the young man with the bow coming round to the back of the jeep and nodding as soon as he saw James Karai, I could not help feeling that earlier in the morning, as soon as we left his Nissen hut to get our food prepared at the hotel, Karai had somehow set the 'telegraph' in motion, perhaps by sending a cyclist to some village off the road near Luganville and getting the drums to relay the message from there. As we drove on, Karai told us that technically, in the eyes of the Joint Court, all the land of Vanofo was French land, on which Jimmy Stevens and his followers had squatted in order to dramatize their claims to unused land. Once the French bulldozers had come as far as the very edge of the community, and Jimmy's followers, a thousand strong, had gathered there expecting a confrontation which they would have sustained to the bitter end, but the bulldozers had turned away, and Nagriamel's domain had been left untouched.

We drove through plantations of bananas and young coconuts, fields of groundnut and sunflowers and sweet potato, and past the biggest banian any of us had ever seen – a veritable skyscraper of a tree, a cathedral in vegetable Gothic, with bamboo benches set among its roots. There, every three months, Karai told us, the Nagriamel Council gathered as a kind of parliament in opposition, and there, each year, the annual festival of the movement was centred.

On the far side of the great open space that began with the banian tree there was a flagstaff from which fluttered the Nagriamel flag, an enlargement of the badge which James Karai bore on his armband, with two tall man-faced slit gongs embedded in the ground beside it. Beyond the flagstaff was the wooden building which served as Jimmy's office and the headquarters both of Nagriamel and of the nuclear commune of Vanofo.

Jimmy was awaiting us with his little court: one of his new wives, who also acted as his secretary; a couple of attendants dressed in shirt and trousers who looked as though they had spent a good deal of their lives in the vicinity of white men; and a thin rachitic old man in a loincloth of flowered print. After Jimmy had welcomed us, read Ramrakha's letter, and then welcomed us again with a fervour not evident before, the old man was the first to whom he introduced us. 'This naked pellow – he call Tom. He chief. Village eighteen mile back in bush,' he added, waving towards the high forested mountains that reared up behind Vanofo. Obviously Tom – or whatever his native name may have been – was presented as concrete and living evidence of Jimmy's influence among the bush folk. Equally obviously, Jimmy had fresh knowledge of our arrival, presumably by runner from the border point, since we had heard no drums beating after we entered the community lands, for he appeared wearing an impeccably pressed and laundered shirt which, in the immense humidity of the day, became quickly soaked with sweat as he stood there talking to us.

Jimmy was a striking, likeable man who tended to overwhelm one's initial mistrust by a charismatic attraction which, since it worked with us who had arrived as somewhat sceptical observers, doubtless worked even more intensely among the native peoples whose thoughts and desires he understood. His Polynesian ancestry – for his mother was Tongan – emerged in his powerful build; at first one did not appreciate his tallness – he must have been nearly six feet – because he was so sturdily architectured. His cast of countenance also was Polynesian; he was pale-skinned, with large and slightly shifty hazel eyes, and a whitening fringe of beard like a nineteenth-century sailor's. His paternal grandmother had been Melanesian, and her influence seemed to emerge in the lower part of his face, the wideness and slight coarseness of nose and mouth. The high, European brow seemed the main contribution of his English grandfather, the original mariner named Stevens. He spoke a quick serviceable English, not pidgin but interlarded with enough pidgin expressions to make it vivid. The idea of destruction, which emerged often in his conversation, was always expressed in the pidgin phrase 'Baggerap pinis' – 'pinis' being the nearest a New Hebridean can get to 'finish'. And his way of describing an active agitational campaign was: 'We go boom – talktalktalk!'

Sitting in his office and looking over the land maps in which he seemed to take a great delight as he expounded the iniquities of the plantation owners and the land speculators, we gradually pieced together a good deal of Jimmy's history and the history of the Nagriamel movement. He had moved more deeply into the white man's world than most of his followers. He worked for the Americans during the war. He had operated a bulldozer, and complained of the atrocious leg pains he still suffered as the heritage of a knee injury incurred at that time. He had been the master of a small trading schooner. He had run a little store in Luganville. He had built up a reputation among white men and educated New Hebrideans for being both shiftless and sly, and yet he was the only outsider who had really made his own the problems of both the bush people and the landless men of the coast.

As Jimmy told it, Nagriamel sprang out of the surge of discontent among the villages of Santo when the plantation owners began to put bush land to use for grazing purposes at the beginning of the 1960s and in the process to displace native villages and destroy native gardens, whose owners were technically squatters on land that belonged to the planters. Some of the bush chiefs, particularly a man called Buluk, conceived the idea of a resistance organization, perhaps inspired by rumours of the recent Marching Rule movement in the Solomons, and in some way which nobody – not even he himself – defined very clearly, Jimmy gravitated to the movement and quickly, because of his sharp, adaptable mind, made himself leader.

As he described it, in 1966 they 'raised the symbol of the united leaves', which signified that they were dedicated to 'custom', or to preserving the traditional way of life instead of that inculcated by the white rulers and the missionaries, and in 1967 a gathering of 1,800 people officially set on foot the Nagriamel movement. In 1968 confrontation with the French gendarmes (the 'sondarms' as Jimmy called them), occurred when the members of the new movement obstructed land-clearing operations for a French cattle ranch, and Jimmy was imprisoned, which did a great deal to consolidate his reputation among the native people. Many native pastors of the Church of Christ gave their support to the movement, and Jimmy claimed that he had a following of 23,000, a quarter of the population of the New Hebrides, scattered over most of the northern islands. In fact, it seems evident that his critics were right when they told us that, though 23,000 people may at one time or another have showed interest in the movement, it was unable to call on more than a small fraction of that movement in any active way. (Several months later, when Mike Poole returned to Vanofo to film the anniversary celebrations, less than 2,000 people appeared, and this probably represents the bulk of Nagriamel's active following.)

It was obvious that what made Jimmy a more effective leader and Nagriamel a more influential movement than most of the other native movements was his firm grasp of the central problem of land. He spoke with contempt of Jon Frum – with whom it was quite evident he did not intend to associate – and of cargo cultists in general. 'I no waiting for steamer. I rather have black steamer than white steamer. Land my steamer.' And his repeated emphasis on *use* of the land as being the criterion of ownership not only followed New Hebridean custom, but also showed him as a reasonable man who was not unwilling to come to an arrangement with the planters based on their giving up title to the lands they did not use.

Jimmy talked angrily about missionaries and the French; sadly about the British, whom he regarded as weak friends of the people, who never lived up to expectations. He rejected the political aspirations of the New Hebridean National Party, on the grounds that Western politics were not for Melanesian people, who should find their own way of organization according to 'custom', and he had set up a kind of state within a state, establishing a series of centres on the islands which sent their representatives to the Nagriamel council or shadow cabinet meeting under the great banian at Vanofo. He had also organized a home guard armed with sticks and cane knives which paraded in Nagriamel villages, and it is possible that this may have been partly responsible for the recent slowdown in the enclosure of land for grazing purposes by the French planters. Jimmy had also tried to induce his followers to boycott schools, and he had even persuaded the people of Ambrim to reject a Condominium offer to build them a road around the island, promising that Nagriamel would see that it was built – a promise he was quite unable to keep.

Clearly one of Jimmy's great problems was the difficulty of co-ordinating people like the New Hebrideans who had no tradition of national or cultural unity, but had always lived in tiny language-groups following local customary patterns. Another was that of uniting what he called 'the men of the mission and the men of the fire' – or the partially acculturated converts of the coast and the pagan villagers of the bush. Jimmy's solution had been the attempt to revivify custom, and he spoke passionately and very interestingly on a past to which, by his mixed ancestry, he hardly himself belonged. I noted what he said in my diary that night, and I cannot do better than reproduce the relevant paragraphs to give some idea of the kind of memories that inspire the leaders of the movements in the South Seas which look backward into the traditional past for a solution to local problems:

'The men of the fire are the custom people who trace their descent and their rights through the ceremonial patterns. When a man hands on the title to land, he gives a fire. "The fire is the name and the name is the land." When a man feels death approaching, he calls witnesses, lights the fire, and passes on his name and his land to the son or the other heir he has chosen. But to validate his title completely, to become a respected chief, the young man must go through five fires, each a ceremony of proving and initiation. The first – his father's fire – takes him "out of the nakamel" – the common folk of the tribe. The second, for which he must kill two or three pigs, is involved with his acquisition of his first wife. He goes on gathering pigs, and passes through the third and fourth fires. Then comes a critical point, for "the nakamel returns", and representatives of the people put the aspirant three searching questions. If he answers two satisfactorily, he goes to his fifth fire, at which 100 pigs will be killed. If he answers only one question satisfactorily, "He all baggerap, he no land, he go back to nakamel, start again." To pass through the five fires can take a man from seven to eleven years.

'It is not only the acquisition of land that requires validation by fire and feast. Pottery can be made well only by those who have acquired the vocation through the fires. Other fires validate the right to perform certain dances, and there was the awful fire of reconciliation when two tribes decided to unite so as to adjust imbalances of land. Then a young woman had to be killed by a member of the other tribe, and to atone for her death compensation passed and over the fire the tribes pledged brotherhood and unity. Later a pig took the place of the young woman. But now the "fire" – or the world of custom – is losing ground as the people steadily drift to the coast for money and education. "There are brothers," says Jimmy. "One come from the fire, one from the school, but now the fire don't come." '

There was a wistful, almost elegiac note in Jimmy's voice as he said that; he may have been thinking that his own advocacy of a return to custom, while it had consolidated the support of bush people like old Tom, had alienated many of his former Christian supporters, so that James Karai was one of the few Church of Christ pastors remaining with him; especially since his acquiring a plurality of wives, the leaders of the Church had begun to denounce his movement as the work of the devil.

Nevertheless, in Vanofo Jimmy still ruled with all the respect that in Melanesian societies is accorded to the big man, who has many adherants, can call in large supplies of goods, and can provide good feasts and lavish hospitality. As we sat in the office, he insisted that the movement had been gathered together entirely by the spoken word, for the written word was alien to their culture; the movement had no periodical and no literature. In fact I did see copies of a printed pamphlet in the office, but Jimmy did not offer one of them, and I noticed they were quickly and deftly whisked away by one of the attendants.

Afterwards Jimmy took us out to the flagstaff to show the star pattern of pebbles in which it was set and to explain the almost monastic regime of the community. Each day began with a compulsory assembly called by the slit-gongs at seven o'clock. Everyone in the community appeared, which at present meant about 250 people, the core of the faithful. There were prayers and hymns and a speech by Jimmy. Then the members dispersed to the tasks which were laid down by a rigid timetable. On Monday everybody did road work, on Wednesday they worked on the land belonging to the Church, on Friday they worked on the communal farm, and on Tuesday and Thursday they worked on their private plots. Saturday and Sunday were days of leisure. We were there on a day of leisure. Few people were around, but those seemed reasonably content. After all, most of them were landless young men who had found a refuge and a sense of purpose in a society where to have no land is to be nameless.

As we returned, jolting back over the rough track between the barbed wire and the trespass signs, I was reminded of the Doukhobor leaders I had known in Canada, peasant sectarians also seeking to revivify a dying traditional world. Jimmy had the same charm as they, and the same masterly evasiveness, so that he could turn a blank face of incomprehension when he did not want to explain or to discuss some embarrassing point. Most amusing was the pose of helplessness he would assume whenever one asked him about his tactics or his plans. 'I no big man. I got no money, got no guns. Just talktalk. That all I do.' Yet one knew that a helpless man, a man dedicated just to 'talktalk', could not have created a movement which, if it has gained little land back from the planters, has at least made them hold back from further enclosures and dispossessions.

Jimmy Stevens was the only one among the several leaders of custom movements in the South Seas whom we succeeded in meeting, and that was doubtless because he was partly European in background and in cast of mind, and liked to impress white men with his reasonableness. We did later on Malekula, indeed, meet militant village malcontents, but that was quite another matter, and we did also on Santo encounter some of the educated Melanesians who were rather forlornly seeking a solution by the use of Western democratic means.

We met one of them, Titus Path, the day after our visit to Jimmy Stevens, when we travelled up to Hog Harbour on the north-eastern end of the island. Hog Harbour had given fuel to the resentments that bred Nagriamel and had created problems for the three various governments of the New Hebrides, because an American speculator named Peacock had managed to acquire a large stretch of land there, and had proceeded to subdivide it and sell it to Americans in Hawaii who had found the forty-ninth State of the Union no longer the Pacific paradise of which they had dreamed. Dreams were dashed, we gathered, at Hog Harbour too, for the purchasers were subjected to the sudden action of the French and British authorities who, faced with the prospect of a whole American suburb complicating their problems, instituted prohibitive taxes on subdivided land sold to any but their own subjects, and refused permanent resident permits to Americans.

It was an extraordinarily pleasant drive to Hog Harbour, up a main road that was given a Gallic look by the tall poplar-like trees which lined it. For a long way north of Santo we drove through large coconutgroves descending to beautiful open bays, and forded clear translucent rivers. Everywhere one saw the metallic debris that commemorated the American occupation, and indeed the road itself was a relic from those days. Land-crabs scuttled every now and again over it, and the beautiful little green and scarlet parrots known as coconut lories squawked and flashed like bright arrows in the crests of the palms. Farther north, beyond the area that had been of wartime interest, the highway dwindled into a coral road and we drove through a jungle densely curtained by vast green draperies of creepers. Great wild taros grew by the roadside. The few small native plantations, half-choked with weeds, seemed only to emphasize the fact that there was land in abundance, if only the ownership could be decided, for the jungle receded over vast areas up the hillsides, and the air was resonant with the singing of birds.

When we reached Hog Harbour we were forced to admire the instinct with which Peacock has chosen his site; Hog Harbour was belied by its name, for it was a magnificently caped and islanded water, certainly the most beautiful spot we had yet seen on Santo, with the land rising around it in such a way as to form a splendid amphitheatre. But despite all the money that had changed hands, there was very little to show. Some roads had been carved through the subdivision, but no houses were visible, and indeed the only sign of life there, apart from the parrots and the phalaropes and the strange spidery grey crabs that flitted over the beach, was provided by a beach hotel in the centre of the bay.

It was run by one of the few Americans who had reached Hog Harbour before the twin governments took their drastic action, and it became evident as we sat drinking with him in his lounge that he was a scared man in an intolerable dilemma. He was a retired army officer who had invested a good part of his savings in the venture; he had spent $10,000 on a house lot and $30,000 on the building of his house on which he had been working for three years; with $10,000 invested in another lot as a speculation it meant he had laid out $50,000. If he went all this would be lost. But he was in the New Hebrides only on sufferance. He was allowed only two-year permits, and the second was due to expire soon. He had almost no real comprehension of the situation in which he was trapped. The local land conflict meant nothing to him, and he imagined that the French and the British had decided to stop the development merely because they feared a third power might make claims in the New Hebrides.

North of the American holdings at Hog Harbour lay the native village, where Titus Path was the Presbyterian pastor. It was built on a wide and more or less open hillside, sloping down towards the sea. The church and the church houses stood on the cool top of the hill, with a pasture, full of cowpats and flies, between them and the houses of the village, which lay nearer the sea. The church was open, and as we went in we saw in the middle of the floor a great pile of large yams and a few sweet potatoes; each of these fruits of the earth was decorated with a little bunch of flowers tied on with raffia. A grey-haired woman came out of the mission house; she was Australian, looked like Margaret Rutherford in her fifties, and introduced herself as Nance Smith. The last white pastor had gone, she explained, a decade ago, but Australians still came out to help the native pastors and she had been a deaconess here for seven years. Titus Path chose to live in a house down in the village among his people and to leave the parsonage to her.

As for the yams we had been admiring, they were connected with the yam festival, which had been the great feast of the year in the old pagan days and now was taken over by the church. The customs were very similar to what they had always been. Before any of the new crop could be eaten in the houses, yams had to be offered in the church, and a yam feast eaten in public.

'The pastor is down there now arranging it. Come and meet him.' So we walked down with her, inordinately pestered by the flies, to the cane-and-thatch village hall under the great banian tree where the feast was being prepared. Titus Path was a small, quick, luminous-eyed man, and he immediately invited us to the feast. We went back up the hillside where the wind was blowing fairly cool, and stood talking to Nance Smith and a young missionary girl on leave from Malekula. 'The bubu will sound,' said Nance, and then, seeing our bewilderment, added, 'the conch, you know.' It sounded strange and portentous, like a calling to judgement, but in fact only a whistle shrilled, and we went down into the hall where long tables had been laid with banana leaves for the first ritual eating of the new yams. The local people had prepared the feast, and a long line of enamel bowls stretched down the table; an enormous red coconut crab formed the main decoration. Except for the three of us and the two missionary women, who were the honoured guests, the table was occupied only by the children; the adults ate standing at tables behind us, for everybody had to partake as of a sacrament. The doxology was first sung, in excellent English, and then we made speeches, Mike and I being by now practised enough to present gems of florid and slightly sanctimonious rhetoric. Some of the bowls were filled with slices of yam cooked in coconut milk, but laplap was the main dish; it was made of grated yam, mixed with cream squeezed from the flesh of the coconut and spread out to the thickness of about an inch between the large leaves of a plant called 'native cabbage', and then baked on red-hot stones. It was a pleasant, bland but extremely stodgy food of which we found that a little went a long way. Yet the children consumed great hunks of it, and I am sure that each of them must have eaten at least two or three pounds, tearing it avidly with their fingers, by the time the feast was ended. The coconut crab, we noticed, was eaten by no one at the table, though the children touched it longingly and the pastor called on us to admire it, remarking that it would taste of sweet coconut. Then it was whisked away and I imagine treated as part of the offering and consigned to the pastor's larder; he certainly deserved it, for throughout the feast he was on his feet, serving the children until they could eat no more.

It was obvious that the condition of the Presbyterian Church was much healthier on Santo than on Tanna, and we suspected that native pastors like Titus Path might have had a great deal to do with the situation when we spent the rest of the afternoon talking with him in his house, a native hut of cane with a corrugated iron roof. We sat at a battered wooden table, while his wife, a massive woman in a shapeless Mother Hubbard, listened to our talk.

Path was a cultured and well-read man. He had been educated in New Zealand, and as an elected member of the Advisory Council, he was one of the many New Hebrideans opposed to Nagriamel. He argued that Jimmy Stevens did not keep his promises, and that while on one side his movement set out to right a notorious injustice, on the other it was concerned merely to put back the clock. Path argued that progress might even be desirable, and in any case it was inevitable; we should accept it and bend it to our wishes. But he feared the possibilities of American incursion, and was glad that the Hog Harbour project had been frustrated.

Path was even more concerned about the economic troubles of his people than about the political ones, though he did not minimize these, for he felt that the New Hebrideans were actually caught between two rival European philosophies of government, of which he and most New Hebrideans found the British the more democratic and sympathetic. Nevertheless he had to admit that the French had recently, as a gesture, given back 2,000 acres of land to his village, and he had persuaded his people to work it as a co-operative plantation rather than fragmenting it between families. One had the impression of talking to a non-political, non-partisan man, illuminated but not dogmatic, who would gladly live at Christian peace with his neighbours, and even swallow a few insults to do so, but who found some of the injustices committed in the New Hebrides beyond even his great forbearance. I went away greatly heartened from having met him, for never in the South Seas did I feel more completely that the barriers of race and culture are without meaning in the meeting of people who seek the truth by inner lights. It seemed appropriate that the evening, driving back down the island, was particularly golden and the world seemed at peace with itself in the great harmony.

More than anywhere else in the South Pacific, more even than in New Caledonia, we were conscious of the weight of alien presence on Santo. We drove westerly along the southern end of the island as far as the road went, crossing one large river by a car ferry operated by three men in ragged shorts and battered straw hats decorated with hibiscus, who worked us over the swift current by pulling on a steel rope. All the way the barbed-wire fences and the trespass signs and the herds of cattle grazing under the coconut trees continued, and twice we met cold-eyed Europeans in bush shirts driving truck-loads of native labourers.

The French were the most numerous foreigners here and elsewhere, and for us the most elusive. We soon began to suspect that they knew we had begun to work with the help of the British agent and avoided us for that reason. Twice when we made appointments with French planters to meet at the Corsica we sat waiting in the bar, drinking Alan Brown's strong Singapore Slings, watching the ants running in and out of the earthquake cracks in the floor, and talking to the bored Australian journalist who was visiting the island on an assignment from *Reader's Digest*; on neither occasion did the planter appear.

Indeed, the only Frenchman with whom we did talk on Santo was a priest at a parish on the far northern corner of the island, a pale man with a twisted mouth and the look of having been brought up in a Parisian working-class suburb. He was living in a special community – a village of people whom the early Catholic missionaries had persuaded to leave a malaria-infested locality for a better setting. The church itself was built on taboo land – land which because of the presence of evil spirits the local people wished to use neither for dwellings nor for cultivation – but the villagers the priests brought with them had no traditional rights in the new locality, and land had been bought from the local tribes. Now no more could be bought, and the community of 600 people was becoming steadily overcrowded and impoverished. It was this situation that made the priest think differently from other Frenchmen. He realized that the planters were sitting on unused land that would have meant for his people the difference between poverty and sufficiency, and he spoke bitterly of the injustices of the past. No one, he remarked, missionary or layman, had stood forward resolutely to defend the interests of the native people at the time when the land-grabs were being made. He pointed across the water to the shadowy outlines of the island of Vao; it had been tribal land, and had been deeded to La Société Française des Nouvelles Hébrides by a single individual who falsely claimed to own it, yet the Joint Court had upheld the deed. To this day, he remarked, the Joint Court had refused to set in motion an inquiry that might give true weight to the Melanesian side of the land question. He ended by requesting us not to ask his name.

It was a further sign of the atmosphere of moral pressure, if not of actual terror, which existed on Santo, that we had the greatest difficulty in finding the President of that constitutionally democratic organization, the New Hebridean National Party, who lived in Luganville and worked for an American-dominated corporation. I refer to him as X, since for all I know he may be subject to the same difficulties as he revealed to us on the evening we finally found him in the Nissen hut which he and his family inhabited. He was clearly reluctant to take us into the hut, so we sat outside on the lawn in the gathering dusk as the mosquitoes began to bite ferociously.

X was a rather pale young man with a round face and a little chin beard that made him look like a young and innocent though rather swarthy Trotsky. But there was nothing Trotskyian in his manner, for a shyer and more tongue-tied political leader it would be difficult to envisage, and we could only think that he had become President of the party by default, a compromise choice to evade the rivalries of more dynamic figures. We had positively to extract answers from his mouth, as if we were verbal dentists, and this was not from hostility or – one felt – from any real unwillingness, but from a freezing embarrassment that we had patiently to thaw.

He confessed that the NHNP was still a movement of the acculturated Melanesians, consisting mostly of clerks, civil servants and teachers, but the village people were beginning to join, encouraged by the fact that the party had gained a significant political beachhead because three elected members of the Advisory Council had joined it and declared their support publicly. Essentially, he remarked, the party was in agreement with Jimmy Stevens that a just solution of the land question might be based on use. They differed from him in rejecting the custom cultism of Nagriamel and in insisting that the aims of the people could best be achieved by enlarging democratic participation in government in a constitutional way.

British officials and even British planters, he remarked, had shown themselves sympathetic to the party. The French planters remained its implacable enemies, and since they were so important to the commercial life of Santo, this had meant that all European employers exerted pressures of various kinds on members of the party. He himself was unable to speak in public because his employer had threatened him with dismissal, and he had a family to keep. The same applied to other leading members on Santo, though elsewhere in the islands pastors and even Catholic priests were advocating the cause from their pulpits; when we went to Malekula we must meet Father Leymang, the first native Catholic priest in the New Hebrides.

Through all this, one was aware of an almost oppressive caution. Certainly there was nothing of the nationalist extremist, of the fiery militant about X. He still talked of giving the governments advice, rather than of making demands, and he understated the interest of his party in actual independence. In the end, when it was almost too dark for us to see each other and the onslaught of the mosquitoes had reached an unendurable intensity, he asked us quietly if we thought he and his party were right in their activities and their aims! In what other land would one meet a nationalist so diffident and so modest?

5

Our departure from Santo to Malekula as eloquently embodied the curious frontier eccentricity of New Hebridean life as anything else that happened to us in that strange uncountry. Our plane was scheduled to leave at 1.30. By 1.00 all the passengers but one were there, and the pilot, a young Australian with a golden pageboy bob, announced that as it was booking-in time and the missing man had not arrived, he proposed to leave. None of the other passengers – regular New Hebrideans – protested, and we were hustled on board, the doors closed and the propellers revved up. The plane was wheeling around into position to take its run up the hill of the landing strip, when I saw a car racing along the lane to the airstrip. I was sitting in the seat behind the pilot, and I leaned over and tapped his shoulder, since he obviously had not seen it. The engines were turned off, and the doors opened to admit the latecomer. What astonished me was the equable way in which everyone took the incident. The pilot did not think it necessary to apologize, and the passenger, a young Frenchman, did not complain. Everyone obviously accepted that this was the way things were done in the New Hebrides, and that a more rigid standard of efficiency would destroy the flamboyance all appeared to treasure as an attribute of a region where an excess of governments seemed often to have the same effect as no government at all and to produce a cavalier if not a positively anarchic attitude towards the regularities proper to bourgeois existence.

Like most people who were young and rebel in the thirties, and who kept up with such manifestations of contemporary intellectualism as the

Left Book Club and Mass Observation, I had always associated Male-kula with Tom Harrisson's *Savage Civilization*, though of that book I had remembered almost nothing but Harrisson's descriptions of the Big Nambas and their graded societies based on the culture of pigs with curved tusks. We had heard in Vila that the culture he saw in the interior of the island was almost dead: that no more than a hundred Big Nambas had resisted the temptations offered by the Seventh-Day Adventist mission on the west coast, and that this hundred lived largely by the cult of primitism, aggressively charging anthropologists and rich American tourists as much as $20 for the right to take a single group photograph; that of the Small Nambas, who lived farther into the bush, only a score or so had not been tempted to the coast, and their culture, with its strange and fragile funerary figures of sticks and painted clay, was at last feeling the impact of European influences. Still, even knowing this, it was something of a surprise to land on the hilltop airstrip at Norsup, and to find a very elegantly built open house of wood and palm-thatch with a waiting-room and bar. Standing there was a Land-Rover sent by the British agent to take us to his station at Lakatoro; the driver was a short dark man named Kilman, a native Malekulan who spoke excellent English.

Norsup was the site of the great 4,000 acre estate belonging to the Plantation Réunie des Nouvelles Hébrides and laid out on land bought by Higginson for a few hundred dollars' worth of trade goods.

We drove along dirt roads through the regimented lines of the vast palm-groves; the lichen-reddened trunks of the trees were banded with shining collars of tin to prevent the rats from climbing up to eat the nuts, and the effect, as one looked into the distances of the grove ahead, was curiously like an extension into infinity of the vistas of Moorish columns in the great mosque at Cordoba, so that suddenly, in this distant and primitive island, one seemed to gain an insight into the motivations of Moorish architectural forms, seeking to make the mosque in visible appearance as well as in poetic metaphor a palmy oasis of the spirit.

Lakatoro lay five miles down the coast from Norsup; beyond the plantation we drove down to a coral beach, forded a river beside a great boulder as green as jade, and continued, through jungle and the native gardens that mingled with it, until we came to a signpost pointing to the British agency, and climbed through an avenue of flowering hibiscus and tree mallow up the great amphitheatral hillside where the agency is built, a scattering of wooden buildings in a park-like clearing, with the jungle above and below, and before one's eyes a wide panoramic view of the coastline of Malekula and of the offshore islands.

At the bottom of the steps leading to the agent's office, stood two men whose faces were more negroid and whose manner more rustic than we had so far seen on Malekula. They were dressed in ragged singlets and drill trousers, and beside them lay two bundles tied up in sheets of plastic and attached to the ends of sticks like the bundles of classic tramps. They came forward to intercept us with a curiously dog-like expression of pleasure, and insisted on shaking our hands with the flabby grip one always experiences among Melanesians, as if they valued the honour of shaking a white man's hand but at the same time were repelled by physical contact with these beings whose flesh their ancestors had found so much less tasty than good dark meat.

'Those, alas, were Big Nambas,' explained the agent, Darvall Wilkins, when we were sitting in his office. 'They are the converts who have been lured away from their villages, and in abandoning their penis-wrappers for trousers seem to have lost any dignity they once had. In fact, they've really ceased to be Nambas, since the word Namba actually means penis-wrapper, and what always distinguished the Big from the Small Nambas was not their stature, which is about equal, but the size and design of their ornamental codpieces.'

Darvall Wilkins was a russet-haired Australian, who had joined the British Colonial Service twenty years ago when its future seemed to be flourishing. He had begun in Africa, and then as the bounds of Empire were set narrower and narrower, he had come to the New Hebrides, first serving on Tanna and eight years ago coming to Malekula, a formerly much-neglected island, to establish the British agency. When we arrived he was coping with an event that would have shocked an earlier generation of South Seas administrators – a strike by the native civil servants who in the British system, by one of the anomalies that resulted from the threefold government, were paid considerably less than their counterparts in the French service. It was a very mild affair, since the police and the health service employees had refused to join in and the strikers, not wishing to embarrass their non-striking colleagues, had decided not to set up pickets. Somehow the three European officers and three VSO volunteers, with Ida Wilkins, the agent's wife, manning the switchboard, were carrying on very satisfactorily. After all, as Wilkins remarked, large districts in Africa had been managed with no greater staff in the early 1950s, but in the Empire's decline the inexorable workings of Parkinson's Law had become evident, and vaster and vaster numbers of officials were appointed to administer ever smaller and smaller territories.

Wilkins loaned us a jeep and a driver for our first day, and told us where to get one for the next. We planned first to go south, visiting planters along the coast and trying – if the rivers allowed – to reach the village of Benbassis where the Small Nambas traded. Afterwards we would visit Father Leymang, the radical-minded native Catholic priest in the north of Malekula, and the militant villagers of Taotu, the place in all the New Hebrides most dramatically harmed by the injustices of the land situation, and the most dramatically resistant.

Our journey southward the next day lay through the ordered disorder of native plantations merging into jungle. Kilman was our driver, and at the very beginning, as we left the agency, we received a curious insight into the sahib-like customs that still prevailed among the British colonial officials, for though Kilman spoke good English, the agent insisted – clearly for the sake of form – on giving him his instructions in pidgin, which at that moment we saw revealed as not merely a lingua franca useful between differing language groups, but also as an imperial language, used (as Father Sacco appears to have understood) to emphasize the difference between the rulers and the ruled.

As we drove, Kilman talked to me, not about himself, since he obviously philosophically accepted that he had risen as far as he ever would by becoming a government driver, but about his children and the education in which they were so notably successful. Here was again the illusion which we had encountered in Samoa and Tonga and the Gilberts, that education is in itself a magic formula which will ensure a man comfort and happiness without relation to whether it is appropriate to the realities of his situation.

Sometimes there were breaks in the jungle, where the land had been burnt off to make a native plantation, and then we were able to see the soaring ridges of the central mountains, out of which many streams ran down to be forded – and ominously they were running high. Our first destination was a plantation that had belonged to one of the few important British planters in the New Hebrides. His daughter, who had married an Australian, now ran the place, and we found them in a primitive plantation house consisting of a converted American Nissen hut which stood in the midst of the area of rough pasture that was surrounded by their coconut-groves.

Mrs. G. was a comely dark woman – half Melanesian – who had obviously been very pretty in her youth; she had a great deal of vitality, and talked of the past in the very pure English which here and there the missionary teachers left behind them, refined in her case by the experience of a finishing school in Melbourne. Obviously the plantation had made a great deal of money in the past, for she and her husband owned houses both in Sydney and on that Australian Bermuda, Norfolk Island; and it was clear that the house in which we visited them, with its ancient rattan furniture and its shelves of shells as decoration, was a place where they merely camped when they came to view the source of their income.

A dry source indeed it had become, with the price of copra in the island at $30 a ton. For two years they had let the nuts fall rather than make copra – the first year because there had been that unheard-of event, a strike among the plantation workers, and the second year because the prices had fallen so far that with plantation workers earning $2 a day and copra cutters $4 a day it was no longer economical to continue in production. Mrs. G. would like to sell out. 'Quite a nice property for anyone who likes bush!' she quipped, but in fact, when she took us through the little belt of mangroves to the mile of beach which the plantation owned on Bushman's Bay, it was obvious that this splendid sickle of sand with hardly a rock to mar the swimming might well have attracted one of the new generation of land speculators, as a possible site for a resort, if it had not been for the fiasco of Hog Harbour.

In any case, no sale could be made until the status of the land was confirmed, and here again – as among the Pauls on Tanna – we came up against the bitter complaint that while the French looked after their own in the New Hebrides, the British did not. All the French titles on eastern Malaita had been confirmed by the Joint Court, Mrs. G. claimed; her father had bought his land from the local tribesmen in 1901 as legally as any Frenchman of the time had done, and yet, in 1972, she was still waiting for the title to be validated. Indeed, it was hardly reassuring that pieces had already been bitten off the plantation and ruled to be native, a fact that embittered Mrs. G., who remarked that as a half-Melanesian she could not complain if the people were given land, but that the giving should be made equal and the French as well as the British planters should be forced to disgorge. Implicit in her remarks was the suggestion that somehow the British were failing in loyalty to their imperial past if they did not find some way of morally obliging the French to abandon the favoured position which their numbers (three French to one British) as well as their greater interests in the New Hebrides conferred on them.

The G.s were examples of the kind of amiable and rather ineffectual gentility that in a second generation of British planters had succeeded the tough capability necessary among those who first settled on a remote and primitive island like Malekula. Among the French the inclination seemed to have been either towards a kind of half-nativist Bohemian-ism, which characterized some of the older planters, or towards a ruth-less efficiency, which characterized many of the younger men who served as managers for the plantation companies. On our way south lay the establishments of men of both types. One of the great eccentrics of the South Seas, said to have been celebrated like Aggie Grey in *Tales of the South Pacific*, was a certain Pierre T., now an old man, who had lived like a Muslim with a harem of four wives, one of them married in church, and the other three bought by regular bride-price payments from local villages and married according to native custom. Altogether – with these women – he had propagated fourteen children. When we drove into the rough yard of his estate, his truck was not there, and only a family of thin jackal-like dogs stirred about the decaying house of planks and an open-ended Nissen hut beside it, with crowded beds open to the air and the sight of travellers. But there was enough to suggest the kind of decline into a parody of savagery which T.'s neighbour on the next plantation regarded as an abdication of the style of life neces-sary for maintaining the superior status of the white man.

Jean P.'s plantation indeed was in better shape than any other planta-tion I saw in the South Seas. A new corral built for the cattle on which the plantation largely depended was well carpentered and creosoted to prevent early decay. The buildings of the plantation complex – the drying kilns, the barns and stores, were in perfect repair, the roads were well drained, the cattle had been efficiently herded to do their job of keeping the grass down, and the new plantation house which Jean P. had built in semi-native style was light, airy and attractive.

P. himself was a compact blond Frenchman from Provence, with steely blue eyes and a sharp cocky manner, who had spent some years in New Caledonia and for this reason spoke his English, rather dis-concertingly, with a pronounced Australian twang. He was obviously lonely and glad to see any strangers, for his wife was away sick in France, his children were at school and he was surrounded only by the Melanesians whom he despised. His efficiency was bound up with a philosophy of toughness that made him an almost too perfect spokesman for the French planter's point of view. Indeed we never heard the unofficial French point of view put forward elsewhere with such arrogant simplicity. P. declared that in his belief any country should be open to those who can best exploit its resources, and that the New Hebrides should be opened wide to foreign capitalists to whom the land and other resources should be made available under the condition that they be used. He argued that native claims were spurious because the natives did not make a proper use of the land that was even now available to them, and this criticism was clearly bound up with his general low opinion of the Malekulans. 'All this business of providing higher education for the New Hebrideans – it's useless !' he argued. 'They have the kind of minds that are incapable of learning beyond a certain point. Very few of them can absorb anything beyond what they're taught in primary school. Why, sometimes they're so stupid that in exasperation I slap their faces, and then they're too spiritless to resist! Do you think a people like that are capable of governing themselves?'

It was obviously time to leave, if we did not want to abuse our role as guests by violent disagreement, and we did so, driving south through the jungle, which on Malekula is much more open and less tangled with lianas and underbrush than on Santo. There were buzzards flying over the forest, and black and white martins racing through the air, and once we saw two brilliant jungle cocks. Eventually, however, we reached a great muddy wallow that submerged the road for many yards. Kilman got out and waded in to test the solidity of the bottom. As he was doing so a man with a long three-pronged bird spear came out of the bush; even if we did get through the wallow, he said, the river beyond it was so high in flood that it could not be forded, and therefore the way to Benbassis was impassable.

We could only return, on the way back visiting two of the inland villages which lay up a narrow road where the cacao fruit hung ripe for gathering in the woods. At the first place, called Fili, we found the villagers busy at work rebuilding their school, which had been blown down by the hurricane. The schoolmasters were working as carpenters, and teachers and parents were giving their labour freely.

One of the teachers at Fili volunteered to accompany us to the next village, which lay in the blunt end of the valley up which the track ran beside a small river. At times the way was so muddy that we had to leave the road and pick a way between the cacao trees. When eventually we did reach the second place, which was called Lingona, the pastor and the few men who were at home came out to welcome us, and accompanied us on a tour of their village, taking us to a hill at the far end so that we could get a view of it.

From above it looked like a Roman encampment, arranged in four-square order on a large grassy rectangle of flat land, with the houses built in regular rows, well spaced apart, and the gardens all outside the actual area of the village. It was, the pastor assured us, a traditional pattern, and certainly, except for the Presbyterian church and the co-operative store, which both had corrugated iron roofs, everything was built in the traditional way with nothing but traditional materials. Indeed, we were able to see the method of construction, at various stages from the first frame of poles to the completely thatched house, since a number of houses which had been destroyed in the hurricane were being rebuilt. Even the life was still mostly unchanged, for the village – as one of the elders complained – did not even possess a truck, and it was obvious that the cultivation of the land was done in time-honoured ways. The wearing of clothes in the Western style seemed the main accommodation to the modern world, and even this was largely nominal, since inside and behind the houses we saw the women making their laplap for the evening meal, clad only in their kilt-like skirts.

Yet even for the people of Lingona life had changed greatly during the present century, for they had followed the general tendency – in response to the security offered by the Pax Comdominica – for bush people to come nearer to the coast. One old man who accompanied us on to the hilltop from which we looked over the village pointed into the hills behind, and told us that when he was a boy the village had been up there on the high ground. The land was fertile, he said, but nobody wanted to stay when they found they could live peacefully in the valley, and now the village was gone and all the gardens had reverted to bush.

Lingona was a village that seemed largely to have escaped the depredations of the land speculators; even in its present position it was on the edge of the coconut growth line, and its setting of a narrow valley made it unattractive for planters anxious to expand into cattle rearing. Taotu, which we visited on our second day, was an extreme and obvious example of a victimized village. The settlement, we found, was situated on a flat point of land entirely cut off by the Norsup plantation. Three hundred people were living there on 100 acres of land. Their gardens were in the hills, and to reach them they had to walk an hour and a half each way through the groves that had belonged to their ancestors. The man who had led the resistance to the French planters was Chief David Williams. We found him working as an orderly in the clinic which the French government had established at Norsup, a tall and burly man, with a great bare belly hanging over the tight shorts that were his only garment, but nevertheless a man of exceptional presence. Chief David seemed to relish the idea of telling the tale of his village, but he felt it should be done in a communal way; we should go to the village and arrange with a man called Kenari Williams for a meeting of the Landing Committee, and then we would hear the voice of Taotu.

So we went into the village, noting the difference between the well-kept plantation roads, and the village roads which were poor because of the marshy nature of the ground and the difficulty of getting enough labour to build them up with coral. Kenari was a young-looking man – with a smooth face that seemed more Polynesian than Melanesian; he suggested that we should meet at half-past three in the afternoon, which would give him time to gather the Landing Committee.

We arrived at the agreed time, and found the ten members of the Landing Committee already sitting in the red-painted meeting hall. They varied from old men in their seventies who carried the memories of the village to men in their thirties who sustained its anger. We sat down, as one always does in the South Seas, in the order decreed by custom. As the white-haired visiting elder, I sat at the table opposite Chief David, and Mike faced Kenari who sat on the Chief's right hand and acted as orator; Inge sat beside me on the right, and the rest disposed themselves behind the Chief and his orator, clearly according to rank. We talked for more than three hours, and what happened was an extraordinary act of communal history-speaking as between them the Chief and his men remembered and pieced together the chain of events from the 1880s.

The history began between 1883 and 1887 when the agents of Higginson and his Compagnie Caledonienne actually 'bought' two pieces of land, one of about 10,000 acres for 690 francs in merchandise and the other of more than 20,000 acres for 849 francs in merchandise, the two lots forming a broad band across the island from the east coast to the west and involving a village to the west called Laravat. The Landing Committee had copies of the deeds, and as they showed us these extraordinary fabrications they pointed out that not all the signatories were people of Taotu or Laravat, but some had come from villages at the north end of Malekula, and that in any case no individual or group of individuals had the right to sell tribal land. It was doubtful in fact if even the living members of a tribe as a whole had the right to do so, since the land belonged to the whole lineage, the ancestors as well as the living.

The land lay unoccupied until 1925, and by that time there was hardly anyone alive who remembered the men who came on a ship so long ago and gave people muskets for putting marks on paper. Then the Norsup Company began to plant its estate, using Tonkinese labourers. They destroyed native houses and gardens in the area marked out for the plantation, and when Kenari's father, who was then Chief, protested, the Tonkinese were used as goons to create a reign of terror, so that only a few men remained in the village to make sure that it too was not destroyed. When Kenari's father refused to cede a small piece of land not included in the deed which the Company wanted to complete its plantation, the Company threatened him with a French warship, and he gave in, no payment being made for the area obtained in this way. Later, in 1932, the villagers worked for the Company, planting coconuts, but did not receive the promised payment, and when they protested, the Tonkinese threatened to 'cut off our necks'.

After that the situation remained dormant, though the villagers felt a growing resentment at having to walk so long each day through the plantation to their gardens. Then, in 1954, a villager cleared a part of the bush just behind the plantation and planted seventy coconut palms there. The French manager, a man named Tanguy, instructed his men to tear out the palms, asserting for the first time since the 1880s the Company's right to the land all the way across the island, and in 1955 the 'spearlines' – to use the expressive pidgin term for surveyors – appeared to mark out the claim. The survey went on for two years, and by the end of the 1950s, realizing that even their existing gardens, in which they had been undisturbed since the 1920s, were imperilled, the villages of Taotu and Laravat both formed what they called their 'Landing Committees'.

The people of Taotu, led by Chief David and Kenari Williams now began to organize with a view to resistance, and, hearing of their mood, the lawyers representing the plantation owners came to ask the villagers to specify the land they needed. The people of Taotu replied that all the land was theirs, including the existing plantation, that they had never sold the land in accordance with their own custom in the first place, and that they refused to accept any division at all. As Kenari put it: 'If you want to take our lands, then you cut off our necks and that ends everything.'

The matter went to the Joint Court and two years later the same lawyers came back and showed them maps of what had been decided, saying, as Kenari translated it into his own colourful language: 'The Joint Court is cutting out your tongue; you cannot say anything.' The map gave the French all the good land and left the hills and the swamps to the people of Taotu; when the villagers protested the French made the derisory gesture of offering them twelve acres of good land.

There was a lull until 1965, and then the French Company proposed to build a road across the island, and put forward such a persuasive argument that the people of Taotu accepted the idea that it would be for the general good, and agreed to provide voluntary labour. But when the spearlines routed the road so that it passed through disputed territory, Chief David withdrew his men and the work ceased. At about the same time the Company fenced off an area of land in the disputed bush for the purpose of rearing cattle.

Realizing that they had no hope of a fair hearing from the French authorities, the people of Taotu took their case to the British agent, who promised help and actually accompanied their representatives to Vila, where they saw the British Resident Commissioner. 'He turn his back. He stand by the window. He look out. He say it is very difficult. He do nothing.' What Chief David and Kenari realized only very dimly, if they realized it at all, was that the ground rules under which the Condominium operated really allowed the British Commissioner little room for action, since decisions regarding land were specifically stated by international agreement to be the responsibility of the Joint Court, and the Court had been provided with no machinery to enforce its decisions. At most the British could apply moral pressure.

Finally, in 1967, frustration began to create a mood of militancy among the people of Taotu. Responding to it, Chief David served notice on Tanguy that he must take up the fence he had erected and that he must refrain from his plan of building a labourers' village in the bush. Tanguy did not build the labourers' houses, but he did not take

up the fence, and after Chief David made another fruitless journey to
Vila in 1968, the villagers decided to take the law into their own hands.
To begin, they drove away some men from the northern end of Malekula whom the Company had hired as labourers, threatening them
with cane knives and axes, and then, in 1969 Chief David precipitated
a major confrontation by warning Tanguy that if he did not take up his
fence, the villagers would do it for him.

Tanguy attempted to repeat history by threatening to call in a
French warship. But the villagers knew as well as he did that the time
of gunboats was over, and finally, their patience ended, the men of
Taotu one day gathered, a hundred strong, armed themselves with
axes, hammers and wire-cutters, and set out to destroy the fence. In a
long day of work they cut the wire up into small lengths so that it
could not be restrung, bent and buckled the metal fence posts with
their hammers, broke the water channels, and set the Company's
steers free to wander through the bush. On their way back they chose
their route and marched defiantly through the Company village at
Norsup. The tiny French and British detachments of police arrived and
barred the way. A man waving an axe advanced upon the cordon,
shouting: 'If you want to talk to us, come to our village!' The crowd
surged forward, the police ranks opened, and the men marched home
in triumph to Taotu. Nobody was prosecuted. Even the French authorities realized that the situation was too complex for force to solve. The
men who had done this, be it noted, were not pagan followers of Jon
Frum or Jimmy Stevens; they were all good, devout Presbyterians.

Since then the Norsup Company and the Bank of Indo-China which
owns it have been embarrassed enough by publicity to make several
offers. Some of these the British officials regarded as very favourable,
since they would have given the people of the village far more territory
than they might use in any foreseeable future. But given the Melanesian
idea of land as a sacred trust from the ancestors, this was not sufficient.
The men of Taotu wanted all their land back, so that they could decide
on its disposition. Then, Chief David assured us, with all the dignity
that his massiveness and his slowness of speech emphasized, they would
be willing to give land for public use; they would even be willing to
lease land on reasonable terms to British planters; but never again
would they have any dealings with the French, to whom he applied,
with great deliberation, the adjective that the French usually apply to
the British; they were perfidious.

One could not say of the men of Taotu that they allowed their material interests to interfere with their loyalty to tradition. Though the Norsup plantation was a ready source of work, and would have been glad to take on people from Taotu, if only for the sake of appearance, only two men out of the whole 300 inhabitants were in its employment. Some worked for the French and British governments and the Condominium. A fair number were earning money in New Caledonia. But many lived from their land up in the hills, selling a little copra and cacao, a few yams and taro.

In the New Hebrides we were certainly learning the permutations of colonial despair. In the very elusiveness of the followers of Jon Frum we had seen the recessiveness of a cult combining a reverence for the lost past of paganism with a millenarianism of the most eccentric kind, based on the presumably endless resources of American capitalism. In Jimmy Stevens we had seen a chiliastic prophet seeking to reinforce a rational approach to the land problem with an emphasis on custom that would enhance his power over the less educated of New Hebrideans. In the deliberately anonymous leaders of the New Hebridean National Party we had seen the ineffectuality of the educated people who were dependent for employment on the alien governments and alien companies and therefore unable to express their convictions effectively. And in the men of Taotu we saw the predicament of men who had tried to play the game as white men taught them, who were dutiful Christians, who had set up a co-operative and a local council, who owned three trucks, and who had proceeded in the faith that the white man's justice would see that right was eventually done, but who found themselves lost in a maze of legalities with no apparent way out but by violence.

After that evening with the men of Taotu, which ended as they walked with us through the gathering dusk along the jungle road to meet our jeep-driver, we began to wonder how far the rational and balanced approach of a man like Titus Path could work in a world where the ethics of European business were still so amoral as to sustain unjust deals made almost a century before, and where the native people still clung, whether they were Christian or pagan, to their ancient concepts of the inalienability of land. I think by the time we went north on Malekula in search of Father Leymang we had given up hope of finding anyone who could offer a solution short of the expulsion of the French, which seemed the least likely eventuality of all.

Father Leymang shared with a New England French Canadian, Father Soucy, the Catholic mission at Wala. When we arrived, Father Leymang was not there, though he was expected back shortly from a trip inland, and Father Soucy was supervising the completion of the roof to the new church, one of those massive concrete constructions by which the Roman Church, like the French state, seems intent on proclaiming its will to remain in the New Hebrides. He showed with pride the stained-glass windows that had been put together by his village workers, and then took us down to his parsonage where he displayed with equal pride the chief's skull he kept in his study to show that the mana of his faith was strong enough to defy the greatest of native taboos. But he could never, he admitted, get even the most outwardly devout of his parishioners to follow his example. They all feared the demits, as they called the spirits of the dead. They avoided taboo places. They always reinforced the attentions of a Western doctor by calling in a native doctor who claimed to exorcise evil spirits. And they all continued to buy brides, at prices that ran as high as $400 in cash and fifteen pigs – a good pig being worth as much as $100. If an unmarried girl happened to be compromised in any way, this was a serious matter, not for moral reasons, but because it reduced her value as a bride, and customary damages were expected of anyone who offended in this way. One young man was seen merely talking to a girl at night; after negotiation his family paid $400 in compensation. Another young man actually got a girl with child, but denied paternity, and the result was a battle between the two clans which ended only after several people had been severely wounded. In marriage as in sickness, the people of Wala liked to follow both ways. The wedding would begin with a church ceremony, and after that would come the custom wedding, with the traditional processions and dances, with great feasting and gifts for all the participants. For this also the bridegroom's family would pay; the bill often came to $750 over and above the actual bride price.

Father Soucy was that quite exceptional man, so far as our experience in the South Seas went, a priest who was frank about the extent to which the old religions still survived under the surface of the new, and he kept us fascinated with this subject until a motor bike roared up the drive to the parsonage, and a figure in a helmet, oily khaki clothes and heavy scuffed boots came stamping on to the veranda. He was Father Leymang, an intense-faced young man who spoke in a quick French, serviceable rather than elegant, which he emphasized with brusque Gallic gestures that suggested that he had spent time in France itself.

Even Father Leymang had no easy solution to offer; perhaps at best he saw complexities more clearly than others. He condemned any too easy talk of independence. 'Independence here is a demagogic word. It has no base to make it a reality.' Not only did the imperial powers show no intention of leaving, but they had created no administrative infrastructure by which a liberated people might be supported. And even the question of land was not so simple as Jimmy Stevens and his supporters represented. Apart from the question of alien land claims, there was the quite different problem of the people from the bush making their way down to the better life of the coast, and finding that wherever they sought land there were coastal people with prior ances- tral claims. If the native people expected justice from the foreigners, they must also be willing to share the land they had with their fellow New Hebrideans. 'But first, of course,' he added wryly, 'we have to convince the New Hebrideans that they are one people. In the past they were just the inhabitants of various islands, speaking different languages, following different customs. It will be a miracle if they do not revert to their separateness.' But, he emphasized, that did not mean he accepted the present situation. 'Le Condominium est un monstre!' he shouted passionately. And he added that he often regretted he was a priest, since it restricted his actions. But what actions he might consider appropriate he gave no hint.

One thing only emerged with certainty from the series of encounters we had experienced on Tanna, on Santo and on Malekula: that no New Hebridean who was conscious of the situation perpetuated by the Condominium was less than acutely discontented with it, and that none had found any effort he made to change the situation leading beyond frustration. What the precise outcome would be it was hard even for those who knew the islands intimately to prophesy, but history seems to suggest that situations where universal discontent meets with universal frustration end usually in tragedy.

PART SIX

The Islands of Solomon

1

By the time we reached the Solomon Islands we were already tired from our months of journeying and talking on other islands, months when every day we would get up hours before the late morning which is our normal habit, and still sit late into the night in whatever room we occupied writing up the diary of the day's impressions and conversations. Even so, and though it meant a renewal of the same rigours, we found the Solomons the most congenial of all the island groups we visited in the Pacific – even more congenial than the Gilberts. On its immense variety of high volcanic islands lived a range of peoples unparalleled elsewhere: light Australoid Melanesians in the east and blue-black Negroid Melanesians in the west; Polynesian vestiges on the outlying islands and Micronesian immigrants. And from such a variety of peoples, combined with the geographical isolation of the islands, and even of remote coastlines or upland valleys on the same island, there has arisen a multitude of languages and cultures probably unrivalled anywhere else in the world. On top of all else, the Solomons present a range of sea and island scenery that I have nowhere found excelled.

Inge and I, having left Mike who was returning to Fiji, flew in from Vila to the Solomons' capital of Honiara on the island of Guadalcanal. Guadalcanal revealed itself from the air as a spine of dark mountains running south-east to north-west with small alluvial plains caught between out-thrusting ridges on the eastern side. The higher mountains were cloaked in cloud, and indeed never emerged while we remained on the island; we could not see the forested ridges of the weather side of the island, but on the lower eastern slopes over which we flew there were large areas of uncultivated savanna, and wide gravelly river-beds meandered down to small deltas on the sea-edge. Near the coast lay coconut-plantations and the squared-off patterns of rice paddies, but most of the island seemed hardly touched by human presence, and indeed we found that, although it is the centre of imperial activity in the Solomons, Guadalcanal contains bush tribes which are less in contact with European civilization and consequently less acculturated than the people on most of the other islands. Guadalcanal at first sight had a somewhat forbidding quality, which one sensed quite apart from any knowledge of its evil history during World War II, and although the place was beautiful enough in its own brooding way, we never liked it as actively as we did the other parts of the Solomons.

We landed at Henderson Field, where the runway was alive with an invasion of small yellow butterflies, found our way easily through the customs and immigration procedures, and, after the sense of tensions unresolved that had built up during our last days in the New Hebrides, felt a sudden relaxation in the human atmosphere.

The hotel we went to in Honiara was named after Mendana, the Spaniard who discovered the islands in 1568 and out of some mad idea that a biblical king had mined his gold there called them the Solomons, a name that has survived because the people Mendana found there had never thought of their islands as one place with a name of its own. The Mendana Hotel was a passable colonial hostelry whose main attraction was the great roofed terrace facing out to the lagoon, where one ate and drank looking across the Sound to the Florida Islands, whose appearance changed constantly; sometimes they were black silhouettes, sometimes they were crests of amethyst decorated with plumes of illuminated cloud, and sometimes, so near to the colour of a luminous sky did the distant sea become, they seemed to float like mirages, detached from earth and sea alike. There were notices on the beach warning swimmers of sharks, and every time we sat on the terrace we would look for the menacing triangular fins breaking the surface, but the most formidable thing we saw was a great stingray leaping blackly and hitting the water with a resounding slap as it descended. Around us as we watched would echo the boom of ageing American voices, broken by staccato Japanese, for Honiara does a modest tourist trade which consists almost entirely of veterans from both sides who return to this town built on their old battlefield, where even now streets are occasionally closed for the disposal of some live projectile a work crew has discovered.

'White man's paradise – black man's hell'; so runs the description of Honiara one hears often repeated by educated islanders in the Solomons, and indeed there is no doubt that more than any other of the South Sea capitals this seems to have been made especially for the comfort and convenience of the imperial rulers. Shoreline Honiara is a place of widely spaced buildings between which one can walk with ease even at tropical temperatures through the great gardens and along the tree-shaded roads. One way from the hotel we could stroll to the government offices. Opposite stood the little museum where we bought shell money and a lozenge-shaped club with incised geometrical decorations that, as it stands upright on my desk, is now often mistaken by visitors unaware of its provenance for an abstract sculpture in the manner of Brancusi. In the other direction we found the scattering of shops, built around a great Quonset hut where the Solomon Islands Trading Company operated its supermarket. Over the river lay the wooden shops and eating places of Chinatown, Old and New; the difference in age between the two was clearly marginal, since neither could have existed before the wartime devastation of the area ended in the 1940s, but in feeling they were distinct. Old Chinatown was run by traders whose veranda'd stores with vast miscellanies of goods reflected the patterns of the pre-war South Seas, and who were quite willing to bargain with native farmers over the small quantities of copra or the bags of forest products they brought down from the hills, while New Chinatown was operated by the smart young Chinese whose businesses catered to the white population. In Old Chinatown all the races of Honiara mingled, and there one would often encounter little groups of bush people, the women with pipes in their mouths and great mops of frizzy, lime-blonded hair, and the men, bare-torsoed, with red lava-lavas, and their mouths almost as red as their kilts from the chewing of betel; each of them would wear, hung round his neck, a little closely woven bag which contained the appropriate ingredients – the fragments of areca nut, the leaves, and the lime in a bamboo tube with a thin stick to dab a white speck inside the cheek while chewing.

The ridges named and celebrated in the histories of the war in the Pacific pressed close in towards Honiara, and high upon them were built the houses of the white government officials (mostly British) and the white businessmen (mostly Australian). Narrow dark valleys separated these hilly promontories, and it was here, strictly observing rank, that little wooden houses had been built for the Melanesian workers – a valley for clerks, a valley for lower ranks, and so on; these settlements, quickly becoming shabby in the monsoon weather, had already the look of slums-to-be, in sharp contrast with the neatness of the native houses in the villages outside Honiara, where the renewable covering of pandanus leaf always gives a look of freshness and tidiness. It was, as a visiting historian remarked when we looked down from the patrician ridges into the plebeian valleys, an almost perfect demonstration of the maxim that 'the mighty shall be exalted.'

We found the British colonial officials in Honiara communicative and informative. There was none of the aggressive unco-operativeness we had encountered in the Gilberts, and obviously no inclination to hide things from visiting inquirers, which was a good thing, since except for a couple of Chinese trading schooners and a mission ship stationed away in the New Georgia group of islands, marine transport was entirely in the hands of the government; so, on the big island of Malaita to which our first trip out from Honiara would lead us, were road transport and the rest houses. Only air transport, consisting between the islands of tiny five-seater Beechcraft Barons, was controlled by the small private firm of Solair.

But, friendly as they were on an operative level, in social terms the officials of Honiara formed a close sahib-like order that was almost impenetrable to outsiders. They seemed to take their tone from the governor, an aloof and inaccessible bachelor who – it was said – would show a warmth of interest only when one talked of the birds he watched with binoculars from the windows of his office; we had no opportunity to exercise our ornithological knowledge at Government House. As for the rest of the civil officers, not only did they never invite one to their homes; they kept even their club inviolate from alien presences, and it was only the native officials and politicians who accepted our invitations to the hotel.

This strange social involution was paralleled by the equally self-contained quality of Honiara itself. One would have thought an effort would have been made to open up the island which was the administrative and commercial centre of the colony. But in fact the only road on Guadalcanal ran for fifty miles along about half the inner coast of the island, with Honiara roughly in the middle. One good reason was the steepness of the inland terrain, whose narrow valleys were divided by sharp high ridges. Even the jeep tracks ended five miles in from Honiara; to go farther inland one had to walk with porters, and to reach the weather coast of the island, where a prophet called Moro was leading an influential custom cult, it would have taken days of trekking over terrain whose steepness would have challenged the endurance of even a young and experienced mountaineer. The only other way to get there – and indeed to any part of the Guadalcanal coast away from the fifty miles of road – was by boat, and the government boats went on rare administrative visits, since the accepted policy had become to leave the more primitive villages to themselves unless some disaster like famine or pestilence appeared likely or some atrocious crime were committed. No boat went to the weather coast while we were on Guadalcanal, though when Gordon Babineau later visited the Solomons with the camera crew he was more fortunate.

Since almost all the coastal road on Guadalcanal ran through plantations – the Lever holdings to the east and a number of large independent estates to the west – and people tended to live here in company settlements rather than native villages, there was not a great deal that was novel to us. The parrots were magnificent, for there were not only the green and red coconut lories, but the even more splendid cardinal lories, their plumage an extraordinary spectrum of vermilion, crimson and scarlet. And when the parrots palled – and there were very few other birds except for the white herons we saw occasionally on patches of damp grassland – we found the people not only much freer in their manner than the New Hebrideans, but also inclined to an extraordinary variety of degrees of acculturation. I quote my diary impressions of one short length of road towards the north-west corner of the island, near the Catholic mission of Visala.

'As we return at evening, the people are coming back from their gardens, with yams and taros and sweet potatoes, with firewood and coconut-fronds and bundles of pandanus leaves, all balanced on their heads. Tractors with trailers drive by, their drivers crowned with chaplets of plaited coconut-leaves, carrying loads of shirted and shorted young men who work in the plantations. A man walks alone along the road in a brilliant aloha shirt, listening to a large transistor radio which he carries, with its aerial extended like a steel fishing rod, in the crook of his arm. No more than a hundred yards away a tall man out of the bush, with tatooed chest and high-frizzed hair, clad only in a red sulu, and with massive shell bracelets on his arm, stands smoking his pipe by the roadside.'

Guadalcanal is traditionally a matriarchal island, and perhaps the most striking personal encounter was with a little roadside procession whose members had come down from some village in the hills; in front walked a young man in a blue sulu with a tightly and obviously artificially frizzed head of hair; behind were two girls in filthy red washed-out rags of dresses, and two completely naked small boys; and in the midst of this entourage and obviously thoroughly in control of it marched a mother figure as archetypal as the Venus of Willendorf, all fat, glossy, chocolate-brown amplitude, with bare papaw breasts and a vast belly jutting over the red kilt slung low on her hips, jangling with many splendid necklaces and stacks of bangles hand-cut from white and red shells.

Between trips into the country that was accessible, and our visits – several a day – to the government offices in an effort to complete the arrangements for our journeys in the islands, we spent the four days before we were able to leave Honiara. We only had one real adventure, when our hired car stalled in the middle of a ford across a wide and fast-running river, but then a jeepload of foresters arrived providentially, towed us back to shore and got the car into operation. And our only meeting of any significance – and that in a rather plaintive way – occurred on our visit, in the company of a native magistrate named Francis Talasese, to the village of Roroni, about thirty miles east of Honiara, where Jacob Vouza, one of the heroes of the Pacific war on Guadalcanal, acted as the village headman.

Talasese was one of the small group of Western-educated Solomon islanders – he had been as far as London in his studies and had been a victim there of the militancy of post-war British racism – and he took a certain pride in the fact that he coined the slogan 'Independence by Seventy Five', though he admitted that if liberation were so hurried the islanders might lose more than they would gain from a gradually relaxed British presence. Like other native university graduates in Honiara, he felt it necessary to dissociate his ideas from those of the radical native politicans in neighbouring New Guinea. The Solomon islanders, he insisted, meant to find their own way, though it did not seem impossible to him that one day, when the Solomons were free and the New Hebrides had shaken off the French, some kind of loose Melanesian federation might emerge, to balance the power of Fiji and the Polynesian countries of Samoa and Tonga, which he felt had grown too influential and too arrogant.

Past Henderson Field and the large Lever plantations, with their company villages and their great taboo notices, we drove to the Guadalcanal Plains, where the mountains recede and give room to pampas-like prairies covered with grasses higher than a man, with tall silvery plumes. Here were the rice fields, divided by their curving dykes into long narrow paddies down which great red combines were reaping and threshing, for all the world as if they were working on the plains of Canada. The rice was being grown by a private enterprise called the Guadalcanal Plains Company, and the complicated transactions that Talasese explained illustrated how different the British handling of the land situation in the Solomons had been from that of the parallel governments and their Joint Court in the New Hebrides.

Some land in the Solomons had been acquired by white planters and missions before land regulation began when the British consolidated their rule early in the present century, but after 1914 native lands were protected. They could only be held by the customary possessors, the landholding lineages, they could not be alienated from them, and they could be leased only to the government, not to individuals. When it was decided that the colony could be made self-supporting in rice if the Guadalcanal Plains were brought under cultivation, it was obvious that this could not be done efficiently by a cluster of clans, and the solution eventually found was for the government to lease the land from the owning lineages and then to sub-let it for a limited period to the Company, which would bring it under cultivation.

A mile or two beyond the rice fields the road ended and we had to travel along a rough lane between grass so high that it shut out everything but the narrow prospect of the lane itself and the mirrors of its puddles. After three miles bumping along this track where two cars could not possibly have passed, we reached Roroni, with its houses scattered among groves of fruit trees and shade trees, on the shores of a river that flowed deeply between eroded banks of mud.

Vouza lived in a house on stilts in the centre of the village, and came out on to the veranda and down the creaky steps to meet us, an erect old man with a bush of crinkly white hair and a clear-eyed open smile that revealed a set of excessively regular false teeth. He welcomed us gravely, and took us to sit in the village assembly place, where benches made of perforated steel track left by the Americans had been set up under the giant banian tree that overshadowed his house. Vouza started off at once, as if some inner signal had been tripped, on the story of his wartime adventures, speaking in a soft voice and a mixture, that at some times became incomprehensible, of English and pidgin. He told the story of his service with the Americans who were already on one end of Guadalcanal, and of his capture, torture and near-killing by the Japanese, the adventure that had brought him celebrity. Vouza had been a policeman with the British; he showed a photo of himself in the pre-war force, a squad of fuzzy-haired tamed wild men clad only in belts and kilts and surrounding a wispy Englishman in white uniform with pith helmet. He had imbibed with great literalness the code of unflinching loyalty which the British had taught him, and had kept to it even when many of his teachers fled before the threat of Japanese invasion. When he was captured spying near their lines, he refused to tell the Japanese anything, pretending constantly that he was kanaka, which in the Solomons means a man of the bush, until they gave him many bayonet wounds and left him for dead. But Vouza had only been pretending death, and when the Japanese had gone he managed to drag himself to the American lines and to present his report on the Japanese position, which had a decisive effect on the fighting in the Solomons.

We could not fail to know, as Vouza kept on talking softly and then took off his shirt to show the scars of his bayonet wounds, that he had told the story often to visitors like ourselves, and yet as he did so the real dignity of the man came through, and the sense that in telling the tale to the best of his ability to mere strangers he was fulfilling the Melanesian sense of hospitality. He took us on to the veranda of his house to show us his relics: the key to the city of Arnhem in California, medals and certificates from the American Marines, a photograph taken in London when he attended the Coronation and shook hands with Queen Elizabeth and Queen Salote of Tonga, who impressed him the more of the two. Vouza apologized for the decrepitude of his house, which prevented him from displaying his relics. And his home, indeed, was in the advanced decay of a superannuated native house, with the roof sagging and the coconut midriff floor of the veranda quaking perilously under the tread.

It was the pathos which all of us sensed in Vouza's condition that opened the floodgates of Francis Talasese's resentment on our journey back to Honiara. He remarked that Vouza was too old now to go out as he would have done in the past and gather the materials that were needed to renew his home. And so this celebrated hero sat in a decaying house that as little as $200 would have refurbished so that the tiny museum of his relics might be properly displayed. Partly the situation was due to the failure of the villagers to help him; he was losing the influence that had been his even a decade ago, largely because of the community disintegration which current circumstances had brought about in Roroni. Some people now commuted to Honiara to earn money. Some had moved away to live on their land. The urge to live in villages and create communities larger than the clan hamlet has always been rather fragile in the Solomons, and unless there is a vigorous leadership, from a mission or some inspired and inspiring individual, villages are likely to disintegrate back into clan hamlets. Roroni had been kept together by the influence and the fame of Vouza in his prime; now Vouza was declining, the place was falling apart.

Still, Talasese argued, this did not exonerate the white people whom Vouza had helped so loyally. The British had a grudge against him, because during the 1940s Vouza had shown sympathy for the anti-governmental Marching Rule movement centred on Malaita; he was the most prominent native of Guadalcanal to become involved. But the Americans, whom he had helped most of all, did not even have that excuse. Twenty years ago they had fêted and honoured him. Now that he was an old man in need they had forgotten him.

The thought of Vouza's plight seemed to excite Talasese, and we ended the journey with an extraordinary outburst against both the British officials and the native politicians who were coming to the front now that the Governing Council was beginning to look like a parliament and the chairman of its committees were assuming roles – in matters of local concern – very similar to those of cabinet ministers.

Talasese accused the British administration of dishonesty in hiding its real motives, and the native politicians of being weak, uneducated men willing to be bought with flattery and – he suggested – with material benefits. He talked of the corruption he had seen through his public employment – though he never gave specific instances – and he announced his intention of going into politics to expose it. I could not avoid feeling that there were deeper motives at work than Talasese's personal feelings, and that his outburst suggested the potentiality of strife between the young men with modern educations – who like Talasese came mainly from the western islands – and the less educated majority who tended to be led by men who had risen by the traditional Melanesian methods of gaining power.

Later, after our return from the outer islands, I met one of these leaders who had risen to power largely because the people of his island of Malaita regarded him as a 'big man'. I found him an impressive political being. He was David Kausimae, who in 1972 was Chairman of the Committee on Natural Resources. The chairmen were appointed by the Governor – though under the new constitution now going into practice they will be picked by the legislature – but even when we visited the Solomons they had authority over the British officials who acted as their heads of departments. Kausimae was not only a shadow minister; he was also, at that time, the man whose name was most often mentioned as the potential Chief Minister when self-government arrived.

I tried several times, without success, to see David Kausimae but a day before we were due to leave the Solomons for New Guinea he finally rang me up, and came to the hotel in the evening. We sat on the edge of the terrace with the beat of the waves that rode in through the broken reef giving an accompaniment to our conversation. Kausimae was a rather shaggy, soft-spoken man, with a nervous laugh and a pleasant manner that did not entirely conceal his great natural shrewdness. He volunteered the fact that he had received no more than a primary education in his village on Malaita, and had the roughly polished air of a man with one foot in the world of custom and one in the world of modern politics and also – considering the relish with which he consumed the Bacardis-and-Cokes we were drinking – in the world of modern manners.

I tried to locate the source of Kausimae's power, which I suspected lay partly in his links with the custom movements, but I found him elusive in his answers. He was willing to talk of the Malaita Marching Rule movement in historical terms. It had arisen, he remarked, as a movement of protest among the chiefs of Malaita when the government sought to vest authority in appointed headmen and thus challenged the traditional ways of rising to positions of influence. The Marching Rule chiefs gathered the people of the coastal regions from their separate hamlets into villages which they fortified with stockades and turned into miniature baronies until the government forces reduced them and the leaders were arrested and imprisoned. However, Kausimae remarked, the ultimate result of Marching Rule had been good, since in 1951 a commissioner came out from Britain, the rebel leaders were released, and the British started on the experiment of local councils which was the first step towards autonomy. The men who went to prison for their Marching Rule activities were still heroes in the eyes of the people, on Malaita at least, and one of them was – in 1972 – the president of the island's district council.

Yet when I asked Kausimae whether the heritage of Marching Rule had anything to do with his own success in politics, he denied it, though I had discovered on Malaita that he was brother-in-law to one of the movement's foremost leaders. Similarly, when I mentioned Moro and his custom movement on Guadalcanal, he denied any knowledge of it, though it was impossible that anyone connected with the government of the Solomons should have been other than acutely aware of this leader with his thousands of followers who was challenging the very idea of establishing an independent country of the Solomons on the basis of a political system borrowed from the British.

I came to suspect that Kausimae did indeed, in his island constituency, seek the support of the traditionalists generally known as 'custom people', and that his links with the leadership of Marching Rule were useful in assuring that support. But at the same time he realized that the way the Solomons were moving towards independence made it necessary to understand and practise politics in the European manner, and in this he certainly seemed to be proving himself an apt student, for everything he said to me was directed towards enhancing his image as a leader who understood both the needs of his people and what could be done within the possibilities offered by the modern world. He talked of the difficulties of reconciling the traditional landholding system with a modern financial system based on individual ownership, which meant that Melanesian farmers could not get loans because they had no individual titles to show for their lands. And he discussed the problems that arose because of the lack of a political party in the Solomons; native members of the Governing Council were elected on personality rather than principle, and made individual promises to their electors which they could not possibly keep. This problem was compounded by the fact that the Solomon islanders had no tradition of unity, and the only way to provide it was by creating a political party with a platform in which people from all the islands agreed on basic aims.

When I said to David Kausimae that he had been mentioned as the probable first Prime Minister, he laughed, not without pleasure, and ordered another Bacardi-and-Coke, over which he uttered the obiter dictum by which I most remember him. 'In the Solomons the two most important things are land and women.'

His party, the Solomons United National Party, was indeed founded, but in 1973 a strange and unexpected thing would happen, for it was not the old-style native leaders with their custom following who then won in the vital elections for the Governing Council that would initiate self-government, but the discontented educated civil servants for whom Francis Talasese had spoken in his passionate outburst, and David Kausimae's abounding hopes were temporarily eclipsed when he became the only member of his new party to be elected. I regretted the news, for in spite of his efforts to impress me as a modern politician, Kausimae seemed to me to have a much closer sense of the islanders' real desires and needs than the bitter ambitious men coming home from the universities.

2

Malaita is not the largest island of the Solomons; Guadalcanal, Santa Isabel and San Cristobal all exceed it in area, but it is the most populous, containing about a third of the population of the colony. This made Malaita a favourite place of labour recruiting ,which sometimes assumed a violent form, the recruiters using blackbirding methods to obtain labourers by force or fraud, and the natives 'cutting out' recruiting ships, massacring their crews and pillaging their cargoes.

Even today, when the recruiters have vanished and blackbirding is merely a bad folk memory, Malaitans still go out in large numbers to the other islands to work as labourers, though the island also contains, in its interior and on some of the artificial islands which give the look of a primitive Venice to the lagoons of Lau and Langalanga, most of the pagans still left in the Solomons. It is this mixture of a good deal of experience of the outside world with an obstinate core of intense traditionalism that has made Malaita the least easy of the Solomon Islands to govern; as well as being the original home of Marching Rule, it was also the site of the last massacre of Europeans in the Solomon Islands, which took place in 1927.

On the morning of our journey to Malaita we flew out over the Iron Bottom Sound (where on a clearer day we might have seen the wrecks of Japanese and American warships lying in the depths like ghosts). A wall of squally rain stretched over in the west, between the tip of the Floridas and the western point of Guadalcanal, and we thought uneasily of the talk of a cyclone wandering in the seas towards the New Hebrides which we had heard at the airport. Two English nurses were sitting behind us, and it was to the tune of their incessant chatter, like the yapping of small dogs, that we flew out over the Floridas, beautiful small islands that could be seen whole and in detail from a low-flying plane. Tulagi lay like a model town on its island in a broad harbour. There were villages scattered on the shores, but none visible in the jungled interior of the islands, though the plumes of smoke rose here and there in the forest to show where land was being cleared for yam patches.

Over the Floridas Malaita came in sight, a long ridge of dark mountains, partly in cloud and stretching to each side of the small coastal point we approached, to land on an airstrip that consisted of a short rectangle of grass crossing the point from beach to beach.

A young government officer named Peter Madden was there to meet us and he took us into Auki to make our arrangements for the journey we were making to Maluu on the north end of the island. Auki is the only town on Malaita, and it exists by virtue of being a government centre; it is a collection of bungalows and office buildings scattered among the remnants of jungle, with a minute main street down by the water with three Chinese stores and a bar. To get our transport we had to go down to the Public Works depot that was run by a squad of Royal Engineers seconded from England on nine-month turns of duty, and there we were given a Land-Rover and a driver, a dour young Malaitan named Stanley who wore gold ear-rings. We went back into the village to buy a box of tinned goods and bread from Quon Hung's trading store to serve for our days at Maluu, and then set out on our journey northward on a well-maintained gravel road. Stanley drove fast but well, with the set scowl which at first we thought was a sign of xenophobic resentment; later we found it was a common Malaitan expression, denoting an essential gravity, but easily dissolved so that a smile could often open the closed face of a man by the roadside. 'The Malaitans are dour and tight-fisted,' one English officer said to us, and Stanley was dourer than most, but even he had become friendly by the time we reached Maluu.

We drove sometimes inland over the small hills near the coast, and sometimes by the sea itself. There were few real villages, but many small hamlets of seven or eight palm and pandanus houses, raised on piles; the neatly spaced buildings with the grass well cut around them reminded us of the kampongs in Malaya. A little way out of Auki the rain began, and this meant we could not stop anywhere by the wayside, since there were three large fords that we had to cross before we reached

Maluu, and the Engineers had warned us that when the weather is bad on Malaita the water comes rushing down in flash floods from the hills and makes the rivers impassable. At any one of the fords we might have been held up a day or more, but we crossed them all in safety, though at the last the current was already strong and the usually crystal-line water was turning mud-brown.

Nearing the north of the island the coast became broken and rugged, with little coves and headlands and small bushy islands. The road ran often so near the sea that spring tides covered it; and there were stretches where we drove over drifted sand and through shallow pools of salt water. On the foreshore the local people had built enclosures of low coral walls to trap the fish that came in on the tides. In the more sheltered bays naked boys were tumbling in and out of the tiny dugout canoes, 4–5 feet long, which they manoeuvred with sureness and dexterity.

This was the lush end of the island, the jungle luxuriant, the road verges screened by matted growths of high grass, and the population densening in proportion to the growing fertility, so that the roadside hamlets often seemed within shouting distance of each other. And here, walking barefoot by the road at a hillman's steady pace, we would see little groups of bush people, men and women clad only in kilts of the red cloth which the bush people seem to love throughout the Solomons. The men always walked in front carrying axes or cane knives, and a dog or two always followed. The women carried the burdens, for Malaita is a patriarchal island, and sometimes they would be bent double under great loads of firewood, or bundles of green bamboo tubes, the ends stuffed with leaves, which were used for carrying water.

Maluu was a tiny town on the beach; a hospital, a couple of Chinese stores, a few shacks. We went into one of the stores to buy beer. Young hill men with mops of frizzed hair and ear-rings of porpoise teeth lounged on the veranda which was piled high with copra bought from the native growers. Here even the Chinese knew no English, and we had to make do with our fragmentary pidgin supplemented by signs. The government station was on the hill above the village, a big grassy space, with the local offices and the police station and the houses of the government servants arranged into a kind of loose street. In one building a native magistrate was holding court, and outside the senior primary school the children in their blue and white uniforms were running and yelling. The rest-house stood on the crest of the hill, a narrow line of rooms with an immense semicircular concrete stoop in front of it, relic of the great thatched District Commissioner's house that had stood there before the road was built and the white officials began to operate out of Auki. The rest-house was already occupied, for Dudley Cook, the Acting District Commissioner for Malaita, a tall Englishman who resembled the young Stewart Grainger, was on tour in the north of the island, and we found him working on the veranda with a sergeant of the Royal Engineers who had come to supervise the provision of water supply for Maluu. There were hurried rearrangements so that a room could be found for us, and then we sat on the edge of the stoop to eat our lunch, looking down the hill through open vistas among the palm-trees to a broad curving bay and a reef paralleling its curve, so that there was a sickle of yellow beach and white surf, and then the varying greens and turquoises of the crescent-shaped lagoon, edged by the white of the reef, and beyond the reef the azures and indigos of the open sea where a flotilla of canoes with triangular sails went travelling northward.

For many years, until the road was opened, the only Europeans actually living in the vicinity of the Lau lagoon were the Catholics who operated the mission at Takwa, and in the afternoon we went there, driving through the densest jungle we had yet seen in the Solomons. The trees had vast umbrella crowns starred over with red and yellow flowers, and their trunks were densely furred with epiphytes; the undergrowth was thick with tree ferns and dwarf wild palms, and ground orchids bloomed by the roadside. The road was particularly populous, with whole clans of bush people wandering along, often carrying bundles of leaves or reeds gathered in the jungle. We overtook two people on a motor bike, a bearded white man and his young wife; they were the Frasers, two New Zealanders who had been working as anthropologist and psychologist respectively at a village down the road, and of whom we had been told.

The Frasers told us that their tour of study was ended; they were on their way to say good-bye at the mission. We arranged to meet them there. In the few moments we talked, a knot of bush people had gathered to stare at us. The men, like male birds, were the most resplendently decorated. Almost all had wide armlets of beads arranged in bold geometrical patterns, and some wore broad-rimmed sunhats rather like sombreros but made of dried coconut leaf, while others had made themselves crowns of hibiscus flowers that looked like flowery bathing caps; one had a necklace of star-shaped clusters of porpoise teeth and an older man whom the others treated with obvious deference had a broad silver armlet that had probably been hammered out of coins.

It was harvest time on Malaita. In the little gardens scattered in the jungle, people were digging manioc roots, and when we reached Takwa we drove to the mission through a field where the schoolgirls, dressed in dirty, ragged blouses and skirts, were digging out the yams; to live by the produce one grows and digs oneself is so habitual a part of Malaitan existence that nobody finds it extraordinary that a child should be expected to work at producing the food he will eat at the school where he boards. There were two girls of exceptional beauty who waved at us as we drove by, sisters with blond hair and pale, refined Latinate features which left no doubt that some trader or seaman had fathered them, or perhaps grandfathered them in the wild black-birding days.

We were drawn to Takwa largely by the repute of Sister Marie Evangeline, who ran the little hospital there with – one had heard – a great understanding of native fears and prejudices, so that she regularly kept pagan women three weeks after their children were born to obviate the need for them to spend that time purging their uncleanness in the insanitary isolation of the village bisi house. But Sister Marie Evangeline was busy with an urgent case, and though we met her for a moment and appreciated her air of brisk, humane efficiency, it was with the priest, Father L., that we spent our time, and this gave us a view of life at the mission through dark eyes of disillusion and depression.

Father L. was hospitable indeed, giving us cakes made by the sisters and coffee with thick cream from the mission herd, a special treat in the South Seas where one rarely gets anything better than Australian condensed milk, and he was obviously pleased to have visitors, particularly when the Frasers arrived to augment the company. Yet the image quickly formed of a defeated man, 'bushed' as Canadians would put it, whose will had been eroded by too much isolation from his kind, for he had been on Malaita for twenty years, and for the greater part as the solitary white man in a remote mission on the rarely visited east coast of the island. He was letting himself go physically, appearing dressed in a filthy pair of shorts and a stained loose shirt whose tail he used as a handkerchief, a napkin and a rag to wipe his hands.

But it was doubt that was gnawing at Father L.; not as far as I could see doubt in the Catholic religion, but doubt in his own powers to serve it. 'I have converted nobody at Takwa,' he said. 'On the east coast I did make a few conversions, but now I ask myself if any of the conversions that were ever made in these islands were really valid. I admit that in the past there were pagans who were taken into the Church and who accepted Christianity with fervour. But have you ever thought why they did so? They did so because they were good pagans and were so passionately aware of a world of spirits that they could easily incorporate Christ as a spirit into their field of reference. Even the pagans who were not converted acknowledge Christ as a spirit; they still do so in the bush, but these see him as an evil spirit and they call him the Big Devildevil. But even that is vanishing now. On Malaita, and in the whole world, the new generation is losing any sense of passionate conviction, because the whole conception of a world of spirits is dying away. Nowadays men are neither good Christians nor good pagans. But what I doubt now after twenty years is that any believing pagan was ever really transformed into a Christian. None of them ever completely forgets the paganism in which his faith began.'

We walked down with Father L. and Ian Fraser to see the freezer plant which had been built at the end of the stone jetty projecting into the lagoon from the mission land. Children clustered round us, many of the boys' cheeks tatooed with a curious circular figures that looked like a wheel symbol. There was a sudden embarrassing moment when Father L. noticed that one of the boys was carrying a yam he had appropriated for himself while digging the harvest earlier in the day. He took the yam away from the child, and reproved him. Then he went into a passionate tirade against the Malaitans, whom he claimed were universally addicted to thieving and deceit.

From the jetty we could look out over the Lau Lagoon, and its artificial islands, of which several were close enough to see their form of construction, which consisted of the building of a mass of dead coral supported on the outside by perpendicular retaining walls of larger blocks. On top of the platform that finally appeared, houses were constructed of the same materials as those on the land, and sometimes trees were grown. On the nearest island there were six or seven buildings, but farther north, we gathered, were villages larger than any on the mainland. Father L. claimed that in terms of Malaitan conditions the islands were excellent inventions. Out on the water they were cool at night, while the anopheles mosquito rarely flew far from shore, so

that they were free of malaria. Refuse and sewage were washed away
by the tide instead of lingering around the houses, while in the old
violent days the islands were readily defensible against would-be
invaders. Finally, the people were near to one of their main sources
of food in the lagoon and on its reefs. There was a strange intensity
about the way he said all this, as if in some way the insularity of the
lagoon-dwellers exorcised his own isolation.

That night at the rest-house Dudley Cook and Isaac Goloni, the
black little native magistrate who came from Choiseul, prepared a
great corned beef curry which we ate with bread fresh out of an oildrum oven and strong Australian beer, and afterwards we sat out on
the mosquito-free hilltop, looking down on the lagoon where the reef-
edge was marked by the orange flare of night-fishing torches. It was an
evening of excellent conversation and narrative, for Isaac Goloni had
his background in the traditions of his own island, while Dudley Cook
had filled many remote assignments in the shrinking Empire, including
the District Commissionership of Christmas Island, where he presided
over myriads of seabirds and vast derelict storehouses full of rusting
British military equipment from World War II, with the isolation
broken once every six months by the arrival of the mailboat.

The Malaita bush, as Dudley Cook described it on the basis of his
periodical foot treks, appeared to be the most ferociously traditionalist
and taboo-ridden region anywhere in the South Seas with the exception
of the highlands of New Guinea. Its religious differences were fanatical
and complicated, since they were built on deep and abiding local and
social divisions that had existed long before the first missionary
arrived. The Christian cults that took hold in the bush were all funda-
mentalist and apocalyptic, and they shared with surviving paganism
a tendency towards the fervent belief in the devil as an active presence,
the main difference being that the leading devil of the pagans was called
Christ and the leading devil of the Christians was called Satan. The
pattern began with the emergence among the labourers in the Queens-
land sugar fields of a native church known as the South Seas Evangelical
Mission, given to apocalyptic preaching and a literalist interpretation
of the Bible. The taste for marginal and fervent versions of Christianity
opened the way to the Seventh-Day Adventists, the Jehovah's Witnesses and the Remnant Church, an extreme offshoot of the South Seas
Evangelical Mission which had repossessed the pagan concept of taboo,
with its emphasis on defilement and purification. Like the pagans,

the Remnant Church villages took elaborate precautions to protect themselves from pollution by unclean outsiders. There seemed to be no evident territorial pattern in the distribution of religions. In fact neighbouring villages tended to adopt different churches almost out of mutual spite, and one would find pagan hamlets and those of the various Christian sects all mingled indiscriminately together.

'And that makes it pretty difficult if you're travelling in the bush,' said Cook, 'and you don't know whether you're on the path to a Christian or a pagan village, particularly as the pagans often have one path for women and one for men. Some of the villages are so extreme in their taboos that they won't consume on village ground anything that has come from the unclean Christian world. It might bring disaster by offending the tutelary spirits. But they still like tobacco and unfamiliar foods, so they build a special house outside the village bounds where they smoke and eat forbidden fare, and then they cleanse themselves in a stream before they go home.'

'Do you observe the taboos?' Inge asked him.

'Yes and no. I don't go out of my way to break special taboos. In fact I once paid $10 as a customary compensation when I sat on a man's ancestral stones. But as the Queen's man I don't accept that there are any villages taboo to me. I go into them, and the people all remember what the gunboats did when the last British officer was murdered forty years ago, and they accept that the Queen's man can call down a bigger devildevil than they can. But I go alone because no Malaita man, however educated and Christian he may appear, is psychologically capable of standing up to a taboo.'

Having listened only a few hours before to Father L.'s laments on the essential unconvertability of the people of Malaita, I asked Dudley Cook if he meant that the Christians still believed in taboo and in the sorcery attached to it.

'We don't talk about sorcery,' he answered, 'since it is illegal, and the grosser forms of it are carried out in secret. But you're right, taboo is really a kind of sorcery since it is supposed to invoke the same spiritual powers, and even the Christians believe in it, and their belief can kill them.'

'Do you know of cases where that's really happened?'

'Know! I not only know; I've seen with my own eyes. Let me tell you one incident. I was in the bush with the headman of a big Christian village. He was a deacon of the South Seas Evangelical Mission and a very active man in church matters. You could travel with him for days and never have any doubt that he was a devout practising Christian with no vestige of paganism left in his mind. And perhaps there wasn't, in his conscious mind at least. But one day we came to a pagan village, and in my usual way I went inside and he waited until I'd shown the flag and came out again. But when we continued we stumbled into an area which the villagers for some reason had tabooed, and he saw the signs when it was too late. I noticed he seemed very preoccupied as we went on. His eyes looked glassy, he began to stumble like an exhausted man, and finally he fell down. He wouldn't get up, his speech became incoherent, and within less than an hour he'd gone into a coma. If I'd left him, he'd have died, so the only thing I could do was to hoist him on my back and carry him back to his own village. It took me half a day, but he was still alive when I got there. As soon as the people knew what had happened they took him into the church, and laid him down there, and they stayed around him for twenty-four hours praying and singing hymns to defeat the devils of the pagan village. And at the end of that twenty-four hours he woke up and thanked me. He knew that if I hadn't taken him back to his church he'd have died. But I could never get him to tell me what went on in his mind after he saw the taboo signs. All he would say was that the devil had possessed him, and if he hadn't been rescued with hymns and prayers he would not only have died; he'd have gone straight to hell. But whether that would happen because of the power of pagan magic, or because he'd been a weak Christian I could never make out.'

Traditionally, on Malaita, the bush people and the coast people are enemies, though whether this is because of different origins no historian or anthropologist has yet satisfactorily determined; the bush people, living in their small clan hamlets, are divided among themselves by jealousies and vendettas, usually about land, which Malaitans like all other Melanesians cherish passionately. Nevertheless, even in such a fragmented society trade was a notable moderator of hostilities, and, as Isaac Goloni explained to us, everywhere in the Solomons there are places neutralized by tradition and taboo where people of all tribes can gather for the rites of commerce. A few miles beyond Maluu on the way to Takwa there was a market site at a rivermouth that had been in use as long as tradition remembered, and we could see it on our way to Solofou, the largest of the artificial islands, which we intended to visit the next day.

Since many of the hill people have to walk for two hours or more over their switchback terrain to reach the coast, the markets do not start early, and when we arrived at the rivermouth at nine o'clock trading was only just about to begin. The taboo ground was a sandy delta, and two high-prowed canoes (rather like gondolas in shape) were being beached by women from the islands of the Lau Lagoon; two other similar boats were coming into the narrow estuary, propelled partly by paddle and partly by a small mastless triangular sail which one of the women held up above her head to catch the breeze blowing in from the sea. As soon as these boats came into running water, the women leapt out and waded along, dragging their boats with them and finally drawing them up on the sand.

Meanwhile the bush people had gathered in a riverside grove over-looking the delta. There were about a hundred of them when we arrived, but others kept appearing, usually in small family groups. There were men, women and children; the women carried the produce they had to sell, mainly the sweet potatoes that grow in the hilltop gardens, wrapped in pandanus-leaf mats; the men carried their weapons – hatchets, a club or two, cane knives, a few rifles, and bows and arrows in the case of the boys. None of the coast men had appeared. Looking from one group to the other, the differences were evident. The coast women were taller and fatter, with the heavy muscular shoulders of canoe people; the bush folk were trim and muscular, with the massive calves of hill walkers. The coast women wore washed-out and shapeless cotton dresses, but the bush women for the most part wore only their kilts. The bush men displayed all their finery of bead armlets and por-poise teeth jewellery, and there was one especially striking dandy who was obviously a 'big man' of some consequence; he wore a black hat garnished with silver braid and with tiny gold- and silver-framed mirrors; his new red kilt was held in place by a wide leather belt studded with silver from which hung a bowie knife in a tooled leather sheath, and from his shoulder hung a rifle and a finely woven and geometrically patterned bag which evidently contained his smoking materials, for he smoked a pipe and unlike most of the other men did not have a mouth red from betel chewing. While the other bush folk merely stared at us under their heavy brows and smiled only if we smiled first, he came silently up to us, shook my hand, elaborately raised his splendid hat to Inge, and turned back to rejoin his friends.

For a little while the two groups remained apart, as the lagoon women unloaded the fresh and dried fish and octopus which they had brought, and then the man in the black hat blew a whistle, and all the hill women went wading through the river to the taboo area. The trading was almost entirely by barter, the garden and forest produce of the hills for the fish of the islands. But out on the outskirts of it all, under the shade of the trees, a different and more modest trading was going on, for five or six Malaitans in European dress of shirts and shorts had opened suitcases and were squatting on the ground beside their stock-in-trade of cigarettes, flashlights, knives, stick tobacco, plastic trinkets, chewing gum, and English biscuits; it was the only part of the market where cash changed hands. What impressed one, in comparison with markets almost anywhere else in the world, was the quietness with which everything went on, the bargaining carried on in subdued voices that were almost whispers. And yet there was a sense of latent violence, projected by the group of armed men, with their great mops of hair and their barbaric jewellery, looking on silently from the shadows of the grove; a whole past of nervous watchfulness seemed to find expression in their attitudes.

We drove on. Ten miles or so beyond Takwa the road ended at a jetty, and facing us, less than half a mile across the water was Solofou, the largest of the artificial islands of the Lau Lagoon, with its dense-clustered roofs of native huts, its shady trees, and above them all the shining roof of the big Anglican church of the Melanesian Mission, towering up like the great basilica at Torcello over its huddle of houses. To the north we could see the dark outline of another village island.

Isaac Goloni had told us that there would certainly be canoemen at the jetty. There was in fact no boatman to be found, and now the real person who lurked behind Stanley's dour exterior became evident, for he went talking to the women in the houses by the jetty, eventually persuading one of them to lend us a small dugout canoe. We put Inge on board with the cameras, and then Stanley and I waded the boat through the muddy shallows until the water deepened enough for us to float over the beds of eelgrass among which lay great greenish sea-slugs and colonies of pink starfish covered with scarlet warts.

We passed a small island where a single family lived on its tiny man-made rock of isolation with three houses and a palm-tree, and then a number of towers on high poles supporting pens of mangrove branches in which pigs were fattening in isolation (a pen-bred pig being more valuable on Malaita than a pig allowed to run freely in the bush). Solofou, we realized when we reached it, was a circular island, perhaps 300 yards in diameter, an intriguing muddle of yellow roofs and walls whose planes would have intrigued Cézanne, perched above the solid coral ramparts that rose perpendicularly from the sea, and approached by ladders of poles spaced out for giants' strides. As we drifted in, men greeted us from the canoes in which they were rod-fishing, and when we pulled our canoe on to the beach a gaggle of children leapt shouting into the water around us and then raced ahead of us up the steps and into the village streets.

And indeed they were streets, for Solofou was quite unlike the villages we had seen on land, since it was not a mere clan settlement, but the centre of a confederation of clans, and as such it was planned with a geometric logic. The church stood in the central space which had formerly been the heart of the pagan village, from which communication lanes radiated and crossed the concentric circular lanes on which the houses were built. There were no gardens or grass plots separating the houses as on the mainland; they were built close together and – again unlike the mainland houses raised on piles – they were built flat on the ground. The houses were shabby; the pandanus walls needed renewal, and the general air of dejection was increased by the absence of any grass; the children, unless they were in the water, looked dusty from playing on the pounded coral.

A man dressed in European clothes and wearing a deerstalker hat came up, and told us that the headman was away; so were most of the other men, working on Honiara. That was why the houses looked shabby, he commented. The women had to fish and trade and look after the children.

'I name John,' the man in the deerstalker explained, but he became evasive when I tried to find out what his role in the village might be. 'I pretty near number one,' he finally conceded, and I suspected that he was a villager who had worked outside and earned enough money to cut a dash at home without greatly impressing his neighbours, for as he walked us through the lanes I noticed that the women looked at him with a curious quizzical silence. John led us into the great cool cavern of the church, where the Anglicans had blended simplicity with elaboration; there were no pews, but the floor of broken coral was scattered with little mats for kneeling, while the font and the pulpit were of intricately carved wood decorated with inlaid fragments of abalone shell as the sacred boats of the village had been in the pagan past.

These boats were now decaying in their old sheds on an area devoid
of houses that lay between the front of the church and the water.
'Before we become Christian,' John explained, 'this place taboo to
women. No longer.' In front of the boatsheds stood a line of elaborately
carved gravestones, just as the sacred ancestor stones had stood there
before the village became Christian.

I was depressed by this decaying corner of the pagan past on Solofou,
and indeed by the joyless atmosphere of the whole village, which
seemed to project an apathy more profound than that caused merely by
the absence of men. Both of us – and I think Stanley also when I
remember the briskness with which he paddled back over the lagoon –
were glad to get away and drive back towards Maluu. On the way
we stopped to visit the Seventh-Day Adventist mission at Kwalabesi.
Already in the Gilberts I had developed an unexpected esteem for the
Adventist missionaries, who differed from the ordinary evangelical
sects by supplementing their preaching of faith with a very generous
emphasis on good works. Adventist missions always seemed to be
cheerful, efficient places, and that at Kwalabesi was no exception. The
school buildings, the lawns and the orchards of citrus fruit gave the
same impression of good care, and when we met Natan Rore, the man
from the western island of Vella Lavella who was in charge of the
mission, we felt an immediate sympathy. He took us into his large
cool house, built by the last European pastor, and his fat wife, in her
brilliant Mother Hubbard, was shyly hospitable, bringing us a great
pitcher of lemonade made from their own fruit.

It was obvious that even for the Seventh-Day Adventists conversion
had been an arduous task. In fifty years of work on Malaita they still
had only a little over 2,000 tithe-paying members, for many of the
bush villages that claimed to follow them were too poor to qualify.
And it was clear that the Adventists relied on American funds to carry
out their considerable educational and medical activities, which on
Malaita alone included two senior primary and twenty junior primary
schools, three clinics, and on the east coast of Malaita a ninety-bed
hospital.

Missionaries have changed, and one rarely encounters the rampant
proselytizers, whose approach now produces steadily diminishing
returns. Nevertheless, I was impressed by Nathan Rore's comprehension of the non-religious needs of his people, and also by his reluctance
to condemn the pagans. He was greatly concerned over the inapplica-

bility of a purely academic education to circumstances in the Solomons. Much better, Rore argued, to recognize that most children in the islands would have no alternative but to work the ancestral gardens, and to educate them with that in view. Already, he remarked, classes in modern agricultural methods were being taught in Adventist primary schools, and a large vocational school had just gone into operation in the western Solomons.

Rore remarked that the pagans attended his clinic, but his house was taboo. They believed that if they stepped over his threshold their own demons would send them a 'big sick', and so whenever they wanted a favour from him they stood outside and called, and talked to him through the window. He described them as 'a people full of fear'. He also described the last killing of a white in the Solomons, which had taken place on this spot as recently as 1964.

'It was a question of land, as most killings are on Malaita. When we built our clinic, we bought the land from a man who was legally recognized as the owner. But there was another man who claimed it, and when he saw us beginning to build, he decided to avenge himself in the Malaita way. So he stole a length of steel reinforcing rod, and sharpened it to a point, and went out one night to find his victim. Under local custom that can be anyone belonging to the clan whose member has offended you, and since the pastor here was then a European, the man decided to kill the first European he saw on what he believed was his land. It happened to be the young doctor. One night he was entering the clinic and the murderer threw his spear. It transfixed him. They sawed off the protruding ends with a hacksaw. The road was not here then, and Father took him down to Maluu by canoe, and he went by jeep to the hospital in Auki. He died there. They say that all through that dreadful journey he laughed and jested, and thought more of the peace of mind of his companions than of his own pain.'

'What was his name?' Inge asked.

A look of distress came over Nathan Rore's face. 'I am ashamed to say that I would have to look it up. You see, we always talk of him as the Doctor Who Died, and everything he did in his life is forgotten. I doubt if anyone even remembers what he looked like except perhaps the Father, who went with him. It is the horror of his death and his bravery at the end that everyone remembers. He accepted his death and he triumphed over it at the same time.'

We returned to Maluu with that grim tale tolling in our minds. Our last evening at the rest-house quickly thrust it into the shadows of memory.

I had difficulty getting the Coleman lamp started, and I took it over to the police station to see if they could fix it. There was no one there, and I was returning past the house of Martin, the government clerk, when the police sergeant came out and asked if he could help me, and got the lamp going. I noticed that there were a number of men in the house sitting around in the dim light of a storm lantern. I returned, hung the lamp from the roof of the veranda; we prepared and ate our dinner, and were washing up when two figures came walking out of the darkness and up the steps of the stoop. The short one was Martin, a stocky babu-like man with blue tattoos over his yellowish cheeks; his taller, darker companion he introduced as Albert, the headmaster of the senior primary school, and, as we realized later, the nephew of David Kausimae and son of one of the principal leaders of Marching Rule. Martin's wife, it appeared, was away, so he was holding a party in his house, to which he invited us, since, as Albert explained, 'It would be a great opportunity for mutual education. You will tell us all about Canada, and we will tell you all about the Solomons.'

It sounded an interesting programme for an idle evening, but we had already invited the Frasers to come for a talk and a drink. Why did not Martin and his guests join our party? The suggestion was accepted, and shortly after the Frasers arrived, Martin and Albert returned, accompanied by the sergeant and the two constables who formed the entire Maluu police force, and our driver Stanley. They were burdened down with cases of beer and Albert's gramophone, and our attempts at mutual education very quickly began to take on a hilarious character.

It is true, there were some promising beginnings. We learnt, for example, about that extraordinary bird, which may well become a national symbol if the Solomons ever becomes a nation, the megapode. The megapode is an almost flightless bird, found in most of the islands, which lays a very large egg that it buries in rotting vegetation or hot sand and then leaves to incubate without sitting on it. In most of the Solomons the megapode's egg is found casually in the bush, but there are two small islands, Sava near Guadalcanal and Simbu in the New Georgia group, where the megapode, if not actually domesticated, is at least treasured and fostered as a provider of food.

The police sergeant was a Sava man, and he told us that there the megapodes lay their eggs in warm sand, and the land where they lay is never cultivated but is divided into squares, each possessed by a man who has the hereditary right to any eggs the megapodes lay there. On Simbu the people actually build shelters over the sand to attract the birds. Nobody possesses the megapodes as they might possess domestic fowl, since it is recognized that the birds are wild and therefore free beings, but a man possesses what they lay on his land, though complicated customary laws forbid the killing of the megapode and dictate that one egg in four must be left to preserve the race. We had been told by an Australian woman in Honiara that the islanders on Sava believed that once a megapode has started to lay her enormous eggs, she will provide one every day for the rest of her life; the sergeant confirmed not merely that this was the belief among his people, but stoutly maintained – and this in the earlier and soberer part of the evening – that he, like all the rest, believed in the megapode's formidable powers.

It was after the talk of megapodes that Martin and one of the police constables began to sing the bitter-sweet love songs of the Langalanga lagoon, which had a pleasant lilting quality, but which in the end seemed monotonously repetitious. It was obvious that the tunes were almost interchangeable, and that the lyrics gave the songs their significance; but to us the lyrics were incomprehensible, and so, we realized, they were to all but the two Langalanga men who sang them. Indeed, as the evening went on and the fifty bottles of beer and two bottles of whisky we had laid in the centre of the circle began to diminish, it was clear that the local differences between Solomon islanders were deep and enduring, and only lightly papered over by education. Of the six islanders present four had been to the same secondary school, and it was obvious that the British were trying to create, as they did elsewhere, an elite of teachers and clerks and policemen who would have enough in the way of a common education to take over after they had gone. But the local differences persisted, and emerged in moments of excitement, and on Malaita, we realized, the differences between districts could be as important as the differences between islands.

At first there was a nostalgic feeling to the evening, as we sat in our brotherly circle, with the black velvet of the night beyond us slashed by the gold of the fishing torches down on the bay, and the frogs and insects sounding a chorus to the Langalanga melodies. But then Albert, who resembled greatly one of those Indian students in whom a Western education releases an irrepressible didacticism, began to lecture us on the merits of rock music, which was belatedly hitting the Solomons, and to play on his gramophone the strident yawpings of the West. The whole atmosphere of the evening shifted. We discovered that the great semicircular stoop was a magnificent dancing ground, and there, all except taciturn Stanley who sat slowly absorbing beer and watching us with a wryly judicious smile, we stamped in a kind of rock war-dance, surging to and fro with arms over each other's shoulders under the blaze of the Coleman lamp, with the policemen emitting savage cries that once, I felt sure, must have inspired the raiding expeditions of their ancestors.

It was all, to begin with, excellent fun, but then, when we slumped down exhausted to drink more beer, the quarrelling became suddenly bitter. Martin and Albert, men from northern and southern Malaita respectively, began to insult each other, the two constables began to squabble in pidgin (they had no other tongue in common), and I remembered against my will the lore that had been pumped into us now by half a hundred Europeans in the South Seas: 'Watch out when the natives get our booze! They can't take it. That's when they become violent! Don't let it ever happen!' And here were we, I thought in that lapsing moment, positively encouraging it to happen. Not that there were any threats to us, but as the next two hours went on, wild dancing alternating with wilder drinking, and maudlin fraternity with regional truculence, the atmosphere grew steadily more tense, until, quite abruptly, the police sergeant asserted his authority and marched his unsteady troop back to Martin's house, where we heard them shouting and breaking bottles far into the night. The next morning, when I went there to pay for our room in the rest-house, I found Stanley sober and enigmatic, and Martin grievously hung over, yet so doggedly loyal to his job that he insisted on groaning over to his office and opening the safe to give me a receipt strictly in accordance with government regulations. For all the noisy truculence of the night before, it was evident that nobody had been hurt by anything but alcohol.

And certainly, when we made our journey south to Auki and spent the day there among the local officials, it all seemed tame after our night at Maluu, and we were glad to board the plane back to Honiara north-west on Sunday morning. There we found that arrangements had been made for us to visit the western islands on government boats. We must be ready to fly out next morning from Honiara to the Short-lands, where we could intercept one of the boats that sail out of Gizo. But we must be prepared for Spartan conditions, and must provide not only our own food, but our own bedding and cooking utensils. We spent our Sunday evening in the stores of Old Chinatown gathering our supplies.

3

Journal of the Island Voyage

First Day. We are up early to get the plane that will take us to Balalei in the Shortland Islands and start us on our voyage through the western Solomons. Dawn begins to break as we drive out to the little Solair airport which stands beside the international airport on Henderson Field. One of the tiny Beechcraft Barons is awaiting us, and the pilot himself takes our tickets and checks our baggage while a single attendant wheels out the plane.

The mist is hanging close, like the fleece over a sheep's back, on the central mountains of Guadalcanal as we fly north-westward over Honiara, which from above actually looks like an octopus, thrusting its tentacles of housing up the twisting valleys that probe into the savanna-green hills. Flying out over the sea and the plumed pyramid of the island of Sava, the plane reaches 8,500 feet. It is a brilliant, pristine morning, and above the luminous sea and the bright islands we have an extraordinary sense of a world new and incomparably fresh.

We fly, without putting down, over the Russell Islands, a scattering of thin wisps and shavings of land, the edges of atolls, with the pale blue of still submerged reefs showing up in the seas around them and here and there sandbanks where new atolls are beginning to form. Over all the dry land in these islands march the great orderly regiments of the Lever plantations, the largest and most carefully managed in all the South Seas, evidence that if small planters are feeling the pinch of a restricted market, the large companies still have faith in the ultimate profitableness of copra in a world where raw materials are becoming steadily more scarce.

Next we come in sight of the atoll barriers that shield the New Georgia group and form the Kolo and Marova lagoons, the most beautiful lagoons, surely, in all the South Seas. Within the sheltering and curving walls of long narrow outer islets, a scattering of many small islets (I count fifty in one alone of the several clusters) shields the massive formations of New Georgia itself, a high volcanic island.

At Munda, on the south-western shore of New Georgia, we land on a pitted, weedy airstrip which has not been improved since the Japanese laid it in World War II; it does for the small planes which are now all that land. There is a Quonset hut, also dating from the last war, with a customs desk that can rarely be used, and posters of Switzerland, and an unattended store with fifty tins piled on the shelves and a couple of carved paddles which I covet; alas, they are too long to carry around with us. We are struck by the difference between the people here and those of Malaita and Guadalcanal. There they were milk chocolate brown; here they are liquorice black, with extraordinarily regular features and large luminous eyes.

From Munda we fly low over the sea and the islands to Gizo, with the vast mass of Kolombangara, the active volcano of the Solomons, rising to the north-west, smoke nestling on its summit. At Gizo the airstrip is on a little island out in the harbour, with the town lining the bay opposite and clambering up the hills of red laterite. A single freighter and a cluster of little island launches are moored along its quays. Up to now we have been the only passengers, but here a priest joins us, going to the Catholic mission at Nila in the Shortland Islands, and two islanders, so that the plane is at last full. We fly off, over the large and forested island of Vella Lavella, and out at a height of 6,500 feet over the open ocean towards the Shortlands, where we circle over the harbour of Nila where a Japanese lumber boat lies like a toy, and down to Balalei, a scrub-covered uninhabited island with yet another broken-up Japanese airstrip. We have been told to go to Nila to pick up the *Waisisi*, but find it is lying off Balalei awaiting us. We pick our way down a rough path through the scrub to a jetty off which, a hundred yards out in the bay, a clumsy, square-ended white boat with awning-shaded decks is lying. A dinghy comes over to the jetty, and a little bearded man – the *Waisisi*'s supercargo – takes us over to the boat which, unlike the *Nivanga*, has at least the luxury of a rope ladder hanging over the side.

When we climb up we realize, with a kind of bruising recognition, that the *Waisisi* is primitive in a classic South Seas manner; the front of the boat is crowded with deck passengers sitting on the hatch covers, and the so-called first-class cabin in the stern has four bunks with bare and filthy mattresses and a young Polynesian lying in one of them. There is a sink and a gas stove, but no cooking utensils, and we are glad of our single saucepan and the camping cutlery and plastic cups we bought almost as a joke in Suva. The crew are all islanders. The boatswain, as the masters of these inter-island boats are called in the Solomons, is a tall man from the Shortlands, black, lofty and stern-looking as a Nubian; the mate is a Gilbertese. The rest of the crew seem to be gathered from all the corners of the Solomons, for they vary from the deepest blue-black to an almost Polynesian fairness.

We sail out from the bay of Balalei south-east toward Choiseul, which is merely a low line on the horizon, but abruptly we right angle on our course and make for Nila. As we approach the reef the sea is suddenly broken by the backs of dolphins, rolling in formation and leaping high into the air before and beside the ship. We pass through them and through the entrance to the reef where the waves break turquoise and white and send a veil of spray leaping far into the air.

Inside the lagoon, the ship lies close off a large village of pandanus-leaf houses while the supercargo puts off in the dinghy to deliver a forgotten box of apples to the mission. Along the village beach are drawn up the outrigger canoes which in the Solomons are peculiar to the Shortlands. The bottom slopes down sharply from the beach, and as we look into the clear depths we see swimming, close in front of the houses, shoals of slender silvery fish with brilliant yellow and blue tails and long sharp snouts like miniature garfish, and below them, in the darker depths, other fish of the shape and size of rock cod.

We sail out, dolphins attending, on an almost due easterly course, south of Faro, the easternmost of the Shortlands, whose small but perfectly proportioned mountains rise sheer from its green and rocky shores. Flying fish skim over the water before us, and suddenly, a mile away, a shoal of twenty killer whales rise out of the water, rolling and leaping in all their black magnitude.

Sailing east, with Choiseul slowly growing from a shoreline to a shore, we develop tentative contacts with our companions: the bearded supercargo who offers Inge his pillow because we have come without one (the islanders usually travel with a simple bedding kit of a pillow wrapped in a mat); the black-faced girls who look pertly at us through the cabin windows and have an impudent air in comparison with the shy Malaitans; the young agricultural officer from Malangolo on Choiseul who tells about the efforts he is making to persuade people to rely less on copra and to grow ginger and turmeric, for which there is a good market. The mate comes to talk about the Gilberts; he is from Kuria, the island of legendary navigators who can travel for hundreds of miles using the stars by night and the set of the waves by day. He tells us that, contrary to what we had been told, the *Waisisi* will not be going to several islands; it will merely be circumnavigating Choiseul. But tomorrow morning they can land us at the bay of Sasamongga, and before the day is over a sister boat, the *Leili*, will be calling in on its way to Vella Lavella, and thence to Gizo.

We eventually touch Choiseul somewhat north of Sasamongga, and coast along, watching the little houses scattered along the beaches and dwarfed by the great green background – a line of palms along the shore, and behind them the tall jungle trees climbing up the steep and pyramidical hillsides in columnar groves, all a splendid golden green in the evening light. An exuberant, Amazonian coast. Choiseul – our agriculturist tells us – is an island of coast dwellers; perhaps there are six villagers in the bush, but essentially the man of Choiseul is a man of the seashore, and the interior is virtually uninhabited.

It is a perfect evening, with a mirror-smooth sea. Frigate birds scream and wheel over a shoal of leaping herring-like fish, and from the galley comes the smell of frying, doubtless the two big deep-bellied fish scaled with burnished brass that were drawn in an hour ago on the lines trolled from the back of the boat. We put in to the shelter of the tight little bay of Malongono.

Here we will spend the night. The agriculturist and the silent Polynesian from our cabin – who has spent almost the whole day sleeping on his bunk – depart, and the crew go off in the dinghy to sleep ashore, as do the deck passengers. We are left alone on the ship except for a watchman. We eat a dull dinner of spam and baked beans, and then sit on the top deck as night falls, with a sky splendidly starful, Venus intensely brilliant, and on the headland, behind which the moon falls, a kind of velvety darkness broken by the lights of people walking along the paths and setting lamps in the houses. There is a curiously intense quietness, for the Solomon islanders are a people who rarely sing or talk loudly; flying foxes squeak and flap heavily among the trees, and occasionally a night bird gives a harsh whirring call, but the people are almost silent and the canoes glide with barely a sound over the moon path on the water. A cool breeze blows from the land, and there are no mosquitoes. It is a time of quiet delight, a tranquillity such as we have rarely enjoyed in these weeks of fervent travel.

Second Day. This morning the *Waisisi* sails round from Malongono to the open bay of Sasamongga. We have decided to take a chance on landing and waiting for the *Leili*. The dinghy takes us ashore, and the supercargo puts our suitcase and our box of stores in the big thatched canoe shed on the beach. He shakes hands, the dinghy chugs back to the *Waisisi*, and almost immediately the boat ups anchor and sails south-easterly out of the bay. We walk to the top of the beach, and look across the curve of the bay, taking in the native houses and the wooden buildings of the United Church Mission, and we have no more time than to say 'What shall we do now?' when a young woman comes walking over from the nearest house, introduces herself as Helen Stringer, the pastor's wife and originally from New Zealand. 'We shall be happy if you will spend today with us,' she said, adding, with a smile, 'or as long as it will take before your boat arrives!'

We walk up with her to the mission house. Her husband, a thin, quiet New Zealander, is there, and so is the Bishop of the local Metho-dist diocese. He is Leslie Boseto, a native of Choiseul, with the peculiar blue sheen to his black skin which is so typical of this island, where purity of the race was rigorously preserved, long into the European era, by the killing and eating of all visitors. With his blue shorts and knitted white shirt and his blue-and-white striped kneesocks, he looks like a champion footballer.

We talk the new ecumenical talk that is sweeping the missions of the South Seas. Stringer claims that the real achievement in the Solomons has not been dramatic conversions, but a slow cumulative change in the lives and attitudes of the people. In the past there were zealous conver-sions, but they were rather like a marshfire, leaving the social and often the moral basis of life totally unaffected. (I am reminded of Father L.'s bitter remarks on Malaita.) There was little real impregnation with the Christian spirit, and in many ways the first converts – however fanatical they might appear – remained half pagan. Now, after three or more generations, he feels that there is at last a shift towards the kind of human relationships basic to the Christian way of life. He does not believe that such changes in values, and particularly such an increased respect for human life, involve the destruction of indigenous traditions. On the contrary, he admits the errors of early missionaries who tried to destroy everything connected with pagan beliefs. He remarks with evident satisfaction that Christian Choiseul men are now leading the movement to revive old customs, to keep the old pan-pipe music and the carving of fine canoes alive at the same time as they are demanding that their sons be provided with the finest of Western education.

302	The Islands of Solomon

Helen Stringer offers to start us on a walk around the bay, pointing out that the mission is unusual in that it has never been built separately from the native village, and now its various units – the manse, the school and the hospital, are scattered along the beach among the native houses, which in various clan hamlets extend the whole length of the bay. It has meant that they have been accepted by the people of Sasamongga as naturalized villagers. But for that acceptance, Bishop Boseto remarks, everyone has to thank Sister Lucy Money, who has run the hospital ever since he was a child playing in the surf of the bay. We set off to meet her.

Sister Lucy, who has been here for twenty years, is one of those wiry antipodean women, their faith as tough as their bodies, who thrive triumphantly in the climate and discomfort of the islands. The hospital, kept going on minimal funds, is not all it might be (Helen Stringer remarks how appalled she was when she first arrived at the thought of bearing a child there) but it is better than the nothing that existed before the missionaries came.

The great change, Sister Lucy insists, is not the physical one – that a woman can come into the hospital and have her child in relative comfort. It is the psychological one – the stirring even in these remote islands of the ripples of feminist liberation. Not only do the women form clubs and societies of their own. They even get on the boats and go off to Honiara for conferences. Ten years ago this would have been unthinkable. But now even the attitude of the men is changing. Only a few ultra-traditionalists still insist on the subjection of women. Most of them have accepted the idea that the expansion of their own mental horizons through education demands – if marriage is not to be irremediably dull – a corresponding expansion in the role of the women.

'Yes, we're making progress,' says Sister Lucy, casting a steely eye at the Bishop, who has just come up. 'But I don't know how Christian that makes us.'

The Bishop rises like a barracuda to the bait: 'We're the only large island in the whole group without a single pagan village!'

'Officially,' chants Sister Lucy. 'Officially! Officially also, there are no more crocodiles!'

The Bishop snorts, Helen Stringer laughs uneasily, and Sister Lucy turns to us and says: 'It's a pity my cook has gone home to her village today. I could have shown you the only woman who has put her head in a crocodile's mouth and survived.'

'Thanks to God's remarkable will,' intones the Bishop.

'Thanks to her own native presence of mind, my dear Bishop,' says Sister Lucy. 'She decided to bathe in a hole in a river just up the coast. She dived and went head first into the open mouth of a crocodile. She realized in a flash what had happened, and pressed down on the beast's shoulders with all her force, and managed to tear her head free. She lost her scalp and one of her cheeks was torn away. But she was alive, and we did what first-aid we could and then because no boat was putting in we took her in a canoe, sailing all night and half the next day over to Gizo, where there's a hospital. After that they took her down to Auckland and did plastic surgery on her, and now she's quite present-able looking, and one day, I'm sure, she'll find a husband. Some man will come along who can't resist the only girl to survive a crocodile!'

Sister Lucy has become in her years in the Solomons an enthusiastic canoe voyager, and she offers to take us along to the far end of the bay where a clan of boat-builders live separated from the rest of the village. They are making a canoe for her which makes a good excuse for her to pay a visit. The Bishop decides to accompany us.

Beyond the hospital the village continues in a kind of open forma-tion, with groups of houses, each group belonging to an extended family in the Melanesian fashion, scattered among the palm groves. The houses vary in looks. All are built on stilts and, with the greater Melanesian sense of privacy, they are not open huts like those of Samoa and the Gilberts, but have walls covered with pandanus leaf, with the light entering through window and door spaces.

Between the hamlets a rough road runs through the groves, with footbridges of flattened coconut-trunks spanning the streams that frequently cross it. At one place we have to wade through a stream that has swept away its fragile bridge, and eventually the road peters out entirely and we proceed along the beach, where walking is hard because of the soft sand, and where all the shells are inhabited by hermit crabs which the Bishop whistles out softly so that they peep at him with astonished stalky eyes. Women are cutting copra among the trees by the beach, and the Bishop goes in to talk to them and returns with his hands full of round white objects, as big as billiard balls. They are the hearts of germinating coconuts – the milk turned into solid tissue, which are articles of food in the islands. We munch them as we walk along; they are vapid in flavour, combining greenness and sweetness, like a vegetable trying to pass itself off as a fruit.

We enter a small clearing just as a man is rushing across the grass with uplifted cleaver, pursuing a lizard at least 30 inches long, which scrambles up the trunk of a palm. The Bishop springs into action, picking up immature fallen coconuts and throwing them in an attempt to dislodge the lizard, but fortunately his aim is poor and the reptile retreats into the tuft of the tree to descend at leisure. The Bishop declares it is an iguana, but as it has none of the iguana's characteristic dewlaps and spines I suspect it is really a kind of monitor. Whatever they actually are, these great lizards are generally detested for their egg-stealing propensities.

Eventually we reach the hamlet of the boat-builders. It consists of three houses and another house half rebuilt. Here live the grandfather who is the head of the clan and his two sons. The son who is the master canoe-maker is away, but the old man and a couple of women are sitting in the shade under one of the houses, which is the custom here in the heat of midday.

The examples of the canoe-builders' craft are there to see, and Sister Lucy proves an eloquent exponent in the master's absence. The biggest of the canoes is a splendid piece of native boatbuilding. It is 33 feet long and wide enough for two people to sit abreast and paddle in comfort. It is carved from a great log that floated over in from Vella Lavella in a hurricane that broke up a logging boom in one of the bays there and provided the boat-builders of Choiseul with enough logs, combed from their beaches and dragged into the shelter of the bush, to last them for several years. Sister Lucy sailed on the maiden voyage of the great canoe to Munda; equipped with an outboard motor, it got there, with a load of twenty-four people, in eight hours, beating the mission ship that set out at the same time. On the way back it was caught in a storm and benighted, but the pilot was a great navigator and a great rider of waves, and brought the canoe home safely by dawn. Such experiences appear merely to stimulate Sister Lucy's zest for canoe-sailing, and she shows us a six-person canoe being built to her order. It will cost her round about £60 to make, including the log.

The canoe-building clan are artists in other ways, for the second son arrives and takes us to his house. His wife appears; like her husband, she wears only a simple skirt of a piece of red cloth wrapped round her waist, and it suggests a world of change in the attitudes of missionaries and hence of their converts that she can appear bare-breasted and without embarrassment before the Bishop and Sister Lucy. As we talk to her – for she speaks a slow but precise mission-school English – we realize how for such people history has been telescoped. There are men still alive in the western Solomons who took part in head-hunting expeditions that terrified the islands around New Georgia, where the chiefs developed a positive avarice for skulls whose accumulation it was believed would increase their store of mana, the spiritual power that is most strongly concentrated in the human head. Such bizarre customs as head-hunting are extinct in the western Solomons, but it is obvious that in their general style of living this woman and her family are still largely in a custom world, dressing and eating and building their houses and canoes and holding their land according to the way of the ancestors. Yet her son, she tells us with pride, is studying at the University of Papua-New Guinea. So in a generation there is a leap from the custom life, barely changed by conversion to Christianity, to a modern university which will almost certainly make the son unfit for a return to village life.

We hurry back along the beach to lunch, and overtake the copra-cutting women who are carrying the product of their morning's work on their backs in sinnet nets whose loops are laid across the brow so that they act like a tumplines.

At lunch there is a brief excitement when a white boat sails across the end of the bay. We are afraid it is the *Leili*, not putting into Sasa-mongga after all, but it turns out to be a Chinese trading boat that wanders erratically around the islands. Then a boy from the other end of the village, where the store is situated, comes in to say that a man has arrived in a canoe from up the coast to travel on the *Leili*, and that it will be arriving before sunset. All this arouses a considerable excitement, for sometimes a month will pass without anything larger than a local canoe putting into Sasamongga, and for three boats to arrive in a single day has never been known before.

Later Helen Stringer takes us through the coconut-groves between the beach and the beginning of the hills. 'I'll take you somewhere that will amuse you,' she says, and leads us on by narrow footpaths and slippery little bridges under the palms, where coconut-lories are chattering excitedly and flying-foxes flop from tree to tree like birds of doom. About half a mile inland we climb a stile and go up a short slope to a hillock with a little cluster of three or four houses. A man with clipped moustache and short hair comes out and speaks to us in excellent English. He was educated for a few years in New Zealand, and instead of getting an office job in Honiara, decided to return to his own hamlet and apply to his land the scientific ideas of farming he learnt abroad. His holding, however, looks little different from the others. He complains that his cats are sick, and attributes it to the spraying of house walls with DDT by the health authorities to reduce the numbers of anopheles mosquitoes. The cats rub themselves against the walls, lick themselves and then sicken and die, and the rats increase.

Helen Stringer points to another clump of houses, five or six of them, on a slightly higher hillock a few hundred yards away. 'That is what I wanted you to see. It has the same name as your city. It is called Vancouver!' We climb up the path to see if we can find any of our fellow Vancouverites, but everyone must be out in the fields, for all we see is the little cluster of pandanus-walled buildings and a sow lying with her farrow in the sun. But the man from the other hamlet, who has come with us, tells us the story of the naming of the place. The spot was originally called the Place of the Giant. But about ten years ago the head of the family decided that such an unlucky name must be the reason why his crops were failing and his children were falling sick, so he went down to the school and asked to see an atlas, which he opened with his eyes closed and blindly stabbed with his finger. Vancouver was the place on which his fingertip rested, so Vancouver became the new name of the Place of the Giant.

At last, round about five o'clock, a white boat anchors in the bay. It is the *Leili*. She will not be leaving until dawn, and the Stringers urge us to stay with them, but we feel we have presumed enough on their time, and go down to the beach in procession, the Bishop insisting on humping our suitcase on his muscular shoulder. The *Leili* is a boat of the same class as the *Waisisi*, but this time we have the cabin completely to ourselves.

We cook our meal of pea soup and tinned asparagus which we eat with butter and cheese, and follow with tinned apricots and coffee. Then we go on to the top deck to enjoy another splendid still evening, the sun setting over the open sea, the whole firmament illuminated by golden cloud, and the Shortlands silhouetted against the horizon in a magnifying blaze of orange light.

Third Day. The *Leili* sails at dawn, and immediately it is evident that the mysterious man who arrived by canoe at Sasamongga and who seems to have come aboard during the night is directing the movements of the ship. We sail across the New Georgia Strait almost due south from Sasamongga to a point near the easternmost tip of Vella Lavella, and then down its south-eastern shore. There is little habitation visible – the occasional house on the beach – against the immense background of green jungle, broken by the white skeletons of giant dead trees, curving back to the black and rain-veiled hills.

Turning Kundumbangara Point, we pass a close-reefed coast, and at our first call, a place named Kolekola, the *Leili* has to execute an extraordinary twisting entry between great masking submerged reefs betrayed by the green of the water, and then, having penetrated this passage, where the swell is high and dangerous, moving inside the reef and then shoreward between two half-submerged shoals on which the waves beat in clouds of fury; the *Leili* points in to the beach along a narrow slot of deep water in which we lie tossing on the high swell and keeping our position merely by the adroit management of steering and engines, directed by the boatswain (a tall man from the Polynesian island of Bellona within the Solomons) who stands on top of the wheel-house and gives his directions through a speaking tube; another lookout stands in the bows watching the colour of the water and the visible pattern of the reefs.

The man who came on board last night now appears, a young man with the paler skins of the eastern Solomons, wearing a check shirt and blue shorts, and goes ashore in the dinghy which is rowed expertly over the high swell by two boys from the *Leili*. He walks up the beach to the plantation buildings that are visible through the palms, and returns with a notebook in his hand. I suspect he is a policeman, and shortly afterwards the mate confirms this, but is either unable or unwilling to say what his mission may be.

When the policeman returns the boat reverses its direction, turns north, and begins to circumnavigate the island in an anti-clockwise direction. During the morning and afternoon we put into four other places on the eastern coast, masked always by reefs whose entrances are at the mouths of rivers or within coves that conceal them from the sea and its weather. The first two places are wretched fishing hamlets built on the edges of mangrove swamps, with decrepit houses on piles, a few canoes on the shore, nets hung to dry, and so poor in garden produce that there is not a piece of fruit to be bought in either of them. In each of these places tall, lean and stork-legged elders appear in dirty loincloths and answer the policeman's questions. The next two places are small plantations hidden in green, tranquil-watered coves, each with its own small colony of neat houses built above the tideline, and from these the boat returns with fruit; for 25p we buy a splendid pineapple and a dozen large and delicious jade-green oranges.

Finally, at evening, we enter a deep inlet and come to a large village protected by a screen of small and narrow islands. There are European buildings on the hill overlooking the harbour, a large launch rides at its moorings, and by the shore and on the sheltering islets are built many native houses. A good number of canoes are drawn up on the beach; clearly this is a village of some size and importance. The policeman comes and stands beside me as the *Leili* draws in to the end of the jetty. 'I think we stay here for the night,' he says, and tells me that the place is called Ndovele, and that it is a Seventh-Day Adventist centre. Then, rather hesitantly, he volunteers the information that he has come to take away the accused and the witnesses in a case that will be tried at Gizo. I ask him what is the accusation. 'A man went to his daughter,' he replies, in the rather biblical English one so often hears in the islands. Then he goes off to sit in the great open-sided building – a church we realize – that stands at the end of the wharf; we see him there in his yellow waterproof taking notes from the people who come to him.

I stand looking down at the life going on abundantly in the clear water beside the wharf. Shoals of herring-sized fish swim around the boat, some of them zebra-barred in black on silver, others a brilliant blue with yellow tails, and yet others, which float near the bottom, black and lozenge-shaped. Long-spined sea-urchins cluster on the pile of concrete that forms the wharf and on the sandy bottom there are great striped sea-cucumbers.

As the sun begins to set the people start to gather for evening service in the church at the end of the jetty; in little canoes they come floating in from the islands, whole families from grey-haired patriarchs to tiny golliwog-eyed infants in muslin dresses; they walk along the shore and down the hillside paths, in starched cotton dresses and long-sleeved white shirts, and some of the younger men in shirts of the most dazzling rainbow colours, but all of them carrying large Bibles that show every sign of use and wear. The Coleman lamps are lit in the church as the light fails, and above the sounds of the *Leili*'s generators we hear their singing, echoing over the water until long after the sun has set. Then they emerge, their shirts and dresses pale spots in the darkness, and, coming down to their canoes, paddle silently across the ship's area of light out into the darkness of the lagoon. I am not sure, but I have the feeling that they have gathered specially on this unusual evening because the ship has come to take one of them away.

Fourth Day. This morning there are lights on the shore and activity on the boat long before dawn, and we leave at 6.30, with a silent little group of men and women standing on the jetty to watch our going. No wild scrambling of children on to the deck as happened yesterday when we docked; no demonstration of any kind; just a voiceless farewell to those who are leaving.

For the accused and the witnesses are now on board. The witnesses are a woman with a child in arms and two teenaged girls, one of whom is presumably the daughter to whom the accused – a skinny middle-aged man with red eyes, barefooted and dressed in a worn red-striped singlet and a pair of grimy khaki shorts – 'went'. Perhaps it is the lithe, older girl with skin like a bloomed damson, but whichever it is, nobody seems very concerned, and all the three women of the party seem more intent on enjoying the outing to Gizo than on lamenting whatever may have happened. There is no attempt to confine the man, and except that he stands apart from the others and exchanges no words with anyone, there is nothing to mark him off; he does not even have the look of a man in trouble, and indeed, from a local point of view, he is not, since if he is sentenced it will merely mean a few months mowing the lawns in Gizo and eating better meals than he would probably get at home. The policeman ignores his charges and spends the day sleeping in a deck-chair on the roof of the wheelhouse.

We sail north from Ndovele and turn the top of the island, around the great reefs that begin at this point and continue as a vast barrier around the western side of the island almost down to its southern extremity. It is a day of exciting sailing, sometimes outside the reef in the heavy swell of the open Pacific, but more often along the deep channels inside the reef where the green water of danger often comes perilously near, and we travel constantly with the boatswain or his mate watching intently from the top of the wheelhouse and speaking instructions down the tube and with another man perched in the bows of the boat.

This western coast of Vella Lavella, with its verdurous cliffs, its mountains and coves, its shielding islands and thunderous reefs, is perhaps the most beautiful of all the Pacific coasts I have yet seen from a sea-level view, and certainly the reef-navigation gives an extraordinary zest to travel here, for there is always peril to be felt, and the relief of escape, and skill to be admired, and, in a vicarious way, the triumph of a risk surmounted and therefore justified. Though it is I who mostly have these emotions, standing all day beside the rail, watching the water and getting burnt by the sun; Inge is not at heart a happy sailor, and she often retreats to the cabin to read, and once comes out to me with a passage from Montherlant about the madness of travel that reminds me of the ambivalence of my own feelings; much as I am enjoying these present hours, I am getting tired of our journeys and shall not be unhappy when we turn homeward.

We put in four times during the day, on each occasion to a plantation sheltered by a headland or an island, and the most attractive of all is a place called Mundimundi, completely hidden within an almost landlocked cove, with well-kept groves, hibiscus lining the shore, a pleasant house a little way up the beach, an air of away-from-the-world sufficiency.

We turn the southern tip of Vella Lavella, and put in to the United Church dock at Bilua; mission buildings on the hill, and a little mission ship lying within the reef. Then we sail southward over the open waters of the Vella Gulf, through a heavy ocean swell, past the dismally logged-off hills of northern Gizo, and into the harbour. We dock at the government pier. The hotel faces on to the beach, a hundred yards away, and a ship's boy carries our bag over. A half-breed servant takes us in. There is plenty of room. Nobody but government servants ever comes to Gizo.

4

It was five days before we could get a plane from Gizo back to Honiara, and we did not look forward to the stay with any pleasure, for Gizo at first sight was one of the least attractive places in the South Seas. The island was small, and whatever native Gizans survived were submerged in a heterogenous population of Europeans, Chinese, Japanese, Gilbertese, Polynesians from the outlying islands of Rennell and Bellona and Tikopia, and Melanesians from every other island of the Solomons who had come to work when Gizo was a prosperous centre for the planters of all the western islands, and who were marooned now that it had become a dying town.

For it was clear that Gizo was moribund. You had only to walk into the shabby lounge of the club, or stroll down the dusty road that served as a main street and look into the Chinese stores with their almost empty shelves, to sense that its life was slowly ebbing away, because the copra trade was failing, because the reefs were too tricky for big ships to enter, because the government was thinking of a new capital for the western islands at Hathom Sound on New Georgia where there was better anchorage and in the meantime was starving Gizo of funds. There had been minor reprieves; a logging company had been working on western Gizo, but soon it would have stripped off all it could take; a Japanese fishing operation was operating from a white mother ship moored off the town; but nobody seemed to have any faith in the future, and there was a certain symbolic appropriateness in the fact that the only building on the island that did not look impermanent was the Catholic cathedral.

Yet the very impermanence that was in the air helped to make our stay in Gizo far more interesting than we had first anticipated, since we were seeing there, in concentrated form, the end of the short era of the white man's glory in the Solomons, the era of the palm and the steeple, when the planter and the missionary had reigned supreme, the era before the bureaucrats came in force to wind up the Raj. Almost everyone we met seemed to be in transit, to be moving towards the end of something, the end of a career, the end of a dream, the end of an Empire. I had that feeling particularly strongly one evening sitting in the hotel with the District Commissioner and an agricultural officer on his way back from Vella Lavella to Honiara. The District Commissioner had been born in Uganda, the son of a British colonial servant; the agricultural officer had been born in Bolivia, the son of a British railway engineer; I had been born in Canada, the son of a British immigrant farmer; and as we talked I realized that there was a tendency, in these last days of the Empire, for those who lingered in its fragments to be men with the virus in their veins, in the sense that they were often the sons of an earlier generation of colonial expatriates; the circle was eddying tighter, but still in various ways we would remain within it to the last.

The man whose fate represented most dramatically the end of the South Seas as a dream was Michael Georgetti, who was managing the hotel. Michael was an immense bearded man who used to stand all day behind the bar in the hotel dining room; he stood because he could not ·

bear to sit – standing or lying were the only postures he found congenial – and as the day went on he would steadily drink his way through
the three bottles of Burgundy he had set aside in the morning; he took
it with ice in large glasses. He listened with a curious bird-like tilt of the
head to everything that was said, and occasionally would interject in a
voice surprisingly gentle and hesitant for so large a man, but when the
bar was empty he would talk to us in a low-toned monologue about
his experiences.

He had come into the islands first in 1949, sailing a yacht up from
New Zealand, and had been wrecked off the Shortlands, where he had
lived for several months in a native village. These months set the com-
pass for his life, for he loved the gentle tempo of existence, and when
he left the Shortlands he drifted for a while into labour recruiting, until
he realized that it was the kind of work that did not fit his nature.
After three or four years of it he went into partnership on a Vella
Lavella plantation, and shortly afterwards, when his partner found
another estate, he began to run the place on his own. It was in fact the
peacefully encoved plantation of Mundimundi which we had found so
appealing on our trip down the west coast of Vella Lavella, and we
could understand how in the high years of copra, with his books and
his drink and the money coming in regularly, Georgetti, who described
himself as a 'lazy man' and who was certainly something of a natural
philosopher, had felt it the life he would never want to leave. 'In
twenty-three years,' he said, 'I went back to New Zealand only once,
for three months, and I've never been so happy in my life as I was
sailing between the reefs back to Mundimundi.' He felt so committed
to the islands, that he married a local girl who was still, when we met
her, a woman of striking beauty, with the finely cut ebony features and
the luminous eyes one sees only among the people of New Georgia.

But now Georgetti was in Gizo, and the dream had faded. Prices fell
until he had hardly found it worth while to cut copra; at the same time
he realized that his trees were getting near the peak of maturity, yet the
prospects of the industry were so poor that he could not lay out capital
on clearing land and planting new trees. And then there was the shifting
political situation, the obvious prospect that in a few years the British
would leave and an era of unpredictable independence would begin;
even before independence, though the land question was not nearly so
acute as in the New Hebrides, the native people were beginning to
resent the strangers who stayed.

'When I went there first, I was just accepted. There was never any sign of hostility. The people had enough land of their own, and they were glad to earn a bit working for me and to trade at my store. But then the co-op came in and the store business went off, and wages went up at the same time as copra prices fell, and all at once Mundimundi changed from a place of contentment to a place of anxiety. It's not much fun to sit day after day on a decaying plantation, worrying about money and with nothing to distract your mind. So I sold out a chunk of the plantation to the natives, and I came over here until we can sell the rest. After all those quiet years on Vella Lavella, even living in Gizo is like being in the front line. But I can't see any future for a white man in the Solomons any more. Perhaps the big corporations like Lever's will carry on until prices rise again, if they ever do. But the small planter's day is ended. There are only three of them left in this whole area now, and they'll all be gone soon.'

'What will you do?'

'I don't really know. It means starting up again in the world I was glad to leave twenty years ago. I don't think there's anything like the South Seas that I knew left anywhere in the modern world. So I'm making my plans, and within a year I'll be gone. I don't look forward to the future, and I'll be sad to leave the islands but . . . I won't be staying any longer.'

Up on the hill behind the town of Gizo, looking out over his palm-trees at the blue channels between the islands and at the great volcanic cone of Kolombangara, lived Georgetti's friend Ernie Palmer, the oldest white man on Gizo, and the only planter on the island. Ernie was not working his plantation; the nuts fell from the trees and rotted in grey piles beside its red earth roads. But unlike Georgetti he had made no plans to leave; there was no point in living out the remainder of his life anywhere else. But he thought his sons – who loved the islands as much as he had done – would probably find it impossible to stay.

And even Ernie, who had been in the Solomons for fifty-three years, and his wife, who had been there for thirty-five, always talked of the South Seas in the past rather than in the present; it was 'I loved', or at best 'I've loved', rather than 'I love'. One had the sense they were looking back on something complete, something already – though they still seemed to be standing in the midst of it – in some strange way distant.

Ernie was a thin, agile, old man who belonged to an earlier generation of South Sea hands than Georgetti, and to him the islands had been not so much a dream as a way of life. When he arrived in the Solomons in 1919 he was still a boy of fifteen, and whatever he had become the islands made him, for he never went back for more than a holiday, and that only once in many years. He began as a recruiter, working first with other men, and later on running his own schooner, which was licensed to carry forty and which he described as 'not much more than a ketch'. He did his recruiting mostly on contract for Lever's, and went usually to the coastal settlements of Malaita, where he would fire cannon to attract the men out of the bush, and make down-payments to the elders in stick tobacco, and if he got a lot of recruits he would sail away quickly in case there was a plot to cut out the boat, for the Malaitans were regarded as violent and treacherous and more than one recruiter Ernie Palmer had known lost his life through lingering too long in the same spot. 'They were worst of all at the time of Marching Rule, because then they began to get cargo cult ideas, and if you went in with a good load of trade goods they'd think they had a right to take it, just like that.'

By Ernie's time the worst features of blackbirding had ended. Men were recruited only to work in the Solomons, and were returned to their home island when the period of their indentures came to an end. They were given food and clothing, medical care and a shack roof over their heads, and at the end of their three years they were paid at the rate of £1 a month in trade goods, which meant the princely fortune of £36, counted out in hatchets and calico and stick tobacco, and taken home in a cheap seaman's chest. Ernie Palmer thought they were treated well. 'You've got to see it their way,' he argued. 'Many a man on Malaita became a big chief by starting off giving away the stuff he took back from the plantation. Thirty-six pounds brought a lot of goods round about 1930.'

After World War II recruiting came virtually to an end. Ernie retired to the plantation he had acquired with the proceeds, and then he took to pearl fishing until the beds were fished out, and his two small vessels lay idle in the harbour. Recruiting – plantations – pearling – all the activities that had brought men like Palmer and Georgetti to the Solomons, and allowed them to live in that sphere of moral independence which is the world of all pioneers, were at an end, and all that remained was to stay as long as events allowed in the compelling beauty of the world one had loved.

The day of the planters had ended, and the last of the colonial administrators were busily preparing for the twilight of their own presence in the islands. The situation of the missionaries seemed more complex. Black pastors were replacing white pastors, black Protestant bishops were even replacing white bishops, but the churches remained the same, shaped by their European origins, and the Catholics, at least, refused to accept any selection of priests that was dominated by merely national or racial considerations. And so Father Meese, the Dominican priest of Gizo who completed the triad of companionship with Georgetti and Palmer, seemed by far the most immovable.

Father Meese was an Australian of Irish descent, a rotund and loud-laughing man whose very presence reminded me that Rabelais too had belonged to one of the begging orders of friars. Father Meese came in the first evening we were staying in Georgetti's hotel, ate and drank prodigiously, swore as violently as the toughest recruiter, and told risqué jokes whenever the opportunity arose. He talked incessantly, but though his tales – particularly of his Irish family – were very amusing at the time, they were quickly obscured in memory by the impression of his earthy and dynamic personality, of his intense practicality, of his glad, frank acceptance of the physical world.

There was much we discovered about this extraordinary man only from others. He never boasted, for example, of his linguistic powers, but we had learnt from other missionaries that he alone knew all the important dialects of New Georgia and Choiseul and Vella Lavella, and could pick up a language effectively in two months. Something of his courage did emerge in the tales he told of his ministry on Choiseul, of his canoe journeys through the difficult waters to bring men on the verge of death to the hospital, and of the harrowing hundred-mile walk through the interior of Choiseul when he was seized so violently with malaria that he never thought he would emerge alive; but it was others who told how often he had saved lives.

But the man of tongues and the man of courage were only two of the masks that Father Meese bore. There was also Father Meese the Universal Agent, who had interpreted the original begging role of the Dominicans in a special way, by progressively appropriating to the greater profit of the church, if not the greater glory, the business infrastructure of Gizo. One by one he had taken over the agencies for the shipping lines and Solair and the only insurance company that operated in the islands, and was representative of a whole cluster of international

corporations from Gillette and Pepsi Cola downwards which filled
with small print his large business card. Whenever a ship arrived or a
plane departed there was Father Meese; even if a European resident
wanted merely a haircut, he set off for the little office beside the parsonage where the Father would very efficiently barber him. And there
was the other side of his activities, represented by the Chinese characters
on the reverse of his card, for he was, as he genially claimed, the
unofficial Chinese consul in Gizo, representing the local merchants in all
their contacts with the official world which they found so bewildering.
Out of this activity came a considerable income for the church, and a
great deal of public service in a town that, even if it was dying, was
still not dead enough to be without the need for at least one honest and
enterprising go-between.

At the same time, one could not dismiss Father Meese merely as the
genial priestly businessman one encountered on the waterfront, or
merely as the Rabelaisian with whom one so amiably ate the excellent
Chinese meals served in Georgetti's hotel and drank his French and
Australian wines. It was impossible to forget the courage and compassion and sense of duty that mingled with his restless energy, or, for that
matter, his sense of the power and seriousness of his vocation, which I
realized when he told me, with an unaccustomed straight face, that
when he went into the public bar of the hotel where the Melanesians,
Polynesians and Gilbertese drank together and where the atmosphere
was always keyed to the edge of inter-racial violence, the noise would
cease at once, not because he was a white, which had ceased to mean
anything, but because he was a priest.

It was this sense of his special role, outside race and politics, combined
with an energy as dynamic as that of any departed blackbirder, that
made one feel Father Meese or another like him would be there in Gizo
long after the last planter and the last white officer had departed.
Beside him were emerging the men who would shape whatever
country might emerge with the end of Empire, the native officials,
and among them the man who most forcibly attracted our attention
was Dominic Otuane, the District Officer in charge of local affairs on
Gizo, a short, fat man with a round intensely black face from the
Shortland Islands. Dominic, one of Father Meese's parishioners, shared
his ability to confound the categories. The Shortland Islands is the one
part of the Solomons where Melanesians live like Polynesians under the
rule of hereditary high chiefs, and Dominic was a high chief's son. Yet

he was highly educated in the Western sense. He had broken away from racial prejudice so far as to marry a Gilbertese girl, with whom he took us one day across the island to see a beachside village of emigrants that, with its great maneaba, might have been transported intact from Abemama or Tarawa. And he possessed such a natural energy and such a sense of duty that – when he could not get the government to allow him to employ enough men to keep the townsite in good order – he would go out himself in his spare hours to push the power mower over the public lawns by the waterside.

In many ways Dominic was a highly Westernized man, and he was convinced that the British system of government was particularly appropriate to conditions in the Solomons, since the development of a party system would create the ideological continuum needed to counter the tendency of the native politicians to be obsessed with local problems and interests. But Dominic accepted Western ideas of political organization, just as he accepted the Catholic faith, without abandoning all his traditional beliefs, and one evening he talked of the shark cult to which by ancestry he belonged, and in whose strange manifestations he believed implicitly and, as he claimed, by right of experience.

Certain lineages in the Shortlands, he explained, refer to the sharks as 'grandfathers', and regard them as the incarnations of ancestral spirits. Families have special sharks who inhabit certain bays, and with these they maintain mysterious links, calling them on occasion, and talking to them when they come into the shallows to be caressed by their 'grandchildren'. Such people, by certain conjurations, can divert a shark from its prey, and Dominic claimed that once, swimming as a child, he was pursued by a shark and saved in this manner. People of shark lineages are feared in the Shortlands, because if they regard a man as an enemy and put a curse on him, it is believed that sooner or later their ancestral shark will encounter and kill him. In spite of their conversion to Christianity, Dominic maintained, none of the Shortland islanders doubted the reality of communication with the sharks, and many people still continued the talking, though nowadays they would do it more secretly than in the past.

5

Dominic Otuane, with his equally strong beliefs in Western democracy and communication with sharks, remained a man suspended between the new and the traditional, and when we looked back over our months in the South Seas, whether we had moved among Polynesians or Micronesians or Melanesians, we realized that we had met no single person, except for the Europeans, who did not live in some degree within the mental world of custom and taboo (in its extended meaning of the traditionally sacred). At the same time, we had not encountered anyone who had not been touched profoundly by the impact of Western ideas and technology. In education, in religion, in trade goods, in means of transport, in medicine, in politics, in one way or another the influence of the outside world has left its mark. Even the celebrated Big Nambas of the New Hebrides were now represented either by the sad figures in baggy European clothes who had shook our hands at Lakatoro or by the showmen in codpieces who posed before the cameras; even the bushmen of Malaita came down from their taboo-ridden pagan hilltop villages to walk to market along a macadam road, dressed in kilts of English cloth and carrying cane knives made in Japan.

PART SEVEN
Testing in the Fijian Fire

1

Fiji was the end as it was the beginning of our journeys in the South Seas, the centre from which we had departed on all our trips, and to which we always returned. We flew back there from Port Moresby, seeing again the jet-height relief maps that were the Solomons and the New Hebrides, dipping down for brief stops at Honiara and Vila. It was my sixtieth birthday, and I was pleased by the good-natured way in which the Fijian hostess embraced me when I told her, but not surprised, for it seemed to me an auspicious and appropriate gesture of greeting on returning to the land whose people we had learnt to like most of all the Pacific islanders.

Yet, even in making that statement of preference, I find myself paradoxically with surprisingly little that I am impelled to say about Fiji. So much of what we saw there had at least been paralleled in the other islands, and the most striking – and depressing – difference was the extent to which Fiji's geographical centrality, its tourist boom over recent years, and the presence of a large expatriate population of Indians, had combined to propel these islands even farther in the direction of modern nationhood than any other country of the South Seas.

Suva is now the largest urban community in the South Pacific outside Australia and New Zealand. Even in 1972 more than 110,000 people were crowded into the city and its growing suburbs, and one sensed the emergence of a kind of metropolitan impersonality that even Nouméa, with its French provincial atmosphere, had so far avoided. The process was not complete, for Suva was still in transition from the former capital of the British territories in the South Pacific to a cosmopolitan town dedicated to tourism and drifting towards industrialism.

Many vestiges of the imperial past remained, for the Fijians value their association with the Commonwealth, are devoted to the Queen whom they regard as their hereditary high chief by virtue of Cakobau's cession of his powers to Queen Victoria, and think of Britain as a possible umpire in the event of acute dissension between them and the other principal race – the Indians. Red-coated and sandalled guards still stamped with British military precision outside Government House, though a descendant of Cakobau now presided there, British officials still lurked in high places in the governmental structure, the colonnaded buildings of the colonial era still gave a touch of grace to the city's façades, and imperial companies like Carpenter, Burns Philp and Morris Hedstrom continued to wield great economic power and not a little concealed political influence. Citizens of British and Chinese origin even held the balance of power in the carefully calculated system of parliamentary representation, which meant that they gave their support to the Fijian high chiefs who had controlled the ruling Alliance party since independence.

Suva had never been, in the native sense, a Fijian town. It was from the beginning a town of British rulers, of Australian merchants, of Chinese and later Indian shopkeepers and artisans, and to this day, under the shallow American veneer which tourism has brought into being, the outlines of the essential Suva can still be detected: the Chinese entrenched in Marks Street and the Indians in Cummin Street, the hilly slopes of the Domain behind Government House occupied by large British houses, and the centre of the town, outside the big international hotels (financed by money from Hawaii, Singapore, Saigon and Sydney), shared out between the three trading races. In feeling the place has more in common with other imperial cities of the Pacific changing into cosmopolitan centres, like Singapore and Hong Kong, than it does with any native Fijian community past or present, and I always felt that the Fijians, with their erect stride, walked as strangers in the capital of their own land. They lived mainly on the outskirts, in shacktowns or in hardly less depressing apartment blocks created for their use by the government. But there was one area of the city that they had made peculiarly their own, at least during the working hours of the day, and that was the waterfront area behind the great covered market.

A Fijian in town is still a village man, possessing some interest in the ground belonging to his mataqali or land-holding lineage. No matter how small his shack or apartment, custom demands that he give hospitality even to his distant relatives if they come to town, but custom equally demands that when he needs he must get his share of produce from the family land, and this means that even in Suva one never sees an undernourished Fijian, or a Fijian who begs. All the beggars are Indian, because Indians have no hereditary land rights to cushion them against want. The Fijian may live in overcrowded conditions and work for wretched wages, he may suffer acutely from anomie when he is away from the intense communal life of the village, but he never wants in a physical way, and if misfortune strikes he can always return to live off the land.

The way in which the solidarity of native society can operate even in an urban situation was illustrated just before we arrived in Suva in a manner that would have pleased the classic European syndicalists. The 1,600 stevedores and coastal seamen of Suva went on strike against the five big overseas companies who control both the Suva waterfront and interisland shipping. On their wages of 30 cents (about 15p) an hour, the workers had been able to build up no strike funds, and it was thought that they would never be able to hold out against the rich and powerful employers. What the employers had left out of consideration was the fact that no Fijian lives entirely in the cash economy, and in this case the custom world, the world of the traditional villages, rose up to defend its prodigal sons who had gone to the city. By truckloads the food came in daily to Suva from all over Viti Levu, and when the employers realized that the workers had something better than a strike fund to support them, it was they who gave in.

But even if native Fijian society shows a power to modify such essentially contemporary situations as those created by labour disputes, the factors of change have for long been more widespread in Fiji than in other Pacific countries with the exception of New Caledonia, and it is only a few of the remoter islands and the mountainous interior of Viti Levu that have sustained tribal traditionalism to any appreciable degree.

Fiji in fact was shaped into its present form by the plantations of the later nineteenth century. The land deals were not nearly so extensive as those in the New Hebrides, and when they came to an end with the establishment of British rule in 1876, more than 80 per cent of the land in Fiji was still in the hands of Fijian clans. Nevertheless, the planters have acquired the good coastal land, and by turning it over to cotton and then, when cotton failed, to sugar, they provided a variation of crops which saved Fiji from becoming dependent entirely on copra like so many of the other South Sea colonies. Economically, Fiji was in fact exceptionally fortunate, since the native people had enough land to sustain an adequate subsistence existence, while sugar provided a reliable balance of trade until the late 1960s, when tourism took its place.

In fact, of course, since the native Fijians were able to feed themselves from their own land throughout the colonial period, and had no need to take up the plantation work which in any case they did not relish, the plantation economy benefited only the Europeans (in which category one must include a fair number of Australians and even some Americans) who set out to profit as planters and traders. And it was to sustain the plantation economy so alien to Fijian inclinations that in 1879 the planters began to import indentured labourers from India. When the system came to an end more than thirty years later, 40,000 Indians elected to remain in Fiji. There were then more than two Fijians to every one Indian, and nobody foresaw that by 1944 the heavy breeding of the Indians would have equalized the ratio, and that today the Fijians would be outnumbered 6:5 by a people whom they did not invite to share their country.

Both the Indians and the Fijians were in fact the victims of the imperial authorities who approved and administered the indentured labour system. But the imperialists have departed, and the two races are left to arrange as best they can a situation that in other former colonies had resulted in bitter racial strife and massive bloodshed. This has not happened in Fiji. But the life of the country has been irremediably modified by the presence of the Indians. Two people and two cultures live within the same land. And rather than continue with the history of that confrontation, rather than recount the inconclusive discussions we had with Fijian politicians and with the professors of the newly founded University of the South Pacific, I prefer to project my image of Fiji and its problems through the narratives of two trips on the main island of Viti Levu – Great Fiji.

2

Singatoka is a small white town about a hundred miles west of Suva along the southern coast of Viti Levu, reached by a highway called the Queen's Road where deep potholes and upstanding rocks compete to imperil the traveller and where the hills in heavy rains turn into slides of slippery red mud. Nevertheless, it is the centre of one of Fiji's new tourist regions, the so-called Coral Coast, where the beaches are somewhat better than the heaps of coral rubble that one encounters so often and so disappointingly in the archipelago. There are resort hotels on the beaches each side of Singatoka, and the town itself has a triple function; it is a market centre for the Singatoka Valley, the largest valley penetrating into the interior of the island; it is a sugar-growing centre linked to the refinery town of Lautoka on the west coast by Fiji's only railway, really a narrow-gauge tramway for transporting sugar cane; it is a miniature Hong Kong where duty-free shops sell electronic equipment and 'French perfumes' to Australian and American tourists. Almost all its inhabitants are Indians whose forefathers came from Gujerat to trade with the indentured labourers.

We had come here with Gordon Babineau, whom we rejoined in Suva after our return from New Guinea; we put up at the Fijian Hotel, an international hostelry to the west of Singatoka whose only difference from similar places in Lebanon and Malaysia was that the staff were Fijian and the entertainment was a localized version of the travesty Hawaiian entertainers have made of traditional Oceanic songs and dances.

The next morning we drove to the government office in Singatoka, carrying our letter of introduction from the Ministry of Fijian Affairs. Fortunately the assistant to whom the letter was addressed was on tour, and the tall, pale-skinned man who received us was Ratu Voisalagi, who combined the hereditary function of paramount high chief of the district with the official rank of Roko Tui, the rough equivalent of District Commissioner. All this we learnt only by a series of circumlocutory inquiries after he had offered to accompany us up the west side of the Singatoka Valley; being, like many Fijian chiefs, of Tongan descent, he observed the Polynesian conventions by which a man of noble birth leaves the singing of his praises to orators and maintains a soft voice and a subdued manner until provoked to anger.

Ratu Voisalagi suggested that we should go into the town and buy powdered yaqonna (or kava) to present to the chiefs we might visit, and as soon as we had bought the brown powder wrapped up in little packets he joined us on the drive to Keiasi, up the upper river, the last village before the road dwindled and split into the trails that wandered to remoter villages.

At the beginning of our journey we were on the western bank of the wide palm-lined river. Low hills clustered fairly close to its banks, but they left little strips and triangles of alluvial land which served as truck

farms, and a larger fragment of flat land had been turned into an agricultural experimentation station. It was a region where bamboo grew
profusely and the river people used it for the rafts they moored in the
stream for fishing and on which they brought down cargoes of bananas
from the hill villages where the road did not reach.

Soon we left the river and drove into the hills where the jungle
survived in pockets and gullies of tall trees and gigantic ferns, but even
here there was a great deal of cultivated land, and many crops were
grown: peanuts and broom corn, tomatoes and cabbages, pineapples
and dry rice, and jade-green fields of young tobacco to be dried in the
steep-roofed tin sheds of the factories which, clustered together, looked
like a Cézanne village turned into shining metal.

Along the road were spaced the real Fijian villages, each methodically
laid out in rows of houses – or mbures – on rectangles of brilliantly
green grass. We saw several mbures in construction; their lower
frames were of coconut-trunks, but their rafters of bamboo, and split
bamboo formed the walls, though the walls of the chief's mbures were
covered with large oval leaves resembling those of the teak tree. We
drove through places with sonorous names – Nakumbuta and Koro-
sagena, Naviaga and Malembalemba, until the conical mountains
closed in, gold-green with plumed grasses that flowed like waves in the
wind.

On the way we passed a faint path that came up to the road from the
direction of the river bank, and continued on the other side into a deep
bushy gorge. The Roko Tui pointed it out. 'We're getting into hill
territory', he remarked, 'and the hill folk in Fiji are the people who
cling to tradition. That path comes from a village called Tuu which
lies beside the river. It is the path by which the dead are carried. The
people of Tuu are almost the last in Fiji who still lay the bodies of their
dead in a cave, wrapped in tapa cloths and fine mats.' There must have
been a taboo attached to the burial caves, for when I suggested to the
Roko Tui that we might walk up to them, since he said they were not
far away, he smiled and shook his head with an air of polite finality.

Eventually we reached Keiasi, a village on a broad bench above the
valley, with the soft-contoured grass hills rising around it, patterned in
green for the damp ground, yellow and brown for the dry ridges, blue
for the distances, with the high-forested spine of the island towering
dark beyond them far inland. We drove through the village to the
government station beyond it to get petrol, and as Gordon attended to

the car's needs, Ratu Voisalagi took Inge and me on to the top of a
hillock beside the station, and showed us the ancient track of prehistoric
days, lacing along the ridgetops and hillsides on the opposite face of the
valley, its ledge picked out by the afternoon sunlight, and then, on the
near side of the river, the humps and shadows on a grassy hillside which
marked the site of an old Fijian fort which the British had to storm and
demolish in the 1870s before they could command the loyalties of the
hill people, then ferociously anti-Christian and cannibalistic. 'They
were the people who ate and killed Mr. Baker, the missionary,' the
Roko Tui remarked in a tone of nostalgic satisfaction, and hastily
added, in a dutiful afterthought, 'It's wonderful what the churches have
done.' He went on to talk about the years he had spent at boarding
school in New Zealand – happy years as he remembered them, and yet,
as he said, he had been glad to get back to the hills of the Singatoka,
which he obviously regarded with a truly poetic affection. 'It can be
very lovely just before sunset. It can also be very lonely in the evening.'
And he talked with satisfaction of walking in the mountains, and of the
light and fragrant air of the high forests. And indeed, even in Keiasi,
we felt a burden lifted from our chests after the humidity of the coast.

We returned to Keiasi and, parking the car on the edge of the village
green, approached the mbure of the village chief, a large leaf-covered
house with heavily thatched and low-hanging eaves, surrounded by
aromatic blue-flowered shrubs and approached by a rough stairway of
boulders. A young man sitting outside had seen us, and we waited for
two or three minutes until he called us in and we entered through the
middle of the three doors that provided light and air. A great mat had
been laid out, and before making any greetings, we sat down in the
positions pointed out to us, Inge and I as the elder guests facing the door,
Gordon on the left-hand side of the mat, and on the right the Roko
Tui and Ratu Mele, the old village chief with his right eye milky with
cataract. Ratu Voisalagi made a short speech announcing the reason
for our visit, and Ratu Mele replied in welcome. Then he hurried out,
and we heard the beat of the wooden lali drum. 'It is always beaten
when strangers come to a hill village,' the Roko Tui explained. 'Once
it meant that there was a choice of war or peace; now it means only
peace.' When the chief returned a number of men followed him and sat
across the end of the hut inside the door. One of them carried a bucket
of water, and then out of a corner of the room the great wooden bowl
for mixing yaqonna was drawn out. It had a cord of sinnet attached to

it on which were threaded some great cowries, and this was stretched towards me. 'You are the guest of honour,' the Roko Tui explained. 'The placing of the cord toward you is a taboo act, and in the old days a man would be killed if he stepped over it or touched it before the yaqonna ceremony ended.'

Except that powdered root in a cotton bag was used, the ceremony was very close to that which had taken place on Apolima. There was a sonorous ritual chant in which all the men took part as the first cup was filled and presented to me. I clapped once before taking it, and the others clapped three times as I drank it in a single draught, all but the last few drops which I shook out on the mat, and then as I handed back the bowl the others clapped five times in a special rhythm, shouting 'Mata! Mata! It is done!' It was stronger and more peppery kava than the Samoan, but though the cup passed three times round the circle, the only effect I felt was a slight tingling numbness at the base of the tongue. The inevitable speeches followed, my own, Gordon's, the Roko Tui's, Ratu Mele's. Ratu Mele told of the man who had come there years ago and had put him into a book; it was, I realized, my friend Cyril Belshaw, who had described this very village in *Under the Ivi Tree*. So much time was consumed by these various courtesies, which in Fiji the traditionalist hill people would be the last to abridge, that very little was left before we had to leave for the Roko Tui's evening appointments. Yet what we did learn was very significant of the changes that were taking place in Fijian village life. For the old chief pointed through the door of his mbure at the village, and told us to observe the spaces where houses had once stood – had stood even ten years ago! Now they were no longer there because people were beginning to move away and to build their mbures on the land they cultivated. That was what the coming of the road had done, he complained. It had made people lose their respect for traditional ways. Now the people who lived on their land no longer took part in the common life of the village except on special occasions like funerals or weddings. It was different in the villages up the river where the road did not go. There people still lived in the old ways.

It was clear that Fijian society was going through a transition from a stage of co-operative agriculture to one of virtually independent peasant farming, and that customary tribal life was suffering. 'It is inevitable,' commented the Roko Tui as we drove back beside the river to Singatoka. 'Our people are beginning to want what only money can buy. They see the Indians who work as individual farmers, and they think that they will do as well. Perhaps they will one day. But I hate to admit that up to the present it is the Indians who make the most enterprising farmers.'

The next day we went on our own up the eastern side of the river, talking to the people we met, sitting over yaqonna in the house of a villager named Tuitonga who earned his living as a porter at one of the coastal hotels, and meeting both Indian and Fijian cane farmers. As always happens in such situations, we listened to conflicting complaints.

By the roadside we met a young Indian cane farmer with a classically beautiful North Indian face framed by a ragged straw hat. His name was Amichand. He was twenty-six, had just married, had just acquired a lease of twenty-five acres of land. His lease, from a Fijian mataqali, ran for ten years, with an option for a further ten. He would have to make all the money he could in that time, since he doubted if the lease would be renewed a second time. The Fijians, he said, were becoming jealous of the Indians, and were taking back the land they had leased to them, under the pretence that they wanted to work it themselves. But – and he pointed to an area of rampant bushes and creepers on the other side of the road – this was not always so; that land had been a flourishing Indian cane farm seven years before, but when it reverted to the Fijians they did nothing with it. So he had been lucky to get any lease at all, though not so lucky as his father, one of the few Indians who owned freehold land; he had bought twenty-two acres when a sugar company had decided to divide up land it had bought in the nineteenth century rather than grow the sugar under estate conditions.

What Amichand told us presented the plight of the Indians in Fiji, who were still forced to remain farmers because there was not enough urban employment, and who were excellent cultivators, but were kept from the land by the laws that forbade the sale of native terrain. The discontent of the Indians with the land laws has become the most potent issue in the hands of the political opposition to the ruling Alliance party.

Yet when we talked to Tuitonga and to a young Fijian cane farmer who came into his house and joined us in the rounds of yaqonna, the Fijians felt their own side of the case equally strongly. They admitted they had been backward in taking to commercial farming, but now they were ready, and the young cane farmer seemed to be making a success of the land he was cultivating. But, Tuitonga remarked, it was difficult now for Fijians to start as farmers, in the Singatoka valley at least, for the best land had been leased to Indians, and only the inferior land remained. In another village along the road, the men told us that they had decided to terminate all leases to Indians as quickly as possible, and to appeal to the courts in the hope of cancelling options on extensions. They complained strongly about the situation in which they were forced to earn money working as servants in the hotels on the coast while others prospered from the lands of their ancestors.

3

The situation between the Indians and the Fijians, though the leaders on both sides have so far prevented violence, is bound to become more tense, as the Indians feel that they are increasingly prevented from using their skills as farmers and the Fijians increasingly desire to move into the cash economy without taking up the demeaning work as servants which the growing tourist industry offers. It is largely because they are haunted by the need to divert attention from the crucial problem of land that the Fijian government has so anxiously welcomed the inflow of foreign capital with little thought of its ultimate consequences, in the hope of developing the country in other directions than agriculture.

But the differences between the Fijians and the Indians go deeper than those relating to land. They are temperamentally and culturally widely separated. In spite of the value which Fijians put on traditional ceremonial, they have largely been assimilated into the missionary culture of the South Seas; the ratio of church attendance is certainly higher than in North America or western Europe. The Indians, on the other hand, have clung to the religions they brought from their homeland; they are devout Muslims, Sikhs and Hindus, and certain ecstatic sects have flowered in an alien environment as they never did in India.

We had heard a great deal of these sects, the devotees of the grim goddess Kali, but it was only two days before our departure from Fiji that we saw their feats of firewalking and self-mortification. We were walking in the morning under the rain trees by the waterfront at Suva when a taxi driver asked us if we would like to see a fire-walking ceremony. We imagined that it was one of the dubiously authentic shows put on for tourists. He assured us that it was nothing of the kind, but the annual ceremony in honour of Kali at a secluded little temple at Waimanu about thirty miles out of Suva. Young men would be

initiated into the cult and sick children would be carried over the fire
in the hope of curing them. We went with him, setting off after lunch
into the flat alluvial country that is devoted to dairy farming and
growing the vegetables for the Suva market. We knew already that the
fire-walking cult flourished mainly among low-caste farmers and
labourers. Its priests or gurus were certainly not Brahmins, and their
temples were usually as poor as the congregations, but there seemed no
doubt that they were centres of extraordinary devotion.

The temple at which we arrived stood in a field beside a dirt road
that ended a mile farther on at Waimanu River. Everyone, Indian or
otherwise, was charged a few cents at the gate to help with the expenses
of the cult. The temple consisted of a small closed sanctuary made of
yellow corrugated plastic sheets, in which were evidently stored the
images of the deities and the sacred objects of the cult. But today the
gods had been brought out, and they were lined up on a roofed platform; there were nine of them, and they were really large wooden
dolls, about 3 feet high, carved in a style of crude rustic fantasy such as
I had seen in Nepalese village temples. A black-faced Kali was the
central figure, Ganesh and Hanuman were recognizable among her
attendants, but the rest were beyond my powers of identification, and
I suspect they were the deities of some rural cult of north India that had
long ago been incorporated into the ever-receptive body of Hindu
belief.

In front of the images was a large oblong pit, about 12 yards long
and 2 yards wide, and in the middle of a large pile of greying ashes
which turned red whenever a wisp of wind licked them. Under a
shelter facing the pit, a few planks had been laid over some logs for
visitors like ourselves, and in a longer shelter parallel with the pit the
Indians were sitting on the ground, women and girls in bright best
saris and men and boys in freshly laundered shirts and trousers. There
was a touch of a church fair about it all, for boys were wandering
around selling pop and Indian sweets and girls were selling raffle
tickets. The ceremony had been timed for 2.30, but the hour came
and went, and there was no sign of activity. A small man in white
trousers and a blue and gold shirt appeared, walking among the people,
chatting to them, until finally he came to us. 'I am priest,' he said, 'I
bid you very welcome,' and shook hands as benignly and matter-of-
factly as if he were a vicar at a bazaar, except that he looked less
sanctimonious than the average vicar, for he had a sharp, bright,

youngish face and hair of normal length, and made no attempt in his
dress or manner to imitate a Brahmin. He explained that one of the
drumheads was broken, and they had sent away for another, which
should be here soon.

The drum at last arrived – it was really a rather large tambourine
beaten with a curved stick – and three young men started to beat out a
high-pitched and emotionally intense rhythm while around the
sanctuary about a dozen devotees – some of them boys of fourteen or
fifteen – put on orange shirts and dhotis; the priest attired himself in the
red of fire. Then they walked in procession before the images, shouting
'Govinda! Govinda!', and marched off in file, out of the field with the
drummers at their head, and down the lane out of sight. The taxi
driver came over and said that they had gone down to the river;
he drove us down as far as the car would go, and then we followed a
sandy path until we came to a broad beach, where the devotees were
assembled. They were kneeling on the sand, decorating trident-headed
staffs with fruit and leaves, and filling brass vases with sacred branches
among which were thrust burning incense sticks. This they did with
great meticulousness, as if the placing of every leaf was important, and
they seemed indifferent to the hoots and laughter of a group of Fijian
youths who had climbed into some trees overlooking the beach.

After all this was done – and it took a considerable time for each
ornament to pass the priest's inspection – he led the devotees into the
river where they immersed themselves as a launch filled with laughing
Europeans curved near them, creating a great swell. They emerged and
knelt again on the sand, and, as the drums beat to a crescendo, the priest
and a tall massive man who acted as his acolyte took handfuls of sharp,
bright steel spikes, like thin skewers with trident heads, in honour of
Siva (whose consort Kali is), and began to thrust them into various
parts of the devotees' faces – through the earlobes, through the thin
loose flesh on the temples, through the cheeks, through the nostrils,
through the lips, until each fire-walker had between four and six of
these glistening spikes securely lodged in his face. I was standing within
five feet of the nearest devotees, in bright sunlight, and I did not see a
trace of blood, nor did I hear the slightest whimper or notice any
actual wince, though it was obvious that the youngest boy was in a
state of great tension, for he was breathing stertorously and his Adam's
apple was agitating in the most extraordinary manner; the rest did not
show even that degree of perturbation.

By the time this ritual had ended, the taxi driver suggested that we should go back to avoid getting trapped in the crowd returning from the beach, and so the devotees remained for ten minutes or a quarter of an hour at the river after we left and what happened in that brief time I cannot say. Certainly it was not long after we had returned to our seats that young men with long rakes began to distribute the piles of ashes into a bed at least six inches deep; the ashes were still so hot that we could feel the warm blast on our cheeks as they were stirred, though we must have been sitting eight feet away from the edge of the pit. Then the sound of the drums began to draw near, battering their hypnotic rhythm up the lane until the devotees appeared, this time dancing with an almost spastic compulsion; the trident spikes glittered on their faces, and they bore on their heads the brass vessels and in their hands the leafy sceptres. They came dancing up to the deities and then around the edge of the pit, so that they passed within five feet of us, and I saw that their eyes were strangely fixed and they had the look of men entranced, all except the priest, who looked as calm and matter-of-fact as he had appeared when he shook our hands. The experienced devotees went first over the fire, the priest and the acolyte leading them to the edge of the pit; they passed over with quick firm steps, yet with no sense of hurrying. When it came to the turn of neophytes, the priest took each of them over the coals individually, putting his arm round the boy's shoulder and dancing beside him. Then they came round again, and again, dancing until they were staggering with emotional exhaustion, while a little man stood splashing honey water out of a bucket with his hand into the gaping mouths of those who seemed near collapse. All the time the drums beat on compellingly, and the red figure of the priest appeared constantly, in total control of himself, carrying child after child in his arms over the coals, dedicating them to the cult or hoping to cure them of ills. At last, when every man must have tramped at least a score of times over the dozen yards of that hot pit, we found the intensity of the scene, the stumbling of the obsessed glassy-eyed figures again and again before our vision, more than we could endure any longer, and we went back to the car and to Suva. That what we saw – the piercing of flesh without evident signs of pain, the repeated tramping on hot coals without burning – was authentic I have not the slightest doubt. There was no possibility of deception in such a clear and open light, and the very ordinariness of the occasion, its banal religiosity, its lack of any drama other than that of the acts themselves, made trickery less likely than the actuality of flesh obeying mind.

Curiously, fire-walking is a point where the two Fijian cultures meet, for there are native Fijian fire-walkers too, who perform their rites on the island of Beqa. The Fijians do their fire-walk on heated coral stones, without added mortifications like the piercing of flesh, nor is there any ceremonial resembling the Indian, but they go into fasting seclusion for at least a day before the walking takes place, and it seems likely that in both cases some form of trance is achieved.

But that, of course, is a speculation, and on a speculative note I choose to end this book, for nothing could be more speculative than the future of the little countries of the South Seas. I would rather attempt an explanation of the strange things I saw that day beside Waimanu River than venture a prophecy of how the people of the Gilberts will avoid the disaster of overpopulation that seems to await them, or when the French will be persuaded to relinquish their miniature empire in the South Seas, or how the disparate peoples of the Solomons can ever create a viable political structure, or whether Indians and Fijians will continue to live in peace. What does seem certain is that the combination of modern technology and the strictly contemporary phenomenon of mass tourism has vastly accelerated the tempo of change, and that traditional ways that survived the blackbirders and the whalers, the planters and the traders, the missionaries and the colonizers, may be more imperilled by these insidious enemies. I am glad to have gone to the South Seas no later than I did. I am not sure that I shall want to return in ten years' time, though if men can learn to walk calmly on hot coals, perhaps they can solve the problems of these beautiful beleaguered islands.

Index